the War at Ellsmere

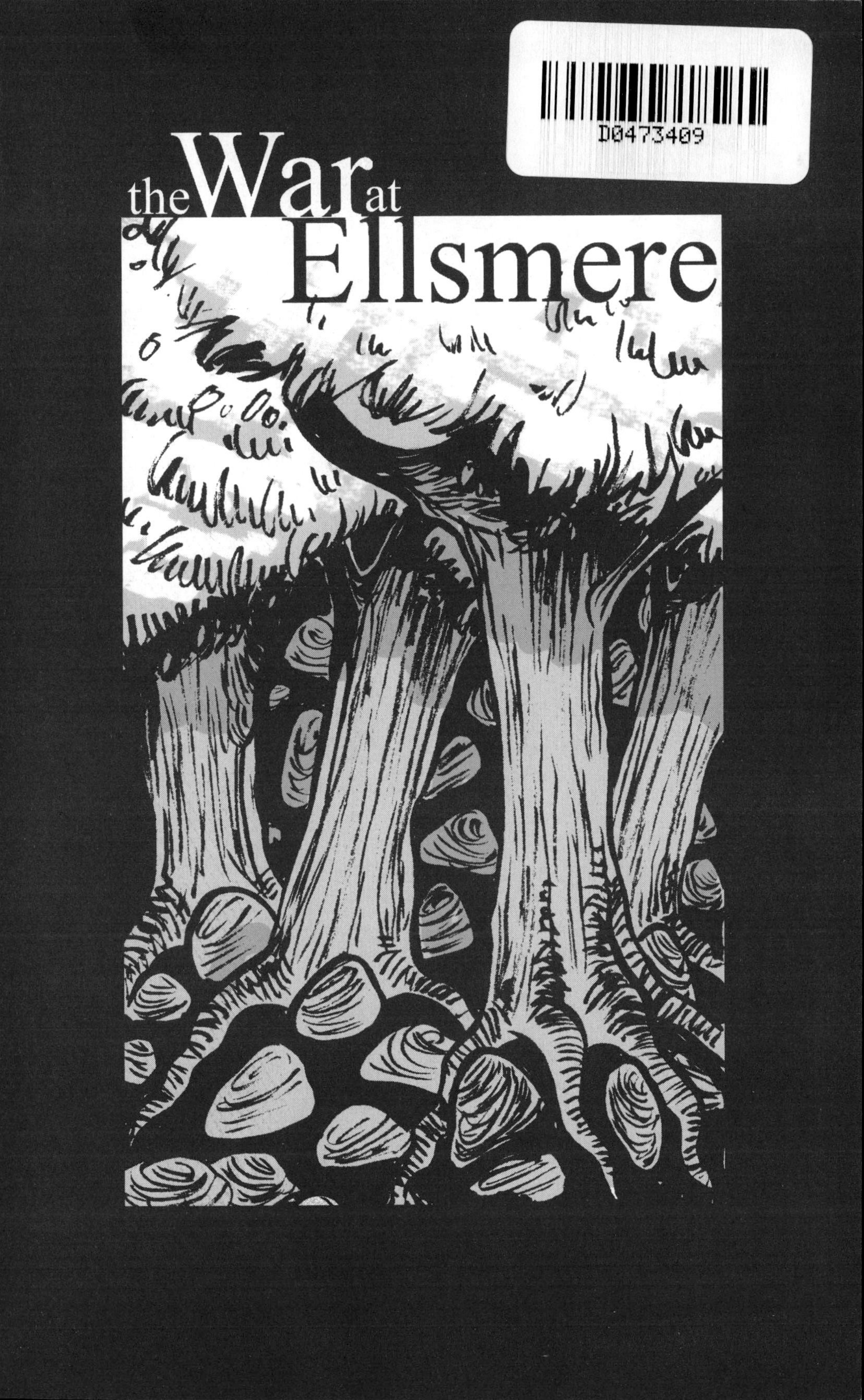

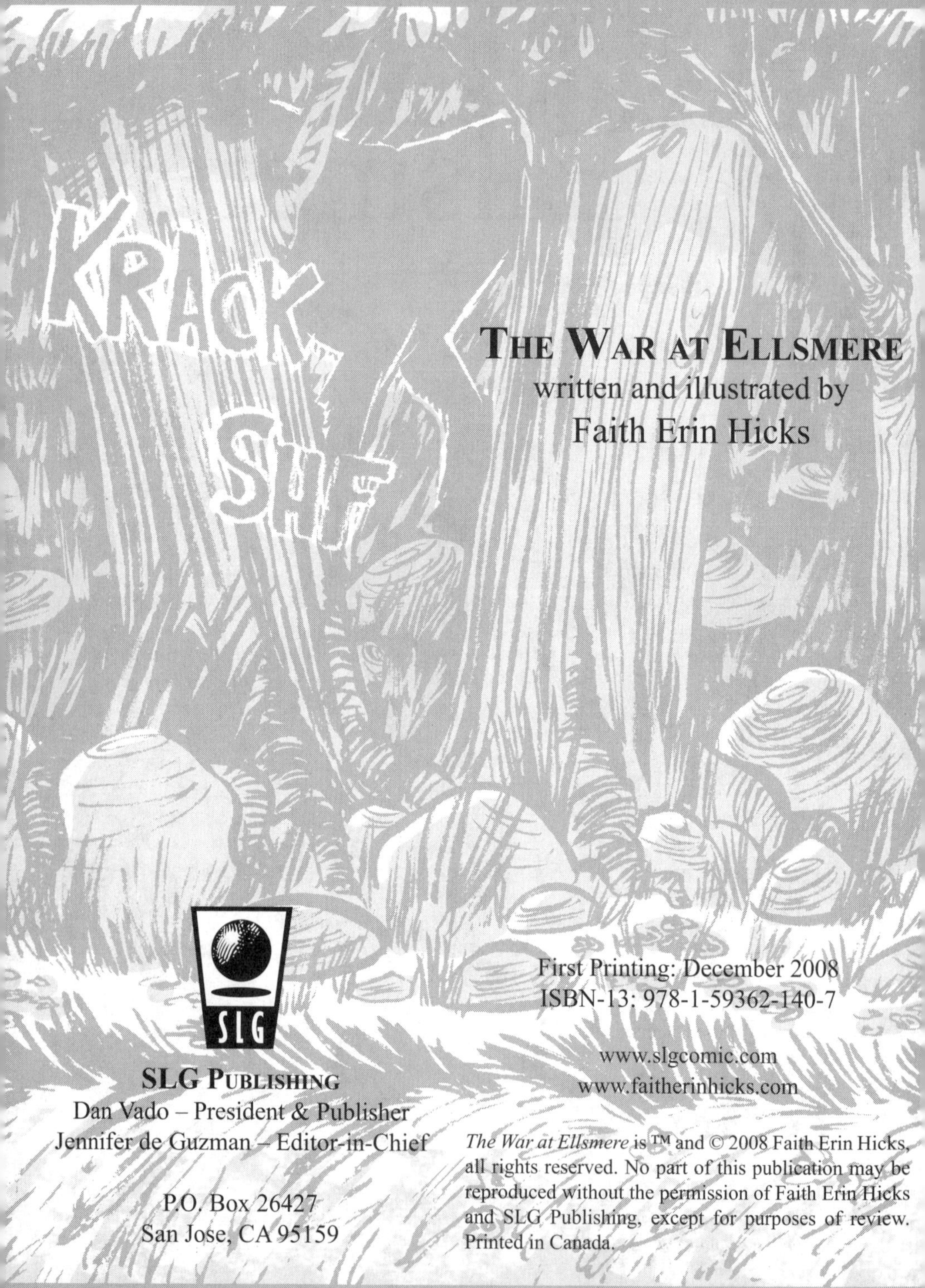
KRACK
SHF

The War at Ellsmere

written and illustrated by

Faith Erin Hicks

SLG Publishing
Dan Vado – President & Publisher
Jennifer de Guzman – Editor-in-Chief

P.O. Box 26427
San Jose, CA 95159

First Printing: December 2008
ISBN-13: 978-1-59362-140-7

www.slgcomic.com
www.faitherinhicks.com

INTRODUCTION by Hope Larson

Boarding school. I get it. In high school, for one lonely year, I did the boarding school thing. It seemed like a shortcut to the smarter, cooler, more worldly person I desperately wanted to become, and I didn't even have to leave home — there was a prestigious boarding school on the other side of town.

The campus was beautiful. The academic buildings, many dating from the early 1900s, sat clustered on a hill beneath huge oak trees. Sporting fields — soccer, field hockey, football, track–rolled away below, eventually giving way to several hundred acres of dense woodlands. The Blue Ridge Mountains were visible in the distance, like the border of an enchanted kingdom. "How wonderful," I thought, "to spend high school here."

I hated it.

The oak trees pelted me with acorns. I always had runs in my pantyhose, and my dress code-mandated navy blue blazer never fit right. I resented mandatory attendance at chapel services. I distinguished myself neither in class nor on the athletic field. I antagonized my French teacher into throwing a book at me. Like Cassie, Jun's roommate, my only real friend was an outcast scholarship student.

I wanted boarding school to change me, but it made me even more inflexible. In the face of so much conformity and expectation, I recast myself as an outsider, a rebel — but a rebel terrified of racking up even one demerit is a pitiful creature, and even I knew that.

Sophomore year I transferred to a day school, and life improved. I made friends, wore jeans and T-shirts, and rediscovered comics. A Junior in my art class lent me the first volume of *Ranma 1/2*, and soon all my allowance was earmarked for manga and anime videos. It didn't go far, so I was thrilled to discover that there were people putting comics on the internet for free.

Bryan Lee O'Malley. Corey Lewis. Faith Erin Hicks. In the late '90s they were just beginners. Their comics were clumsy, and (Faith excepted) they never finished the stories they started, but I read everything they drew and it was never enough. They were my heroes. If I'd known that a few years later I'd be married to Bryan and friends with Faith, that I'd be drawing comics, too, I would have been over the moon. It's funny that I'm writing a foreword for one of Faith's books, because it should be the other way around.

Faith has been drawing comics more than twice as long as I have, but she wasn't published until SLG released *Zombies Calling* in 2007. Considering the quality–and particularly the quantity — of *Demonology101* and the rest of her early work, this is shocking. Not only is she prolific, professional, and capable of drawing at the speed of light, she has the rare knack of crafting stories with realistic female protagonists that are equally enjoyable for everyone. Faith didn't fall into the "girl cartoonist" trap, and that takes real skill. She's got the magic touch.

I wish I'd had her books in ninth grade. I would have read them to pieces.

I moved back to my hometown last year, to a house near my old boarding school. The school gymnasium is my assigned polling place. I was there a few months ago, voting in the Primary, and the grounds look the same as they did when I was a student. It was nice to see the place again, but it was nicer to leave, and close that book.

And open this one.

Hope Larson
October 28th, 2008
Asheville, North Carolina

Hope Larson is the author of the graphic novels Salamander Dream, Gray Horses *and* Chiggers. *Find out more about her and read her web comics at www.hopelarson.com.*

chapter one

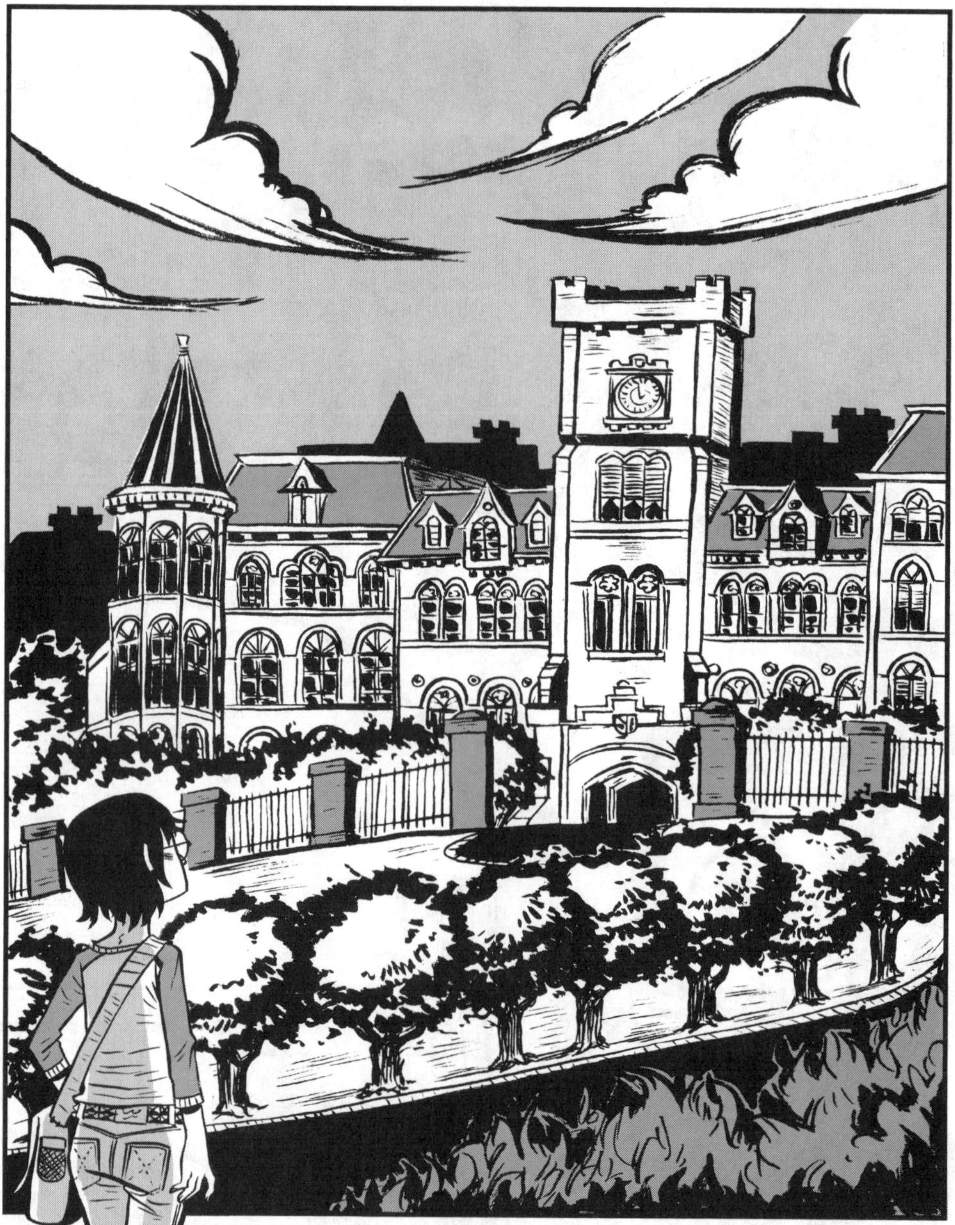

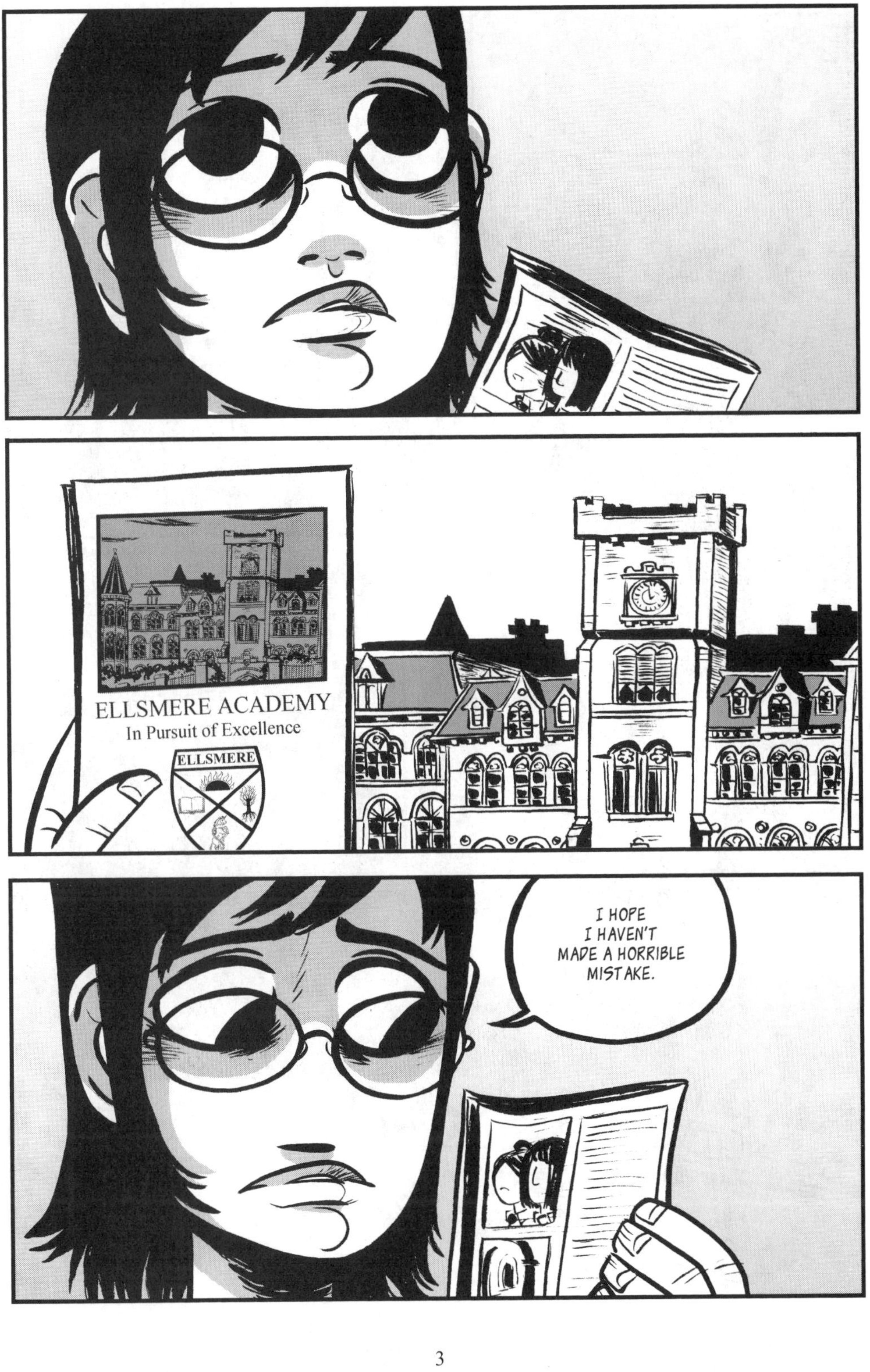
ELLSMERE ACADEMY
In Pursuit of Excellence
ELLSMERE
I HOPE I HAVEN'T MADE A HORRIBLE MISTAKE.

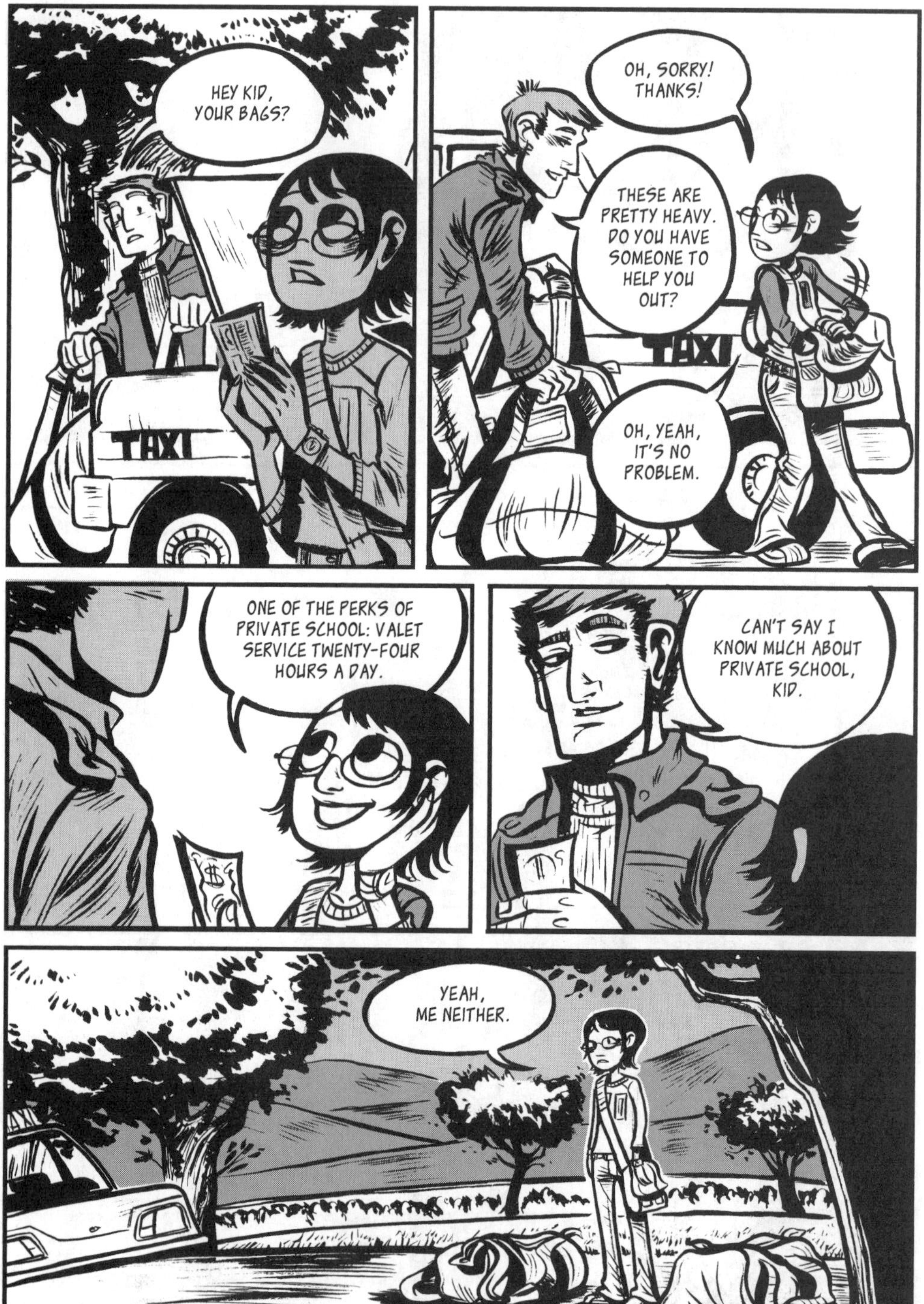
HEY KID, YOUR BAGS?
OH, SORRY! THANKS!
THESE ARE PRETTY HEAVY. DO YOU HAVE SOMEONE TO HELP YOU OUT?
OH, YEAH, IT'S NO PROBLEM.
TAXI
ONE OF THE PERKS OF PRIVATE SCHOOL: VALET SERVICE TWENTY-FOUR HOURS A DAY.
CAN'T SAY I KNOW MUCH ABOUT PRIVATE SCHOOL, KID.
YEAH, ME NEITHER.

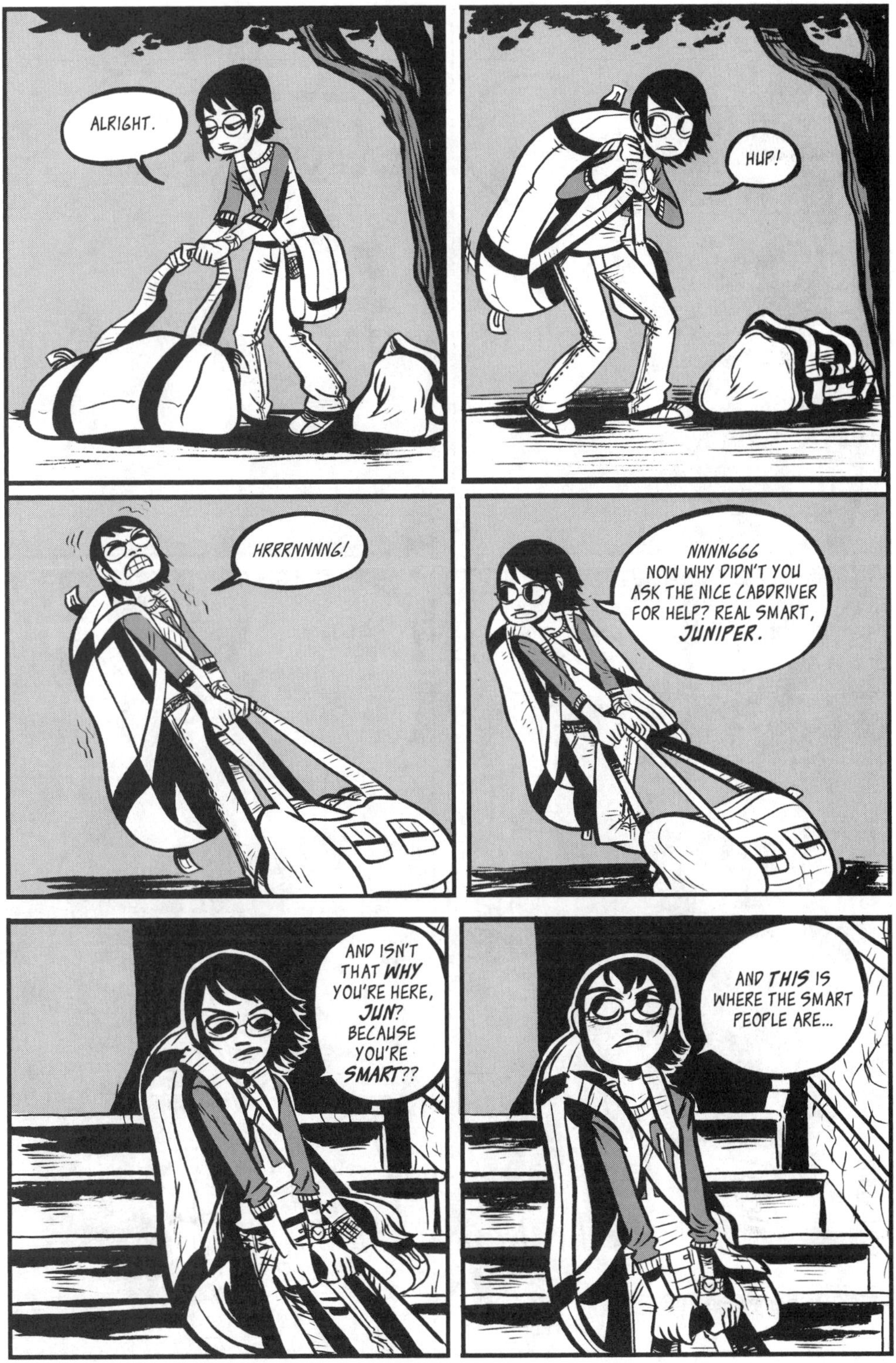
ALRIGHT.
HUP!
HRRRNNNNG!
NNNNGGG
NOW WHY DIDN'T YOU ASK THE NICE CABDRIVER FOR HELP? REAL SMART, JUNIPER.
AND ISN'T THAT WHY YOU'RE HERE, JUN? BECAUSE YOU'RE SMART??
AND THIS IS WHERE THE SMART PEOPLE ARE...

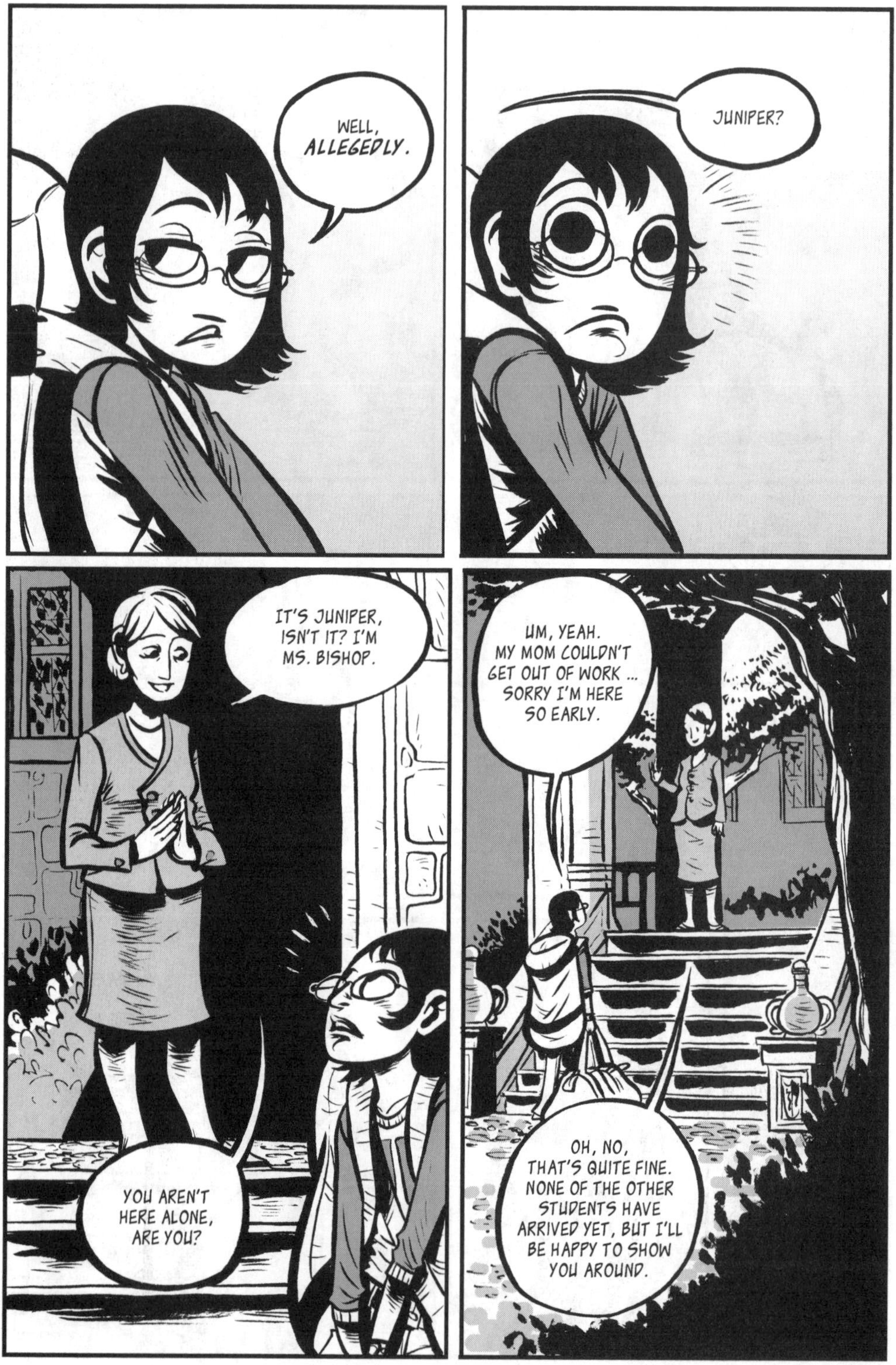
WELL, ALLEGEDLY.
JUNIPER?
IT'S JUNIPER, ISN'T IT? I'M MS. BISHOP.
YOU AREN'T HERE ALONE, ARE YOU?
UM, YEAH. MY MOM COULDN'T GET OUT OF WORK ... SORRY I'M HERE SO EARLY.
OH, NO, THAT'S QUITE FINE. NONE OF THE OTHER STUDENTS HAVE ARRIVED YET, BUT I'LL BE HAPPY TO SHOW YOU AROUND.

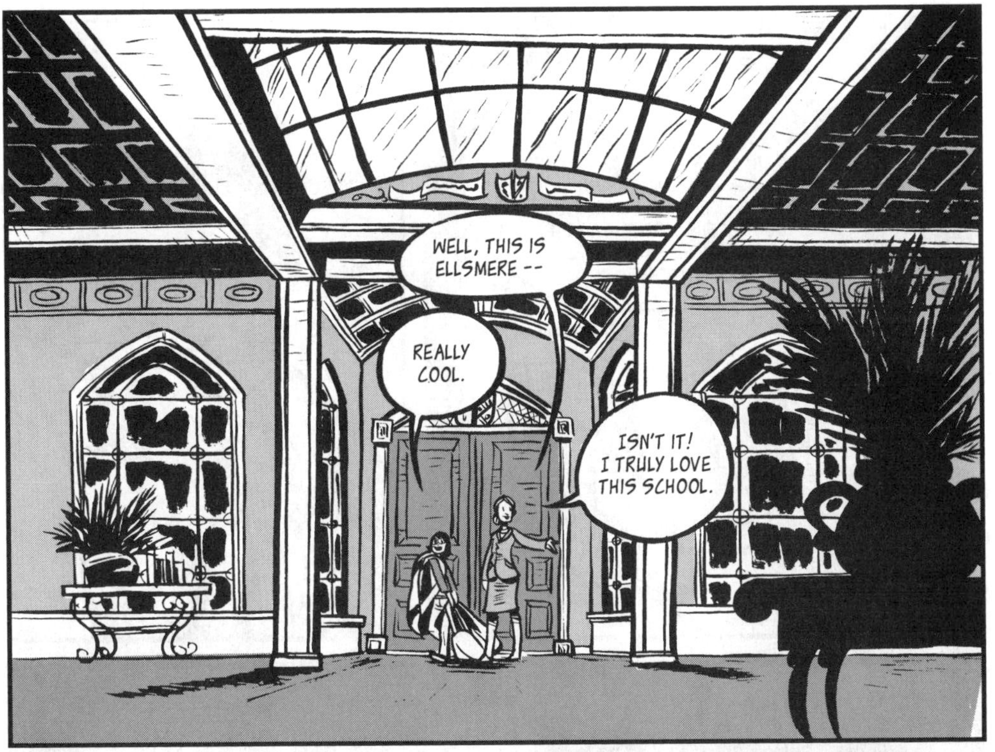
WELL, THIS IS ELLSMERE --
REALLY COOL.
ISN'T IT! I TRULY LOVE THIS SCHOOL.

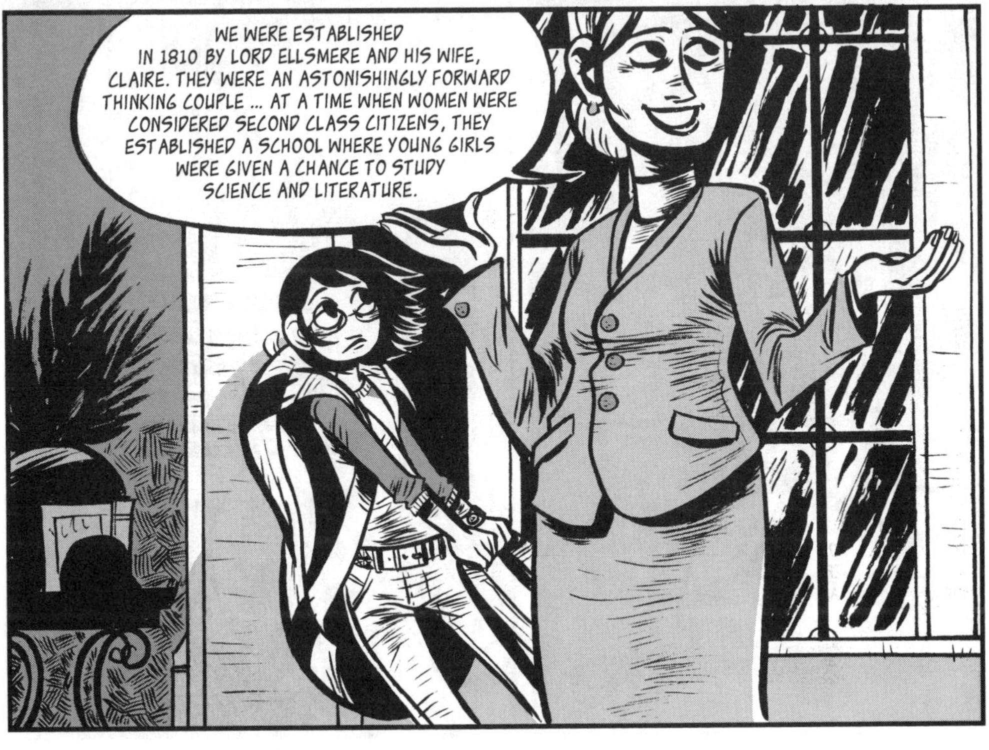
WE WERE ESTABLISHED IN 1810 BY LORD ELLSMERE AND HIS WIFE, CLAIRE. THEY WERE AN ASTONISHINGLY FORWARD THINKING COUPLE ... AT A TIME WHEN WOMEN WERE CONSIDERED SECOND CLASS CITIZENS, THEY ESTABLISHED A SCHOOL WHERE YOUNG GIRLS WERE GIVEN A CHANCE TO STUDY SCIENCE AND LITERATURE.

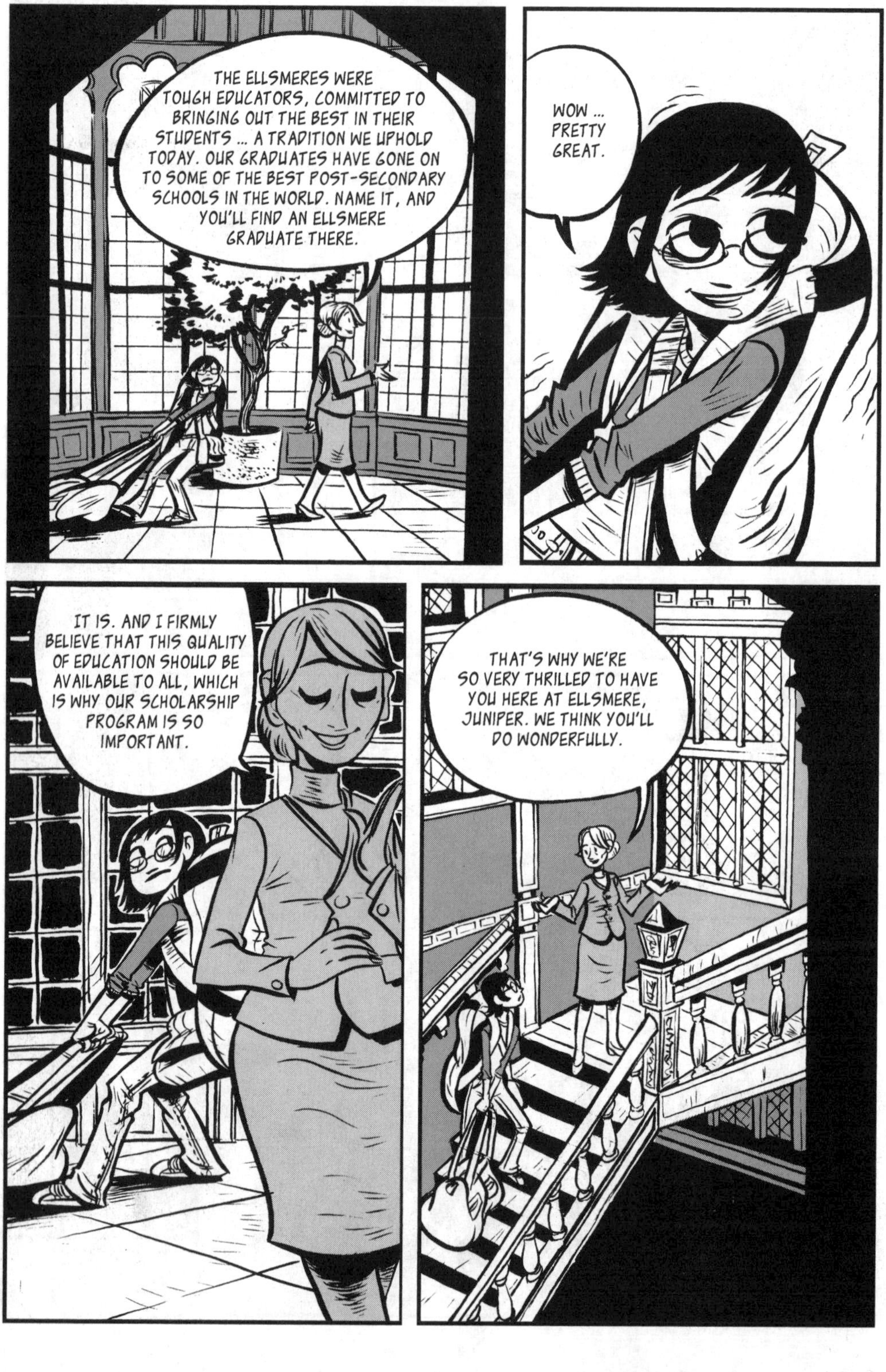
THE ELLSMERES WERE TOUGH EDUCATORS, COMMITTED TO BRINGING OUT THE BEST IN THEIR STUDENTS ... A TRADITION WE UPHOLD TODAY. OUR GRADUATES HAVE GONE ON TO SOME OF THE BEST POST-SECONDARY SCHOOLS IN THE WORLD. NAME IT, AND YOU'LL FIND AN ELLSMERE GRADUATE THERE.
WOW ... PRETTY GREAT.
IT IS. AND I FIRMLY BELIEVE THAT THIS QUALITY OF EDUCATION SHOULD BE AVAILABLE TO ALL, WHICH IS WHY OUR SCHOLARSHIP PROGRAM IS SO IMPORTANT.
THAT'S WHY WE'RE SO VERY THRILLED TO HAVE YOU HERE AT ELLSMERE, JUNIPER. WE THINK YOU'LL DO WONDERFULLY.

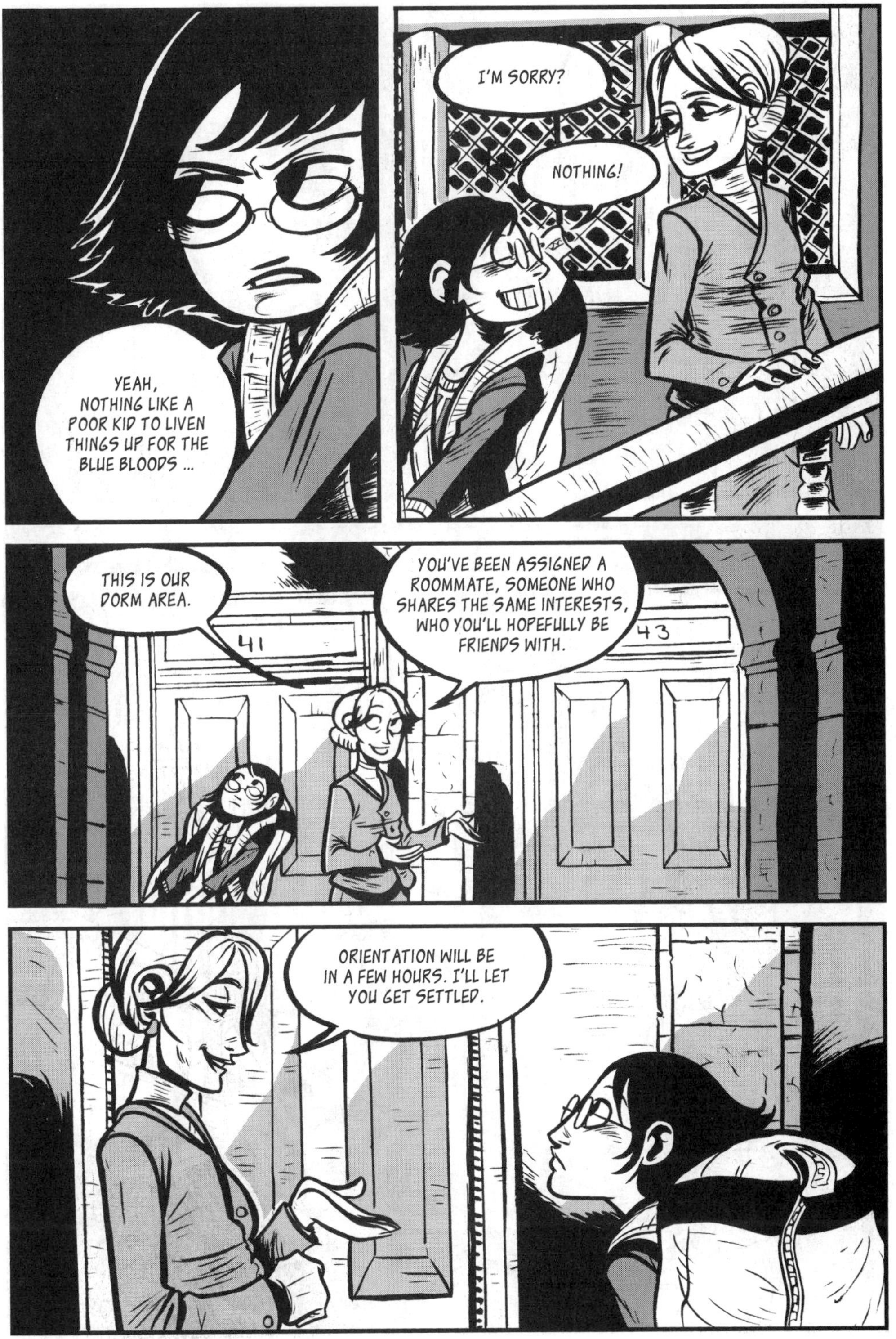
YEAH, NOTHING LIKE A POOR KID TO LIVEN THINGS UP FOR THE BLUE BLOODS ...
I'M SORRY?
NOTHING!
THIS IS OUR DORM AREA.
YOU'VE BEEN ASSIGNED A ROOMMATE, SOMEONE WHO SHARES THE SAME INTERESTS, WHO YOU'LL HOPEFULLY BE FRIENDS WITH.
41
43
ORIENTATION WILL BE IN A FEW HOURS. I'LL LET YOU GET SETTLED.

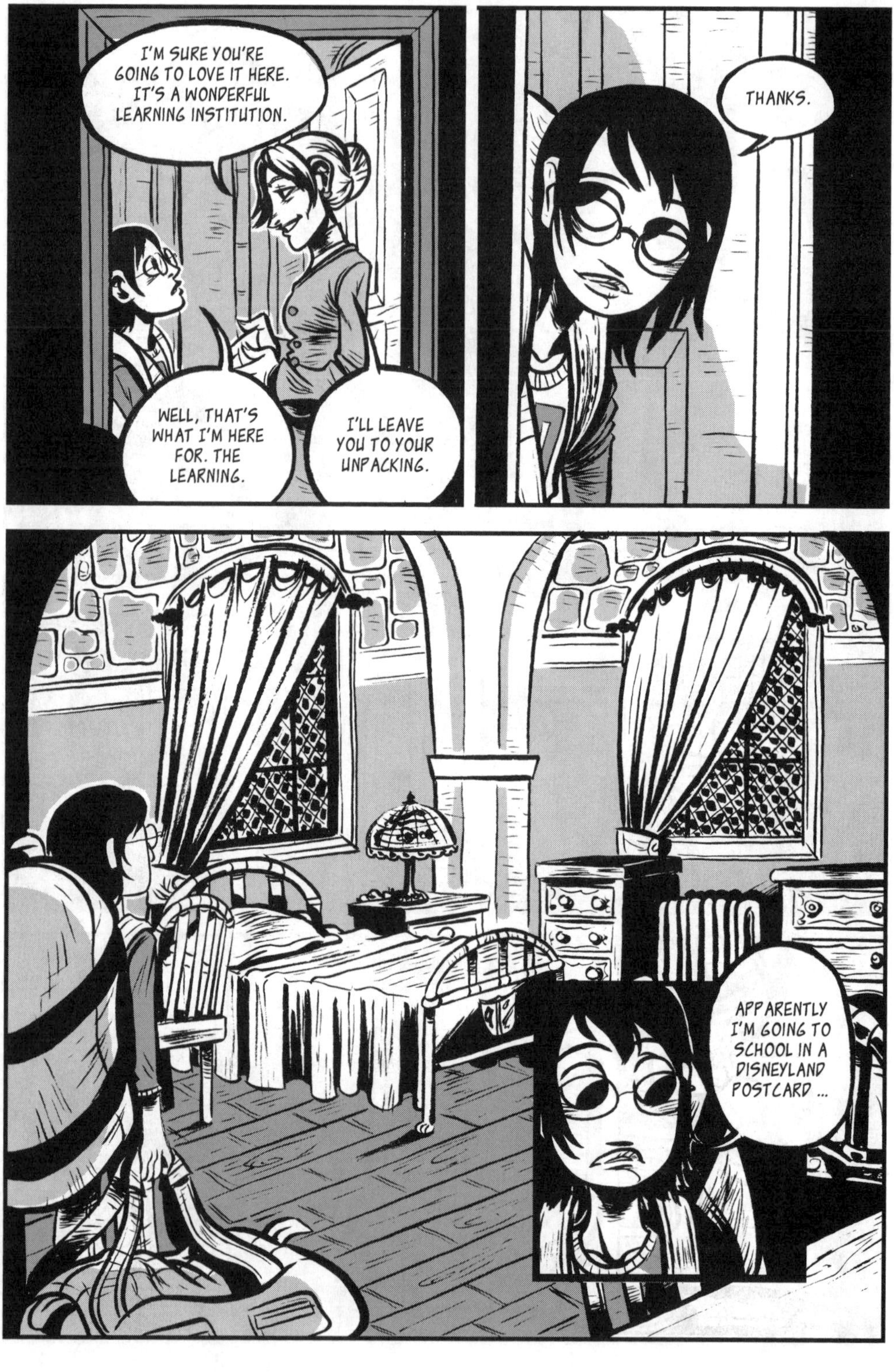
I'M SURE YOU'RE GOING TO LOVE IT HERE. IT'S A WONDERFUL LEARNING INSTITUTION.
WELL, THAT'S WHAT I'M HERE FOR. THE LEARNING.
I'LL LEAVE YOU TO YOUR UNPACKING.
THANKS.
APPARENTLY I'M GOING TO SCHOOL IN A DISNEYLAND POSTCARD ...

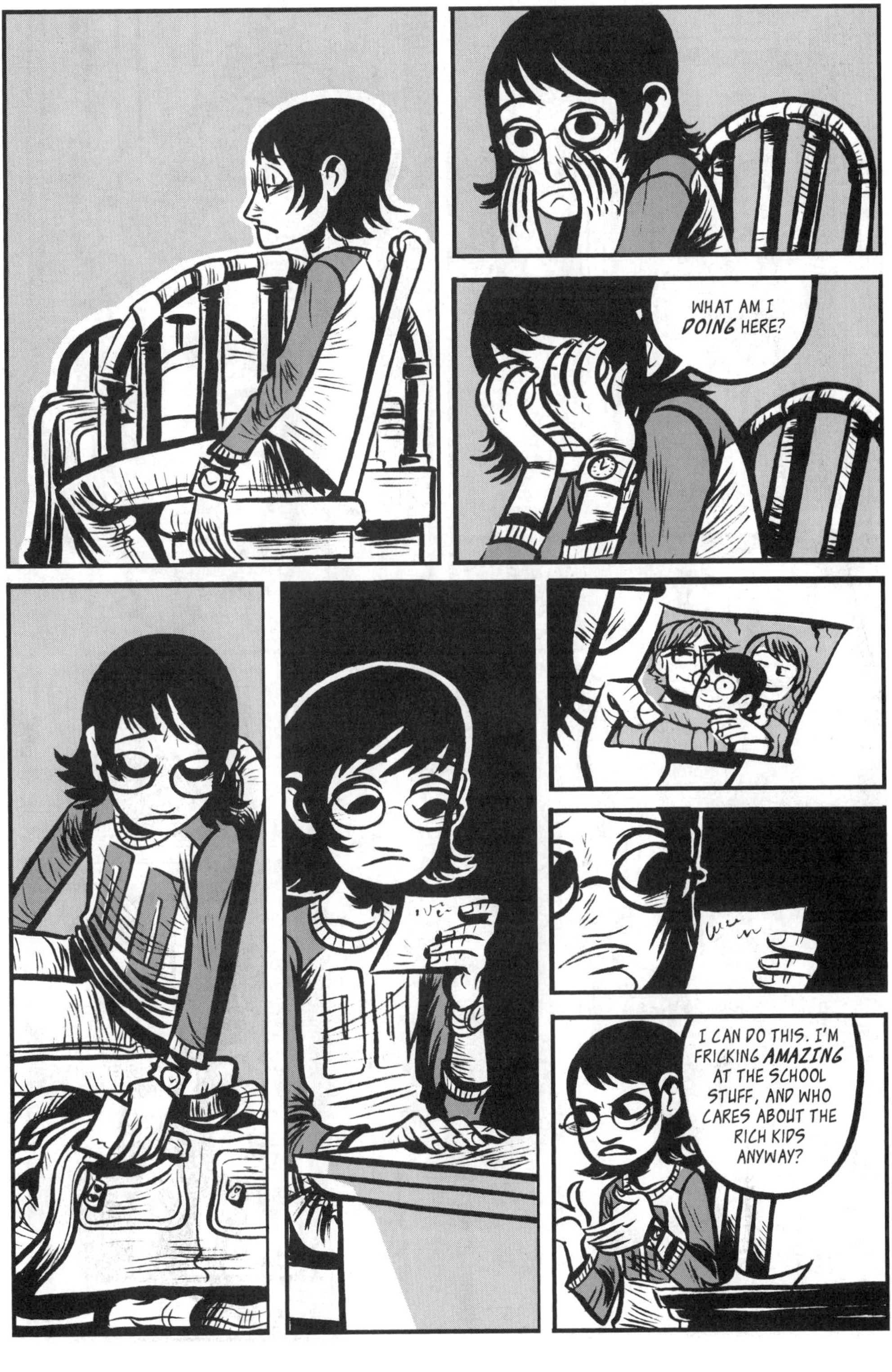
WHAT AM I DOING HERE?
I CAN DO THIS. I'M FRICKING AMAZING AT THE SCHOOL STUFF, AND WHO CARES ABOUT THE RICH KIDS ANYWAY?

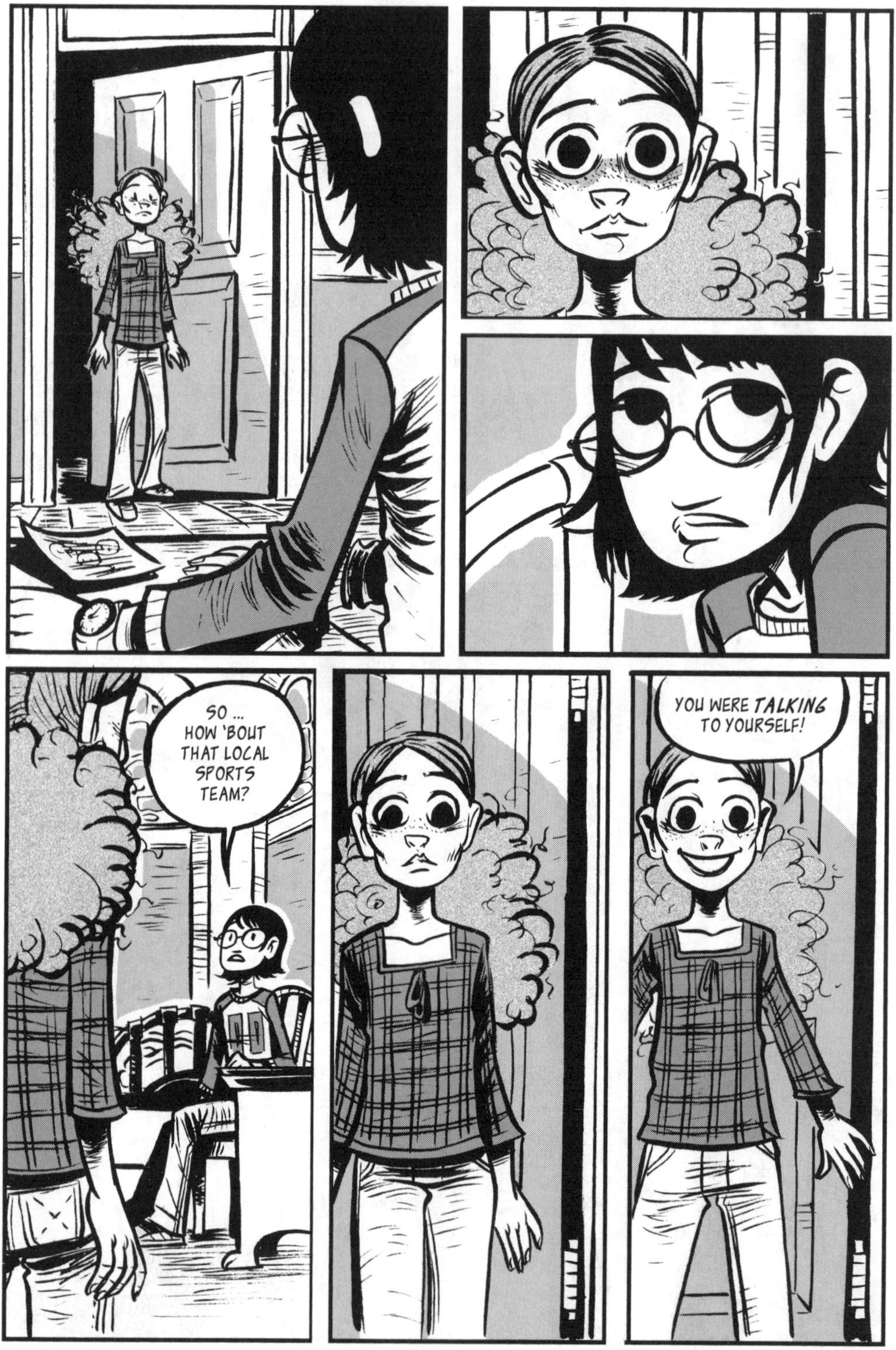
SO ... HOW 'BOUT THAT LOCAL SPORTS TEAM?
YOU WERE TALKING TO YOURSELF!

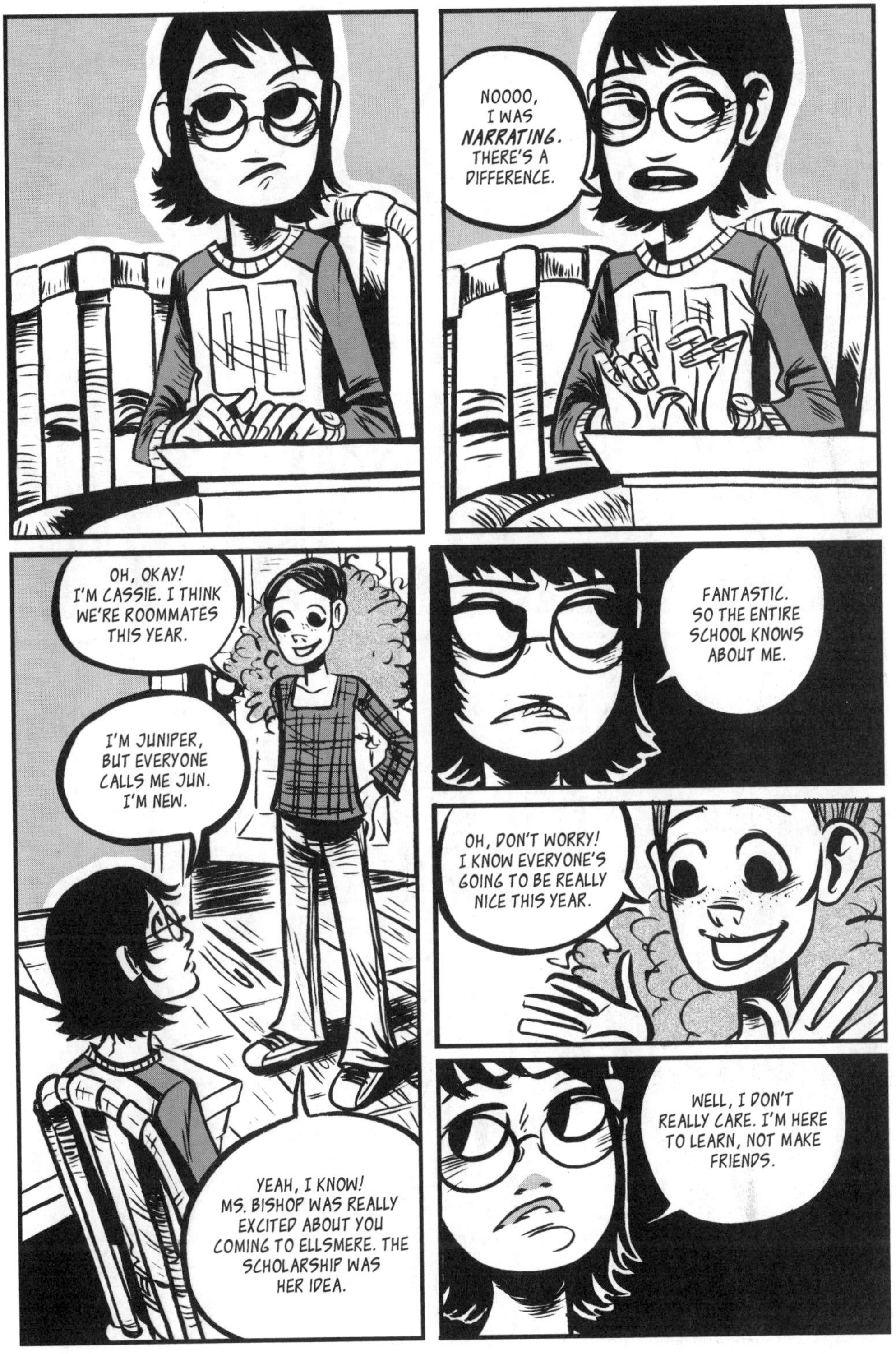
NOOOO, I WAS NARRATING. THERE'S A DIFFERENCE.
OH, OKAY! I'M CASSIE. I THINK WE'RE ROOMMATES THIS YEAR.
I'M JUNIPER, BUT EVERYONE CALLS ME JUN. I'M NEW.
YEAH, I KNOW! MS. BISHOP WAS REALLY EXCITED ABOUT YOU COMING TO ELLSMERE. THE SCHOLARSHIP WAS HER IDEA.
FANTASTIC. SO THE ENTIRE SCHOOL KNOWS ABOUT ME.
OH, DON'T WORRY! I KNOW EVERYONE'S GOING TO BE REALLY NICE THIS YEAR.
WELL, I DON'T REALLY CARE. I'M HERE TO LEARN, NOT MAKE FRIENDS.

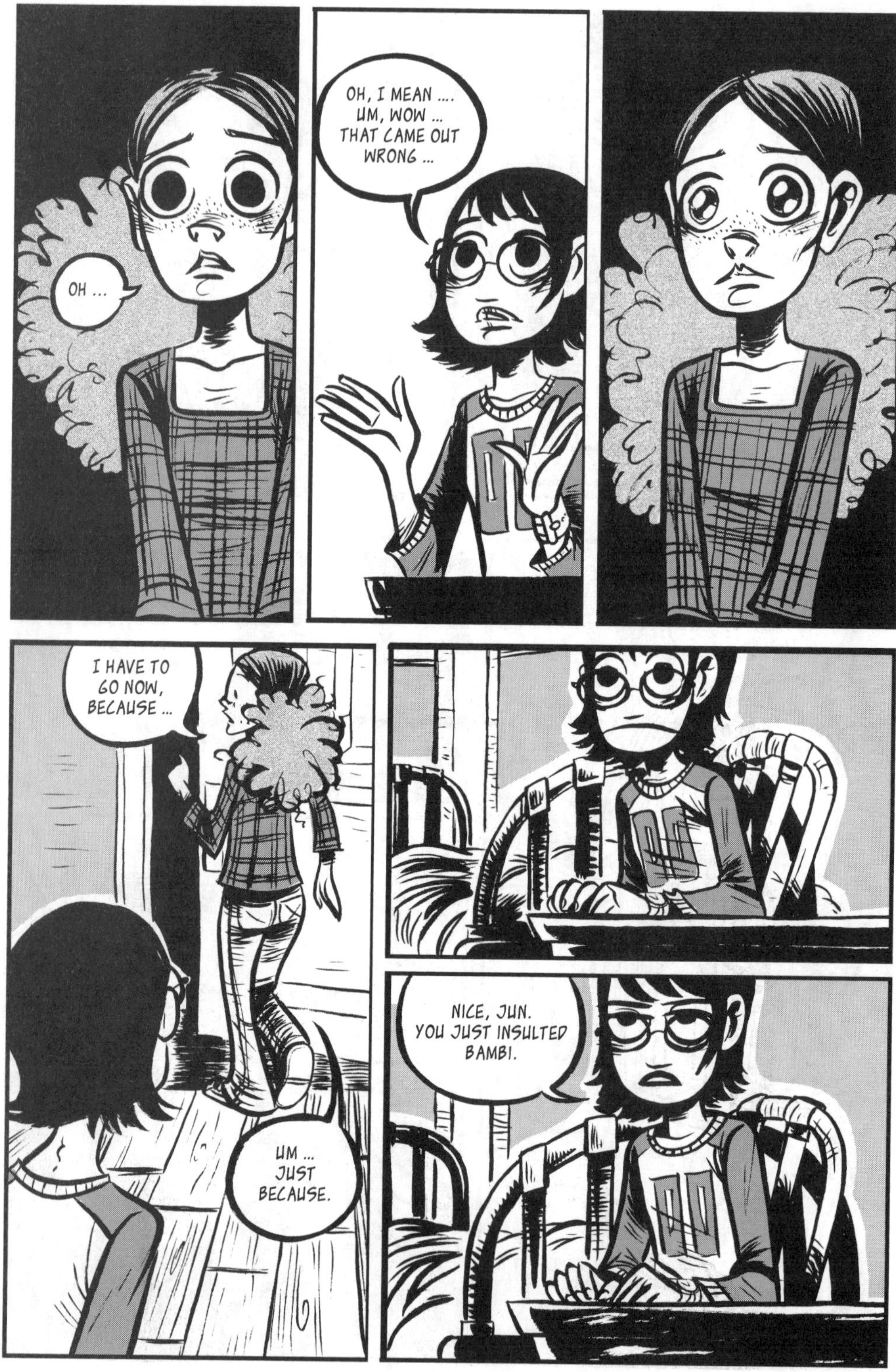
OH ...
OH, I MEAN .... UM, WOW ... THAT CAME OUT WRONG ...
I HAVE TO GO NOW, BECAUSE ...
UM ... JUST BECAUSE.
NICE, JUN. YOU JUST INSULTED BAMBI.

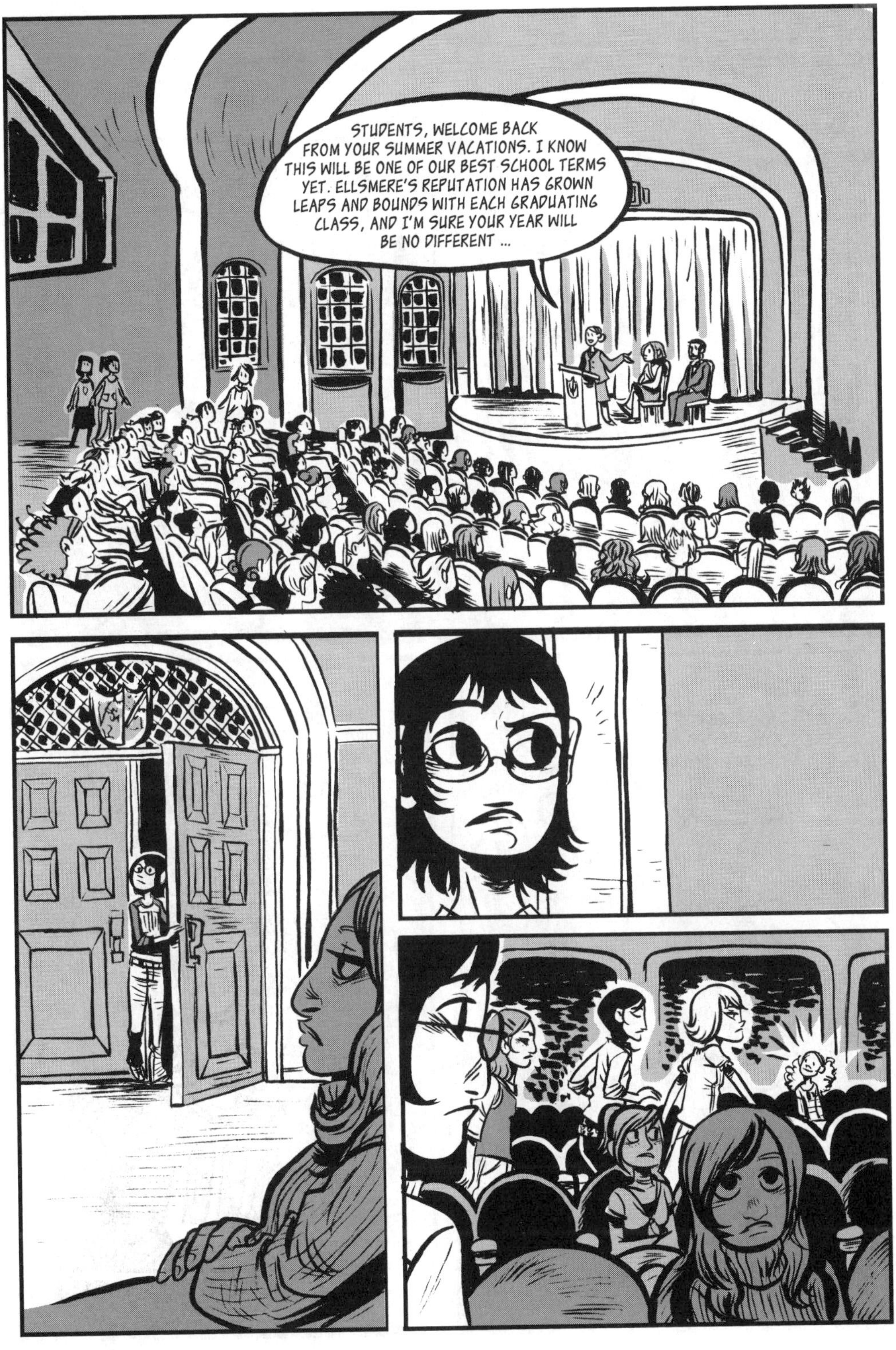
STUDENTS, WELCOME BACK FROM YOUR SUMMER VACATIONS. I KNOW THIS WILL BE ONE OF OUR BEST SCHOOL TERMS YET. ELLSMERE'S REPUTATION HAS GROWN LEAPS AND BOUNDS WITH EACH GRADUATING CLASS, AND I'M SURE YOUR YEAR WILL BE NO DIFFERENT ...

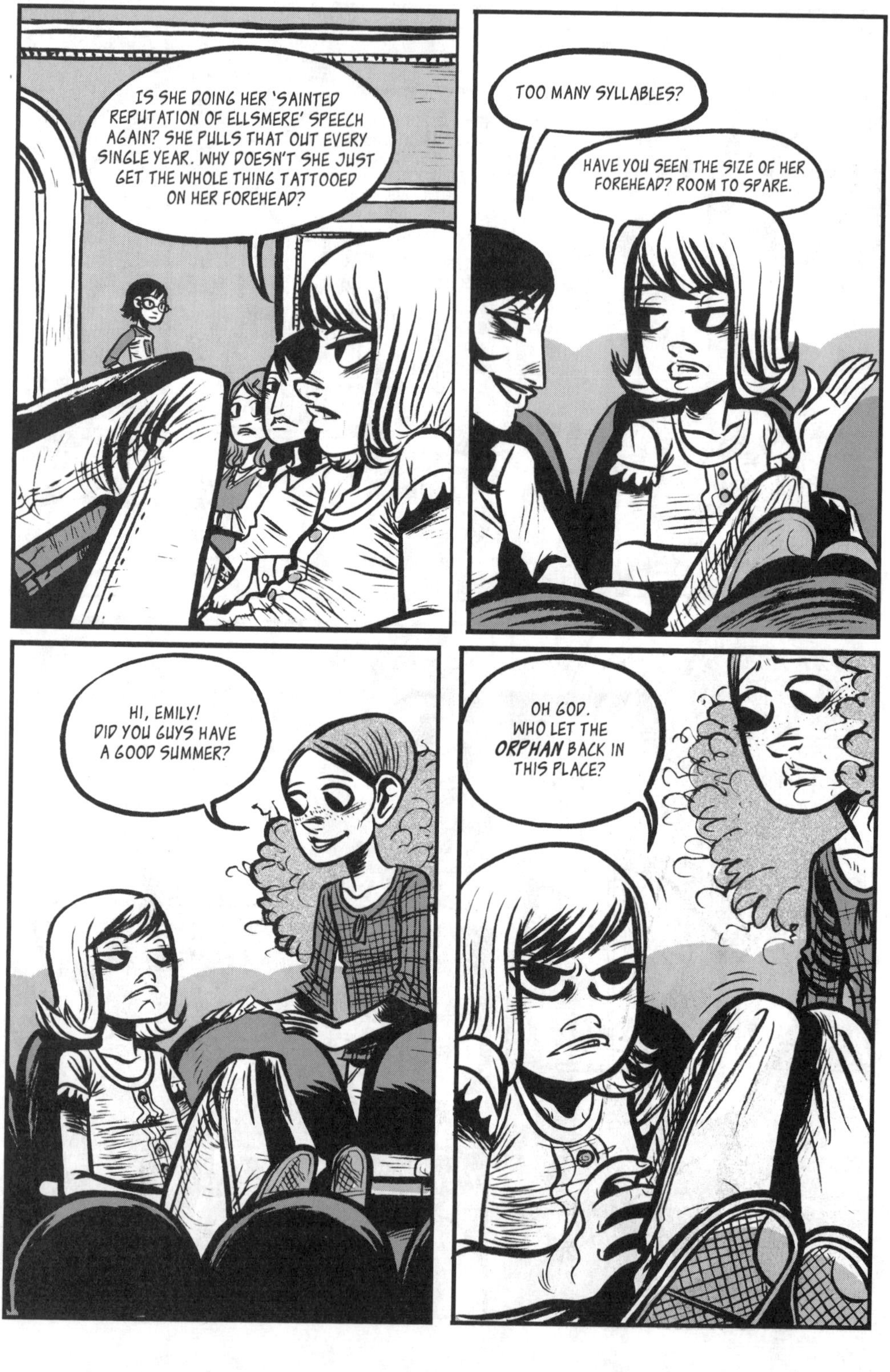
IS SHE DOING HER 'SAINTED REPUTATION OF ELLSMERE' SPEECH AGAIN? SHE PULLS THAT OUT EVERY SINGLE YEAR. WHY DOESN'T SHE JUST GET THE WHOLE THING TATTOOED ON HER FOREHEAD?
TOO MANY SYLLABLES?
HAVE YOU SEEN THE SIZE OF HER FOREHEAD? ROOM TO SPARE.
HI, EMILY! DID YOU GUYS HAVE A GOOD SUMMER?
OH GOD. WHO LET THE *ORPHAN* BACK IN THIS PLACE?

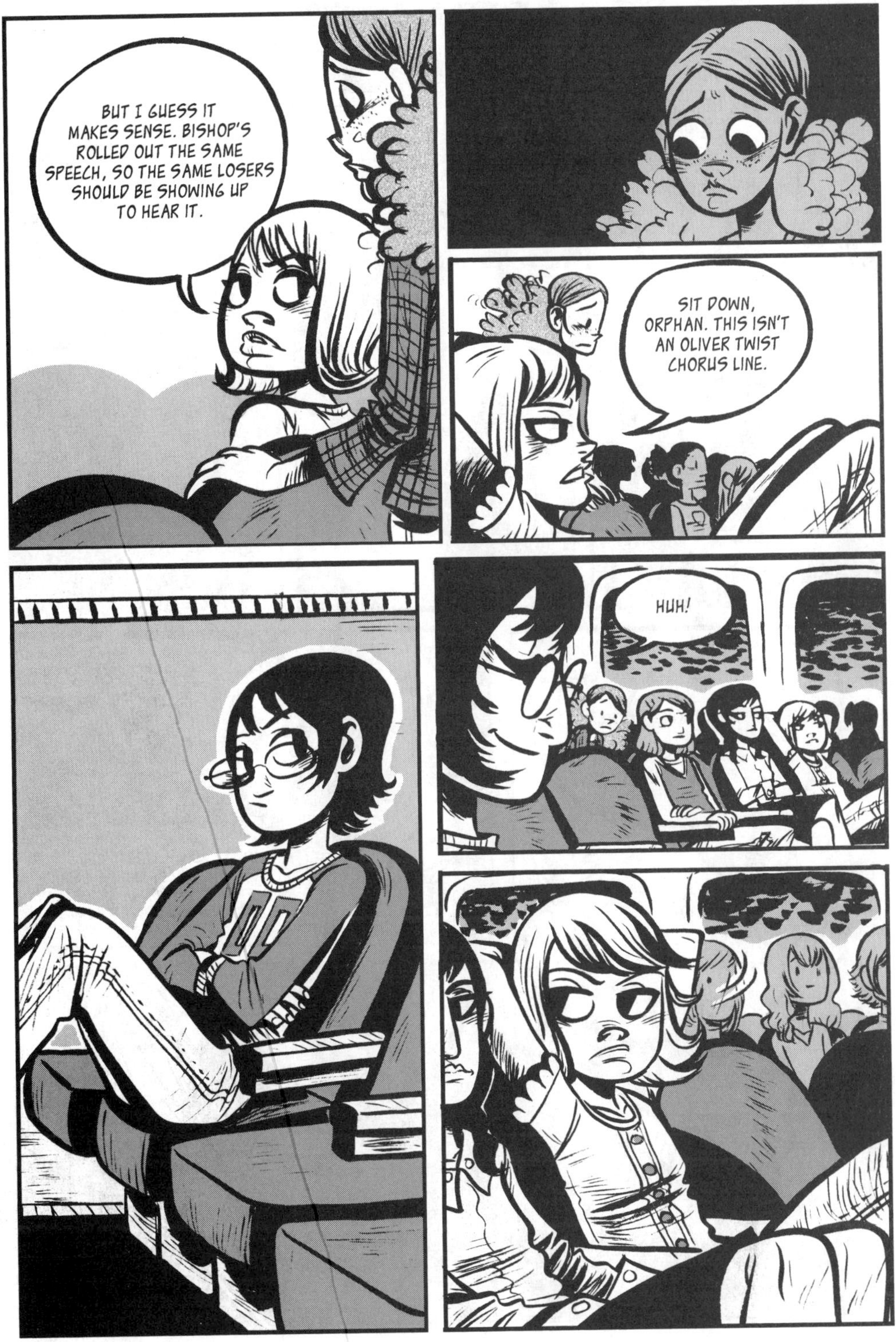
BUT I GUESS IT MAKES SENSE. BISHOP'S ROLLED OUT THE SAME SPEECH, SO THE SAME LOSERS SHOULD BE SHOWING UP TO HEAR IT.
SIT DOWN, ORPHAN. THIS ISN'T AN OLIVER TWIST CHORUS LINE.
HUH!

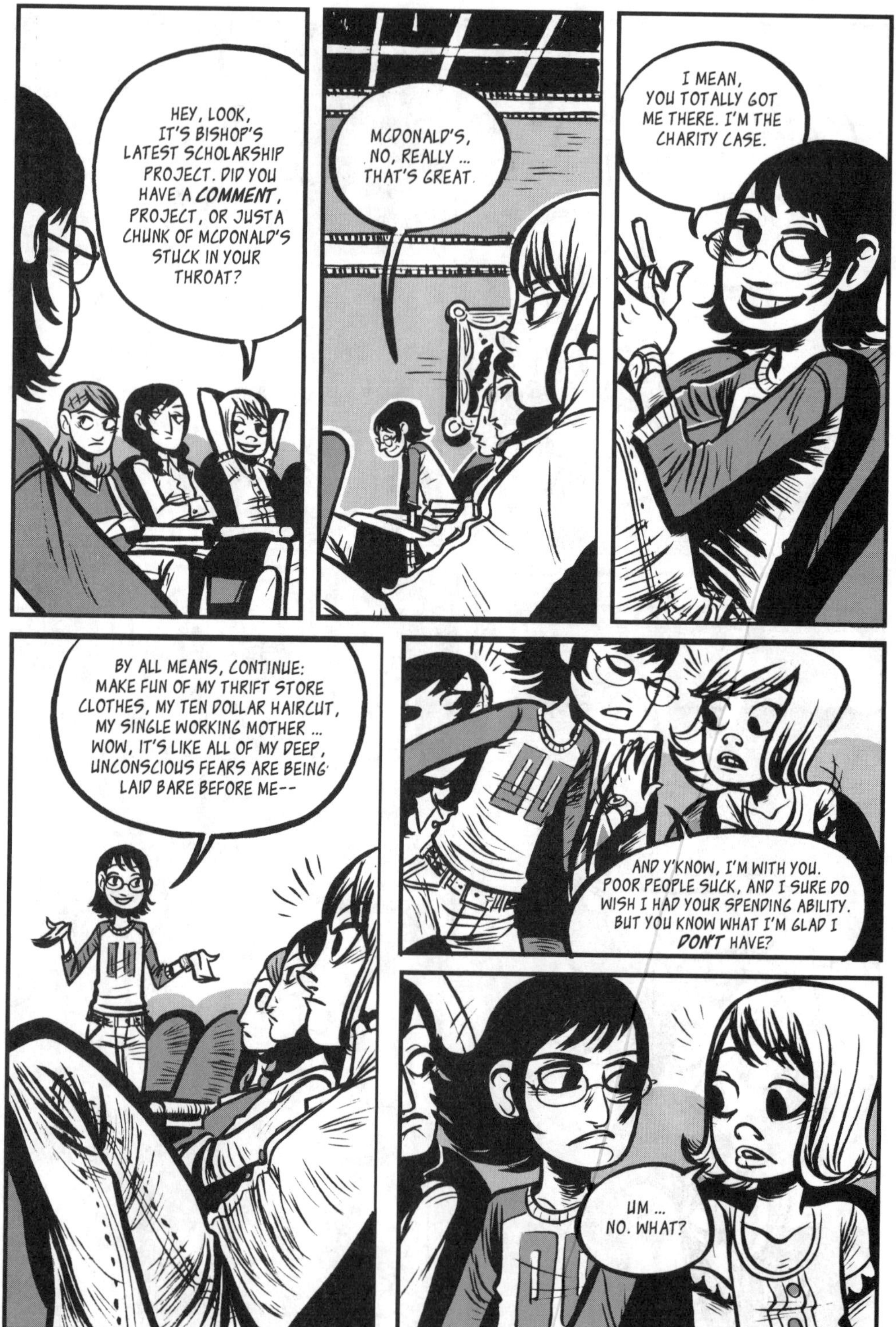
HEY, LOOK, IT'S BISHOP'S LATEST SCHOLARSHIP PROJECT. DID YOU HAVE A **COMMENT**, PROJECT, OR JUST A CHUNK OF MCDONALD'S STUCK IN YOUR THROAT?
MCDONALD'S, NO, REALLY ... THAT'S GREAT.
I MEAN, YOU TOTALLY GOT ME THERE. I'M THE CHARITY CASE.
BY ALL MEANS, CONTINUE: MAKE FUN OF MY THRIFT STORE CLOTHES, MY TEN DOLLAR HAIRCUT, MY SINGLE WORKING MOTHER ... WOW, IT'S LIKE ALL OF MY DEEP, UNCONSCIOUS FEARS ARE BEING LAID BARE BEFORE ME--
AND Y'KNOW, I'M WITH YOU. POOR PEOPLE SUCK, AND I SURE DO WISH I HAD YOUR SPENDING ABILITY. BUT YOU KNOW WHAT I'M GLAD I **DON'T** HAVE?
UM ... NO. WHAT?

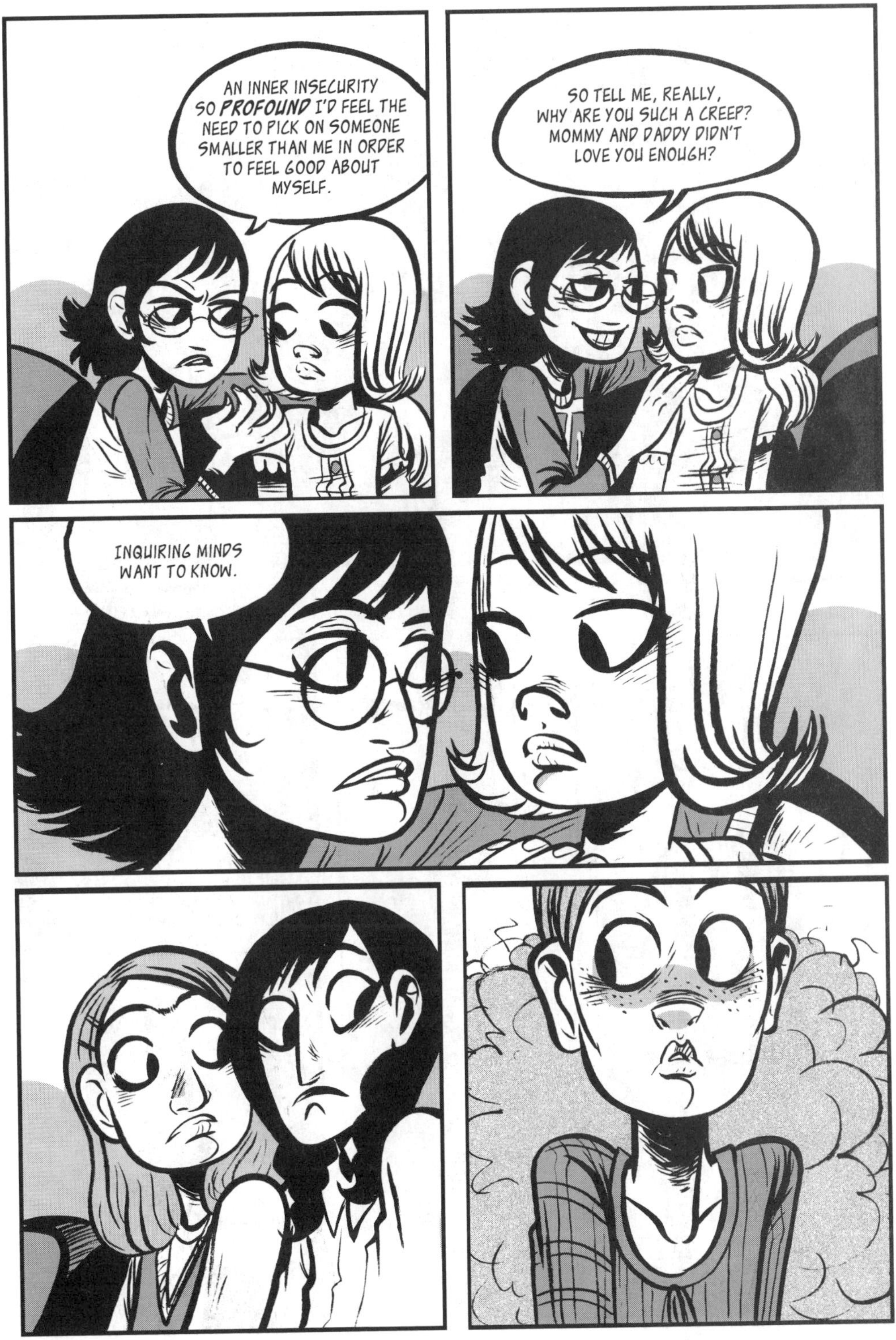

AN INNER INSECURITY SO **PROFOUND** I'D FEEL THE NEED TO PICK ON SOMEONE SMALLER THAN ME IN ORDER TO FEEL GOOD ABOUT MYSELF.
SO TELL ME, REALLY, WHY ARE YOU SUCH A CREEP? MOMMY AND DADDY DIDN'T LOVE YOU ENOUGH?
INQUIRING MINDS WANT TO KNOW.

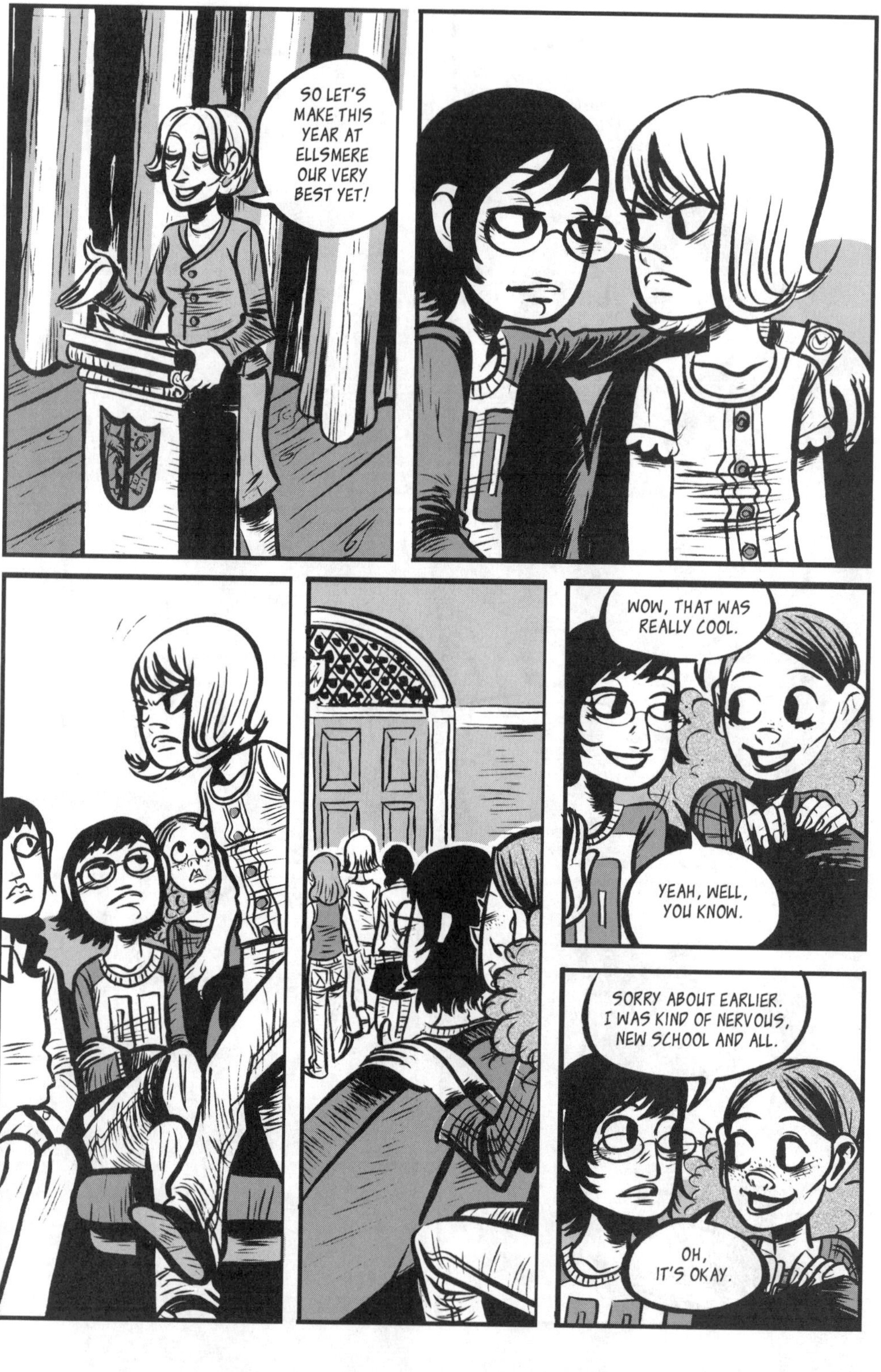
SO LET'S MAKE THIS YEAR AT ELLSMERE OUR VERY BEST YET!
WOW, THAT WAS REALLY COOL.
YEAH, WELL, YOU KNOW.
SORRY ABOUT EARLIER. I WAS KIND OF NERVOUS, NEW SCHOOL AND ALL.
OH, IT'S OKAY.

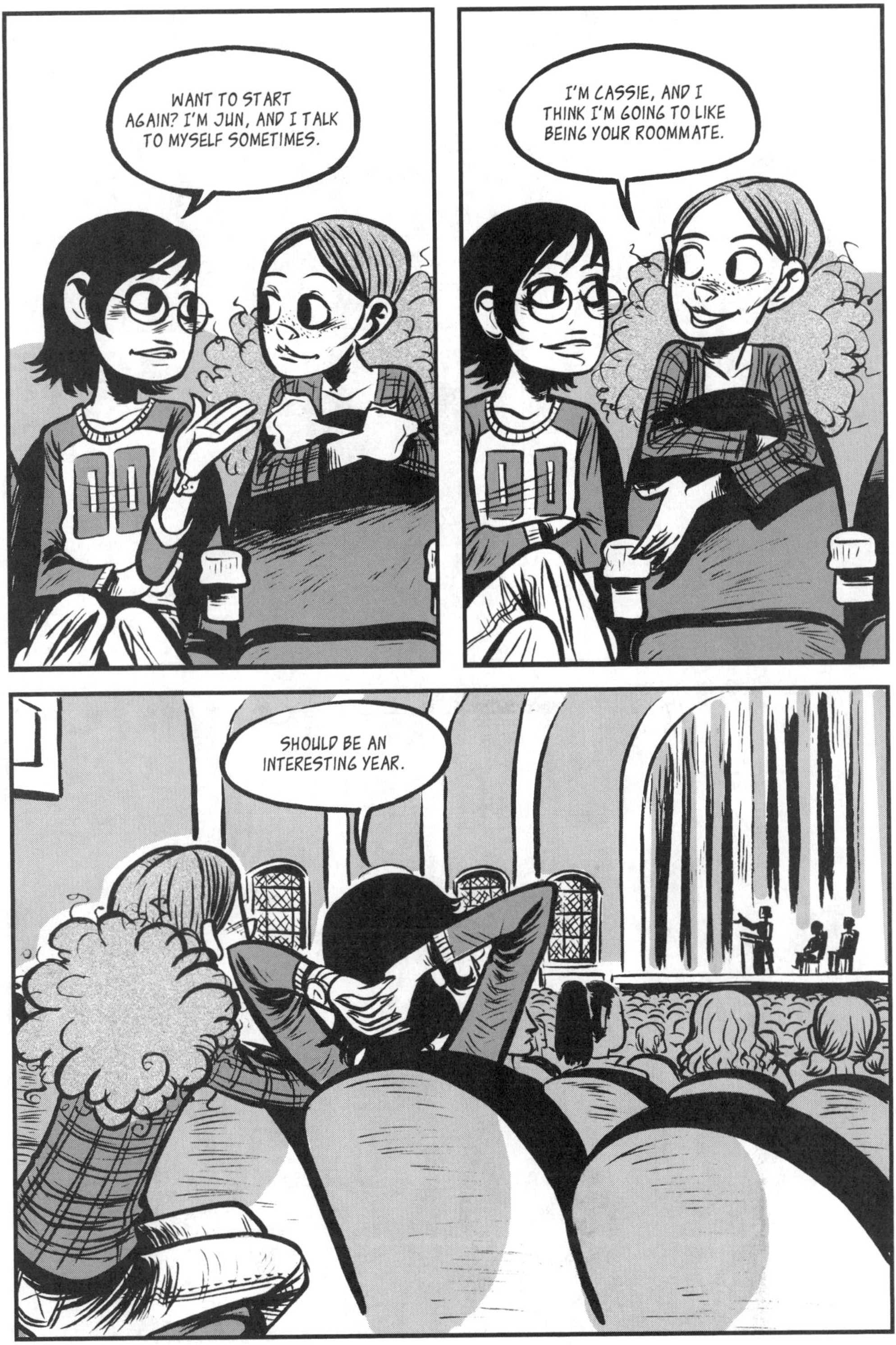
WANT TO START AGAIN? I'M JUN, AND I TALK TO MYSELF SOMETIMES.
I'M CASSIE, AND I THINK I'M GOING TO LIKE BEING YOUR ROOMMATE.
SHOULD BE AN INTERESTING YEAR.

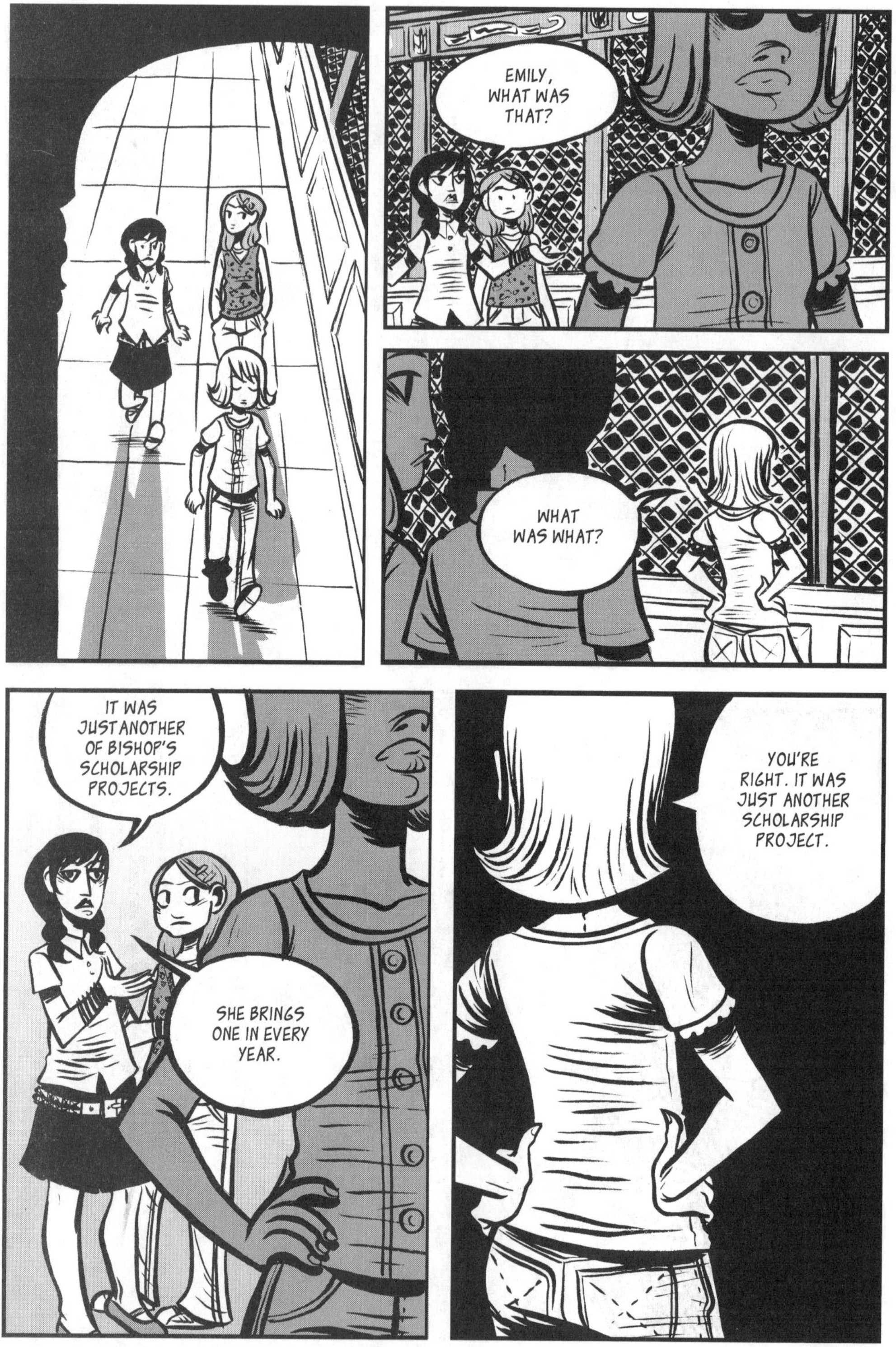
EMILY, WHAT WAS THAT?
WHAT WAS WHAT?
IT WAS JUST ANOTHER OF BISHOP'S SCHOLARSHIP PROJECTS.
SHE BRINGS ONE IN EVERY YEAR.
YOU'RE RIGHT. IT WAS JUST ANOTHER SCHOLARSHIP PROJECT.

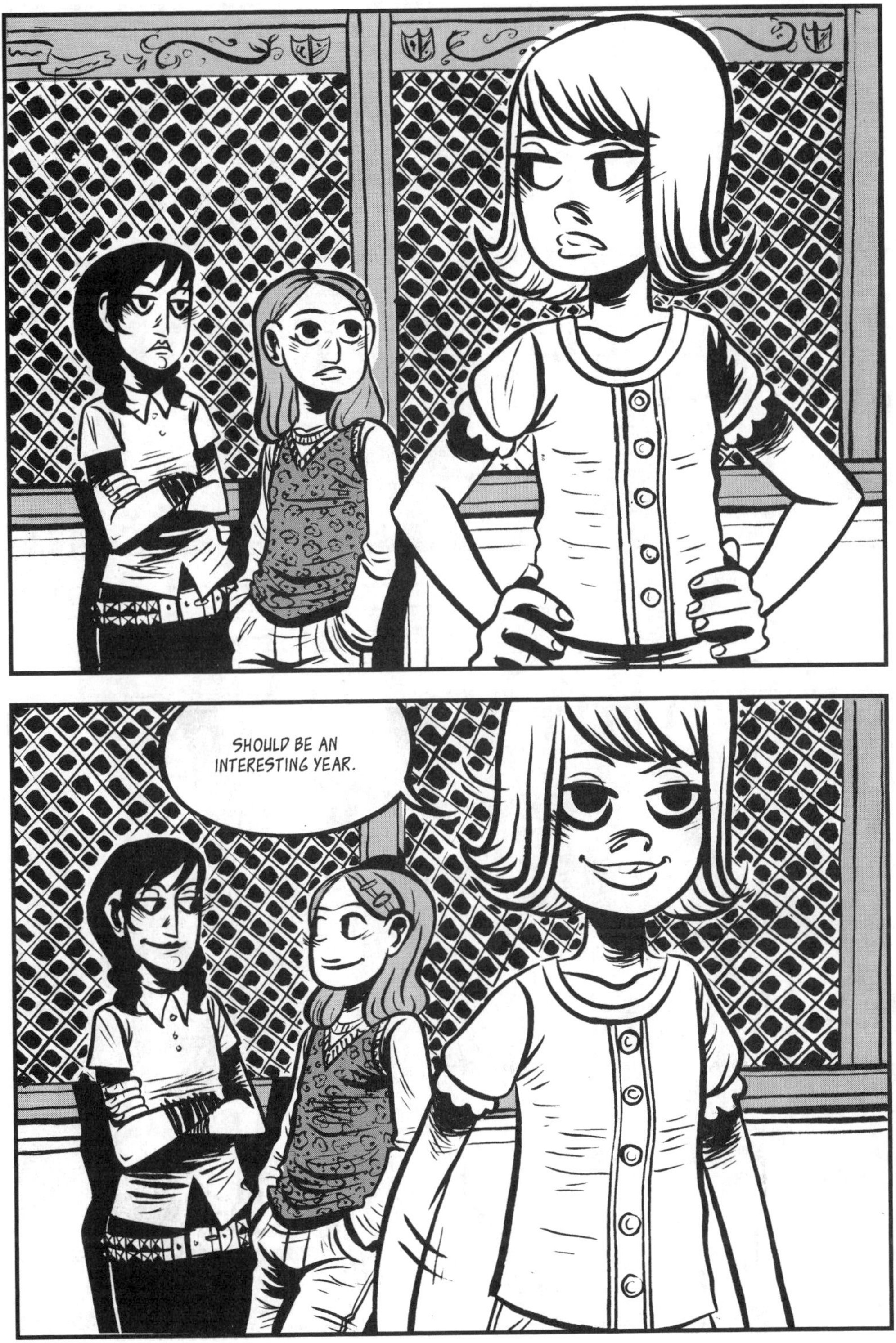
SHOULD BE AN INTERESTING YEAR.

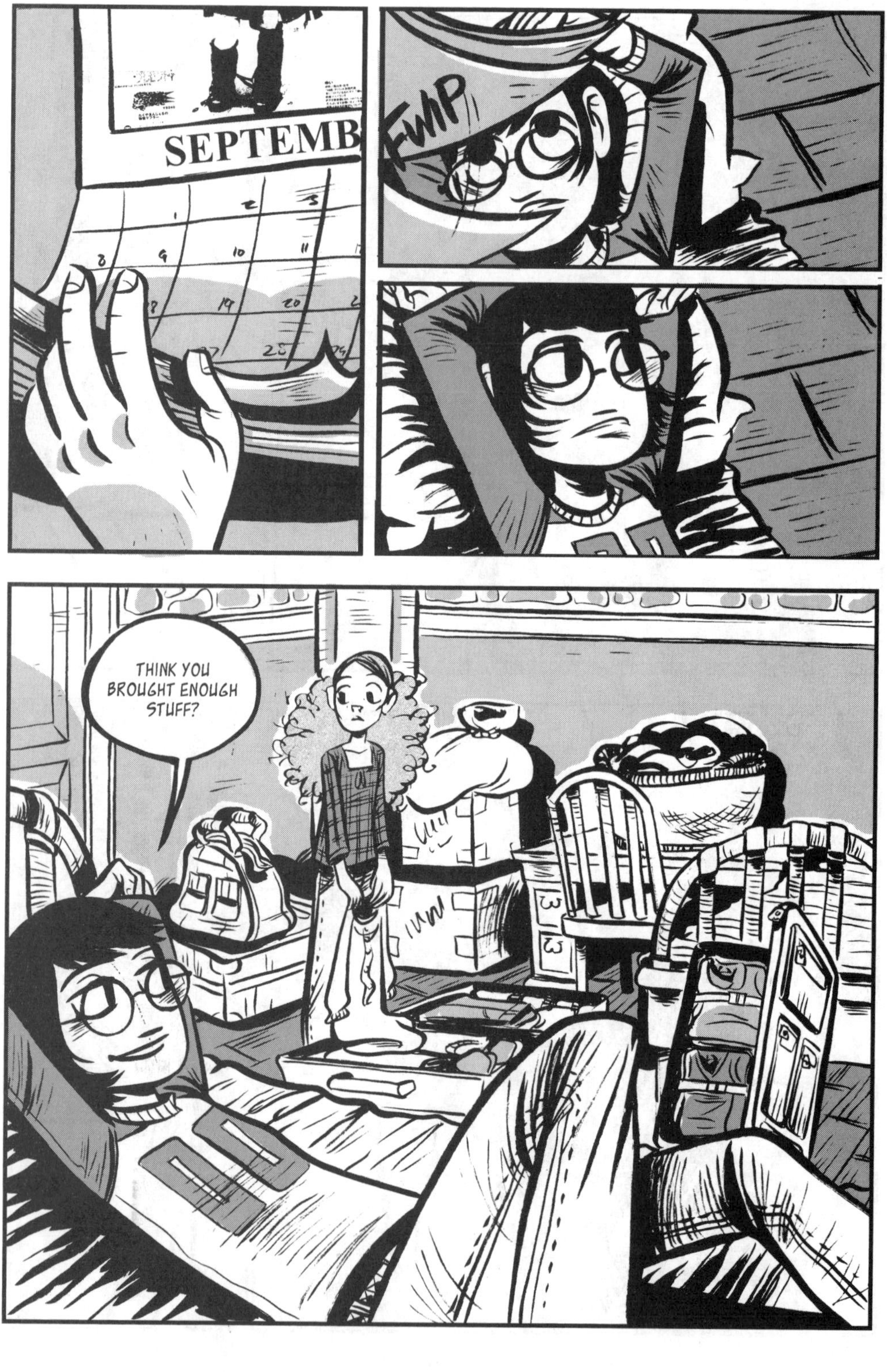
SEPTEMB
FWIP
THINK YOU BROUGHT ENOUGH STUFF?

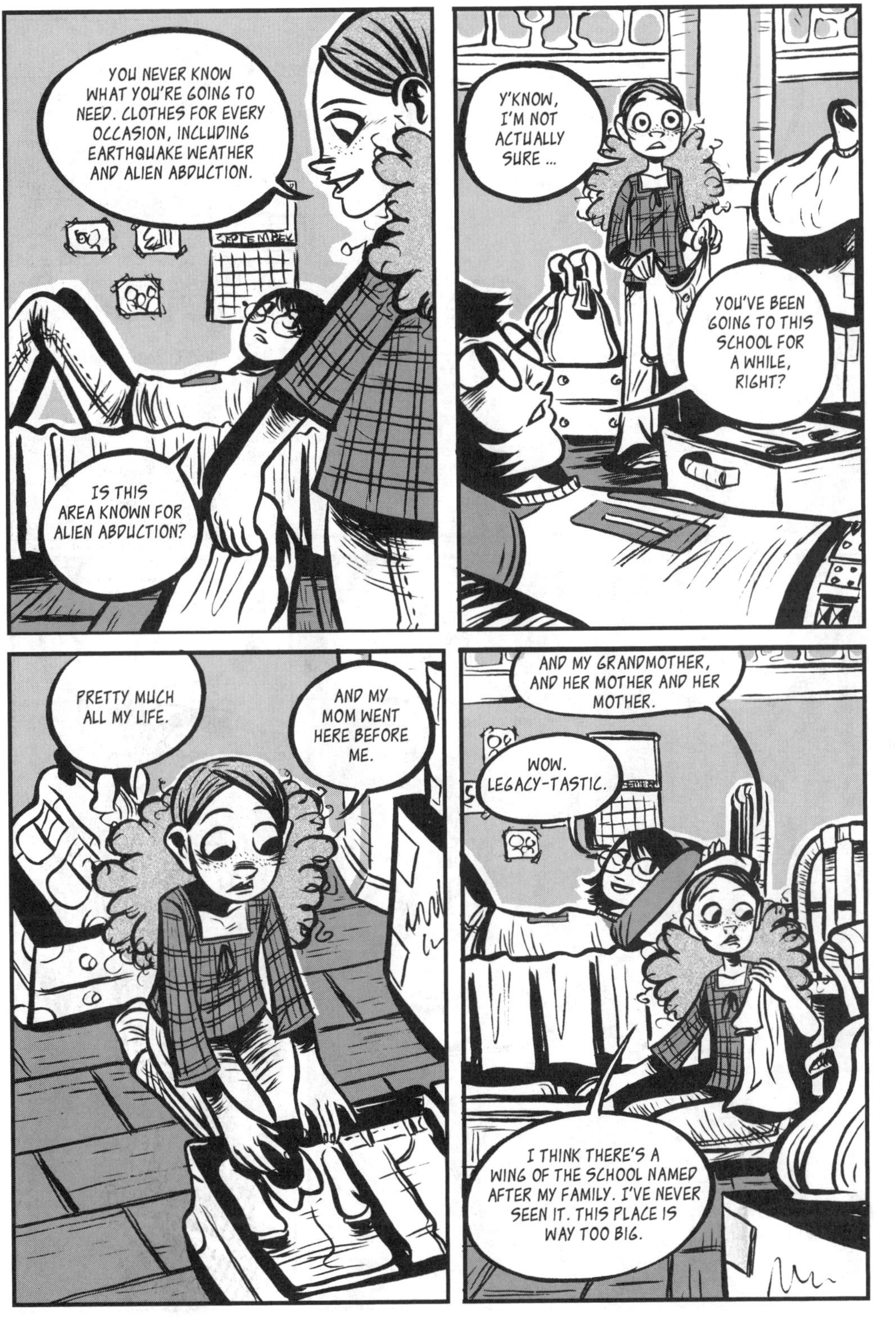
YOU NEVER KNOW WHAT YOU'RE GOING TO NEED. CLOTHES FOR EVERY OCCASION, INCLUDING EARTHQUAKE WEATHER AND ALIEN ABDUCTION.
SEPTEMBER
IS THIS AREA KNOWN FOR ALIEN ABDUCTION?
Y'KNOW, I'M NOT ACTUALLY SURE ...
YOU'VE BEEN GOING TO THIS SCHOOL FOR A WHILE, RIGHT?
PRETTY MUCH ALL MY LIFE.
AND MY MOM WENT HERE BEFORE ME.
AND MY GRANDMOTHER, AND HER MOTHER AND HER MOTHER.
WOW. LEGACY-TASTIC.
I THINK THERE'S A WING OF THE SCHOOL NAMED AFTER MY FAMILY. I'VE NEVER SEEN IT. THIS PLACE IS WAY TOO BIG.

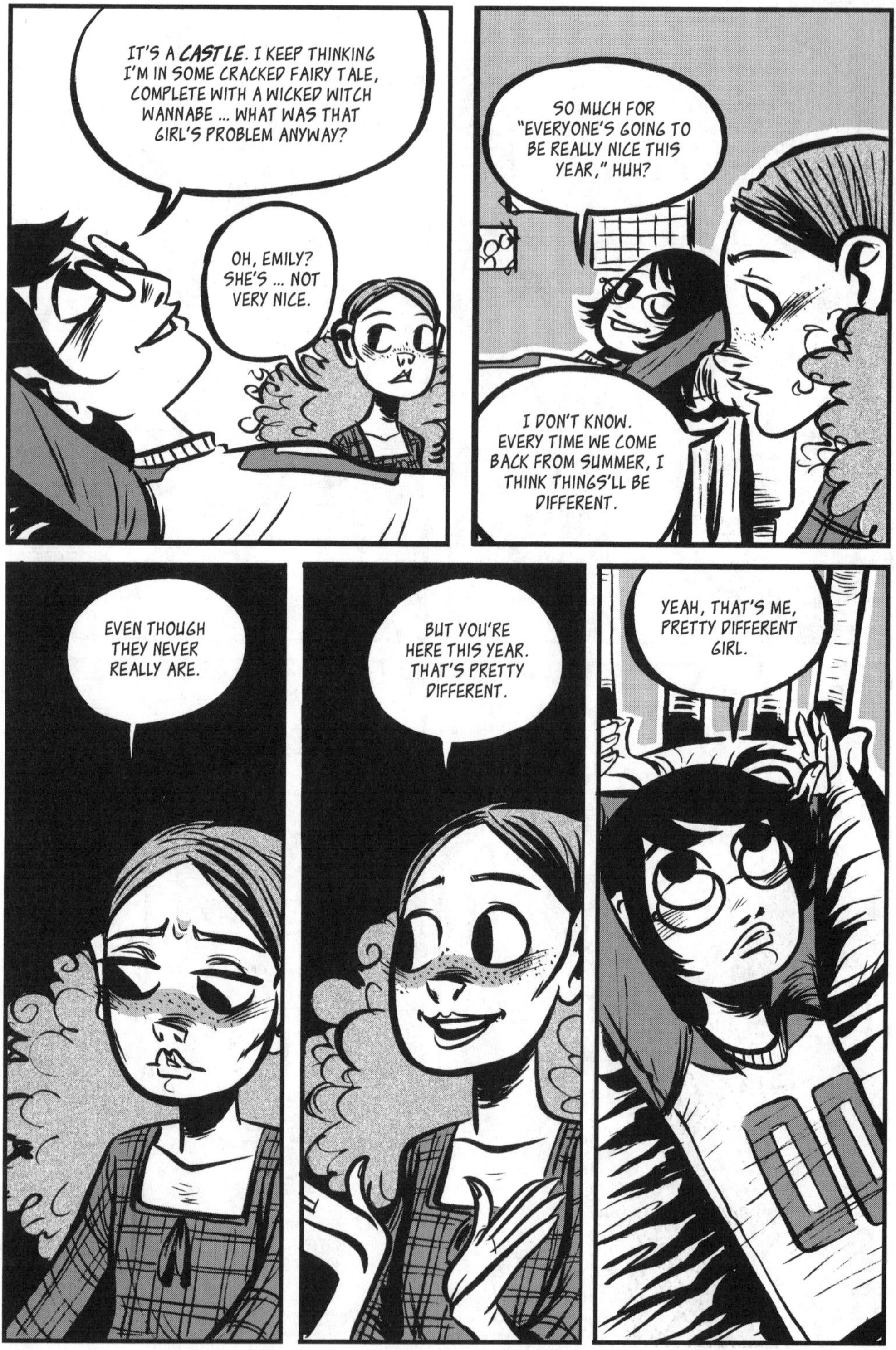
IT'S A CASTLE. I KEEP THINKING I'M IN SOME CRACKED FAIRY TALE, COMPLETE WITH A WICKED WITCH WANNABE ... WHAT WAS THAT GIRL'S PROBLEM ANYWAY?
OH, EMILY? SHE'S ... NOT VERY NICE.
SO MUCH FOR "EVERYONE'S GOING TO BE REALLY NICE THIS YEAR," HUH?
I DON'T KNOW. EVERY TIME WE COME BACK FROM SUMMER, I THINK THINGS'LL BE DIFFERENT.
EVEN THOUGH THEY NEVER REALLY ARE.
BUT YOU'RE HERE THIS YEAR. THAT'S PRETTY DIFFERENT.
YEAH, THAT'S ME, PRETTY DIFFERENT GIRL.

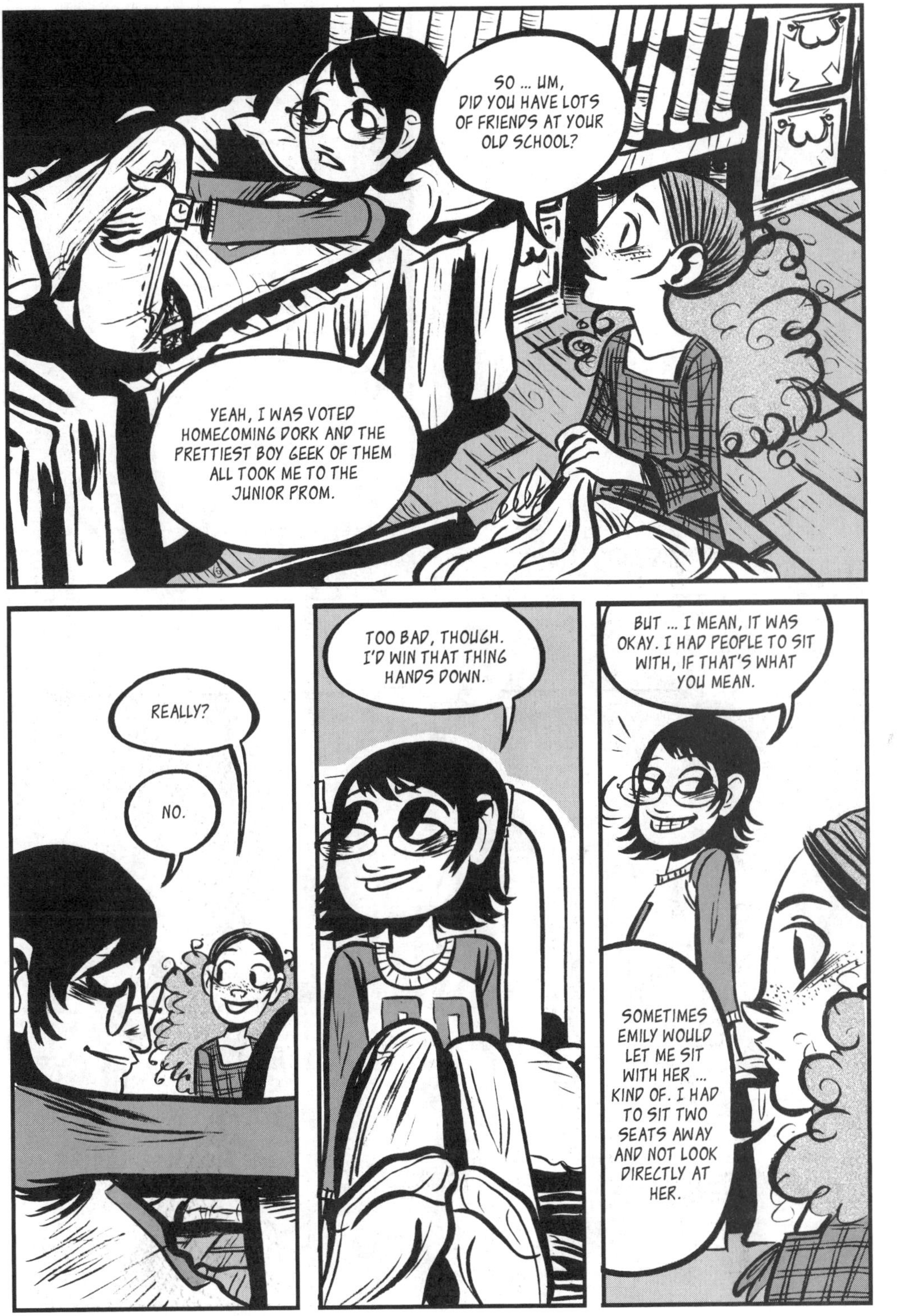

SO ... UM, DID YOU HAVE LOTS OF FRIENDS AT YOUR OLD SCHOOL?
YEAH, I WAS VOTED HOMECOMING DORK AND THE PRETTIEST BOY GEEK OF THEM ALL TOOK ME TO THE JUNIOR PROM.
REALLY?
NO.
TOO BAD, THOUGH. I'D WIN THAT THING HANDS DOWN.
BUT ... I MEAN, IT WAS OKAY. I HAD PEOPLE TO SIT WITH, IF THAT'S WHAT YOU MEAN.
SOMETIMES EMILY WOULD LET ME SIT WITH HER ... KIND OF. I HAD TO SIT TWO SEATS AWAY AND NOT LOOK DIRECTLY AT HER.

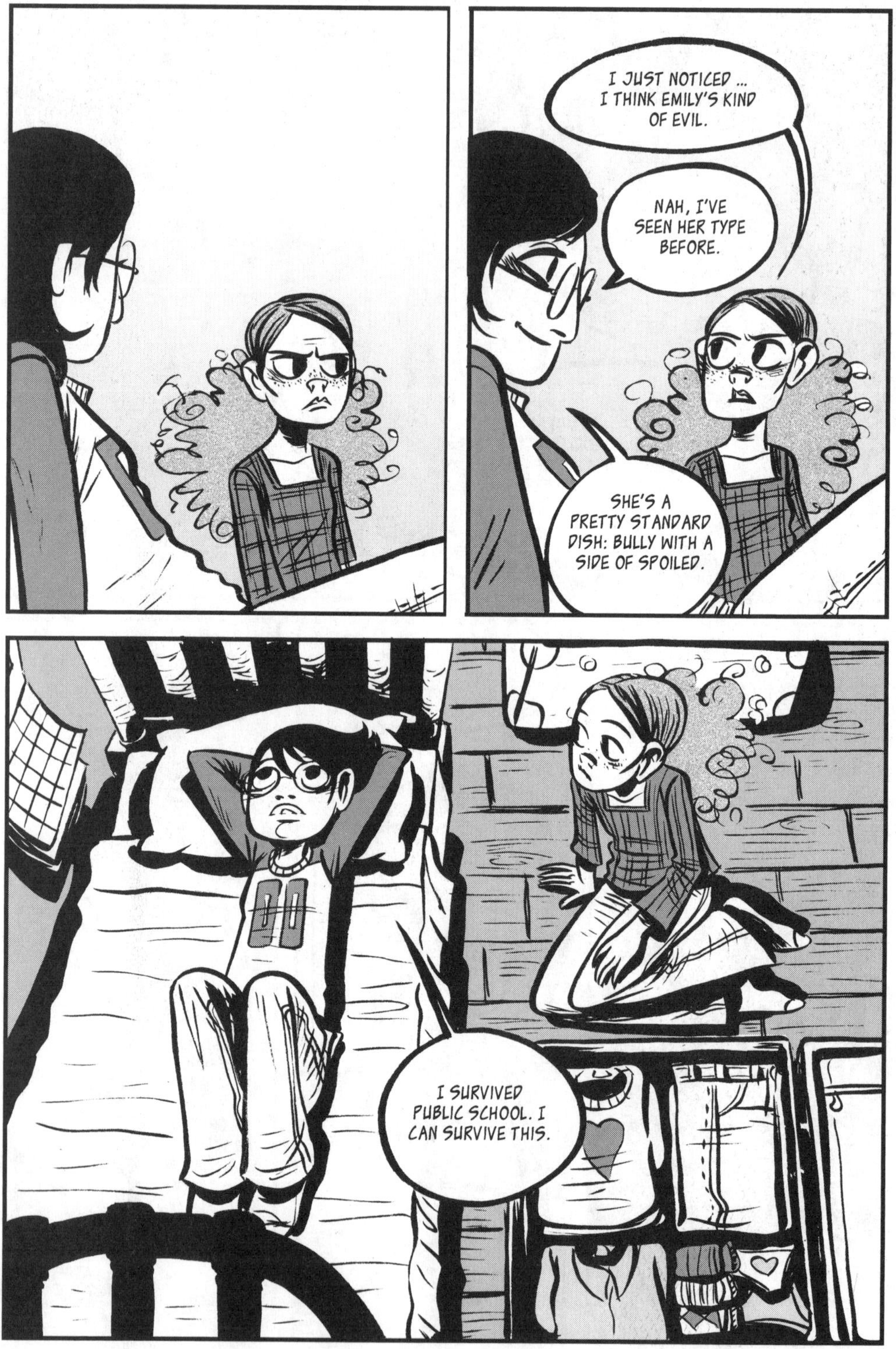
I JUST NOTICED ... I THINK EMILY'S KIND OF EVIL.
NAH, I'VE SEEN HER TYPE BEFORE.
SHE'S A PRETTY STANDARD DISH: BULLY WITH A SIDE OF SPOILED.
I SURVIVED PUBLIC SCHOOL. I CAN SURVIVE THIS.

chapter two

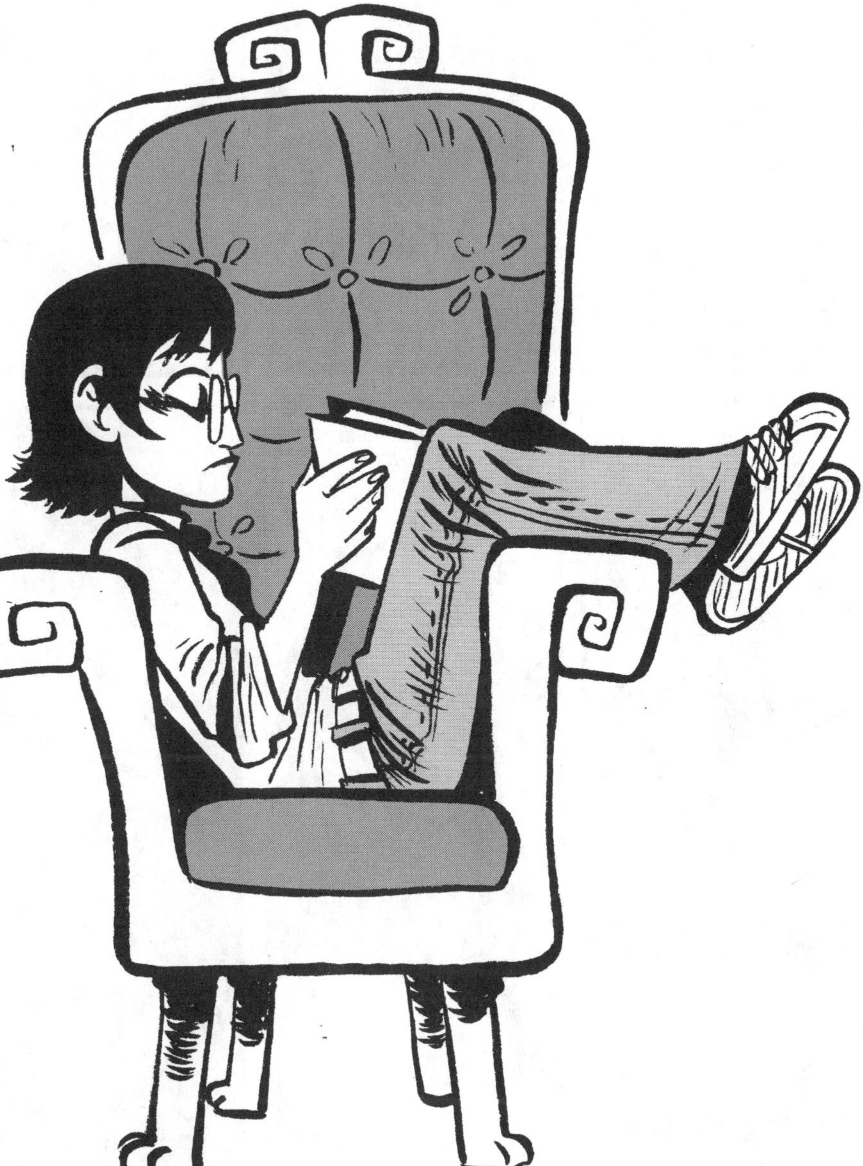

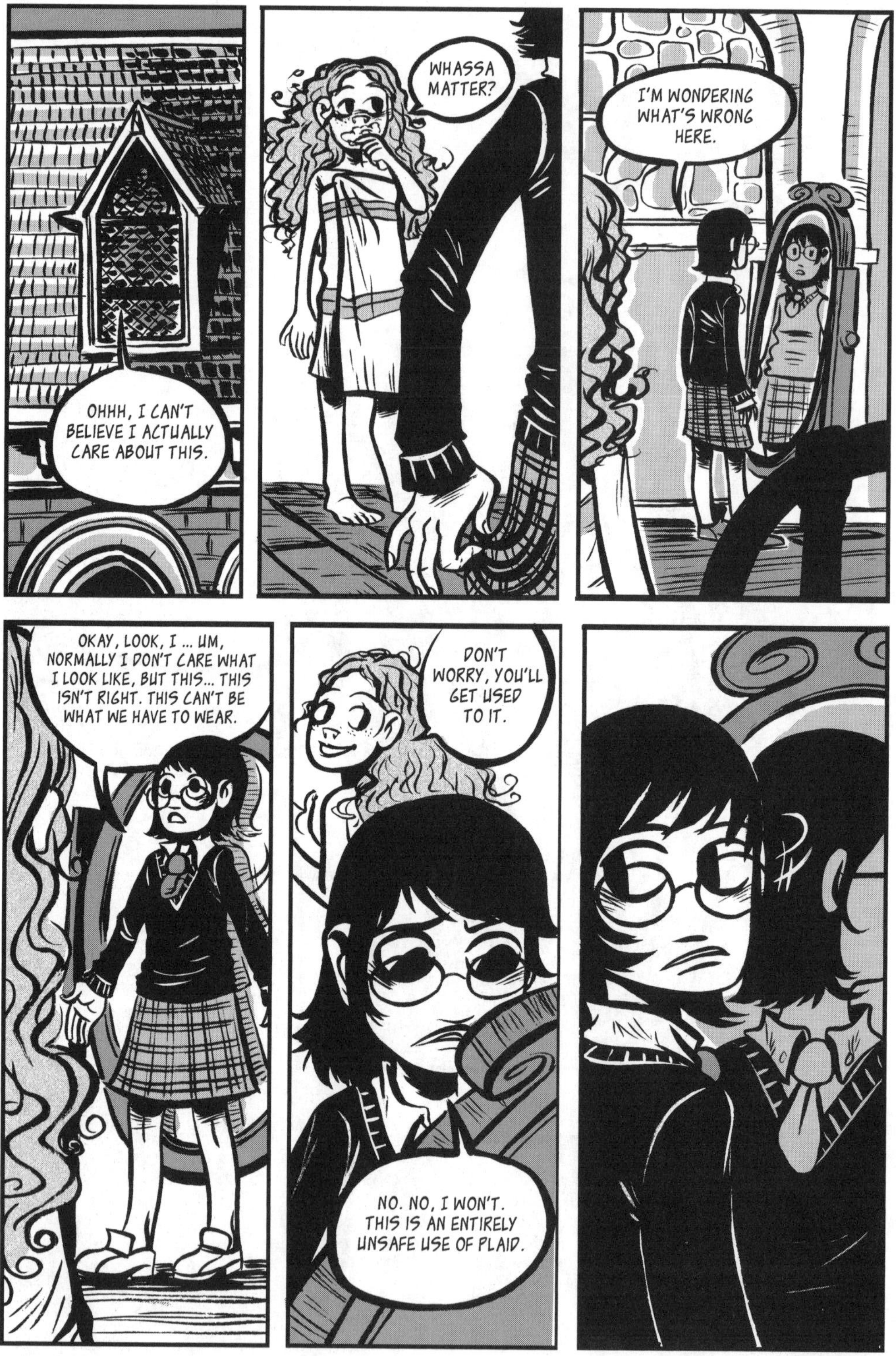
OHHH, I CAN'T BELIEVE I ACTUALLY CARE ABOUT THIS.
WHASSA MATTER?
I'M WONDERING WHAT'S WRONG HERE.
OKAY, LOOK, I ... UM, NORMALLY I DON'T CARE WHAT I LOOK LIKE, BUT THIS... THIS ISN'T RIGHT. THIS CAN'T BE WHAT WE HAVE TO WEAR.
DON'T WORRY, YOU'LL GET USED TO IT.
NO. NO, I WON'T. THIS IS AN ENTIRELY UNSAFE USE OF PLAID.

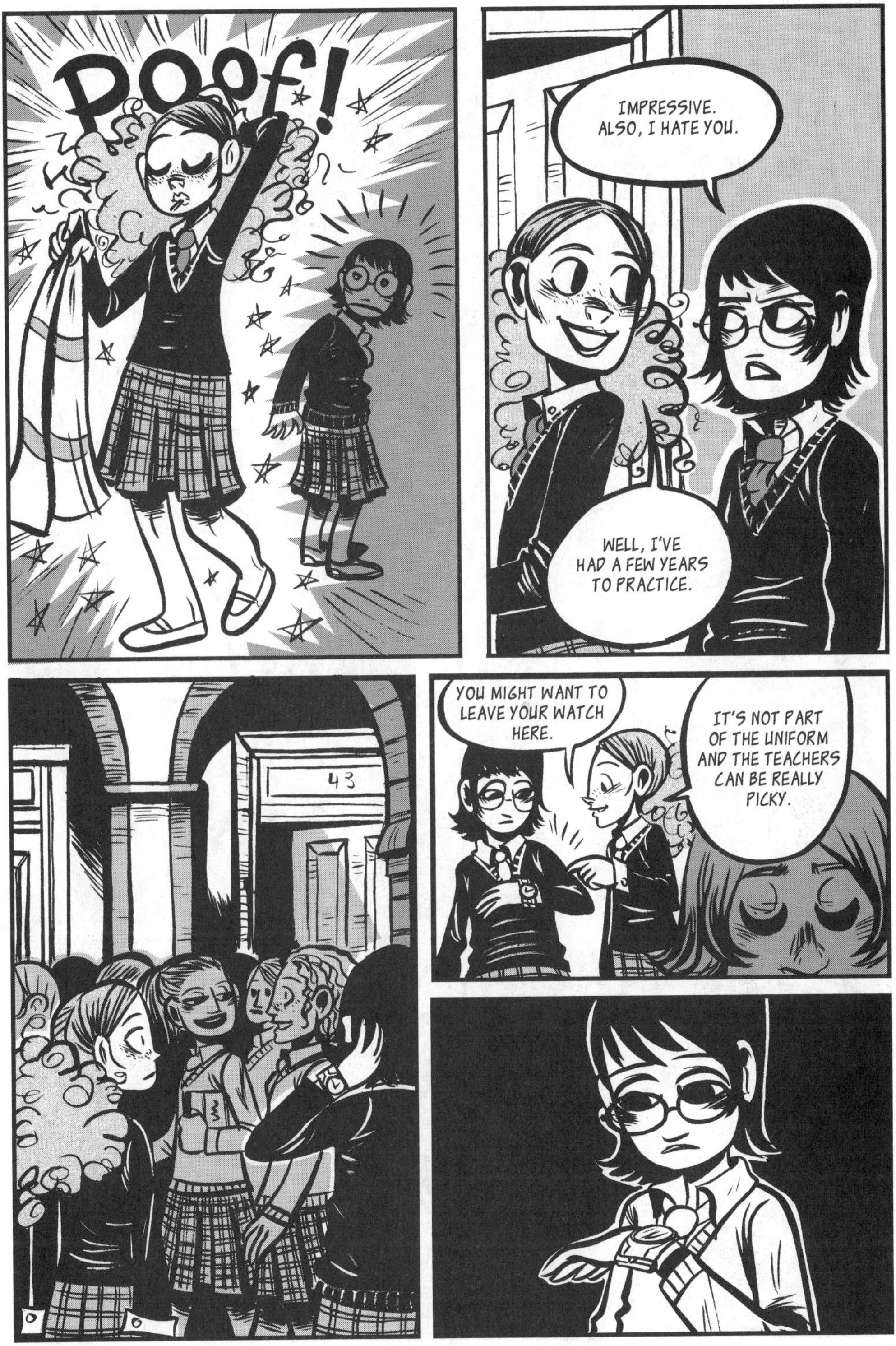
POOF!
IMPRESSIVE. ALSO, I HATE YOU.
WELL, I'VE HAD A FEW YEARS TO PRACTICE.
43
YOU MIGHT WANT TO LEAVE YOUR WATCH HERE.
IT'S NOT PART OF THE UNIFORM AND THE TEACHERS CAN BE REALLY PICKY.

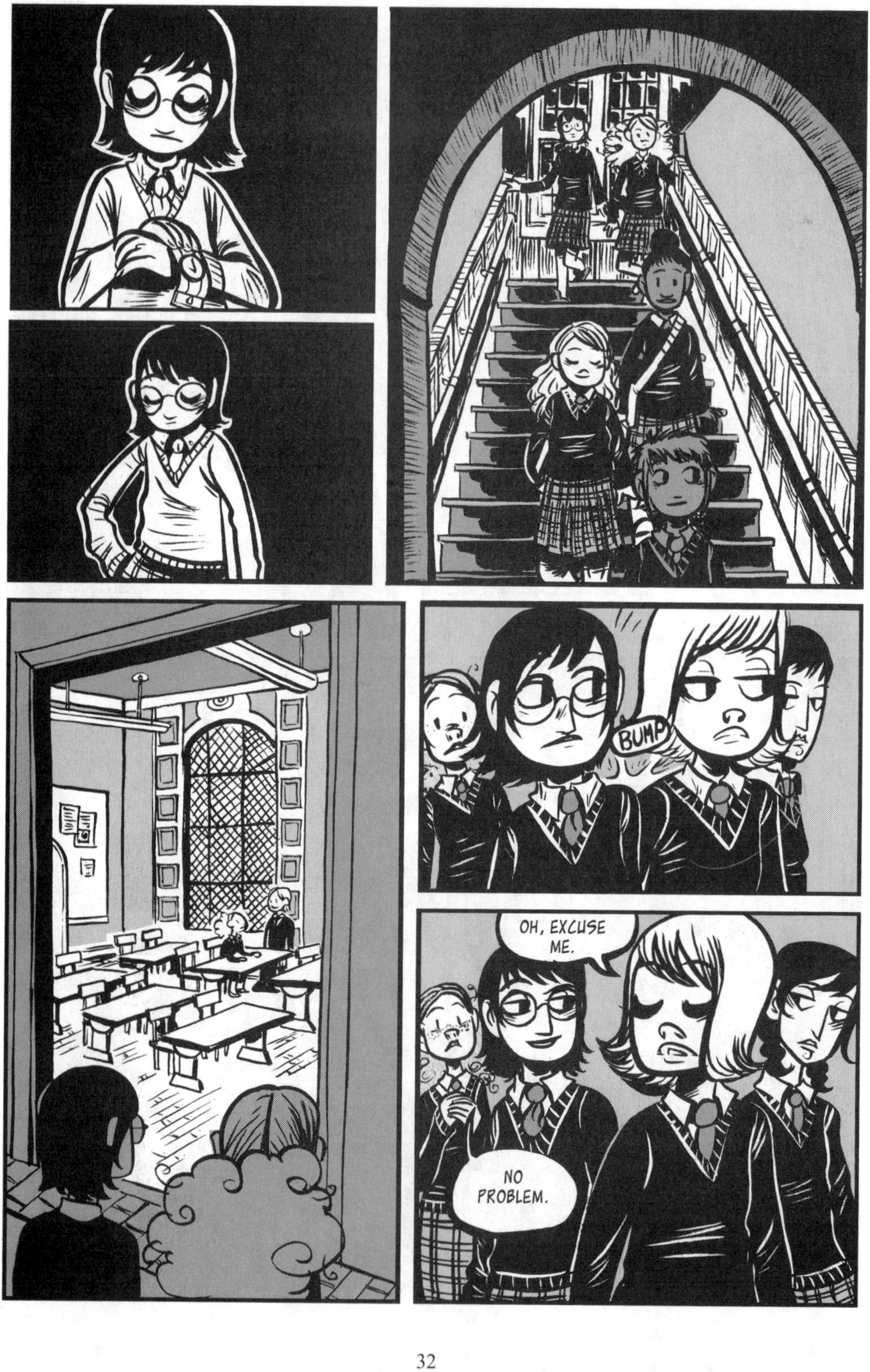
BUMP
OH, EXCUSE ME.
NO PROBLEM.

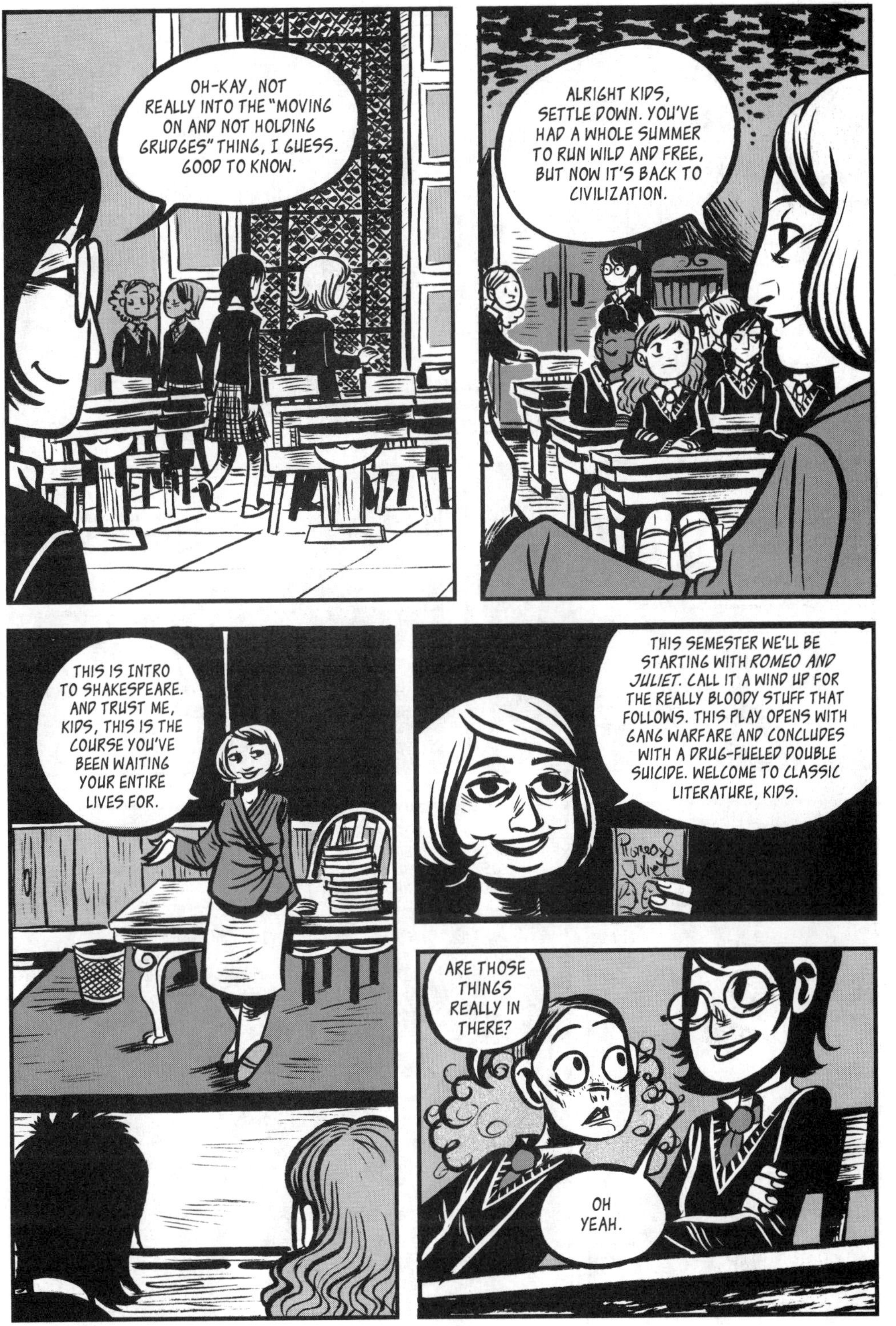
OH-KAY, NOT REALLY INTO THE "MOVING ON AND NOT HOLDING GRUDGES" THING, I GUESS. GOOD TO KNOW.
ALRIGHT KIDS, SETTLE DOWN. YOU'VE HAD A WHOLE SUMMER TO RUN WILD AND FREE, BUT NOW IT'S BACK TO CIVILIZATION.
THIS IS INTRO TO SHAKESPEARE. AND TRUST ME, KIDS, THIS IS THE COURSE YOU'VE BEEN WAITING YOUR ENTIRE LIVES FOR.
THIS SEMESTER WE'LL BE STARTING WITH *ROMEO AND JULIET*. CALL IT A WIND UP FOR THE REALLY BLOODY STUFF THAT FOLLOWS. THIS PLAY OPENS WITH GANG WARFARE AND CONCLUDES WITH A DRUG-FUELED DOUBLE SUICIDE. WELCOME TO CLASSIC LITERATURE, KIDS.
Romeo & Juliet
ARE THOSE THINGS REALLY IN THERE?
OH YEAH.

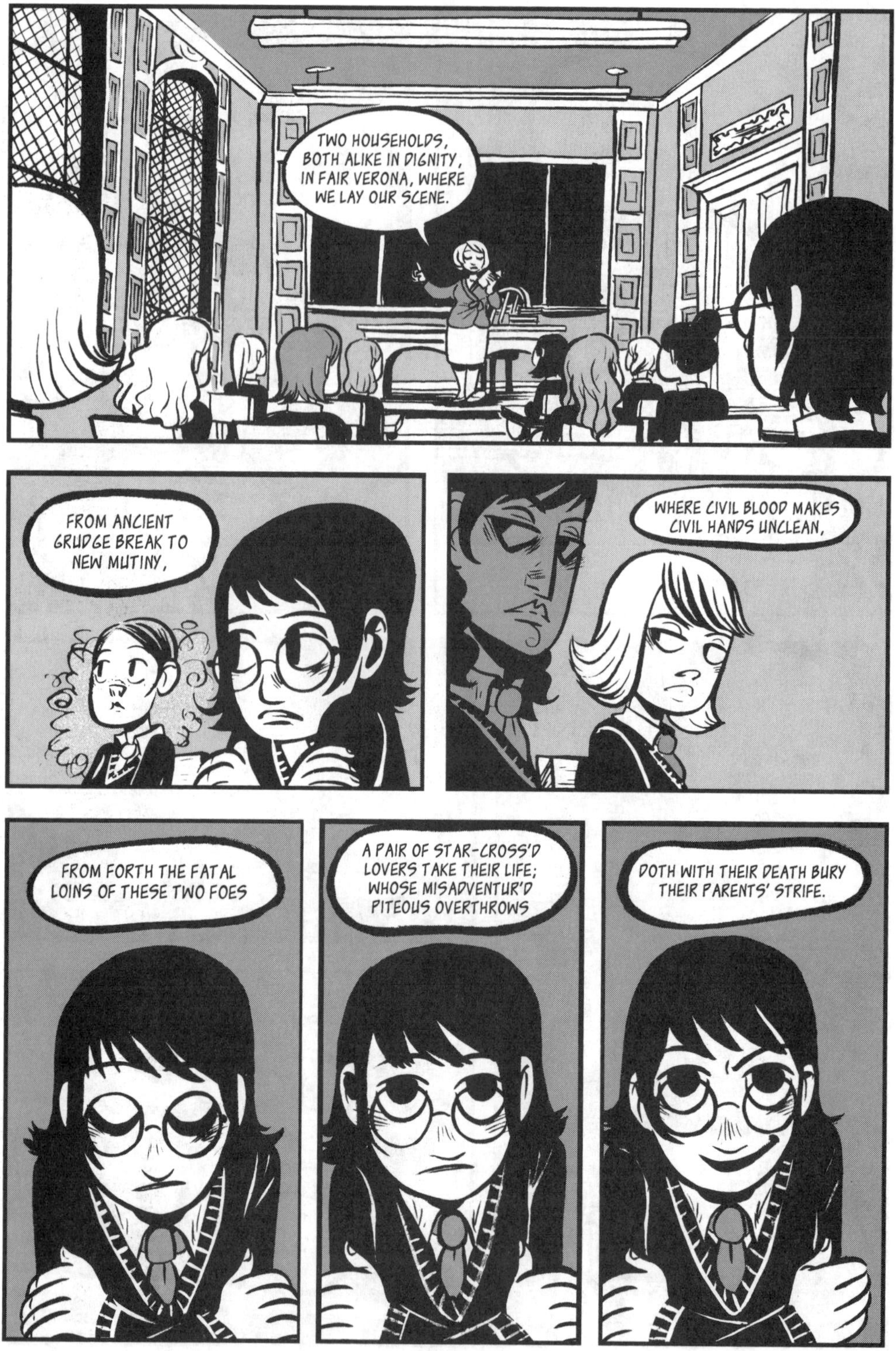

TWO HOUSEHOLDS, BOTH ALIKE IN DIGNITY, IN FAIR VERONA, WHERE WE LAY OUR SCENE.
FROM ANCIENT GRUDGE BREAK TO NEW MUTINY,
WHERE CIVIL BLOOD MAKES CIVIL HANDS UNCLEAN,
FROM FORTH THE FATAL LOINS OF THESE TWO FOES
A PAIR OF STAR-CROSS'D LOVERS TAKE THEIR LIFE; WHOSE MISADVENTUR'D PITEOUS OVERTHROWS
DOTH WITH THEIR DEATH BURY THEIR PARENTS' STRIFE.

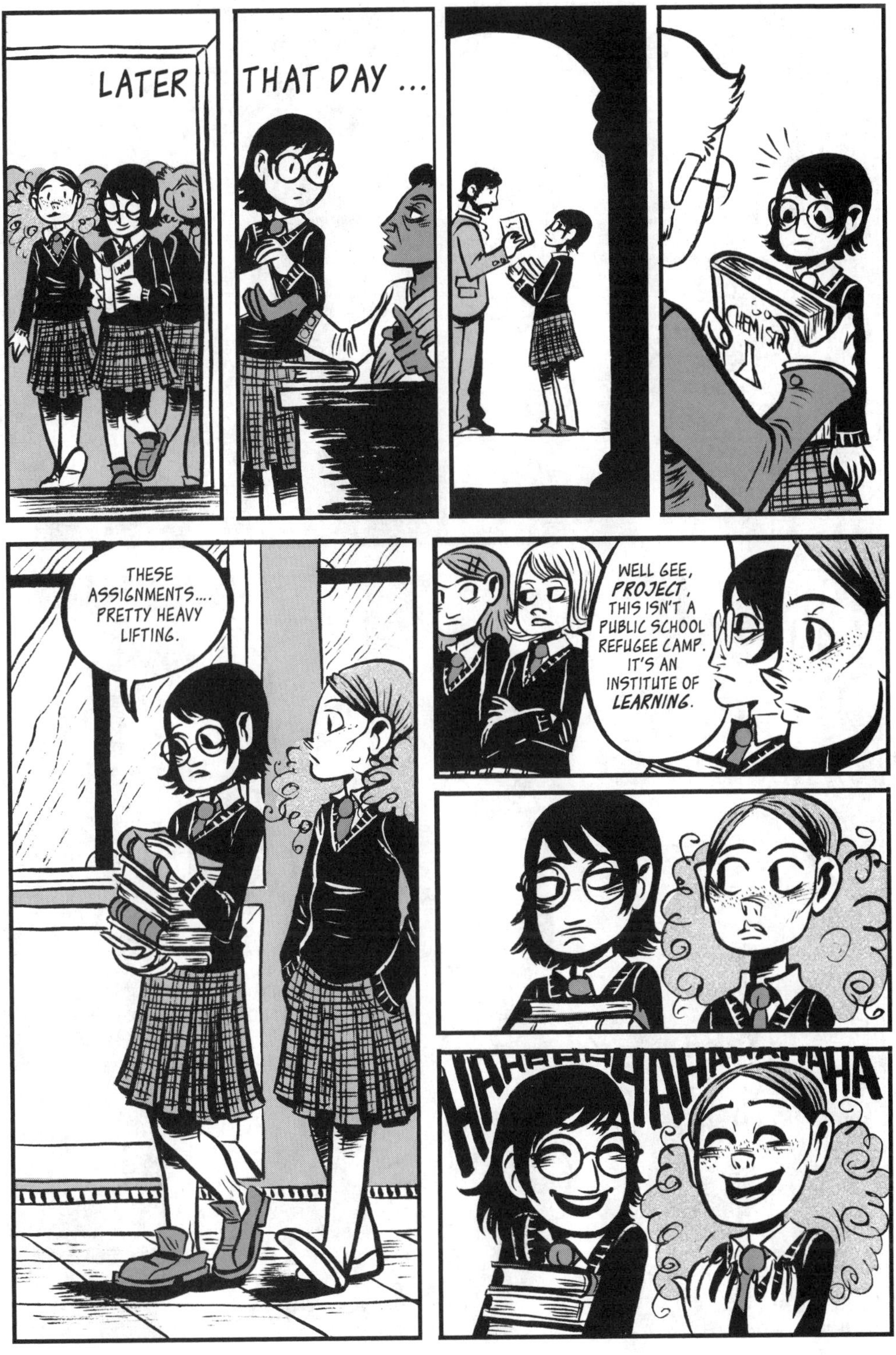
LATER
THAT DAY ...
CHEMISTR
THESE ASSIGNMENTS.... PRETTY HEAVY LIFTING.
WELL GEE, **PROJECT**, THIS ISN'T A PUBLIC SCHOOL REFUGEE CAMP. IT'S AN INSTITUTE OF **LEARNING**.
HAHAHAHAHAHAHAHA

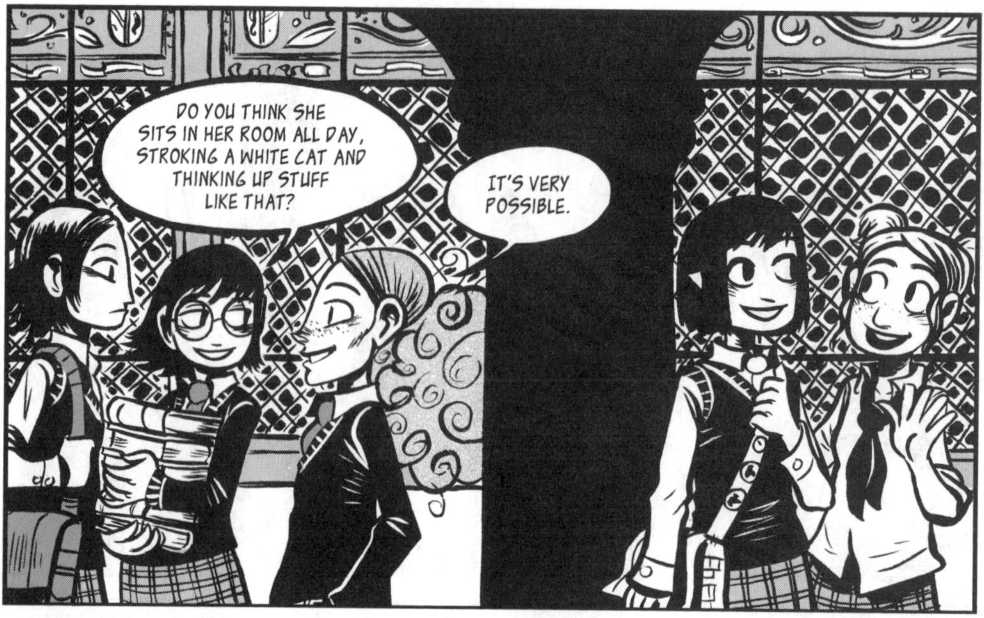
DO YOU THINK SHE SITS IN HER ROOM ALL DAY, STROKING A WHITE CAT AND THINKING UP STUFF LIKE THAT?
IT'S VERY POSSIBLE.

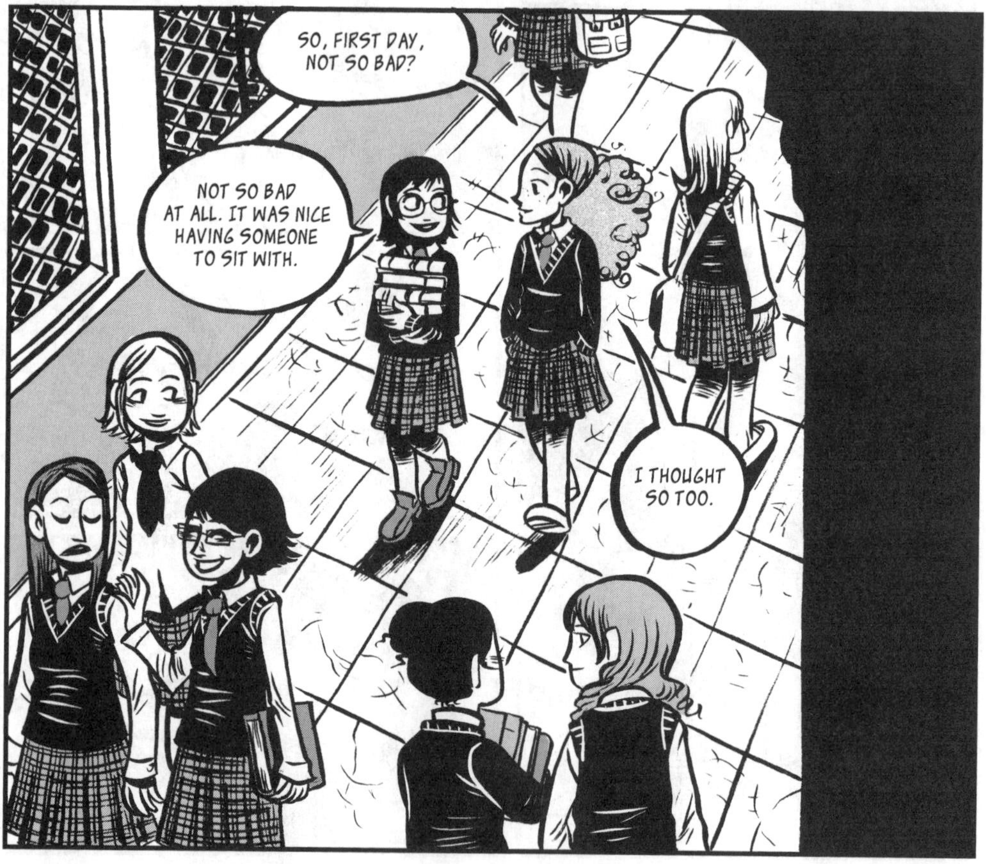
SO, FIRST DAY, NOT SO BAD?
NOT SO BAD AT ALL. IT WAS NICE HAVING SOMEONE TO SIT WITH.
I THOUGHT SO TOO.

chapter three

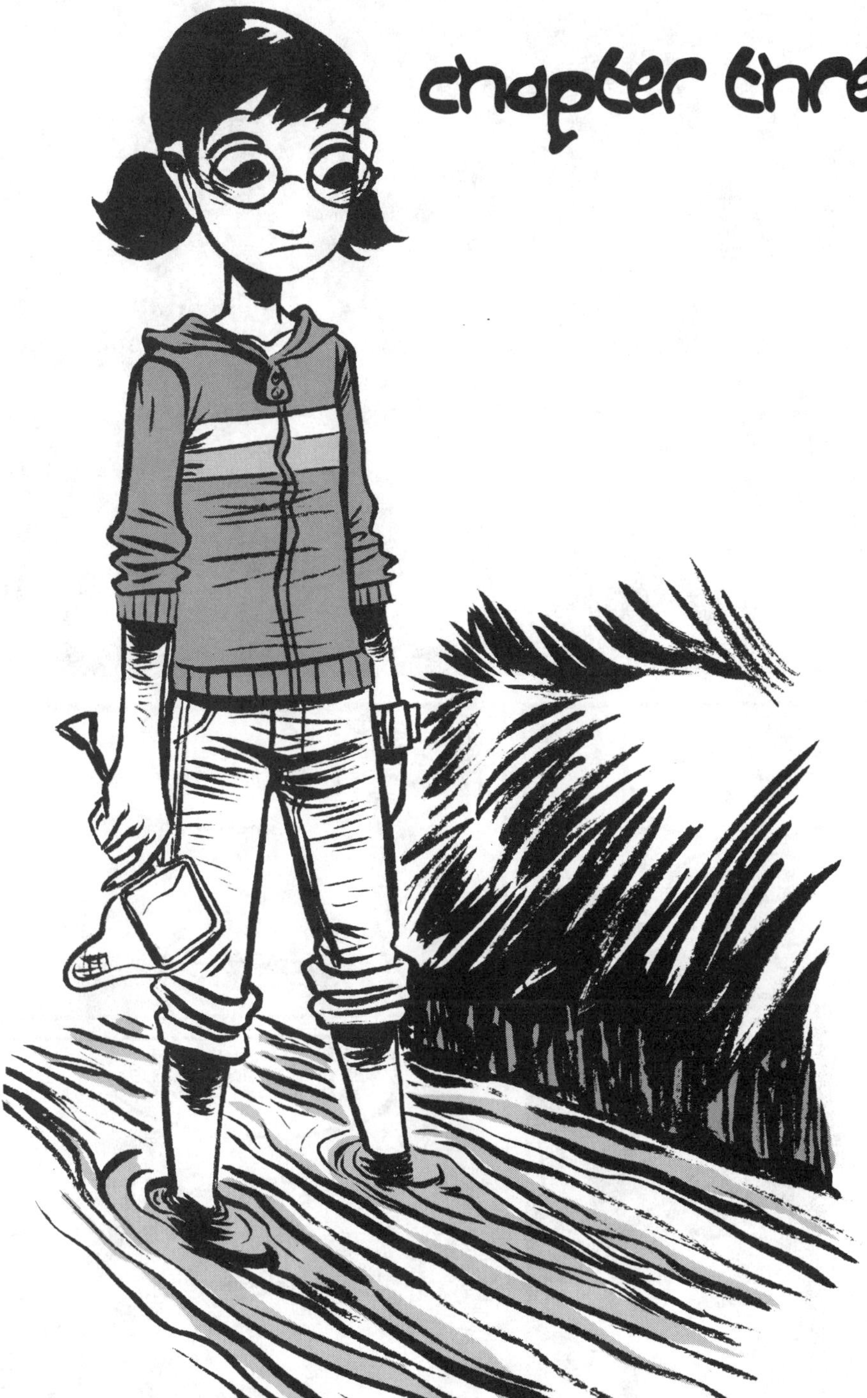

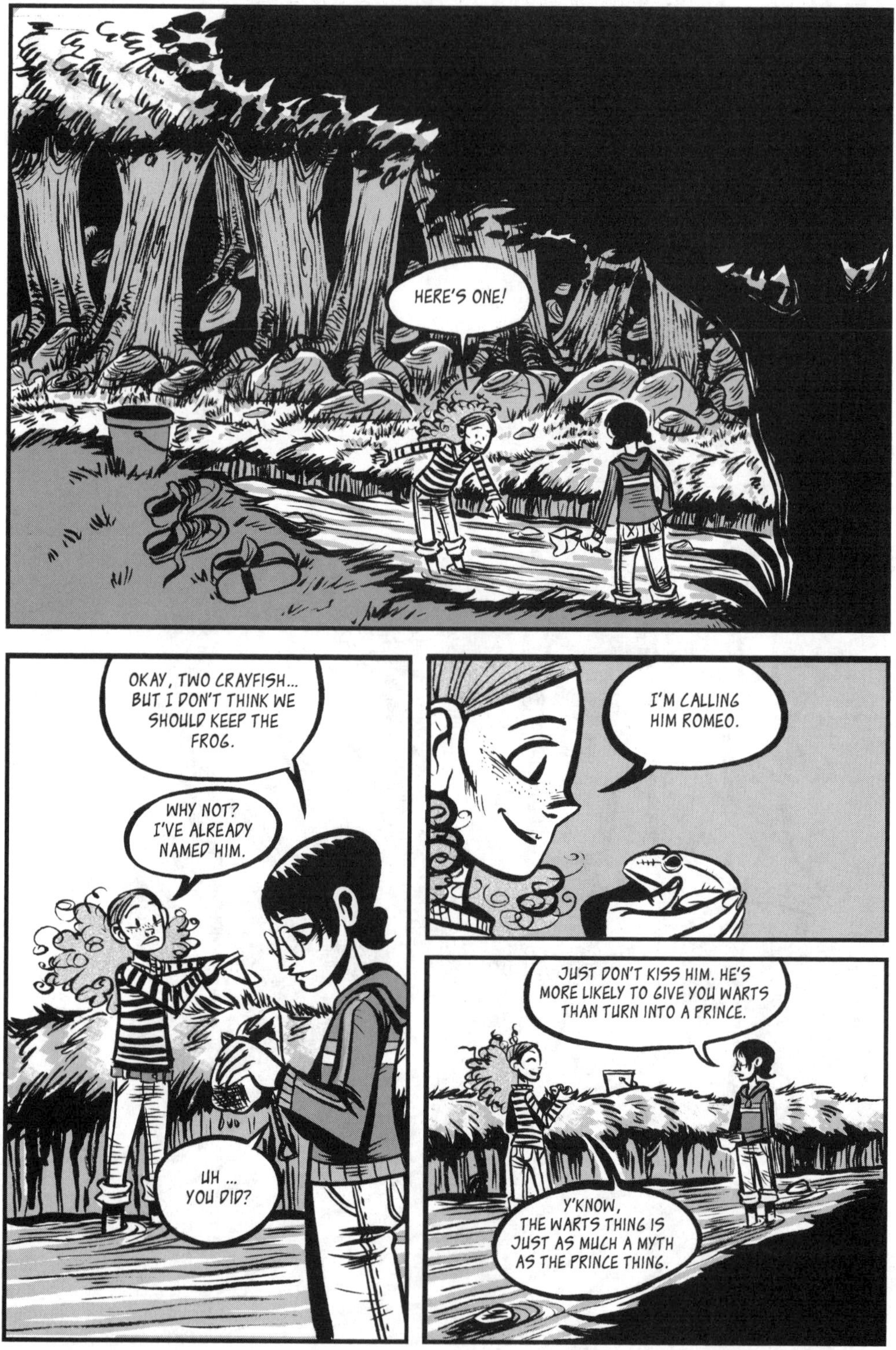
HERE'S ONE!
OKAY, TWO CRAYFISH... BUT I DON'T THINK WE SHOULD KEEP THE FROG.
WHY NOT? I'VE ALREADY NAMED HIM.
UH ... YOU DID?
I'M CALLING HIM ROMEO.
JUST DON'T KISS HIM. HE'S MORE LIKELY TO GIVE YOU WARTS THAN TURN INTO A PRINCE.
Y'KNOW, THE WARTS THING IS JUST AS MUCH A MYTH AS THE PRINCE THING.

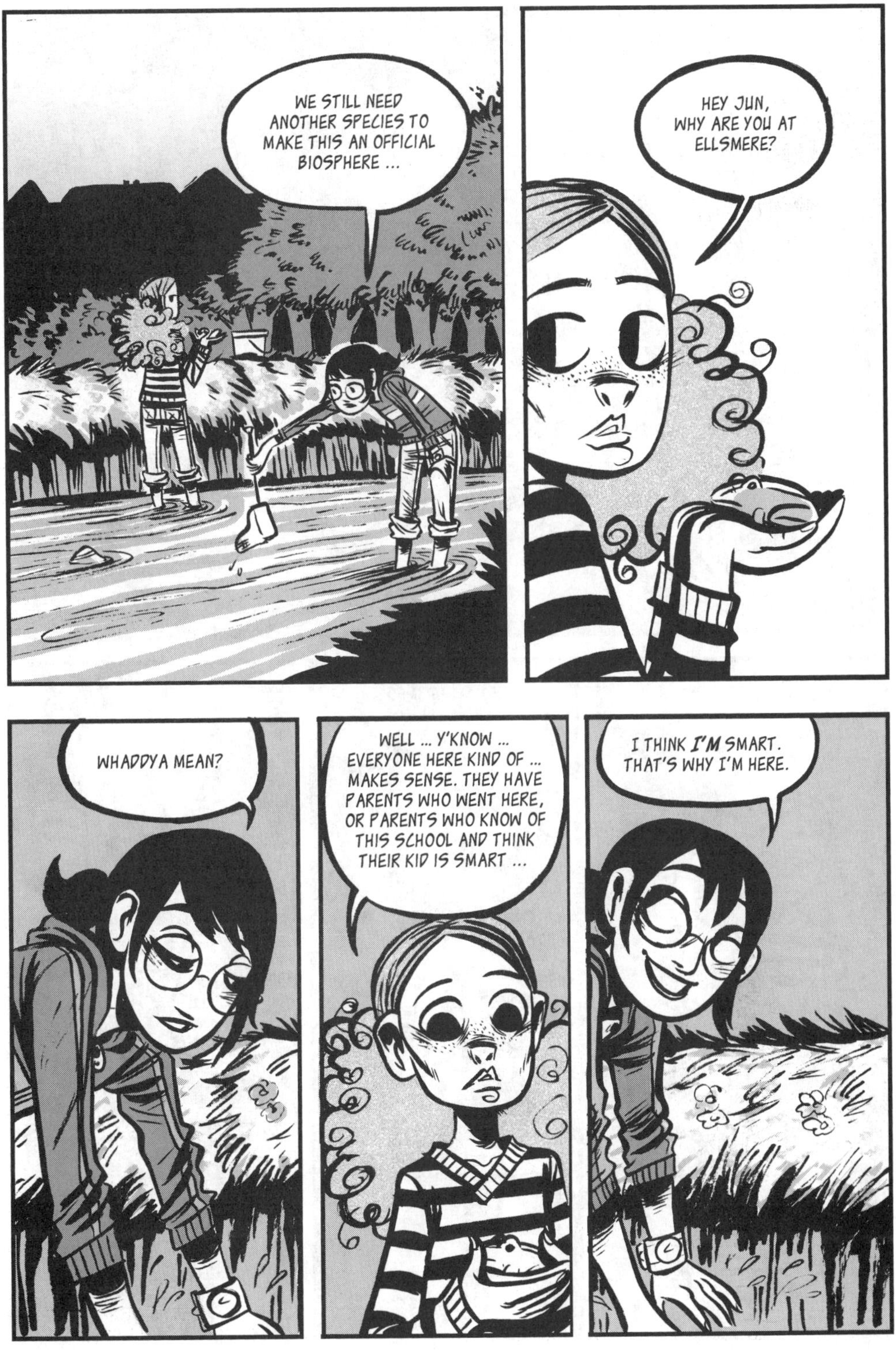
WE STILL NEED ANOTHER SPECIES TO MAKE THIS AN OFFICIAL BIOSPHERE ...
HEY JUN, WHY ARE YOU AT ELLSMERE?
WHADDYA MEAN?
WELL ... Y'KNOW ... EVERYONE HERE KIND OF ... MAKES SENSE. THEY HAVE PARENTS WHO WENT HERE, OR PARENTS WHO KNOW OF THIS SCHOOL AND THINK THEIR KID IS SMART ...
I THINK ***I'M*** SMART. THAT'S WHY I'M HERE.

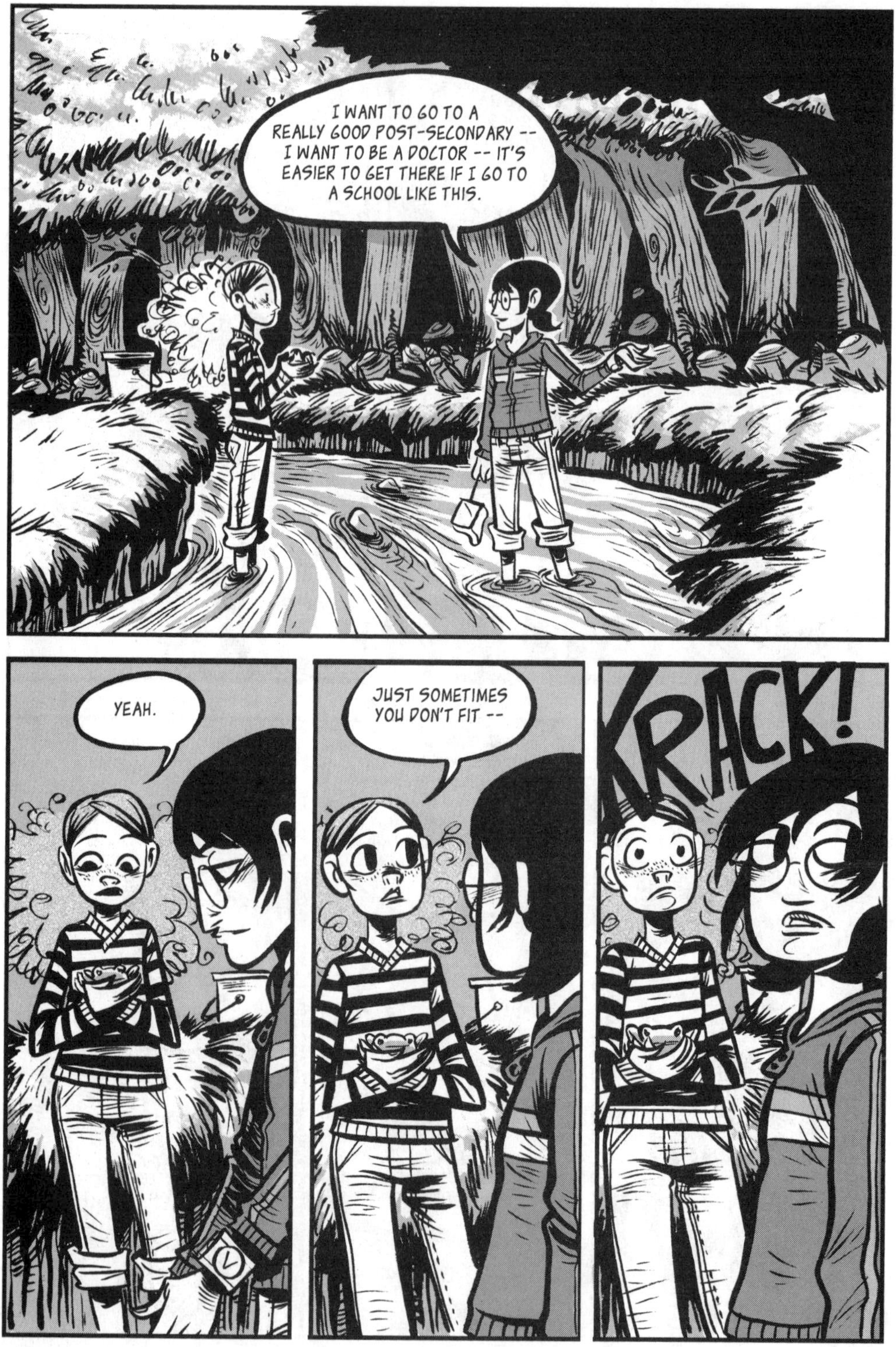
I WANT TO GO TO A REALLY GOOD POST-SECONDARY -- I WANT TO BE A DOCTOR -- IT'S EASIER TO GET THERE IF I GO TO A SCHOOL LIKE THIS.
YEAH.
JUST SOMETIMES YOU DON'T FIT --
KRACK!

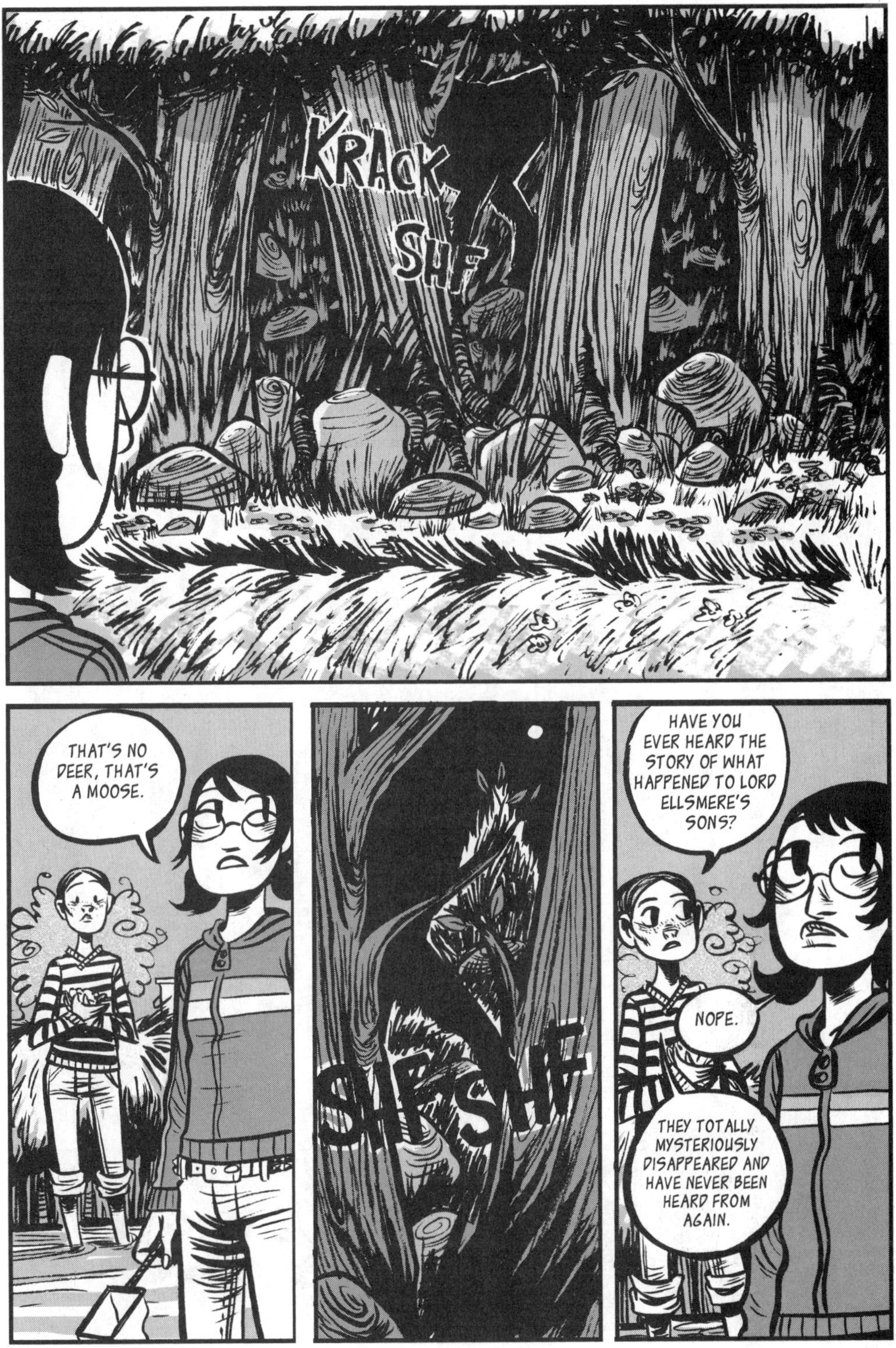
KRACK
SHF
THAT'S NO DEER, THAT'S A MOOSE.
SHFSHF
HAVE YOU EVER HEARD THE STORY OF WHAT HAPPENED TO LORD ELLSMERE'S SONS?
NOPE.
THEY TOTALLY MYSTERIOUSLY DISAPPEARED AND HAVE NEVER BEEN HEARD FROM AGAIN.

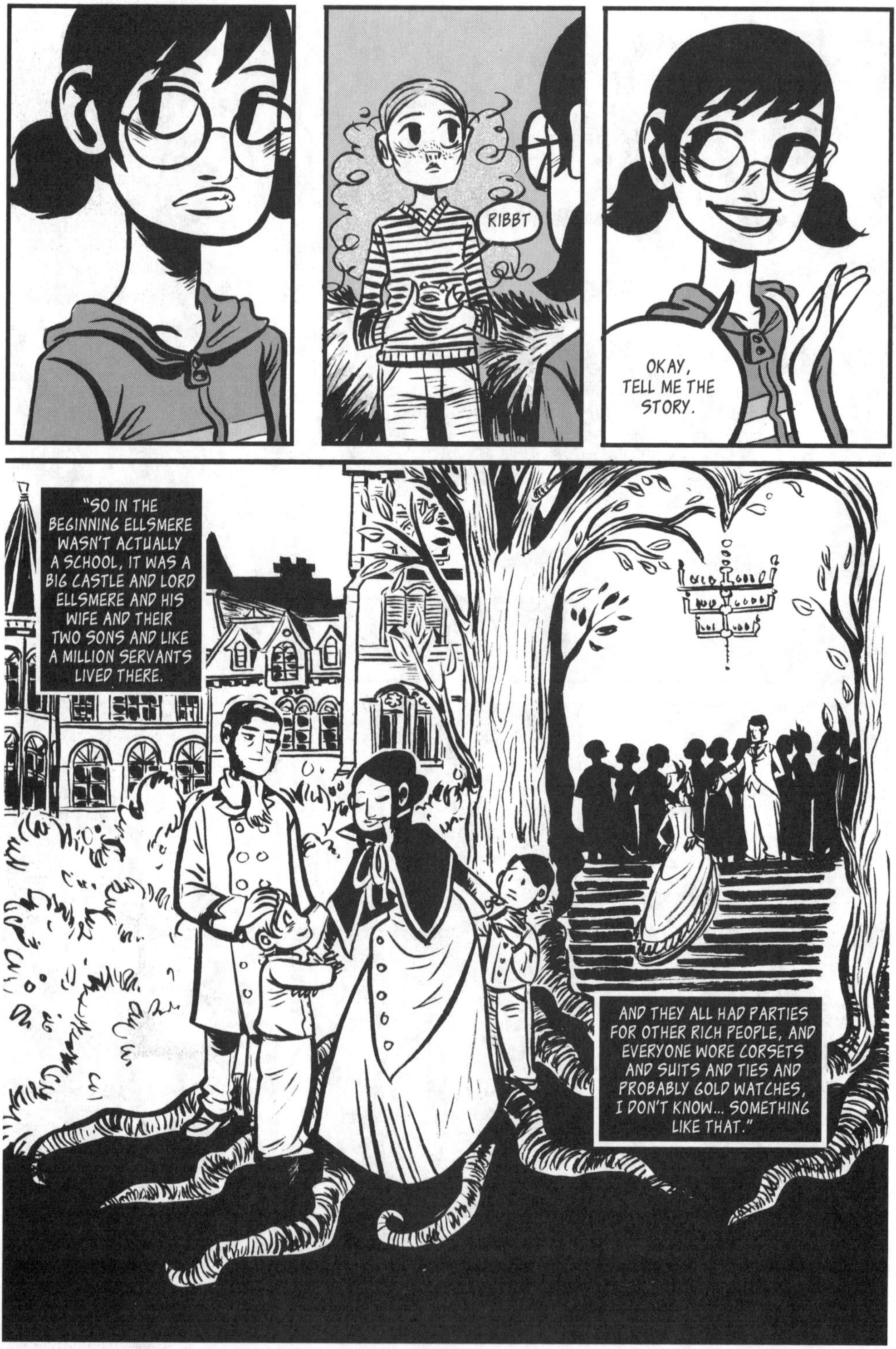
RIBBT
OKAY, TELL ME THE STORY.
"SO IN THE BEGINNING ELLSMERE WASN'T ACTUALLY A SCHOOL, IT WAS A BIG CASTLE AND LORD ELLSMERE AND HIS WIFE AND THEIR TWO SONS AND LIKE A MILLION SERVANTS LIVED THERE.
AND THEY ALL HAD PARTIES FOR OTHER RICH PEOPLE, AND EVERYONE WORE CORSETS AND SUITS AND TIES AND PROBABLY GOLD WATCHES, I DON'T KNOW... SOMETHING LIKE THAT."

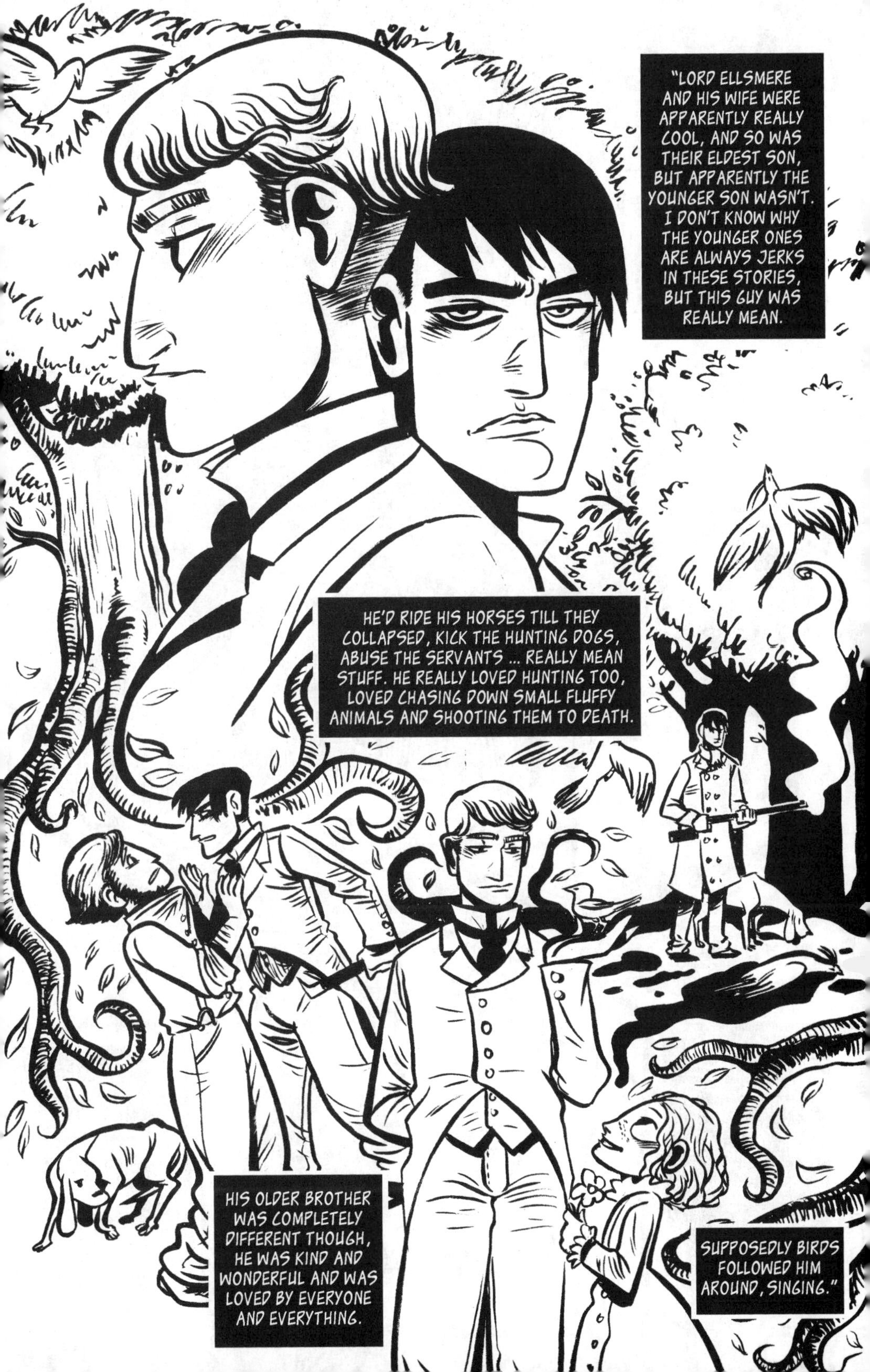
"LORD ELLSMERE AND HIS WIFE WERE APPARENTLY REALLY COOL, AND SO WAS THEIR ELDEST SON, BUT APPARENTLY THE YOUNGER SON WASN'T. I DON'T KNOW WHY THE YOUNGER ONES ARE ALWAYS JERKS IN THESE STORIES, BUT THIS GUY WAS REALLY MEAN.
HE'D RIDE HIS HORSES TILL THEY COLLAPSED, KICK THE HUNTING DOGS, ABUSE THE SERVANTS ... REALLY MEAN STUFF. HE REALLY LOVED HUNTING TOO, LOVED CHASING DOWN SMALL FLUFFY ANIMALS AND SHOOTING THEM TO DEATH.
HIS OLDER BROTHER WAS COMPLETELY DIFFERENT THOUGH, HE WAS KIND AND WONDERFUL AND WAS LOVED BY EVERYONE AND EVERYTHING.
SUPPOSEDLY BIRDS FOLLOWED HIM AROUND, SINGING."

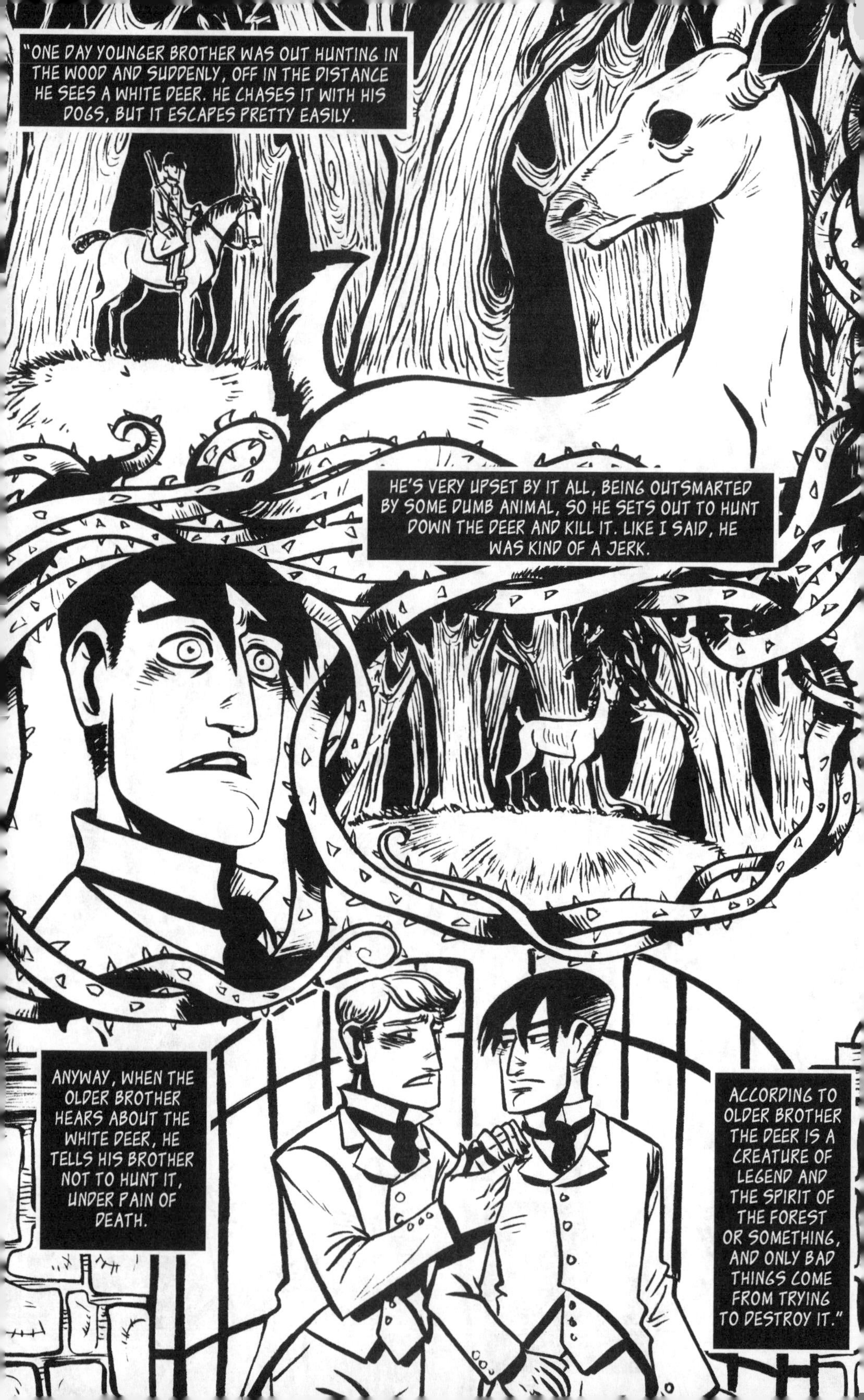
"ONE DAY YOUNGER BROTHER WAS OUT HUNTING IN THE WOOD AND SUDDENLY, OFF IN THE DISTANCE HE SEES A WHITE DEER. HE CHASES IT WITH HIS DOGS, BUT IT ESCAPES PRETTY EASILY.
HE'S VERY UPSET BY IT ALL, BEING OUTSMARTED BY SOME DUMB ANIMAL, SO HE SETS OUT TO HUNT DOWN THE DEER AND KILL IT. LIKE I SAID, HE WAS KIND OF A JERK.
ANYWAY, WHEN THE OLDER BROTHER HEARS ABOUT THE WHITE DEER, HE TELLS HIS BROTHER NOT TO HUNT IT, UNDER PAIN OF DEATH.
ACCORDING TO OLDER BROTHER THE DEER IS A CREATURE OF LEGEND AND THE SPIRIT OF THE FOREST OR SOMETHING, AND ONLY BAD THINGS COME FROM TRYING TO DESTROY IT."

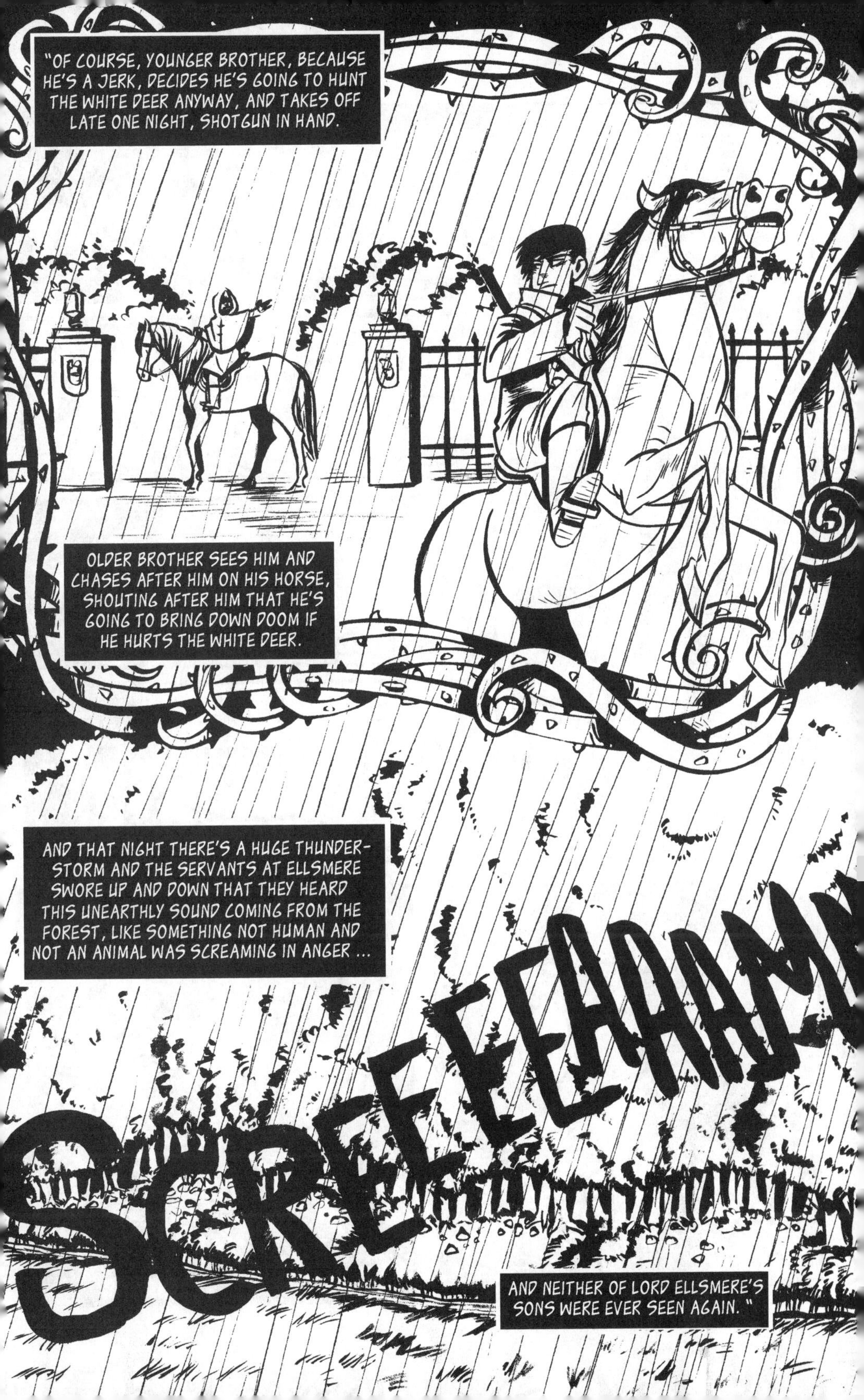
"OF COURSE, YOUNGER BROTHER, BECAUSE HE'S A JERK, DECIDES HE'S GOING TO HUNT THE WHITE DEER ANYWAY, AND TAKES OFF LATE ONE NIGHT, SHOTGUN IN HAND.
OLDER BROTHER SEES HIM AND CHASES AFTER HIM ON HIS HORSE, SHOUTING AFTER HIM THAT HE'S GOING TO BRING DOWN DOOM IF HE HURTS THE WHITE DEER.
AND THAT NIGHT THERE'S A HUGE THUNDER-STORM AND THE SERVANTS AT ELLSMERE SWORE UP AND DOWN THAT THEY HEARD THIS UNEARTHLY SOUND COMING FROM THE FOREST, LIKE SOMETHING NOT HUMAN AND NOT AN ANIMAL WAS SCREAMING IN ANGER ...
SCREEEAAAM
AND NEITHER OF LORD ELLSMERE'S SONS WERE EVER SEEN AGAIN."

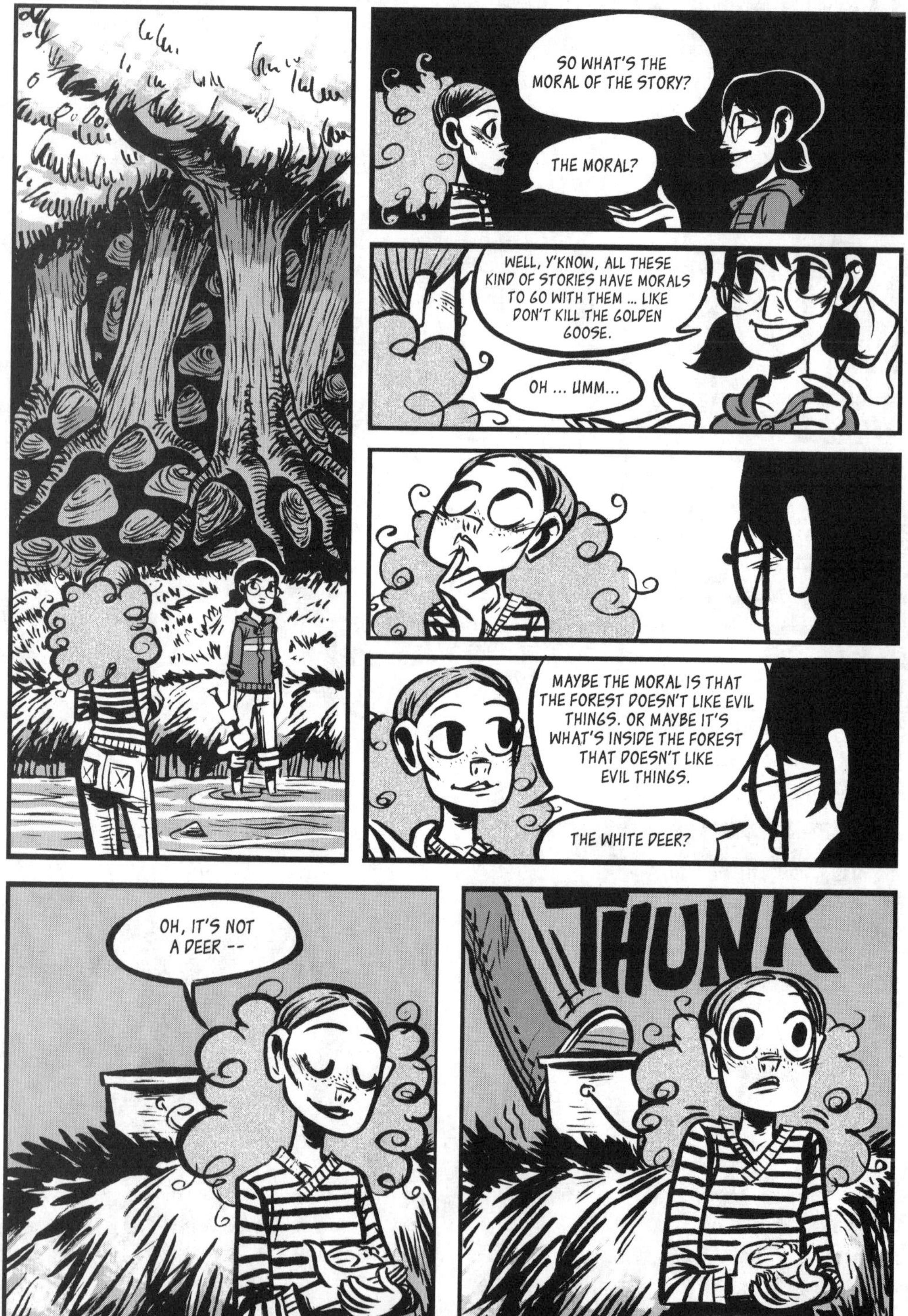
SO WHAT'S THE MORAL OF THE STORY?
THE MORAL?
WELL, Y'KNOW, ALL THESE KIND OF STORIES HAVE MORALS TO GO WITH THEM ... LIKE DON'T KILL THE GOLDEN GOOSE.
OH ... UMM...
MAYBE THE MORAL IS THAT THE FOREST DOESN'T LIKE EVIL THINGS. OR MAYBE IT'S WHAT'S INSIDE THE FOREST THAT DOESN'T LIKE EVIL THINGS.
THE WHITE DEER?
OH, IT'S NOT A DEER --
THUNK

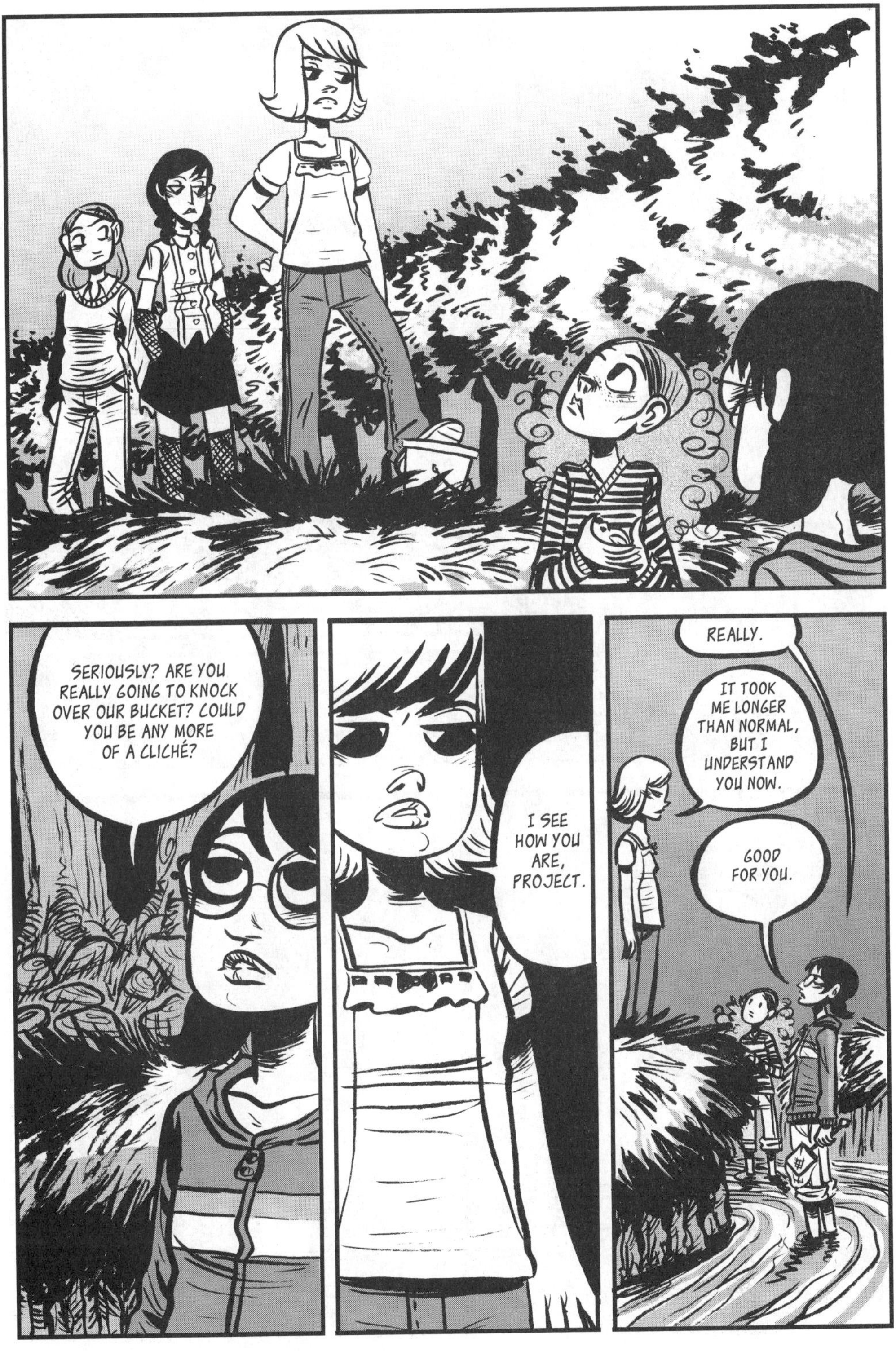

SERIOUSLY? ARE YOU REALLY GOING TO KNOCK OVER OUR BUCKET? COULD YOU BE ANY MORE OF A CLICHÉ?
I SEE HOW YOU ARE, PROJECT.
REALLY.
IT TOOK ME LONGER THAN NORMAL, BUT I UNDERSTAND YOU NOW.
GOOD FOR YOU.

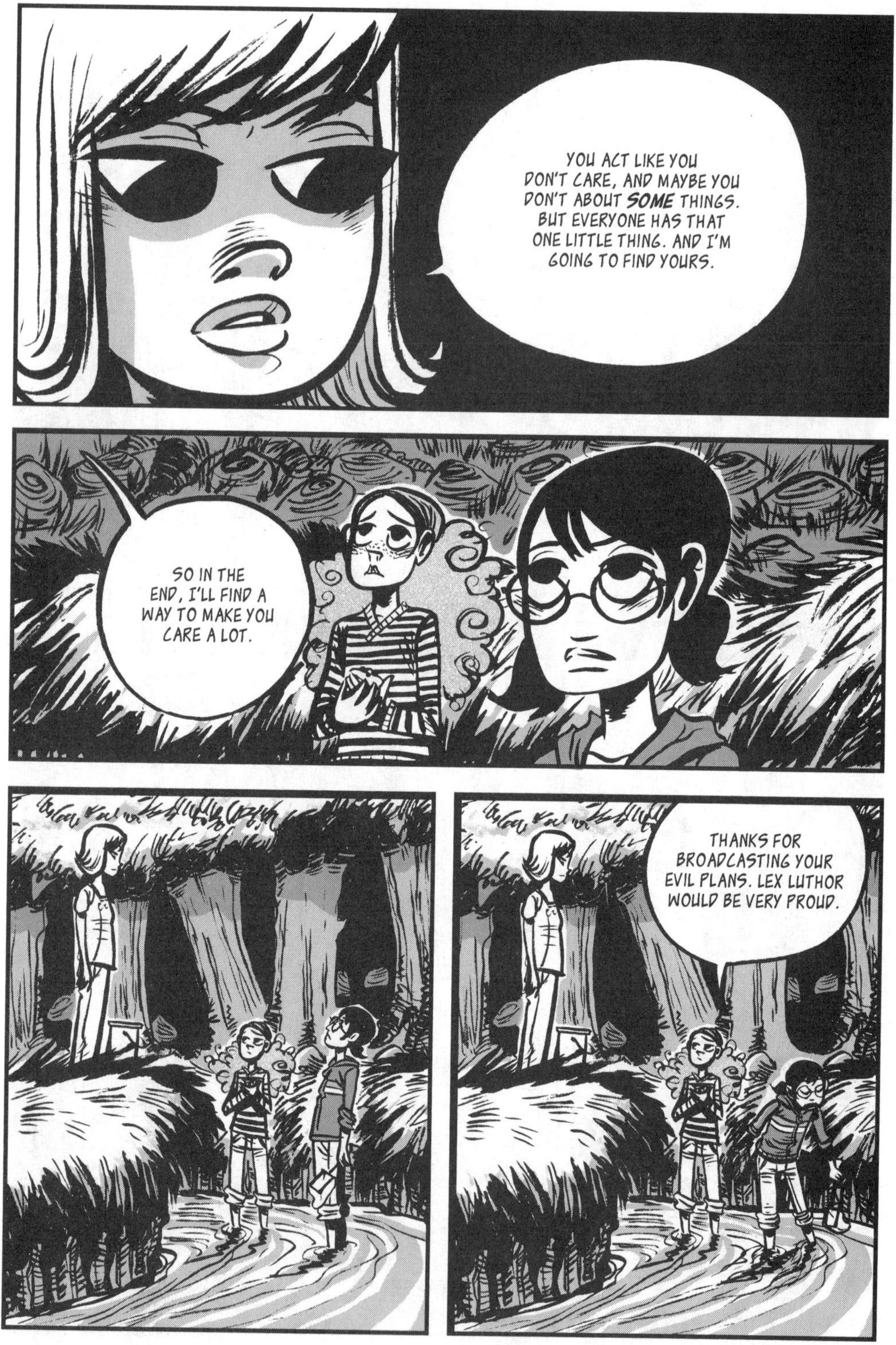
YOU ACT LIKE YOU DON'T CARE, AND MAYBE YOU DON'T ABOUT **SOME** THINGS. BUT EVERYONE HAS THAT ONE LITTLE THING. AND I'M GOING TO FIND YOURS.
SO IN THE END, I'LL FIND A WAY TO MAKE YOU CARE A LOT.
THANKS FOR BROADCASTING YOUR EVIL PLANS. LEX LUTHOR WOULD BE VERY PROUD.

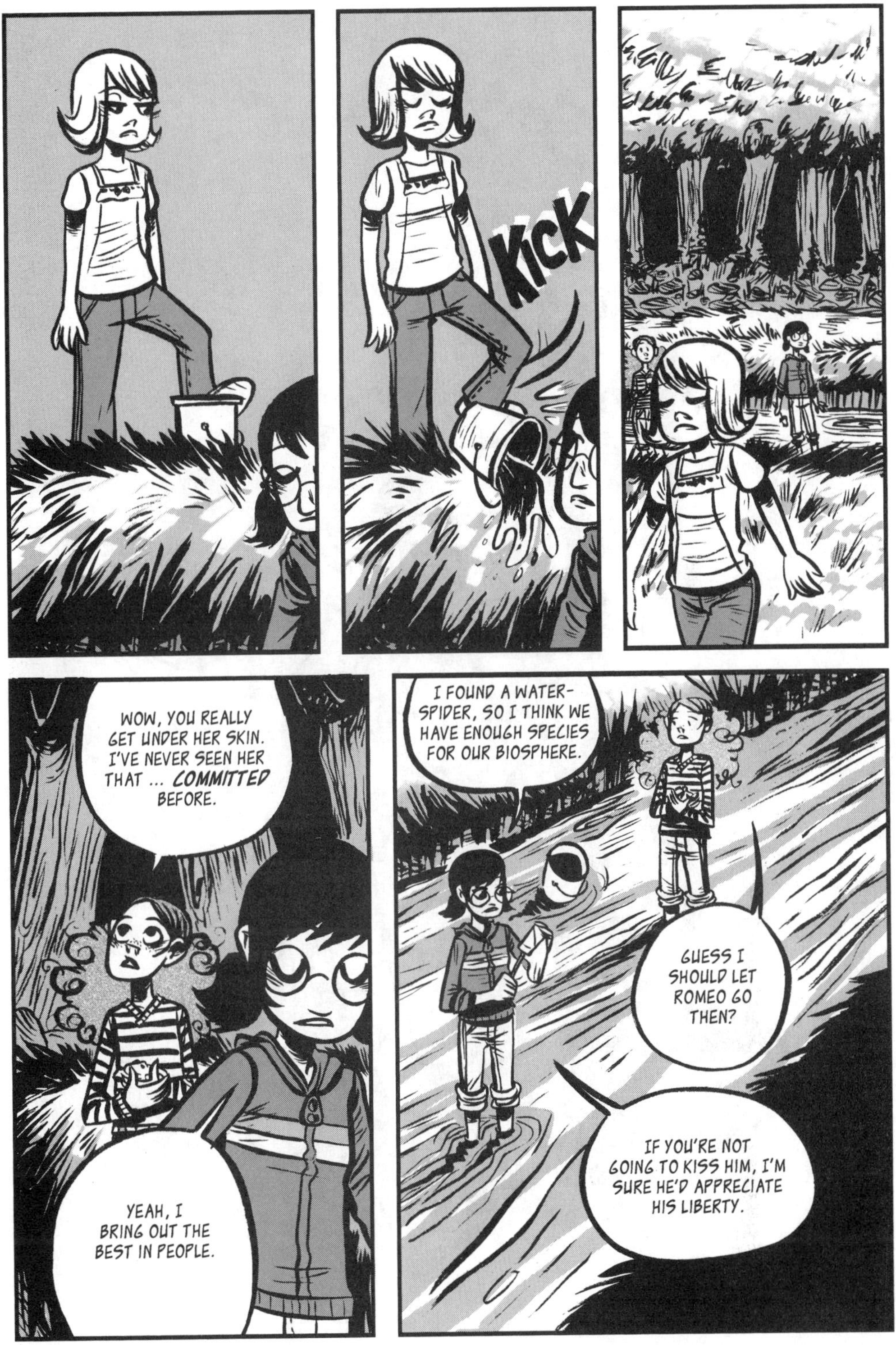
KICK
WOW, YOU REALLY GET UNDER HER SKIN. I'VE NEVER SEEN HER THAT ... *COMMITTED* BEFORE.
YEAH, I BRING OUT THE BEST IN PEOPLE.
I FOUND A WATER-SPIDER, SO I THINK WE HAVE ENOUGH SPECIES FOR OUR BIOSPHERE.
GUESS I SHOULD LET ROMEO GO THEN?
IF YOU'RE NOT GOING TO KISS HIM, I'M SURE HE'D APPRECIATE HIS LIBERTY.

chapter four

YAWN

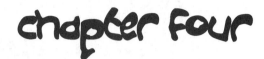

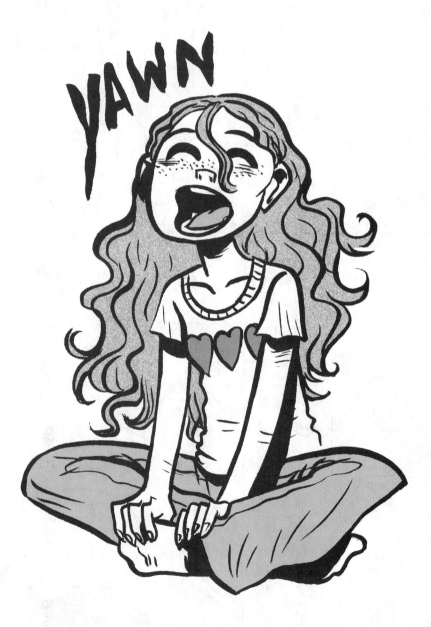

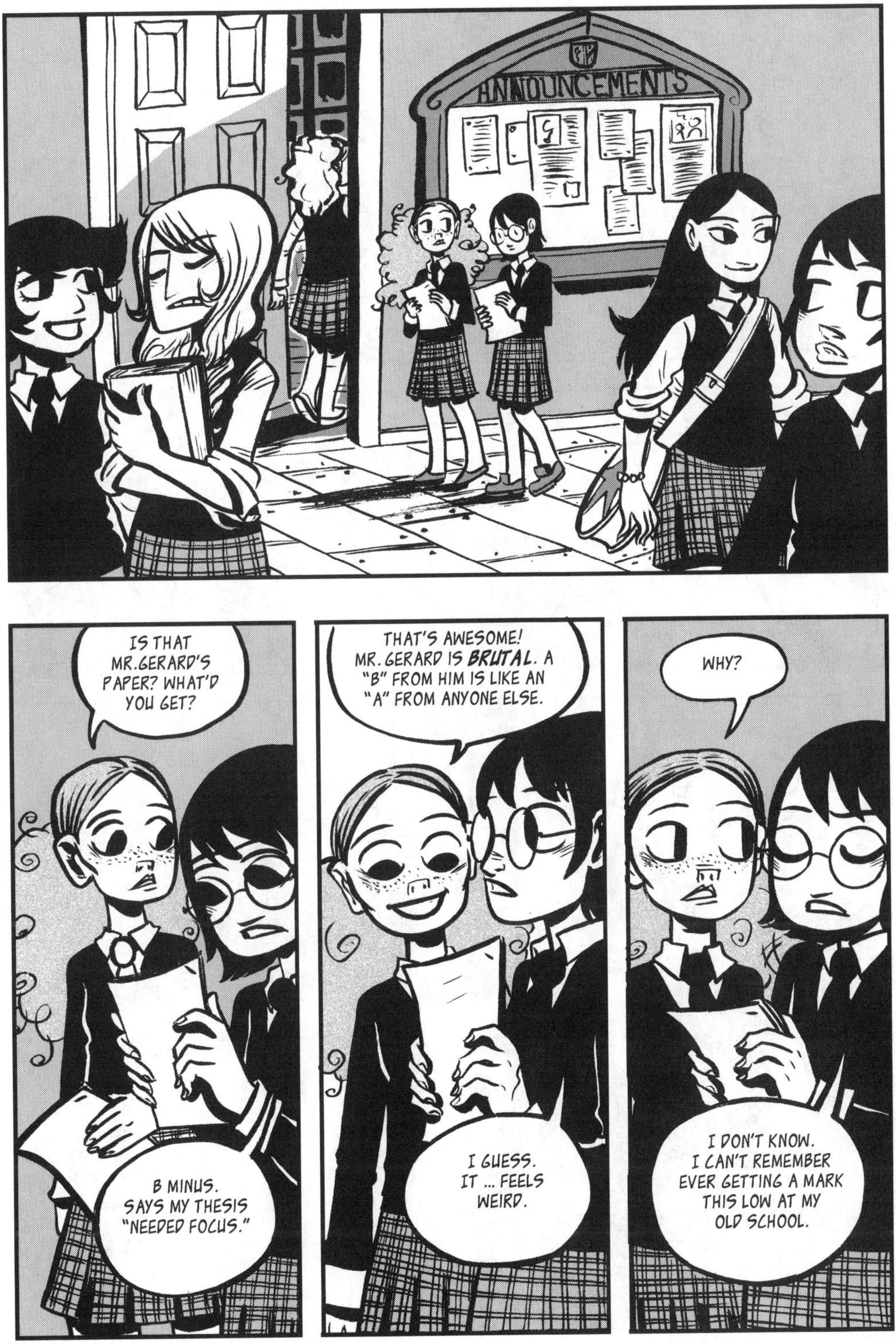
ANNOUNCEMENTS
IS THAT MR.GERARD'S PAPER? WHAT'D YOU GET?
B MINUS. SAYS MY THESIS "NEEDED FOCUS."
THAT'S AWESOME! MR. GERARD IS **BRUTAL**. A "B" FROM HIM IS LIKE AN "A" FROM ANYONE ELSE.
I GUESS. IT ... FEELS WEIRD.
WHY?
I DON'T KNOW. I CAN'T REMEMBER EVER GETTING A MARK THIS LOW AT MY OLD SCHOOL.

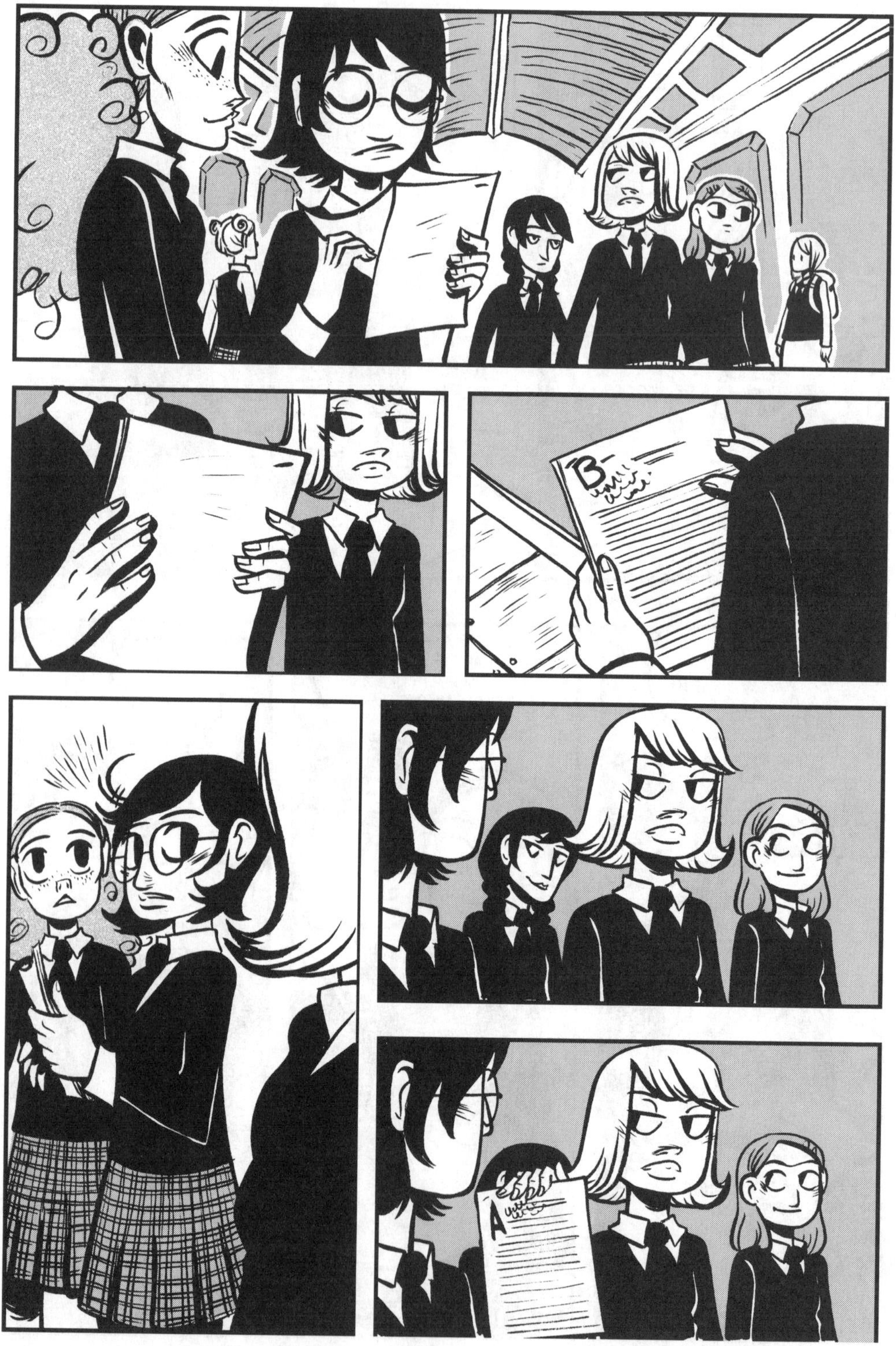
B
A

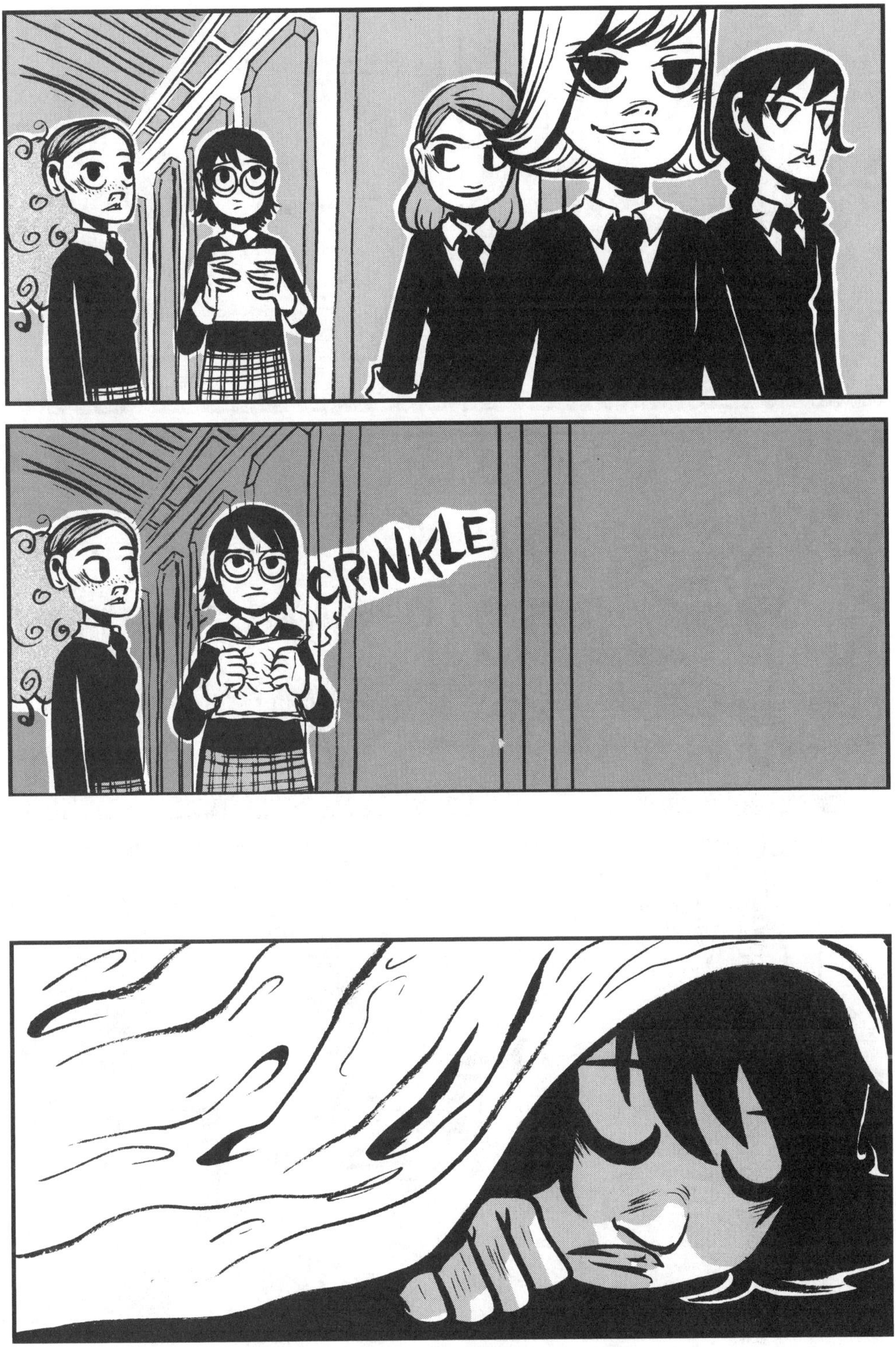
CRINKLE

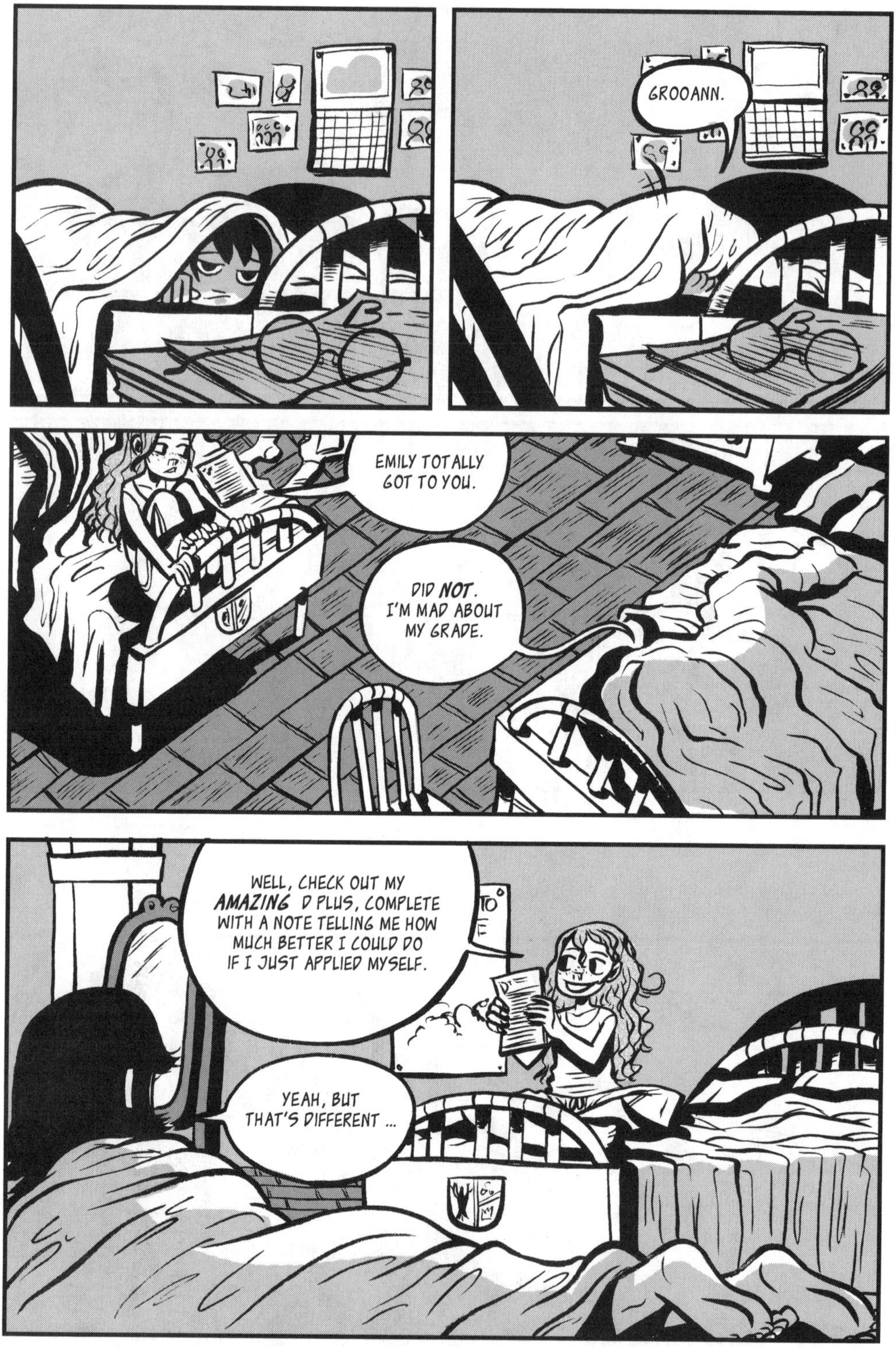
GROOANN.
EMILY TOTALLY GOT TO YOU.
DID NOT. I'M MAD ABOUT MY GRADE.
WELL, CHECK OUT MY AMAZING D PLUS, COMPLETE WITH A NOTE TELLING ME HOW MUCH BETTER I COULD DO IF I JUST APPLIED MYSELF.
YEAH, BUT THAT'S DIFFERENT ...

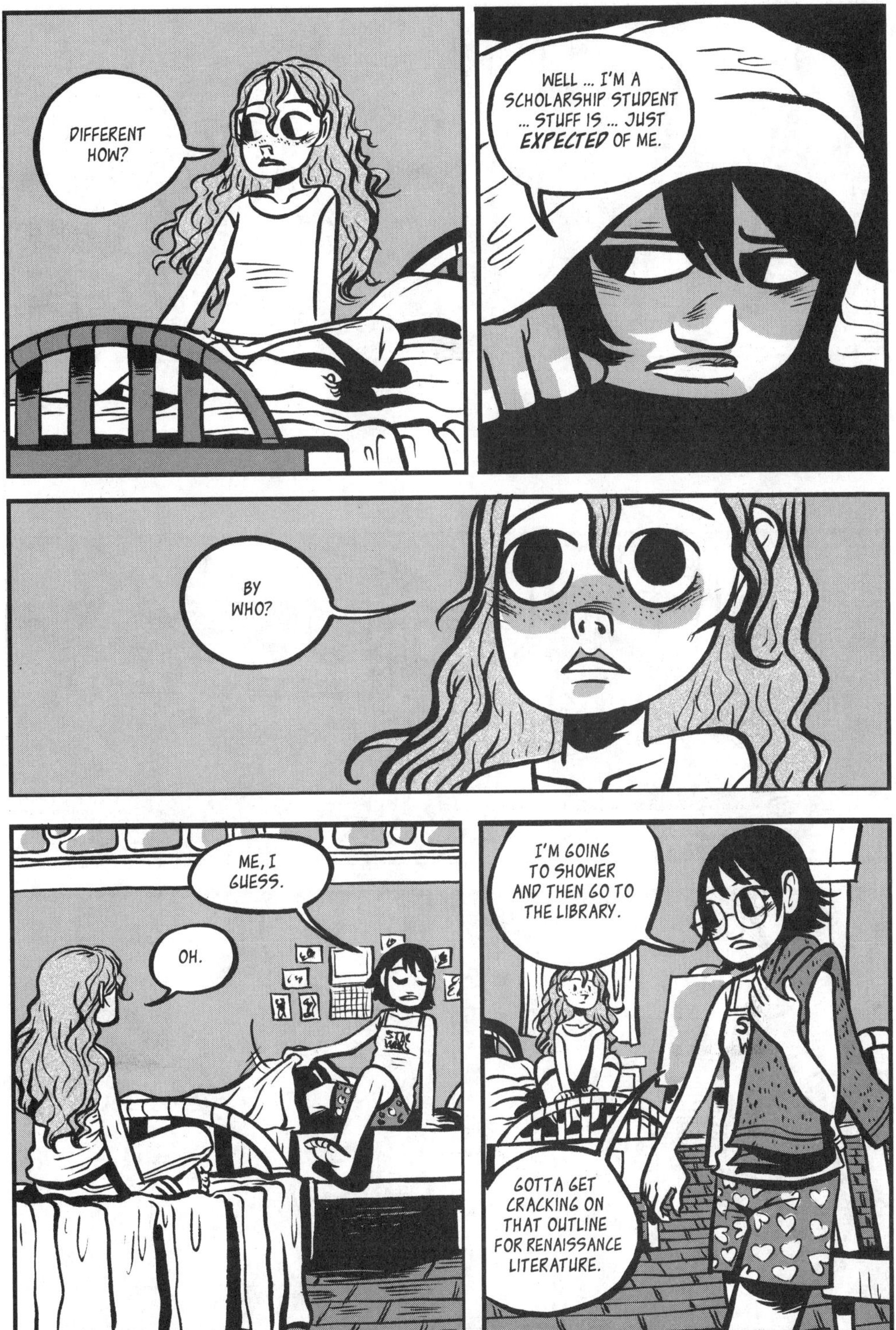
DIFFERENT HOW?
WELL ... I'M A SCHOLARSHIP STUDENT ... STUFF IS ... JUST **EXPECTED** OF ME.
BY WHO?
ME, I GUESS.
OH.
I'M GOING TO SHOWER AND THEN GO TO THE LIBRARY.
GOTTA GET CRACKING ON THAT OUTLINE FOR RENAISSANCE LITERATURE.

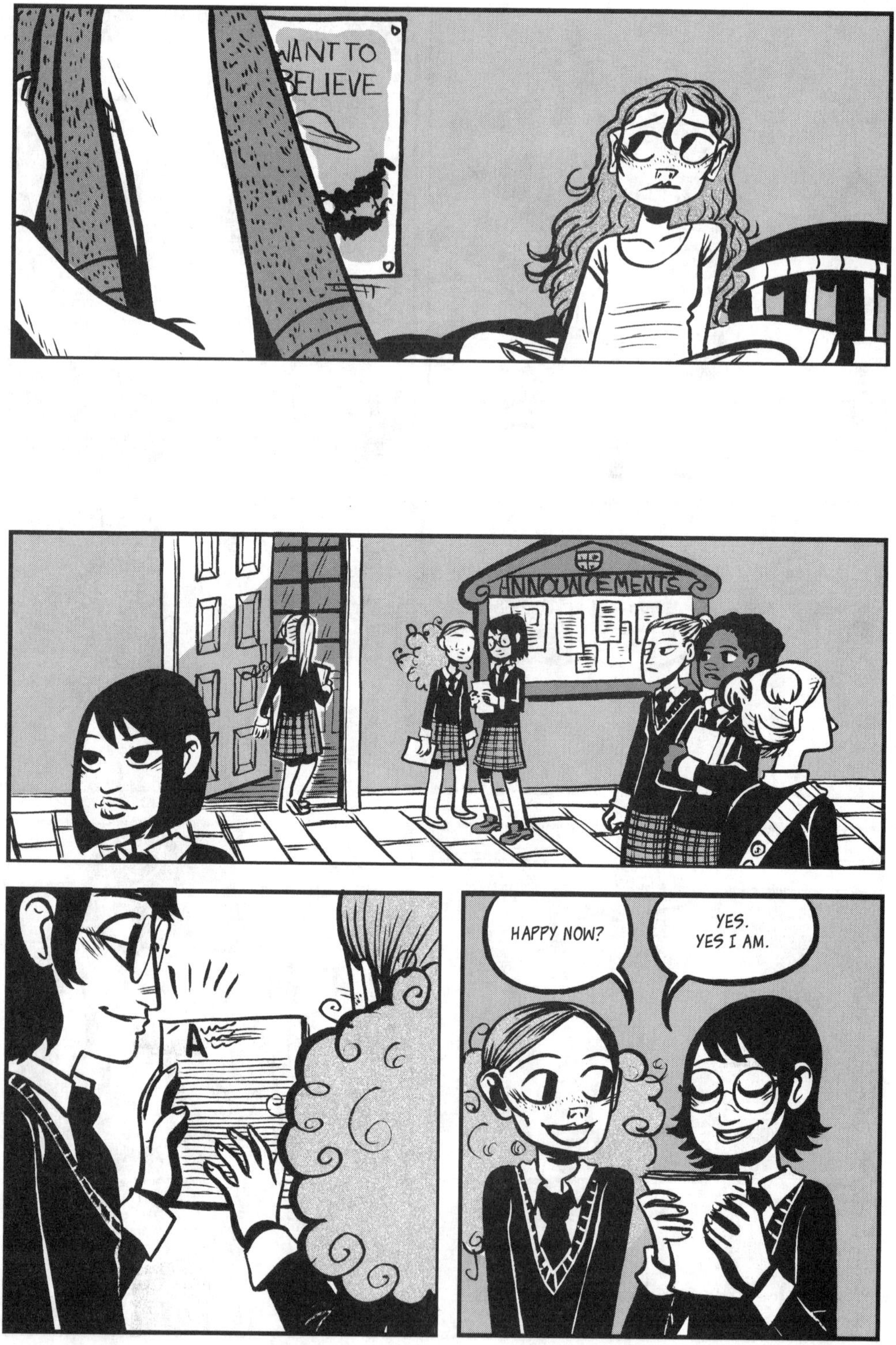
WANT TO
BELIEVE
ANNOUNCEMENTS
A
HAPPY NOW?
YES.
YES I AM.

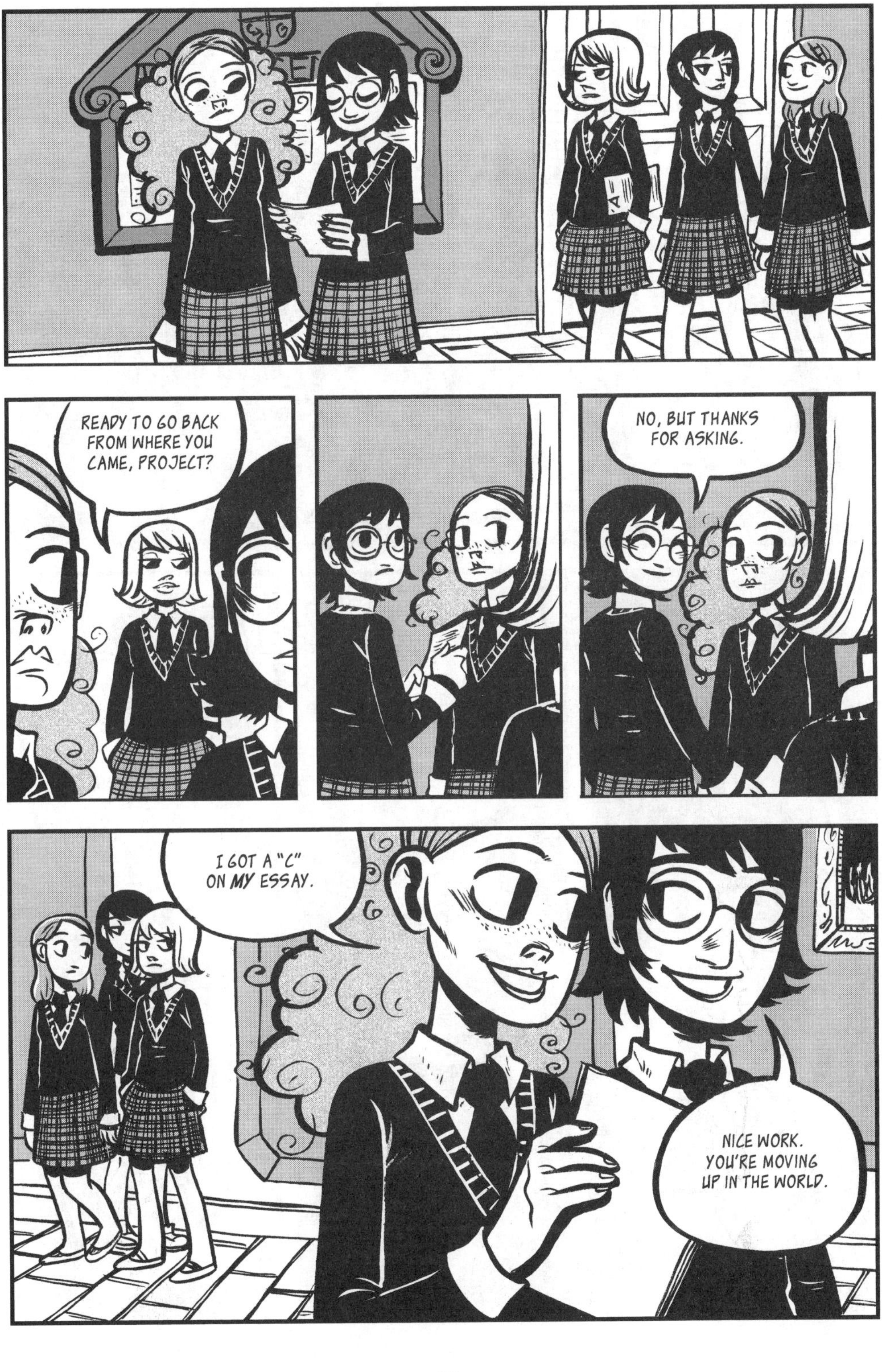
READY TO GO BACK FROM WHERE YOU CAME, PROJECT?
NO, BUT THANKS FOR ASKING.
I GOT A "C" ON *MY* ESSAY.
NICE WORK. YOU'RE MOVING UP IN THE WORLD.

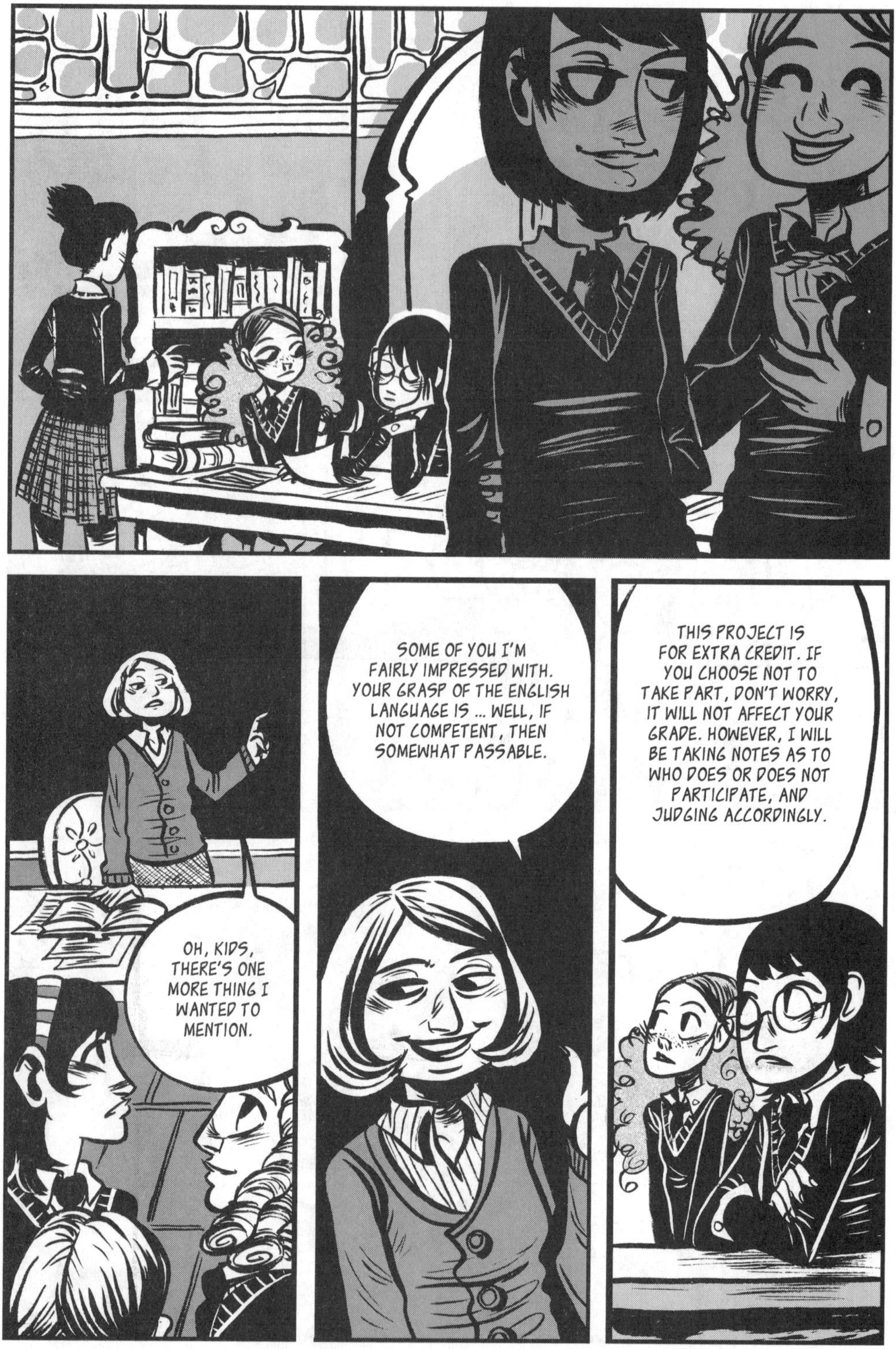
OH, KIDS, THERE'S ONE MORE THING I WANTED TO MENTION.
SOME OF YOU I'M FAIRLY IMPRESSED WITH. YOUR GRASP OF THE ENGLISH LANGUAGE IS ... WELL, IF NOT COMPETENT, THEN SOMEWHAT PASSABLE.
THIS PROJECT IS FOR EXTRA CREDIT. IF YOU CHOOSE NOT TO TAKE PART, DON'T WORRY, IT WILL NOT AFFECT YOUR GRADE. HOWEVER, I WILL BE TAKING NOTES AS TO WHO DOES OR DOES NOT PARTICIPATE, AND JUDGING ACCORDINGLY.

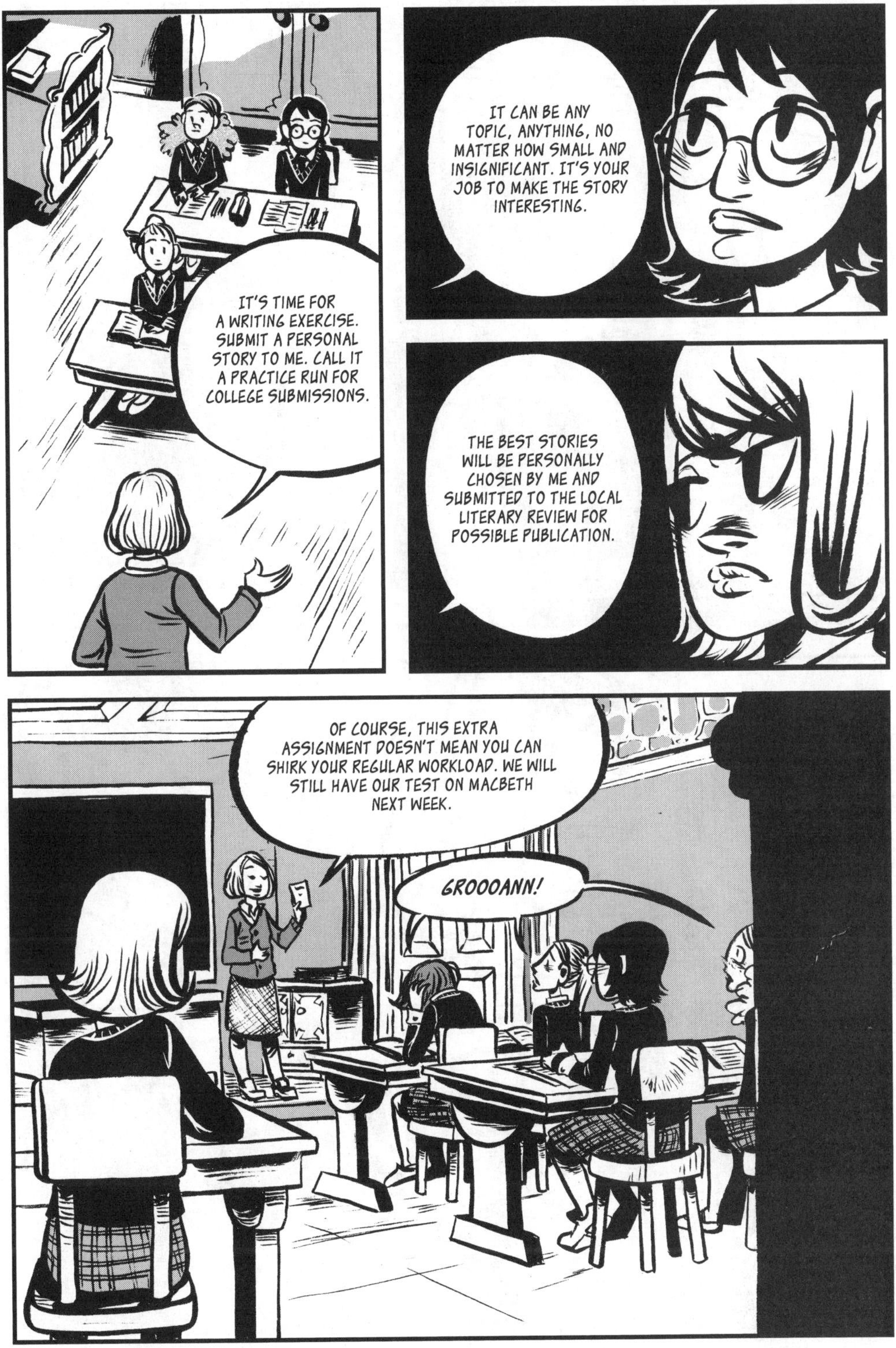
IT'S TIME FOR A WRITING EXERCISE. SUBMIT A PERSONAL STORY TO ME. CALL IT A PRACTICE RUN FOR COLLEGE SUBMISSIONS.
IT CAN BE ANY TOPIC, ANYTHING, NO MATTER HOW SMALL AND INSIGNIFICANT. IT'S YOUR JOB TO MAKE THE STORY INTERESTING.
THE BEST STORIES WILL BE PERSONALLY CHOSEN BY ME AND SUBMITTED TO THE LOCAL LITERARY REVIEW FOR POSSIBLE PUBLICATION.
OF COURSE, THIS EXTRA ASSIGNMENT DOESN'T MEAN YOU CAN SHIRK YOUR REGULAR WORKLOAD. WE WILL STILL HAVE OUR TEST ON MACBETH NEXT WEEK.
GROOOANN!

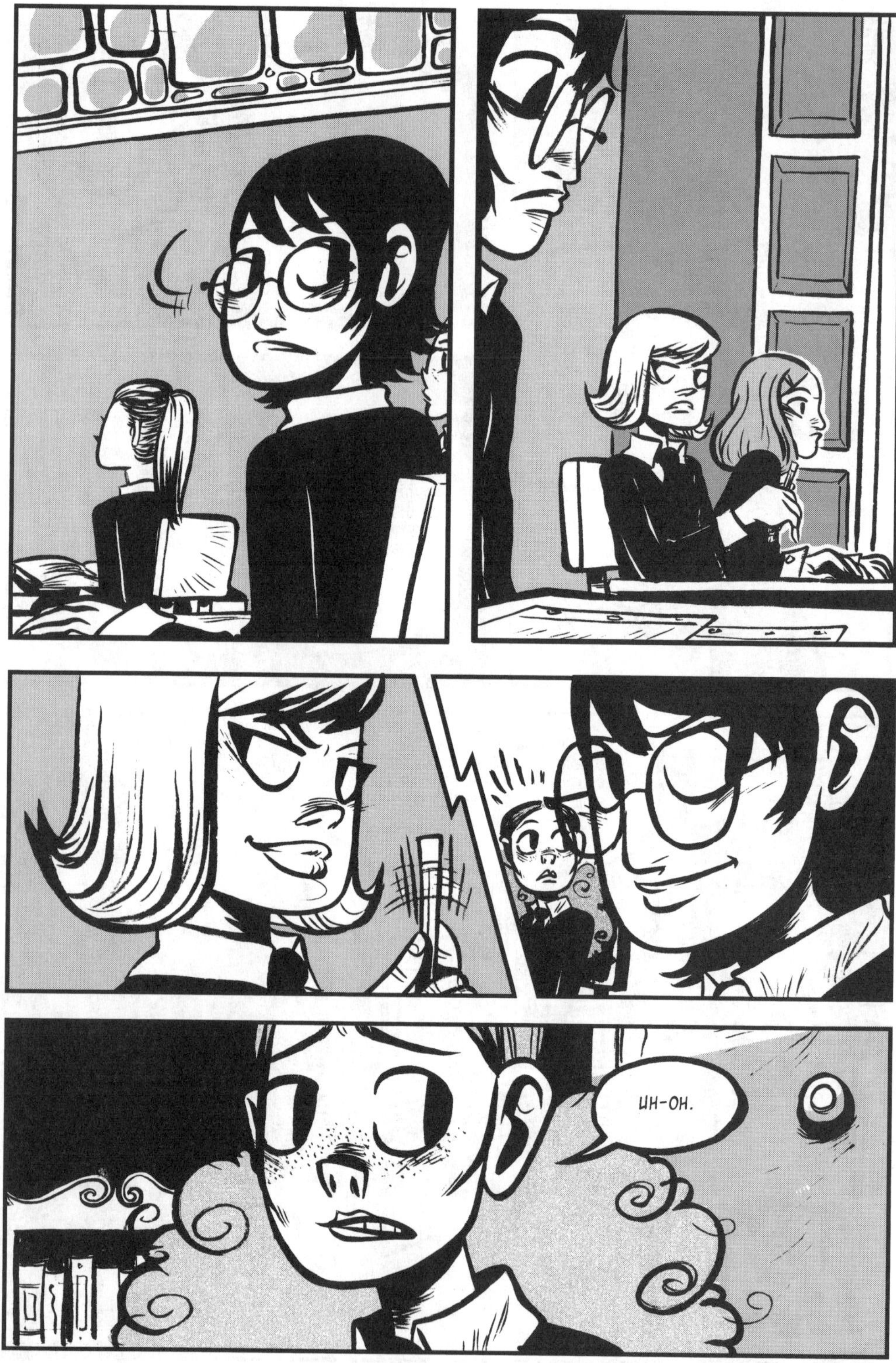
UH-OH.

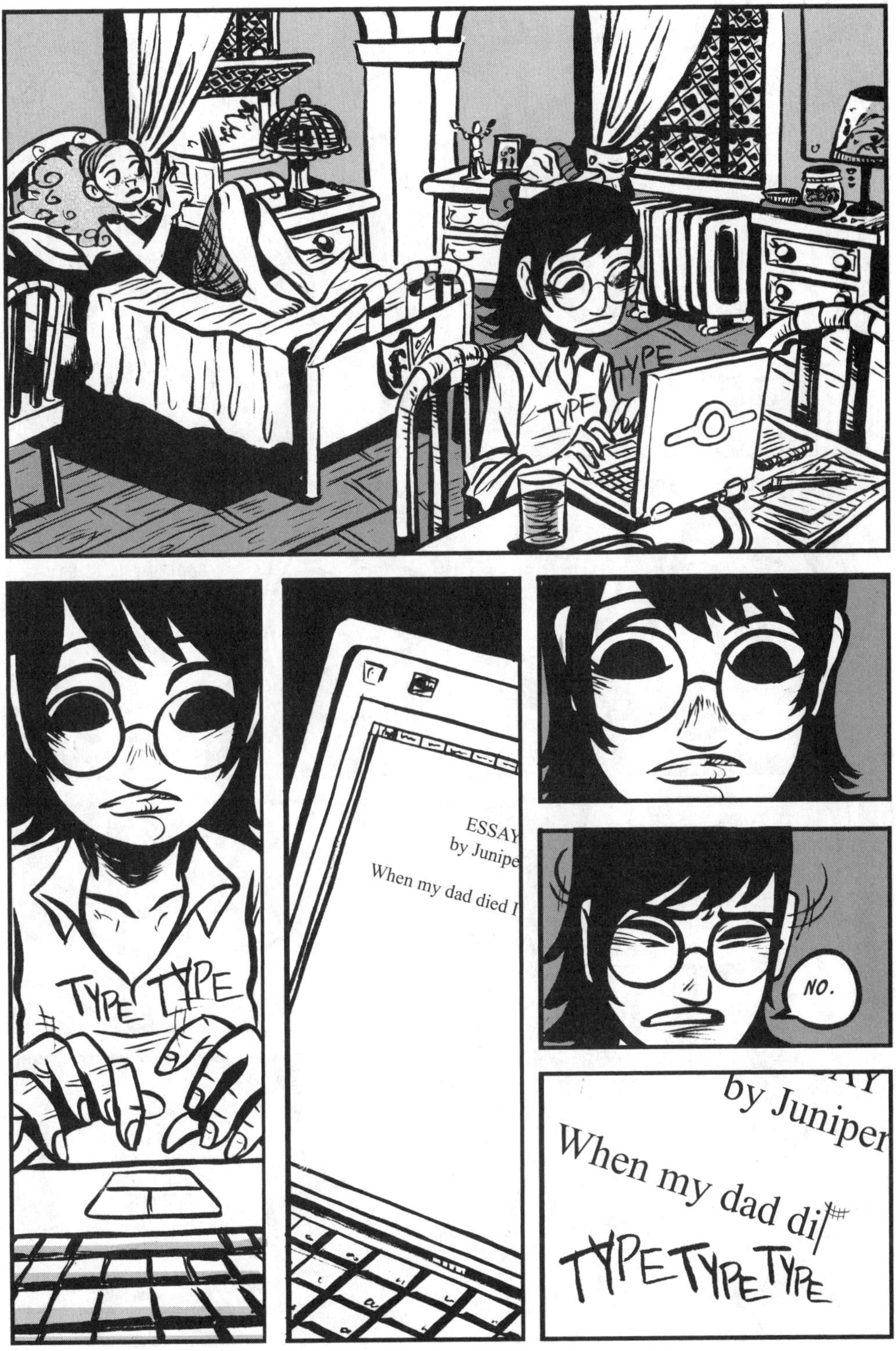
TYPE
TYPE
TYPE TYPE
ESSAY
by Junipe
When my dad died I
NO.
by Juniper
When my dad di
TYPETYPETYPE

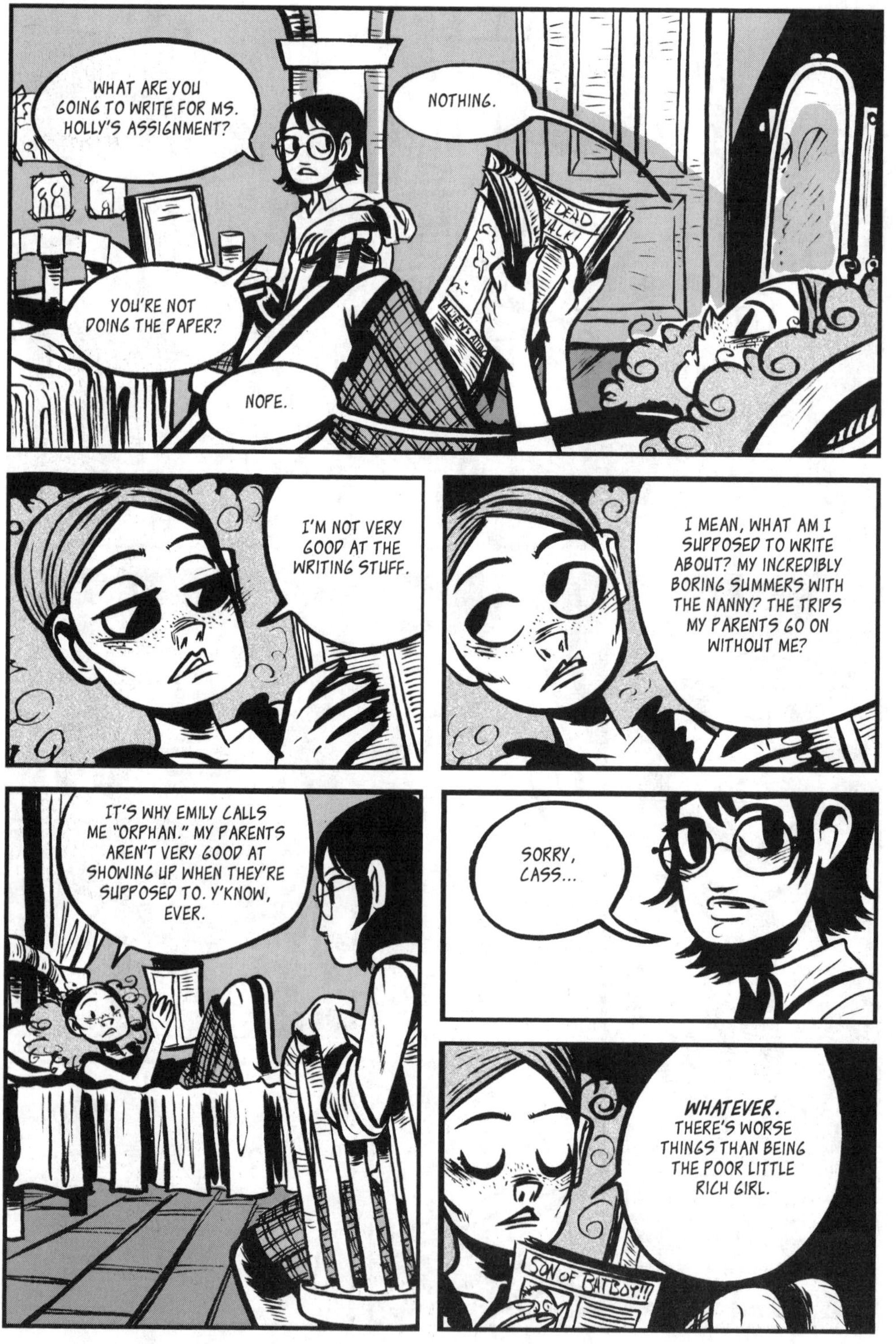
WHAT ARE YOU GOING TO WRITE FOR MS. HOLLY'S ASSIGNMENT?
NOTHING.
THE DEAD WALK!
YOU'RE NOT DOING THE PAPER?
NOPE.
I'M NOT VERY GOOD AT THE WRITING STUFF.
I MEAN, WHAT AM I SUPPOSED TO WRITE ABOUT? MY INCREDIBLY BORING SUMMERS WITH THE NANNY? THE TRIPS MY PARENTS GO ON WITHOUT ME?
IT'S WHY EMILY CALLS ME "ORPHAN." MY PARENTS AREN'T VERY GOOD AT SHOWING UP WHEN THEY'RE SUPPOSED TO. Y'KNOW, EVER.
SORRY, CASS...
WHATEVER. THERE'S WORSE THINGS THAN BEING THE POOR LITTLE RICH GIRL.
SON OF BATBOY!!

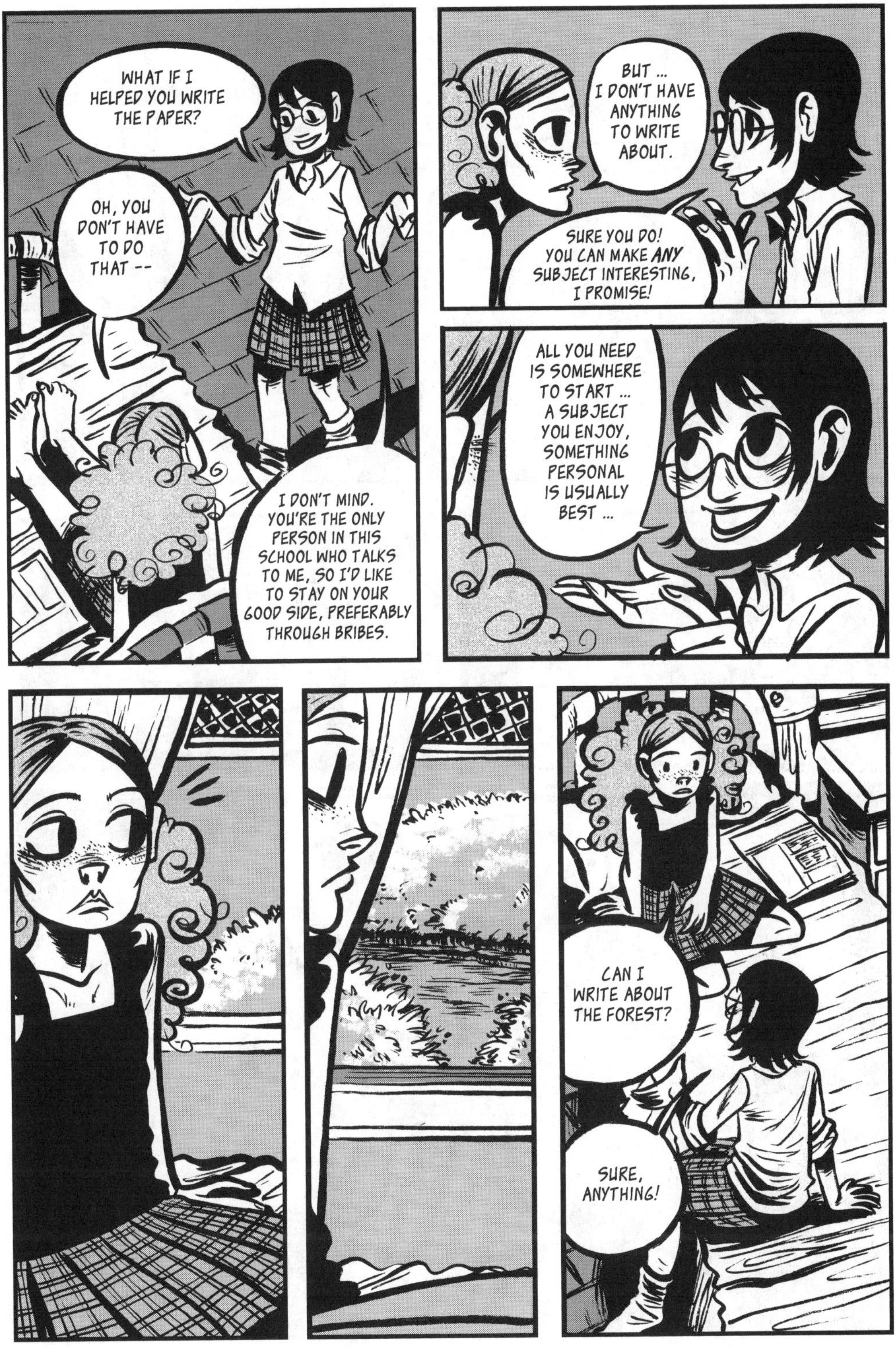
WHAT IF I HELPED YOU WRITE THE PAPER?
OH, YOU DON'T HAVE TO DO THAT --
I DON'T MIND. YOU'RE THE ONLY PERSON IN THIS SCHOOL WHO TALKS TO ME, SO I'D LIKE TO STAY ON YOUR GOOD SIDE, PREFERABLY THROUGH BRIBES.
BUT ... I DON'T HAVE ANYTHING TO WRITE ABOUT.
SURE YOU DO! YOU CAN MAKE ANY SUBJECT INTERESTING, I PROMISE!
ALL YOU NEED IS SOMEWHERE TO START ... A SUBJECT YOU ENJOY, SOMETHING PERSONAL IS USUALLY BEST ...
CAN I WRITE ABOUT THE FOREST?
SURE, ANYTHING!

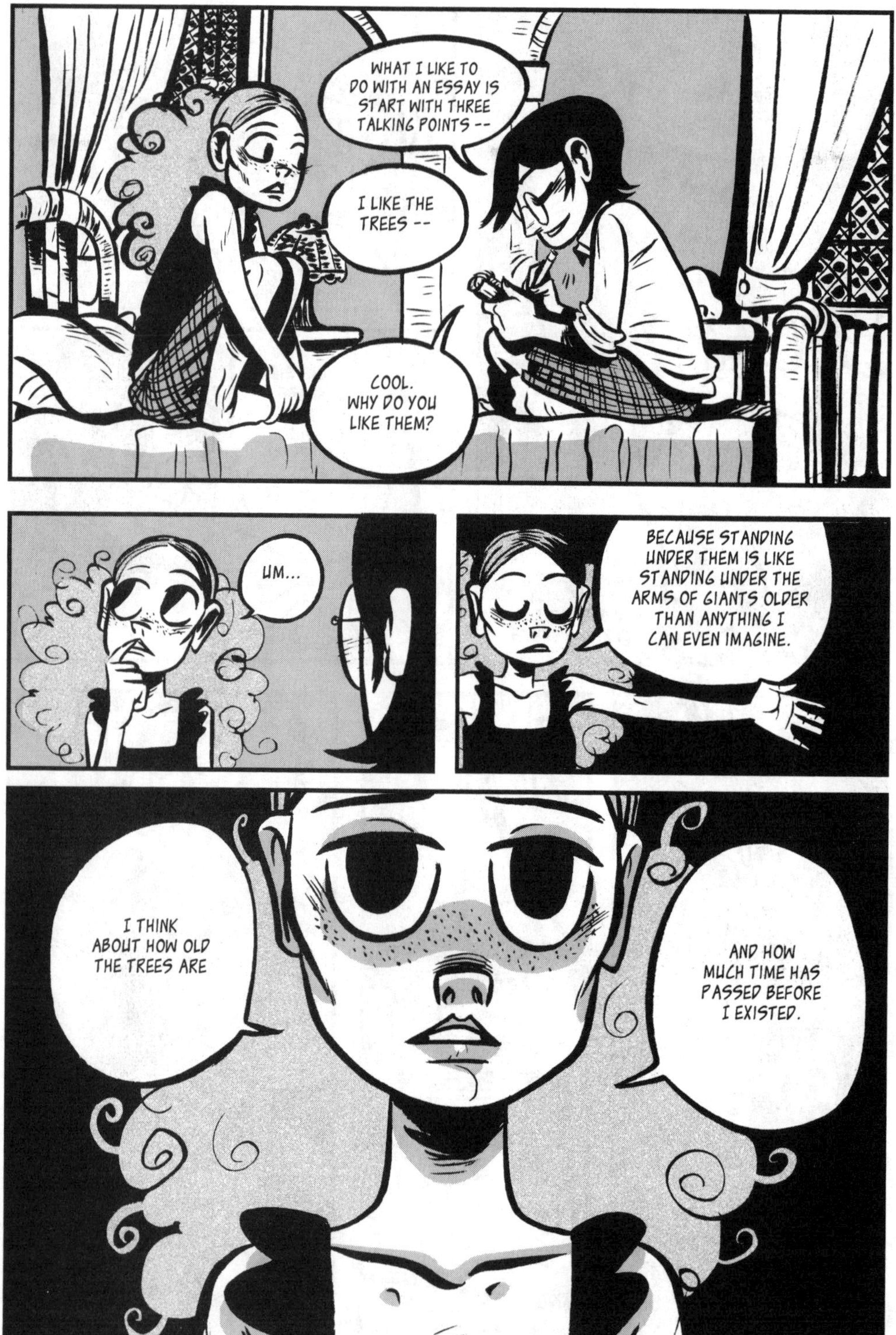
WHAT I LIKE TO DO WITH AN ESSAY IS START WITH THREE TALKING POINTS --
I LIKE THE TREES --
COOL. WHY DO YOU LIKE THEM?
UM...
BECAUSE STANDING UNDER THEM IS LIKE STANDING UNDER THE ARMS OF GIANTS OLDER THAN ANYTHING I CAN EVEN IMAGINE.
I THINK ABOUT HOW OLD THE TREES ARE
AND HOW MUCH TIME HAS PASSED BEFORE I EXISTED.

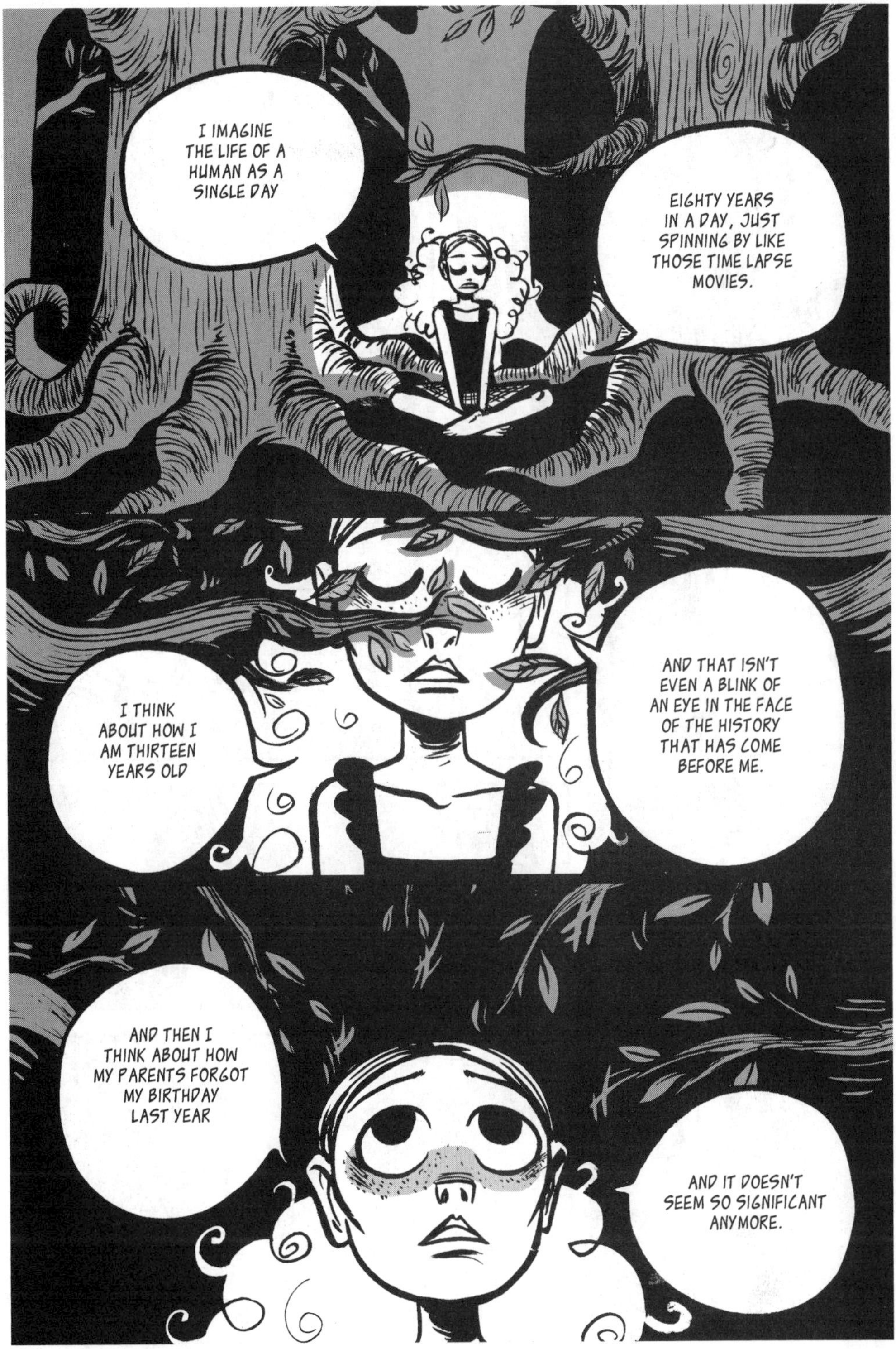
I IMAGINE THE LIFE OF A HUMAN AS A SINGLE DAY
EIGHTY YEARS IN A DAY, JUST SPINNING BY LIKE THOSE TIME LAPSE MOVIES.
I THINK ABOUT HOW I AM THIRTEEN YEARS OLD
AND THAT ISN'T EVEN A BLINK OF AN EYE IN THE FACE OF THE HISTORY THAT HAS COME BEFORE ME.
AND THEN I THINK ABOUT HOW MY PARENTS FORGOT MY BIRTHDAY LAST YEAR
AND IT DOESN'T SEEM SO SIGNIFICANT ANYMORE.

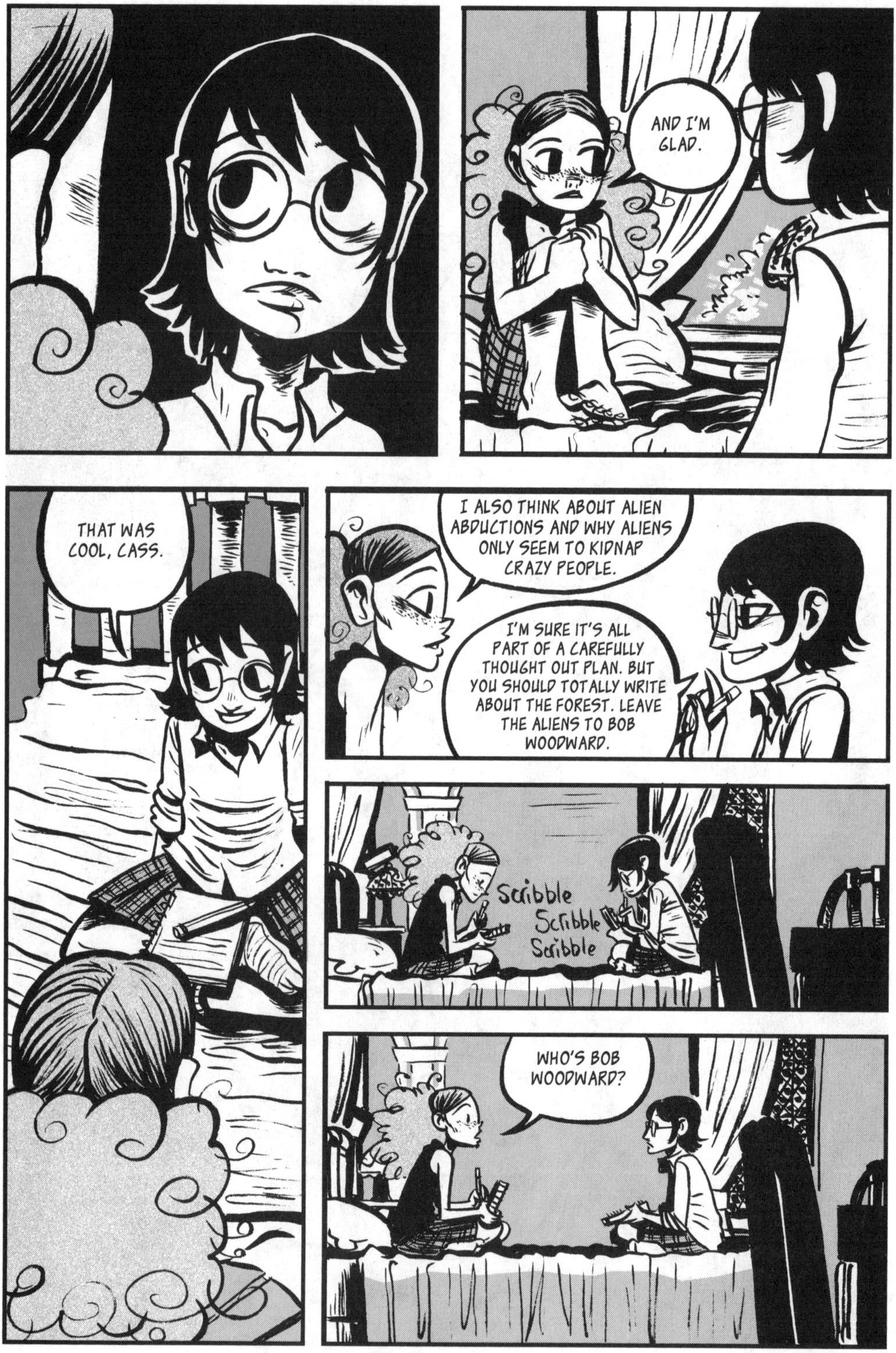
AND I'M GLAD.
THAT WAS COOL, CASS.
I ALSO THINK ABOUT ALIEN ABDUCTIONS AND WHY ALIENS ONLY SEEM TO KIDNAP CRAZY PEOPLE.
I'M SURE IT'S ALL PART OF A CAREFULLY THOUGHT OUT PLAN. BUT YOU SHOULD TOTALLY WRITE ABOUT THE FOREST. LEAVE THE ALIENS TO BOB WOODWARD.
Scribble Scribble Scribble
WHO'S BOB WOODWARD?

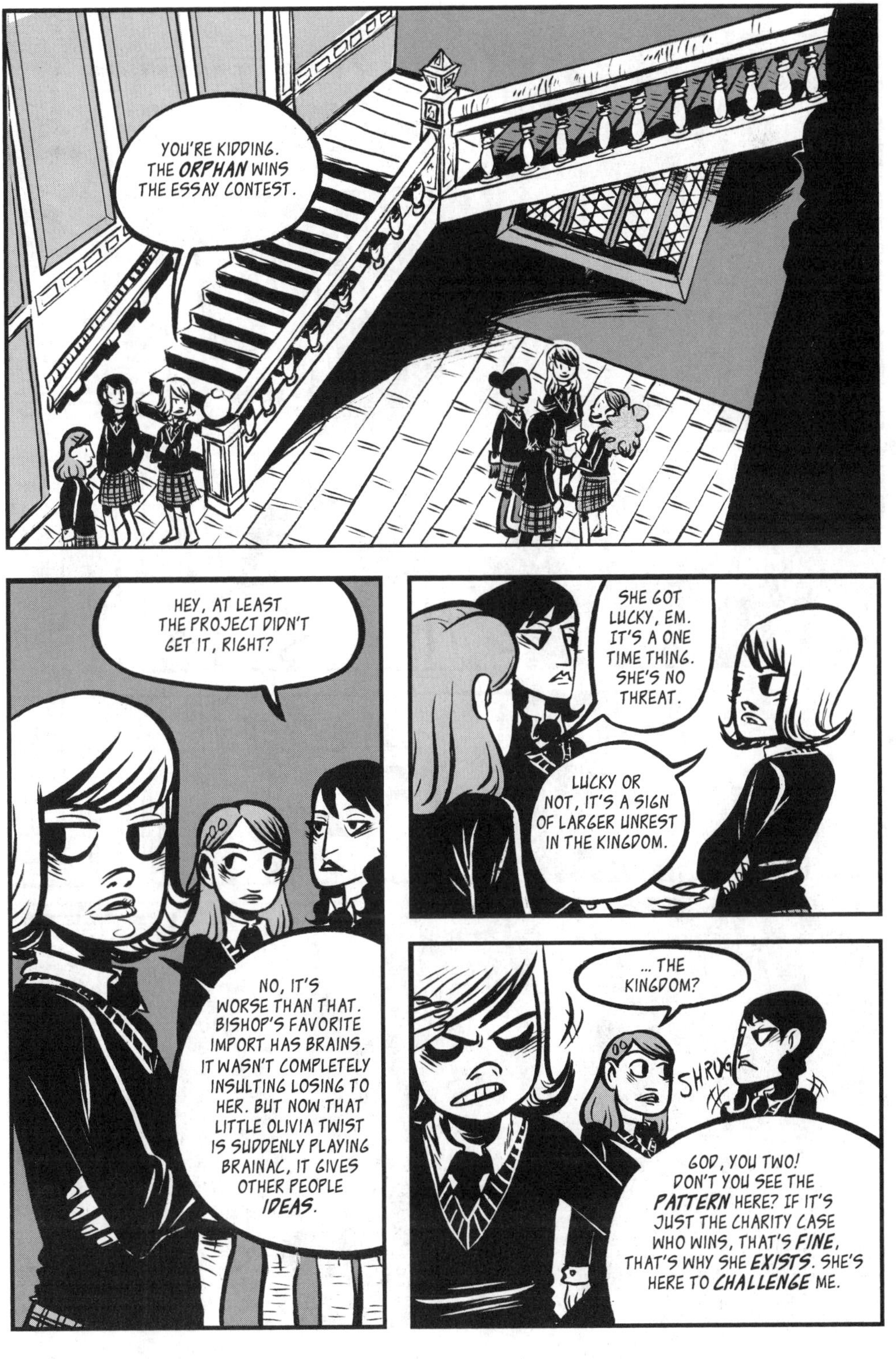
YOU'RE KIDDING. THE ORPHAN WINS THE ESSAY CONTEST.
HEY, AT LEAST THE PROJECT DIDN'T GET IT, RIGHT?
NO, IT'S WORSE THAN THAT. BISHOP'S FAVORITE IMPORT HAS BRAINS. IT WASN'T COMPLETELY INSULTING LOSING TO HER. BUT NOW THAT LITTLE OLIVIA TWIST IS SUDDENLY PLAYING BRAINAC, IT GIVES OTHER PEOPLE IDEAS.
SHE GOT LUCKY, EM. IT'S A ONE TIME THING. SHE'S NO THREAT.
LUCKY OR NOT, IT'S A SIGN OF LARGER UNREST IN THE KINGDOM.
... THE KINGDOM?
SHRUG
GOD, YOU TWO! DON'T YOU SEE THE PATTERN HERE? IF IT'S JUST THE CHARITY CASE WHO WINS, THAT'S FINE, THAT'S WHY SHE EXISTS. SHE'S HERE TO CHALLENGE ME.

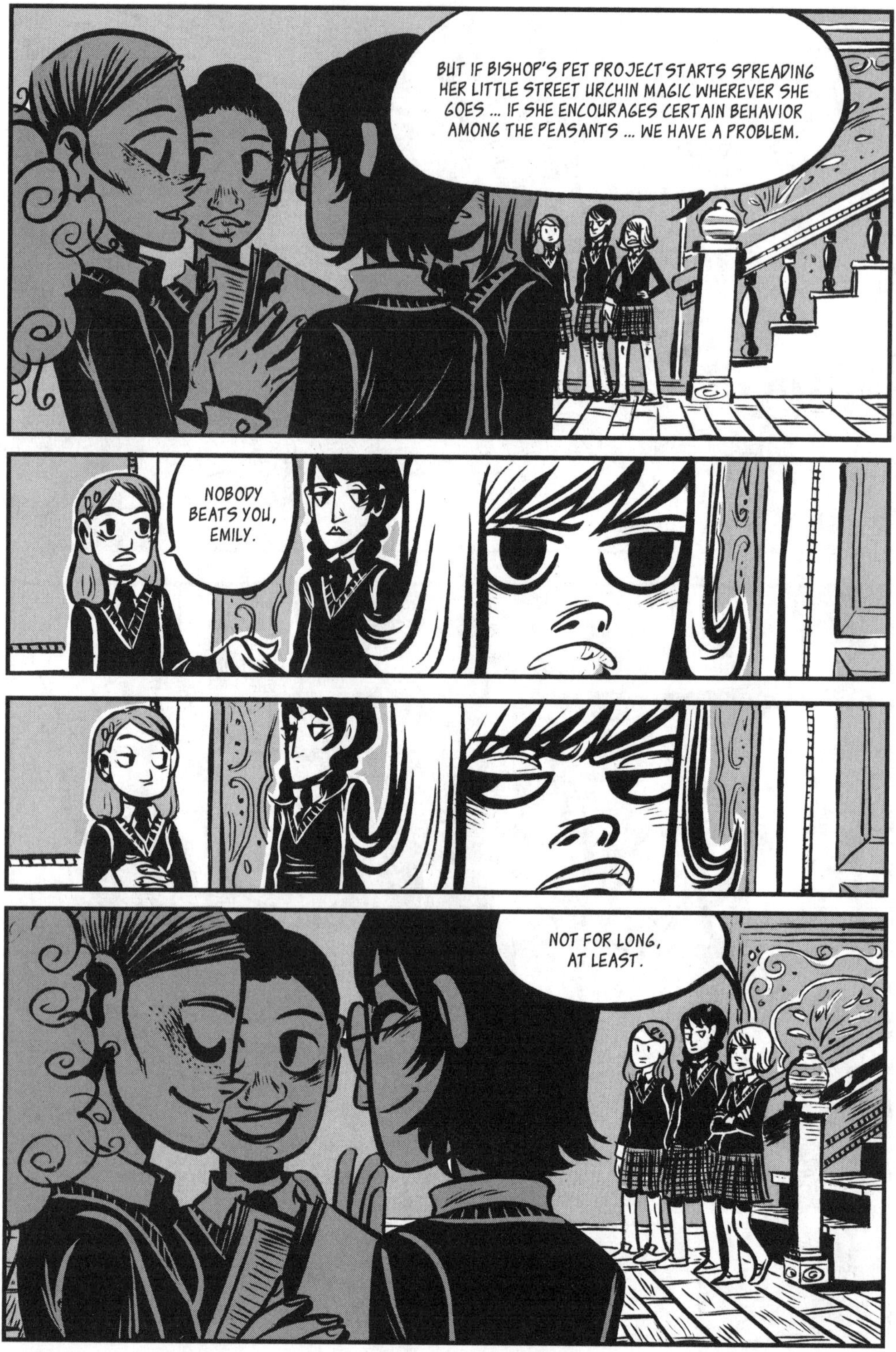
BUT IF BISHOP'S PET PROJECT STARTS SPREADING HER LITTLE STREET URCHIN MAGIC WHEREVER SHE GOES ... IF SHE ENCOURAGES CERTAIN BEHAVIOR AMONG THE PEASANTS ... WE HAVE A PROBLEM.
NOBODY BEATS YOU, EMILY.
NOT FOR LONG, AT LEAST.

chapter five

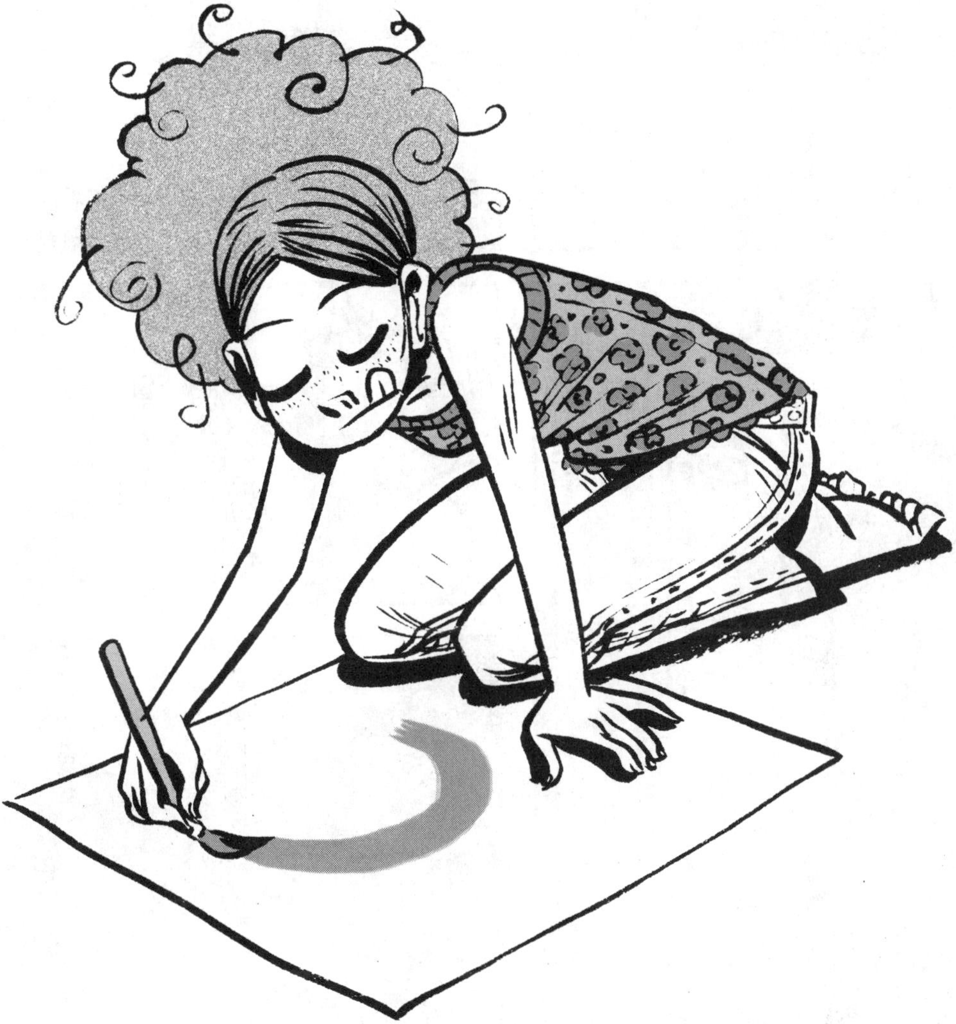

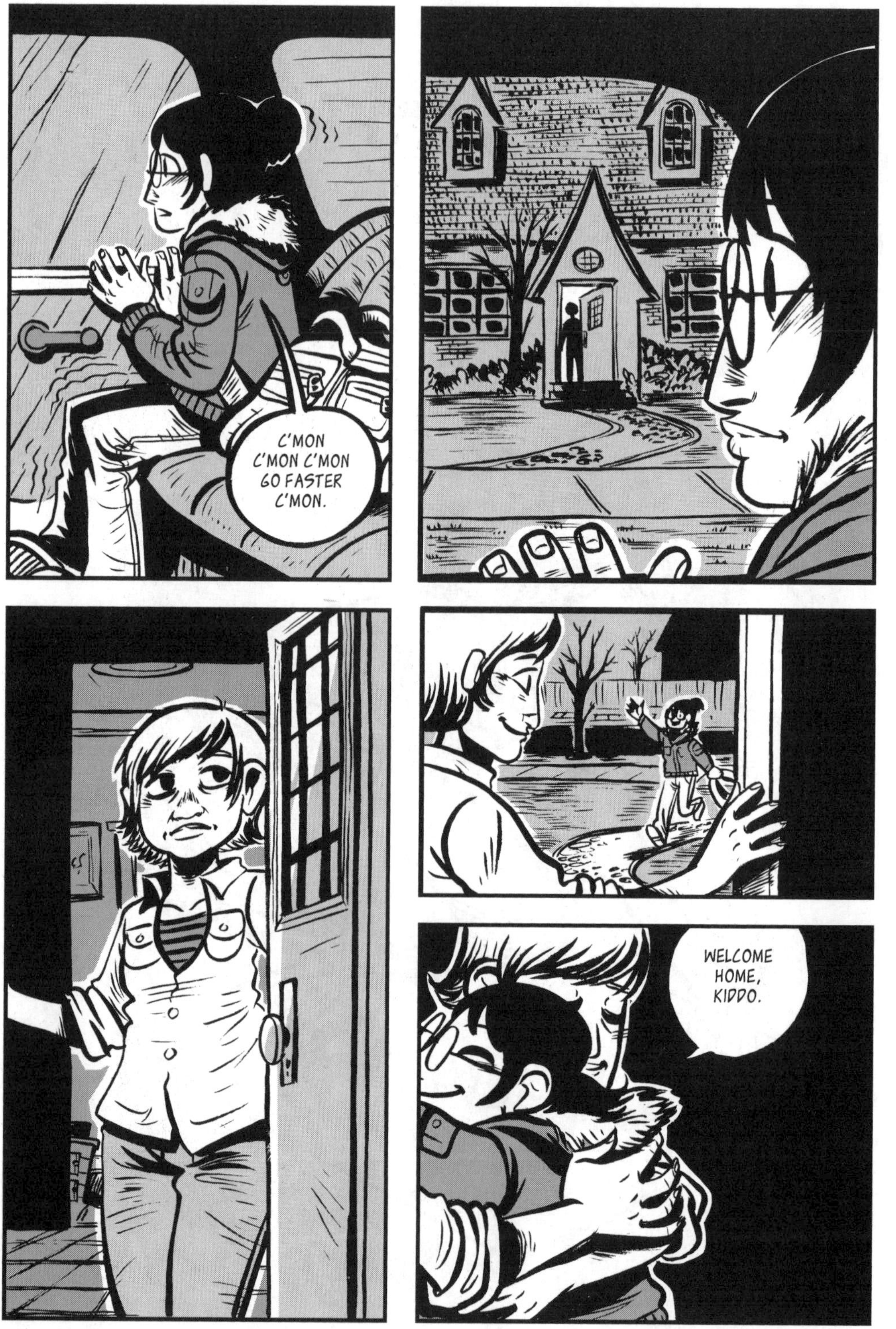
C'MON C'MON C'MON GO FASTER C'MON.
WELCOME HOME, KIDDO.

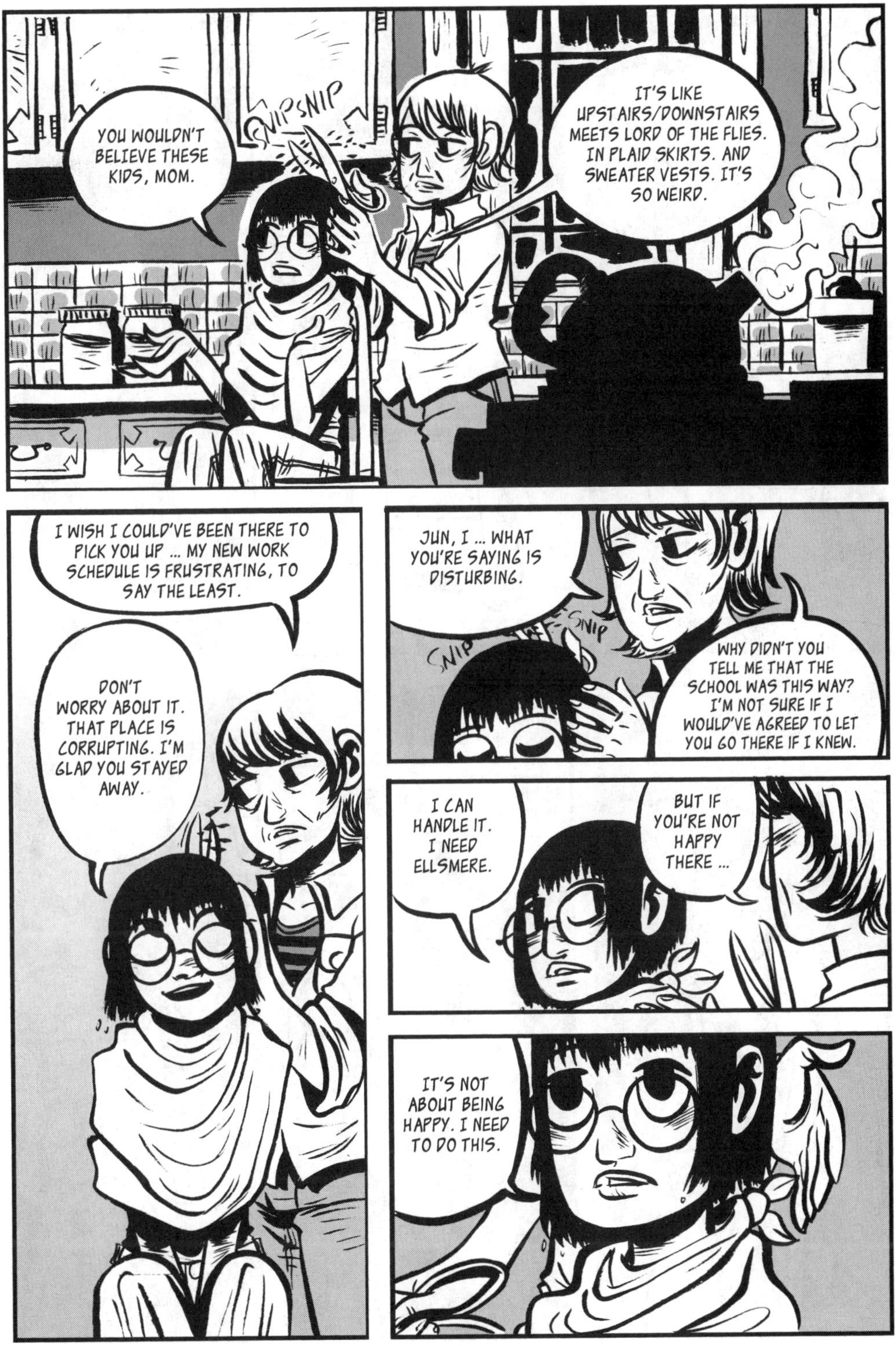
YOU WOULDN'T BELIEVE THESE KIDS, MOM.
SNIPSNIP
IT'S LIKE UPSTAIRS/DOWNSTAIRS MEETS LORD OF THE FLIES. IN PLAID SKIRTS. AND SWEATER VESTS. IT'S SO WEIRD.
I WISH I COULD'VE BEEN THERE TO PICK YOU UP ... MY NEW WORK SCHEDULE IS FRUSTRATING, TO SAY THE LEAST.
DON'T WORRY ABOUT IT. THAT PLACE IS CORRUPTING. I'M GLAD YOU STAYED AWAY.
JUN, I ... WHAT YOU'RE SAYING IS DISTURBING.
SNIP
SNIP
WHY DIDN'T YOU TELL ME THAT THE SCHOOL WAS THIS WAY? I'M NOT SURE IF I WOULD'VE AGREED TO LET YOU GO THERE IF I KNEW.
I CAN HANDLE IT. I NEED ELLSMERE.
BUT IF YOU'RE NOT HAPPY THERE ...
IT'S NOT ABOUT BEING HAPPY. I NEED TO DO THIS.

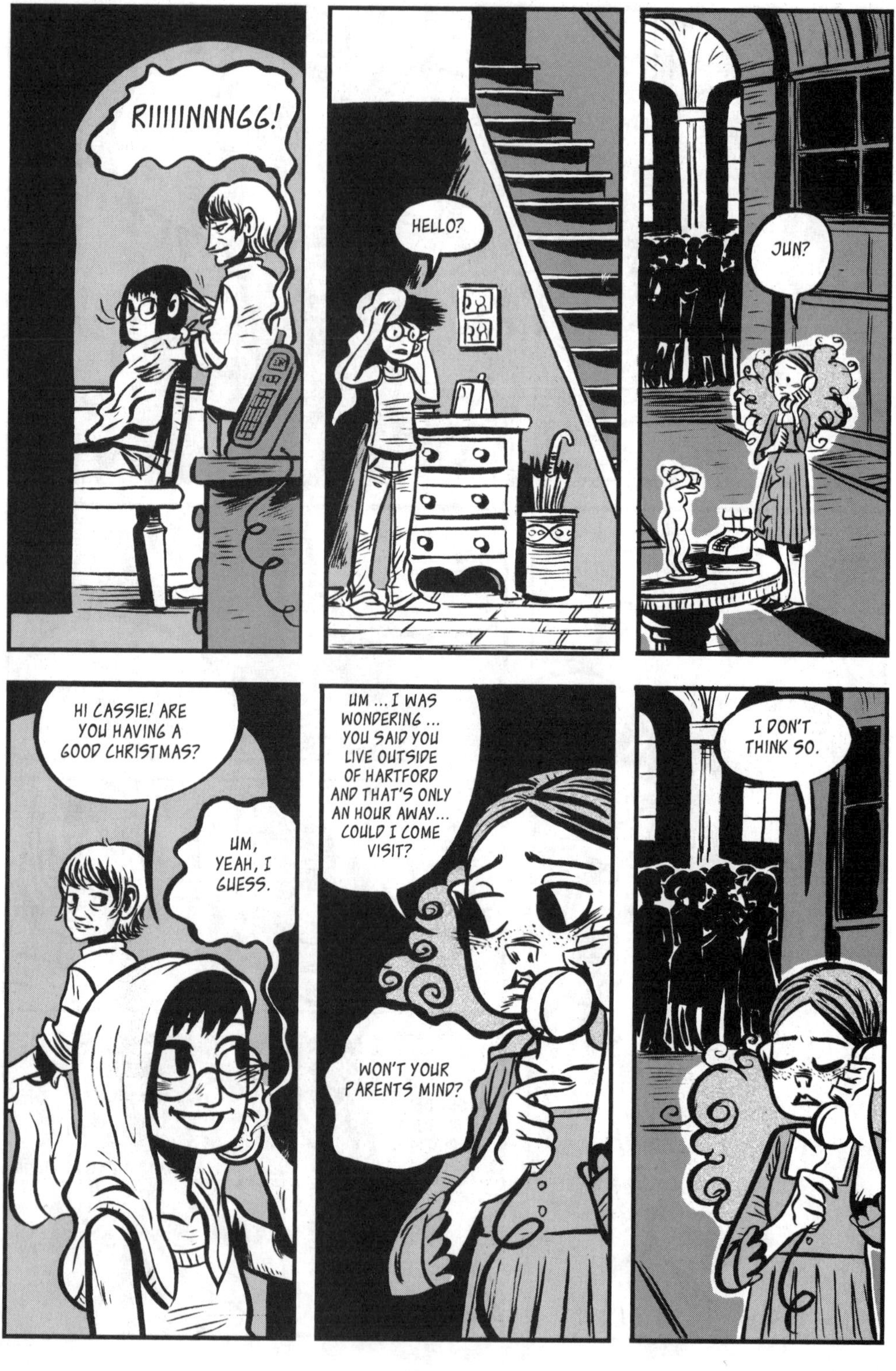
RIIIIINNNGG!
HELLO?
JUN?
HI CASSIE! ARE YOU HAVING A GOOD CHRISTMAS?
UM, YEAH, I GUESS.
UM ... I WAS WONDERING ... YOU SAID YOU LIVE OUTSIDE OF HARTFORD AND THAT'S ONLY AN HOUR AWAY... COULD I COME VISIT?
WON'T YOUR PARENTS MIND?
I DON'T THINK SO.

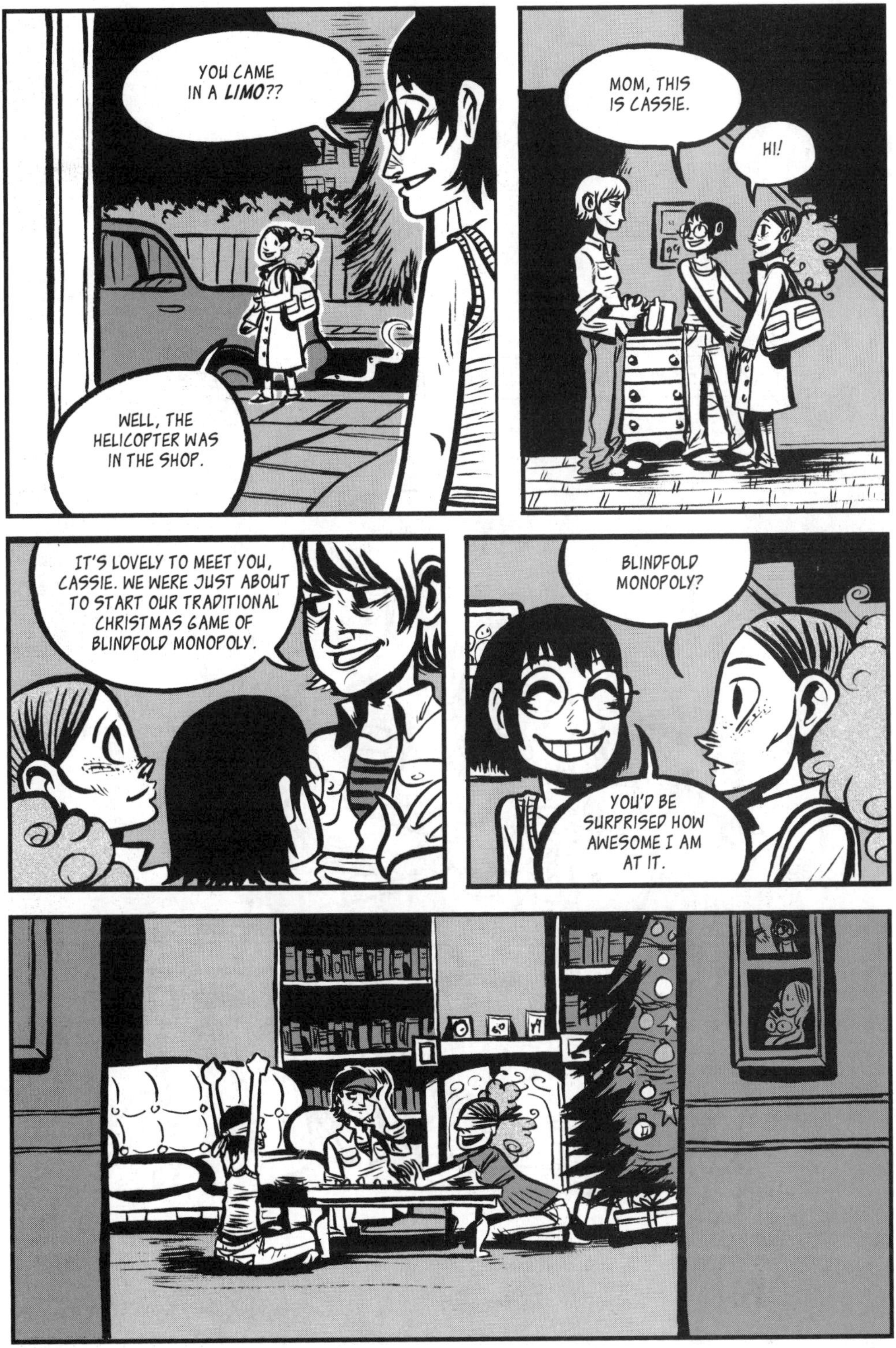
YOU CAME IN A LIMO??
WELL, THE HELICOPTER WAS IN THE SHOP.
MOM, THIS IS CASSIE.
HI!
IT'S LOVELY TO MEET YOU, CASSIE. WE WERE JUST ABOUT TO START OUR TRADITIONAL CHRISTMAS GAME OF BLINDFOLD MONOPOLY.
BLINDFOLD MONOPOLY?
YOU'D BE SURPRISED HOW AWESOME I AM AT IT.

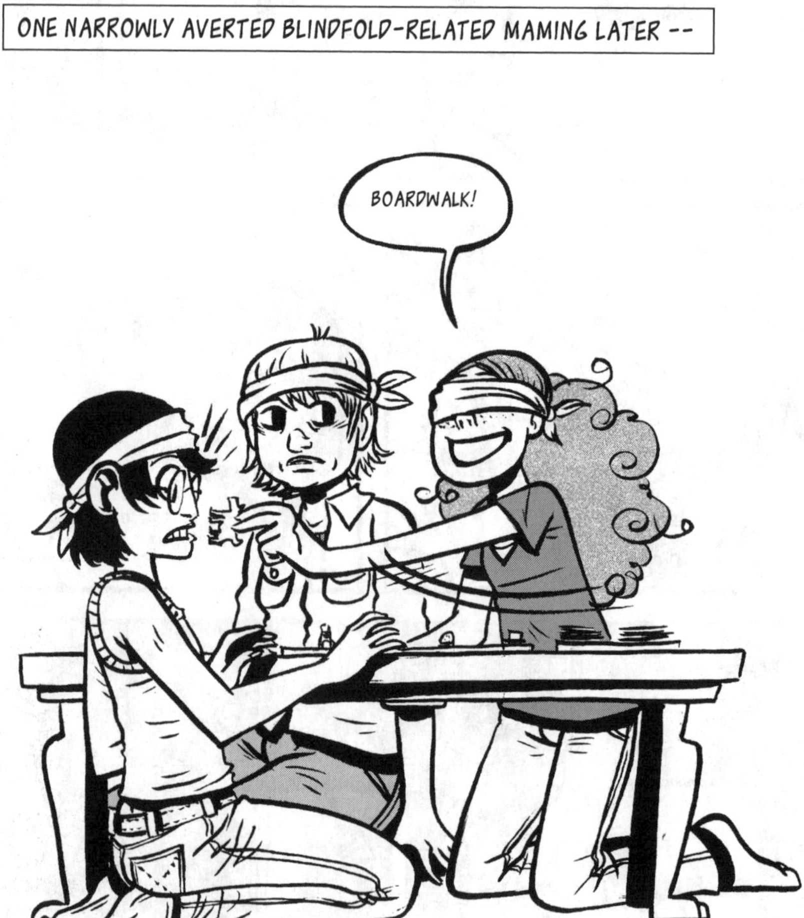
ONE NARROWLY AVERTED BLINDFOLD-RELATED MAMING LATER --
BOARDWALK!

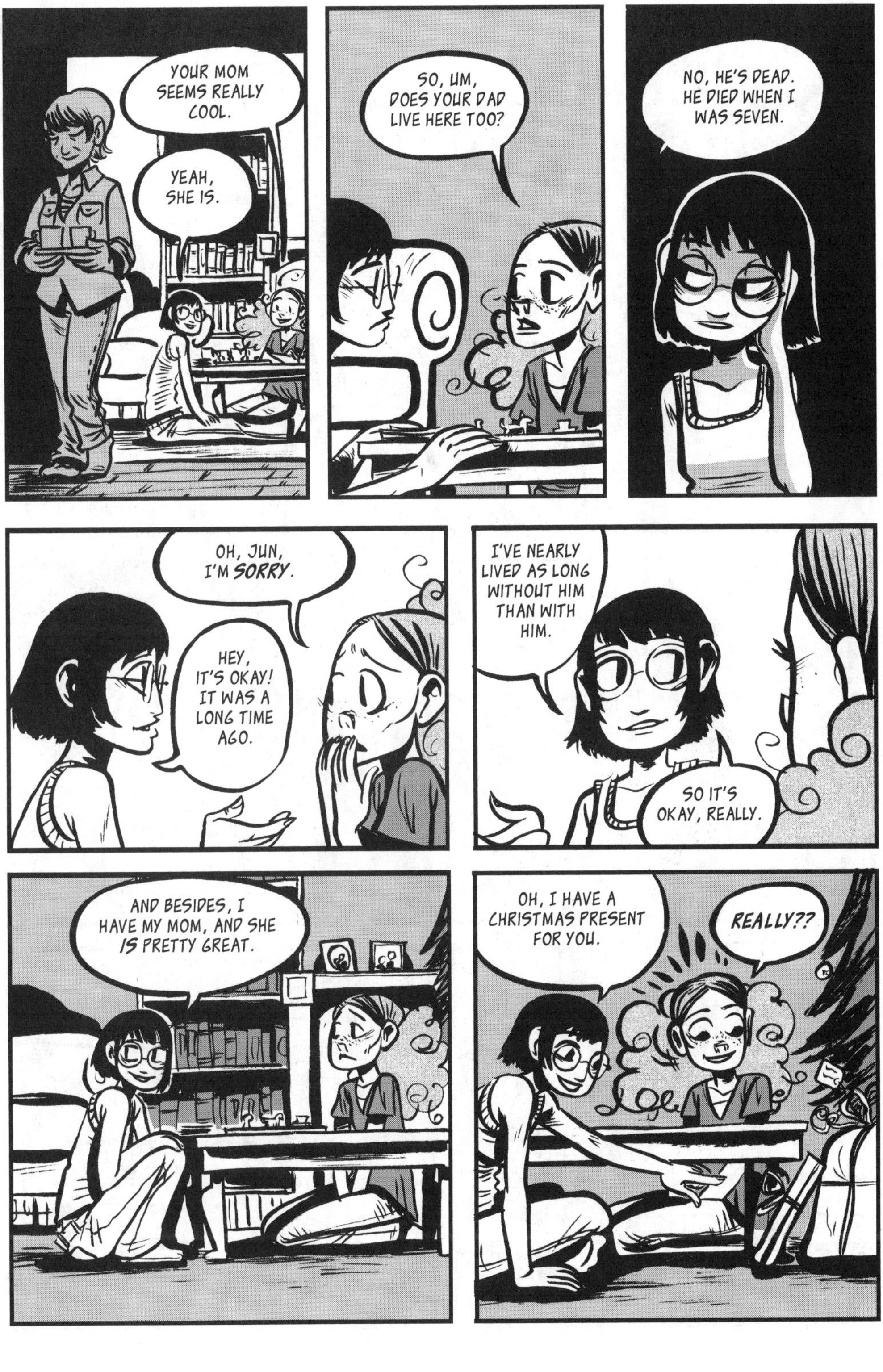
YOUR MOM SEEMS REALLY COOL.
YEAH, SHE IS.
SO, UM, DOES YOUR DAD LIVE HERE TOO?
NO, HE'S DEAD. HE DIED WHEN I WAS SEVEN.
OH, JUN, I'M *SORRY*.
HEY, IT'S OKAY! IT WAS A LONG TIME AGO.
I'VE NEARLY LIVED AS LONG WITHOUT HIM THAN WITH HIM.
SO IT'S OKAY, REALLY.
AND BESIDES, I HAVE MY MOM, AND SHE *IS* PRETTY GREAT.
OH, I HAVE A CHRISTMAS PRESENT FOR YOU.
REALLY??

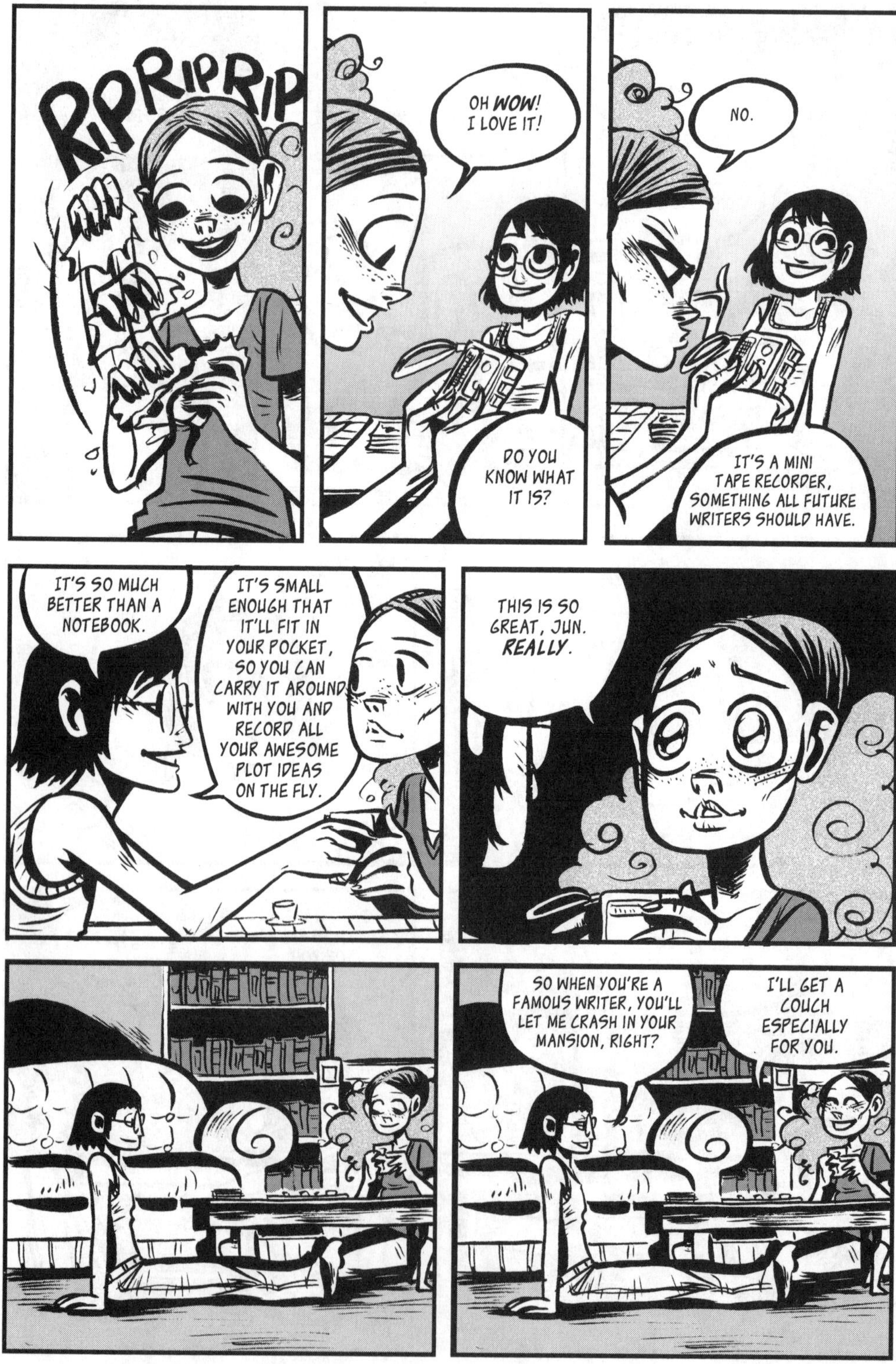
RIPRIPRIP
OH WOW! I LOVE IT!
DO YOU KNOW WHAT IT IS?
NO.
IT'S A MINI TAPE RECORDER, SOMETHING ALL FUTURE WRITERS SHOULD HAVE.
IT'S SO MUCH BETTER THAN A NOTEBOOK.
IT'S SMALL ENOUGH THAT IT'LL FIT IN YOUR POCKET, SO YOU CAN CARRY IT AROUND WITH YOU AND RECORD ALL YOUR AWESOME PLOT IDEAS ON THE FLY.
THIS IS SO GREAT, JUN. REALLY.
SO WHEN YOU'RE A FAMOUS WRITER, YOU'LL LET ME CRASH IN YOUR MANSION, RIGHT?
I'LL GET A COUCH ESPECIALLY FOR YOU.

chapter six

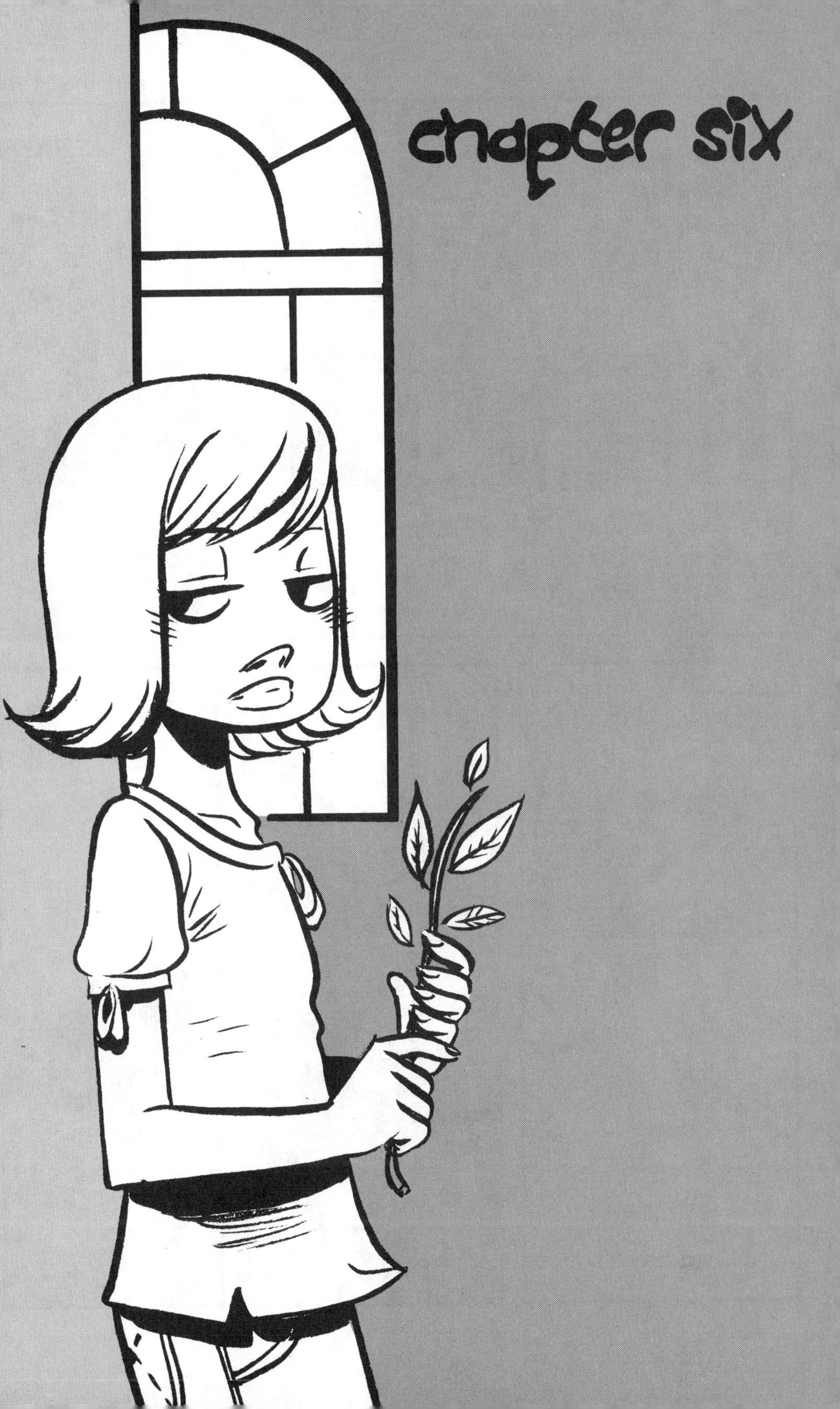

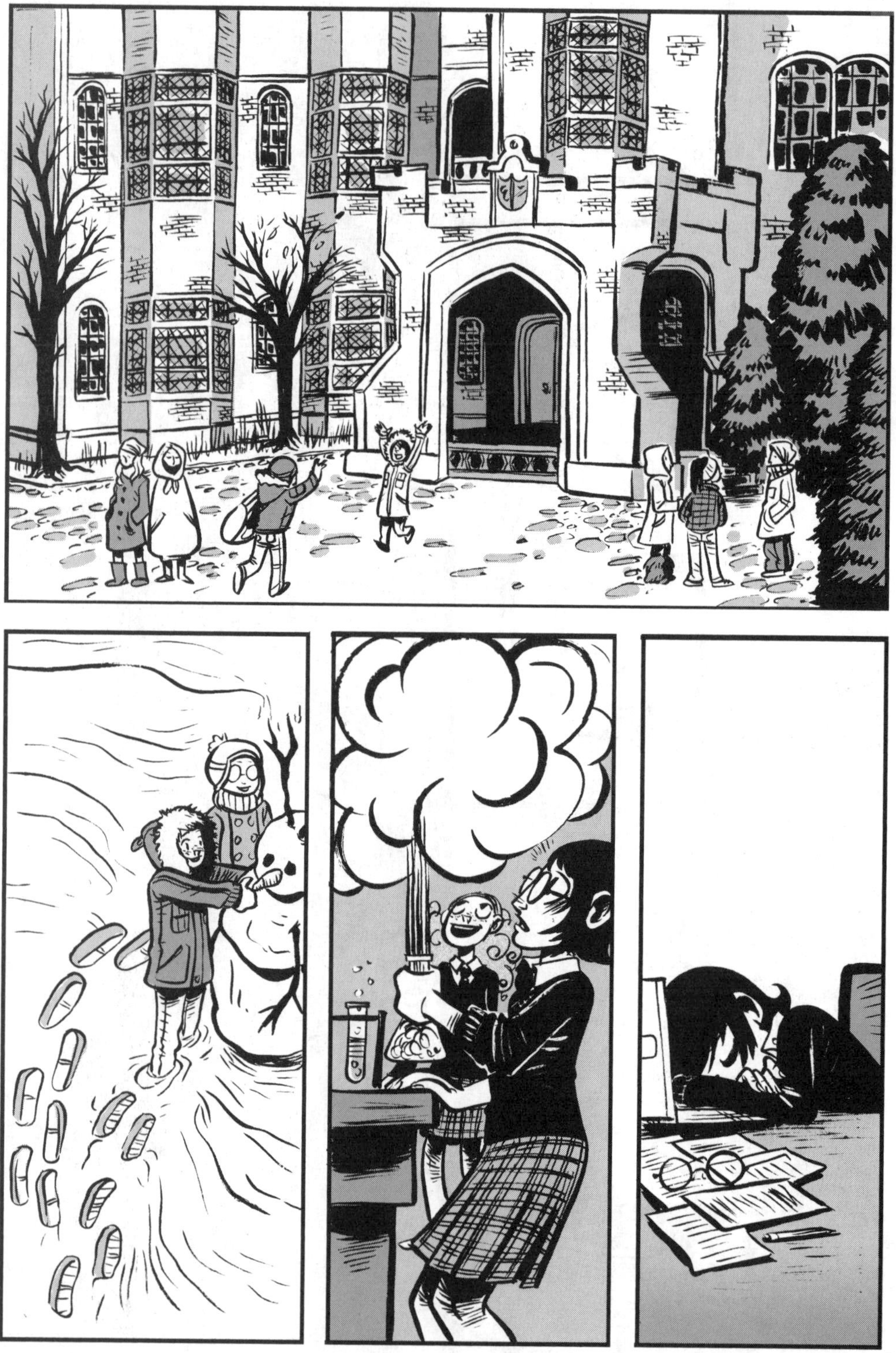

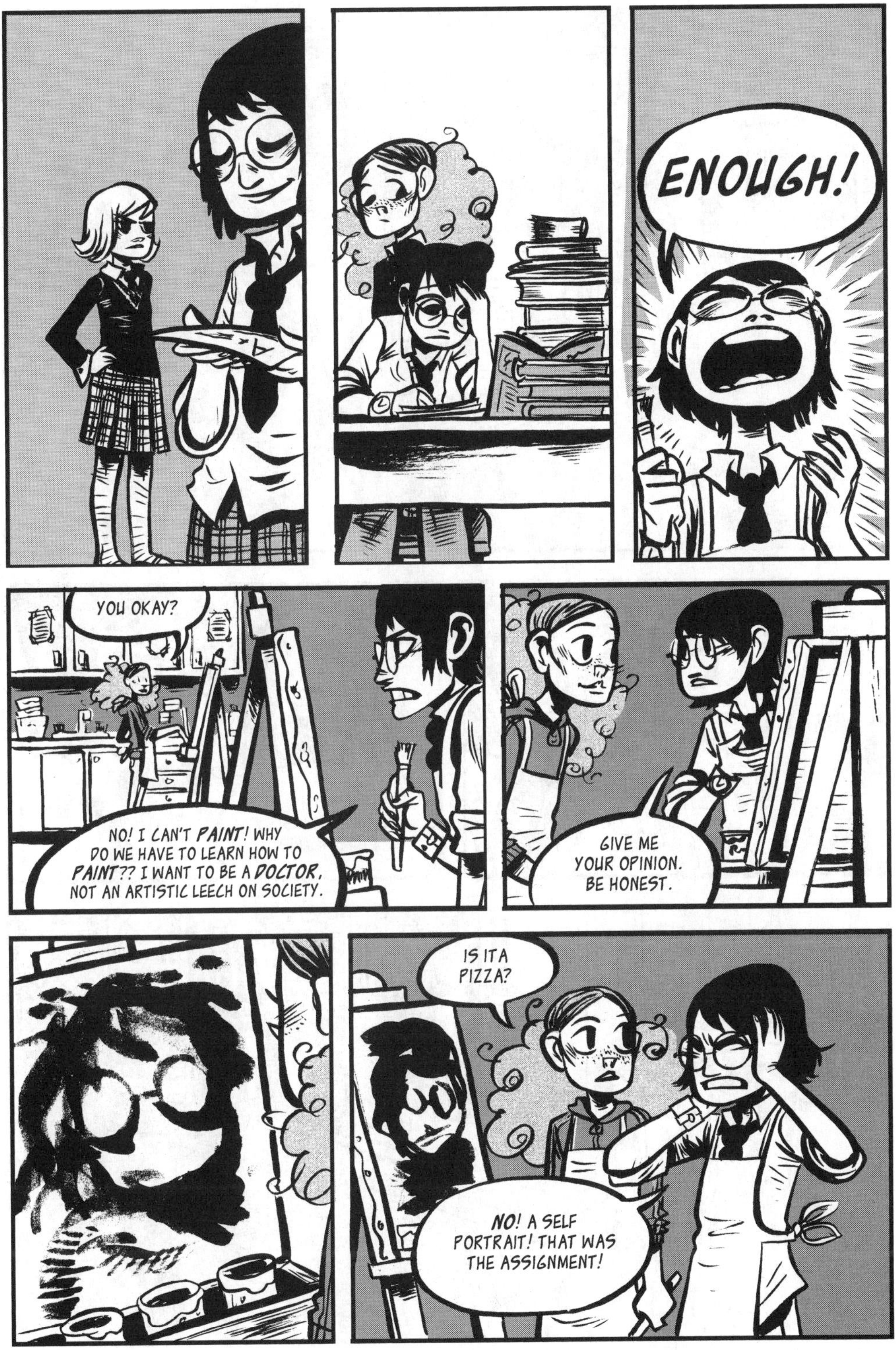
ENOUGH!
YOU OKAY?
NO! I CAN'T PAINT! WHY DO WE HAVE TO LEARN HOW TO PAINT?? I WANT TO BE A DOCTOR, NOT AN ARTISTIC LEECH ON SOCIETY.
GIVE ME YOUR OPINION. BE HONEST.
IS IT A PIZZA?
NO! A SELF PORTRAIT! THAT WAS THE ASSIGNMENT!

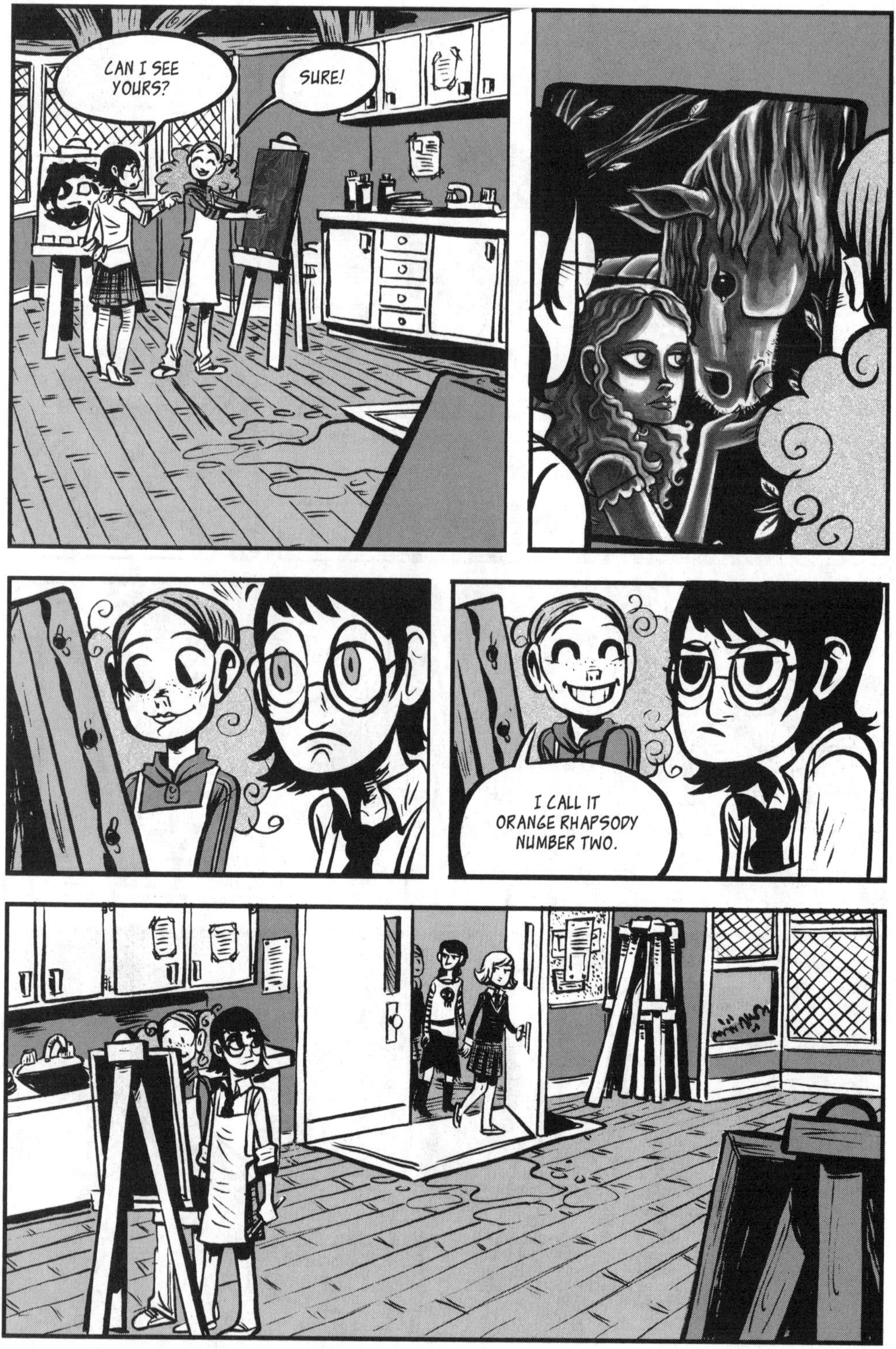
CAN I SEE YOURS?
SURE!
I CALL IT ORANGE RHAPSODY NUMBER TWO.

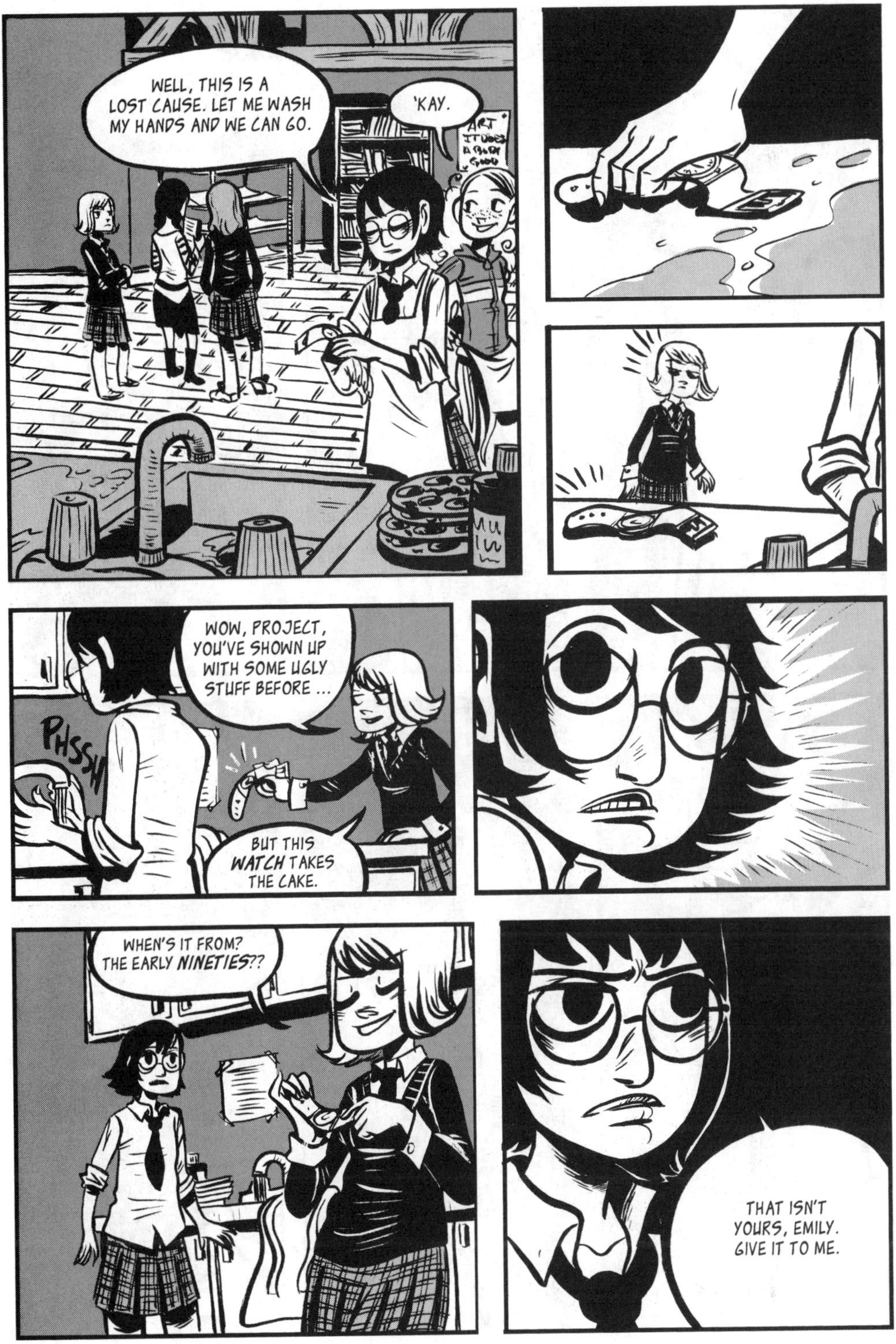
WELL, THIS IS A LOST CAUSE. LET ME WASH MY HANDS AND WE CAN GO.
'KAY.
WOW, PROJECT, YOU'VE SHOWN UP WITH SOME UGLY STUFF BEFORE ...
PHSSSH
BUT THIS *WATCH* TAKES THE CAKE.
WHEN'S IT FROM? THE EARLY *NINETIES*??
THAT ISN'T YOURS, EMILY. GIVE IT TO ME.

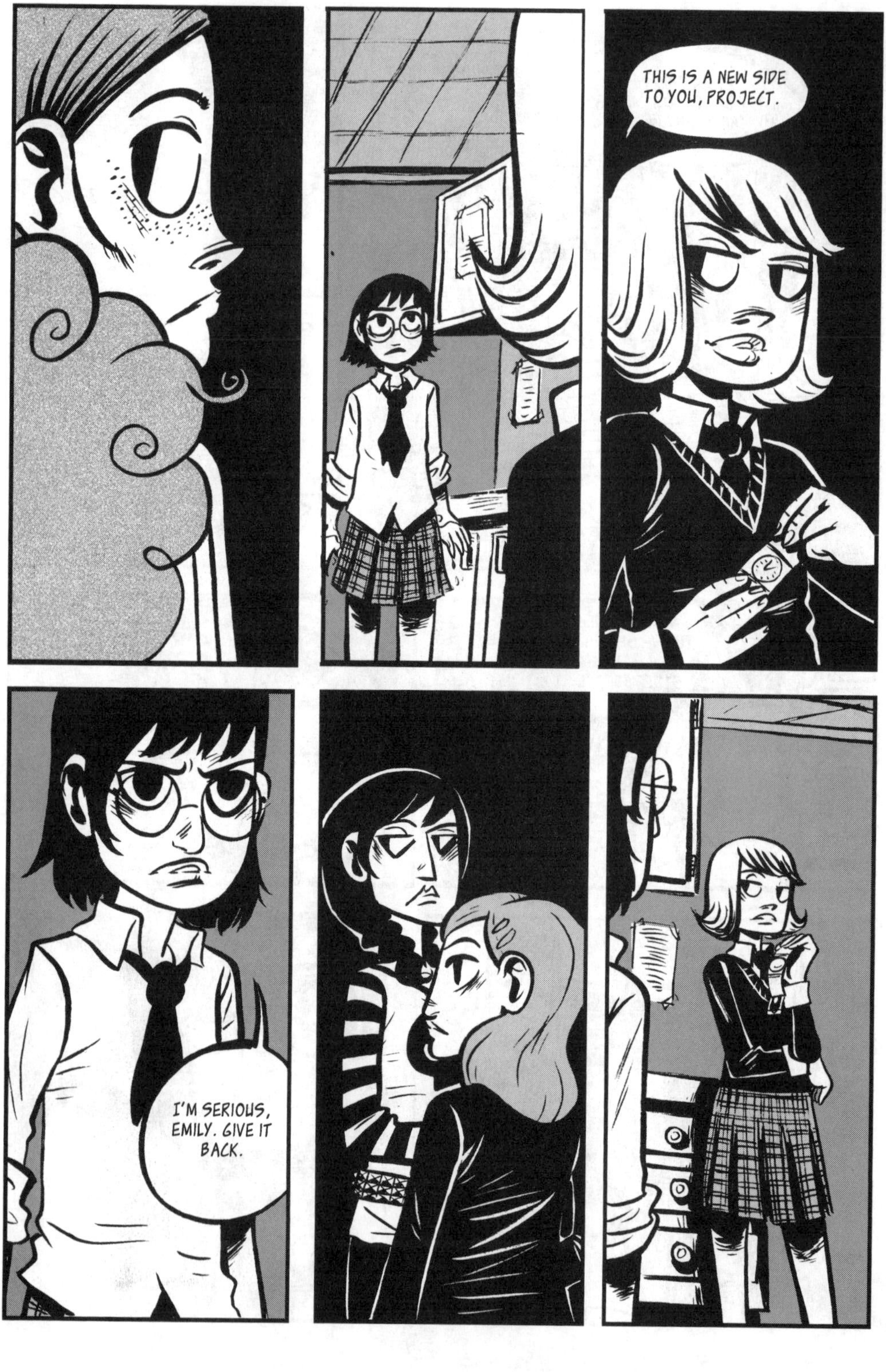
THIS IS A NEW SIDE TO YOU, PROJECT.
I'M SERIOUS, EMILY. GIVE IT BACK.

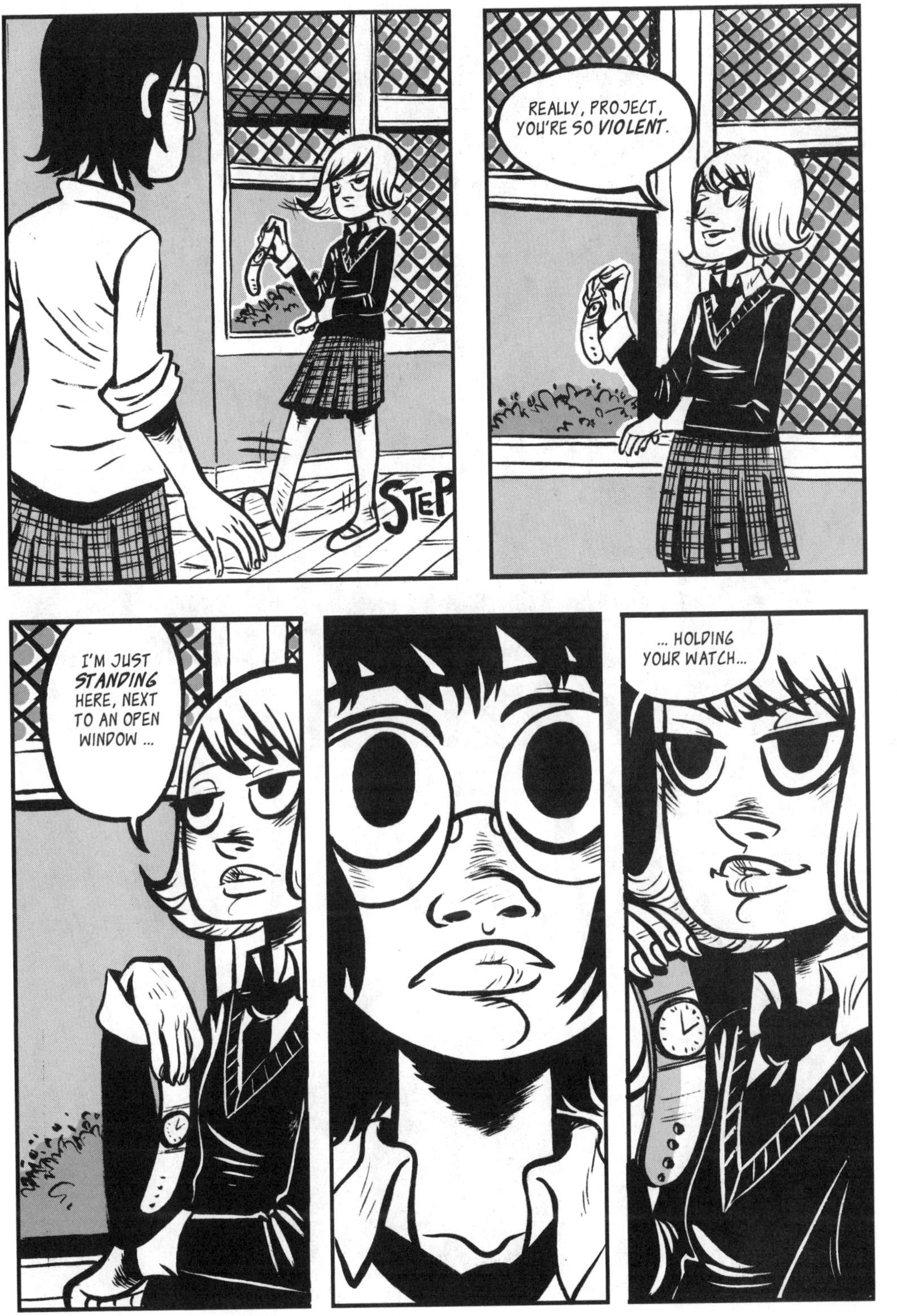
STEP
REALLY, PROJECT, YOU'RE SO **VIOLENT**.
I'M JUST **STANDING** HERE, NEXT TO AN OPEN WINDOW ...
... HOLDING YOUR WATCH...

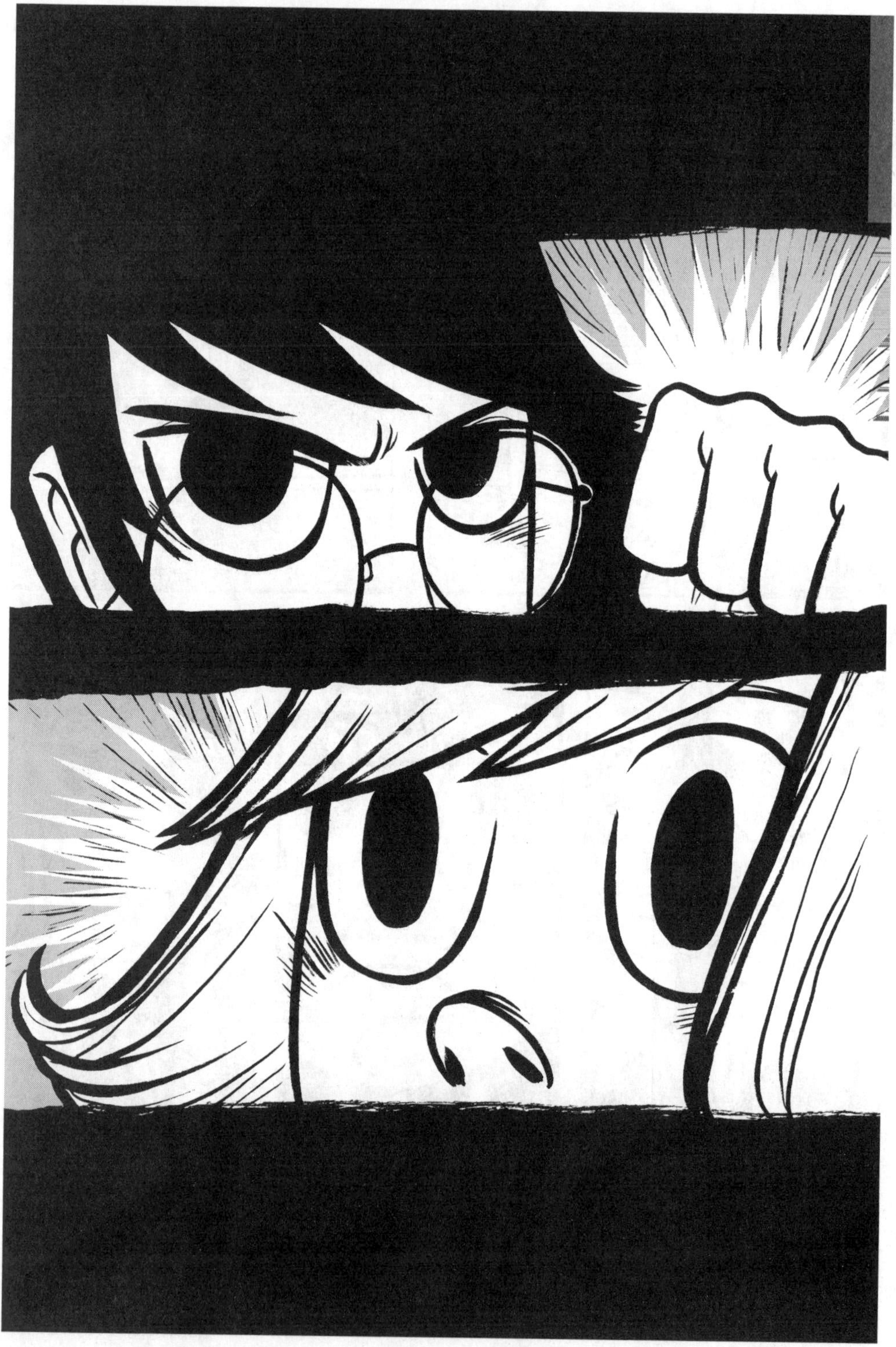

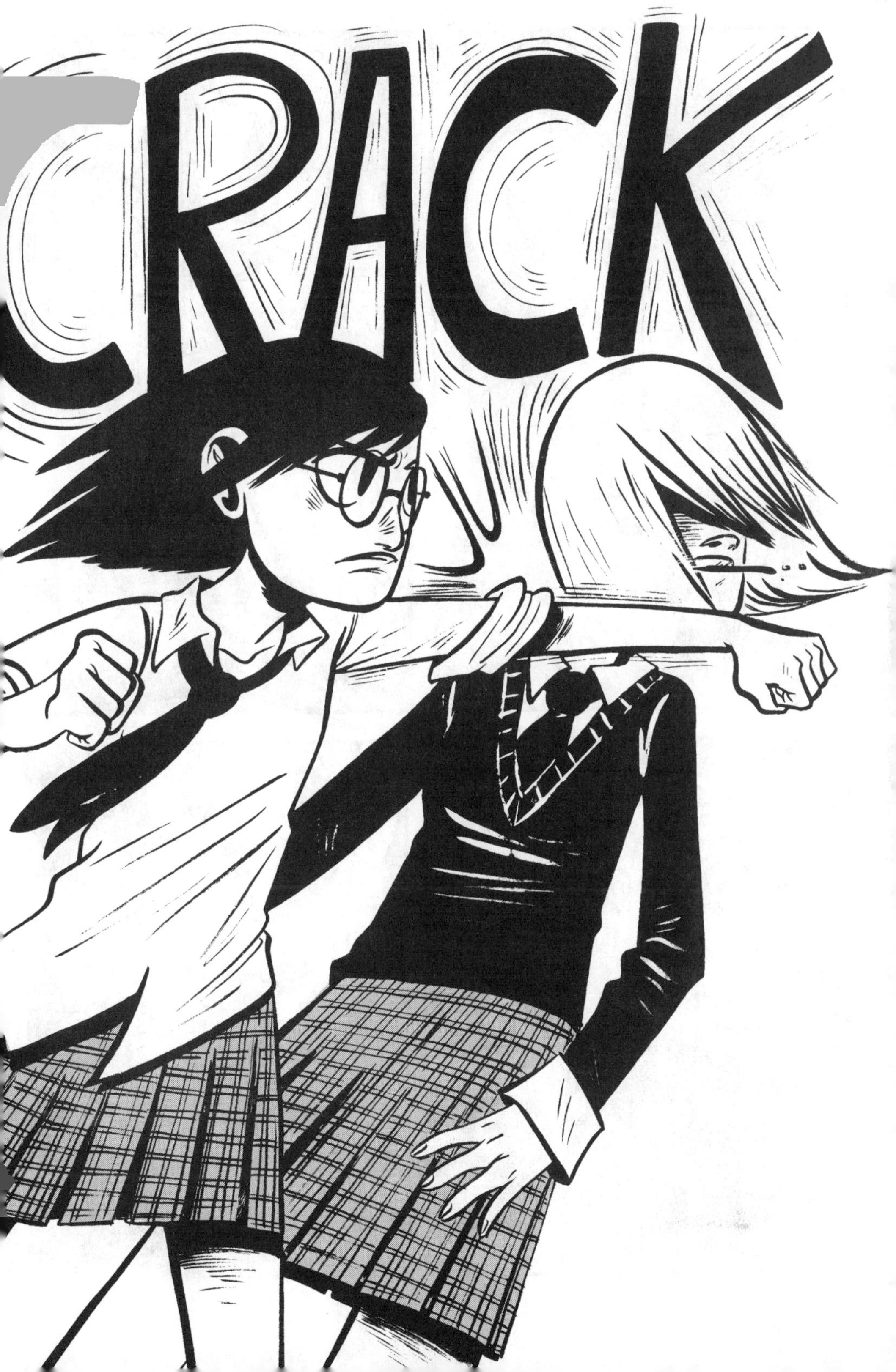
CRACK

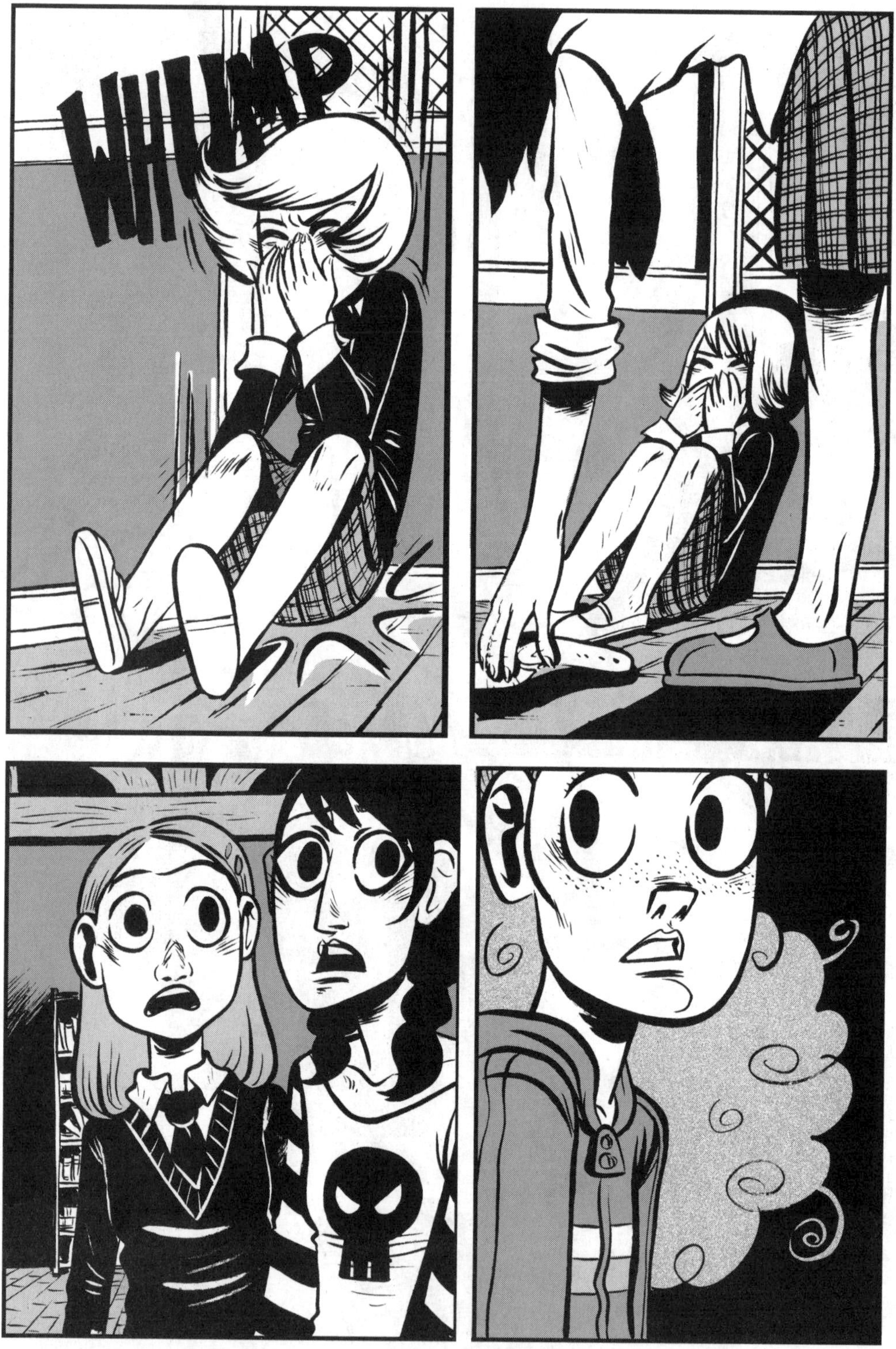
WHUMP

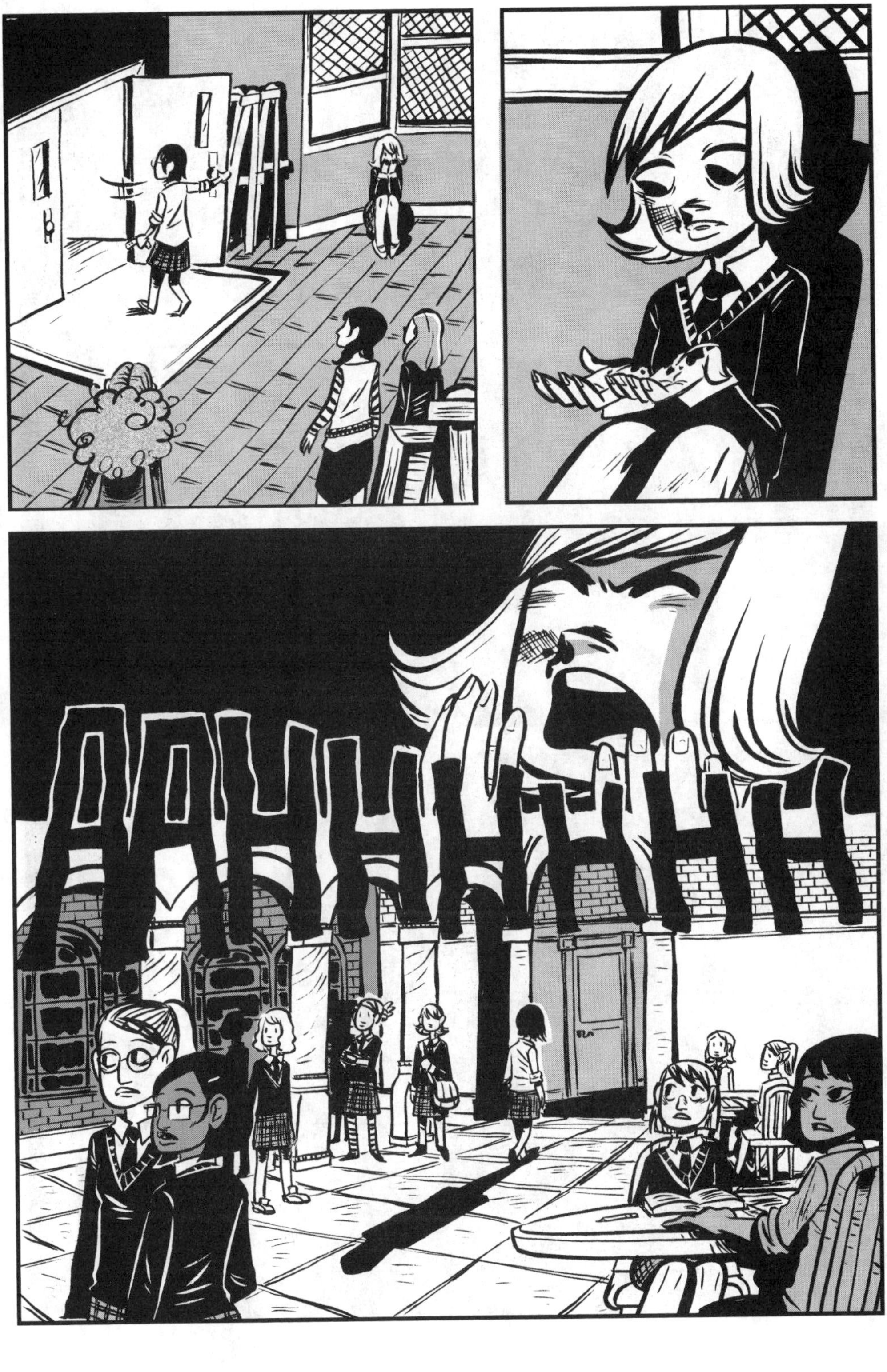
AAHHHHHHHHH

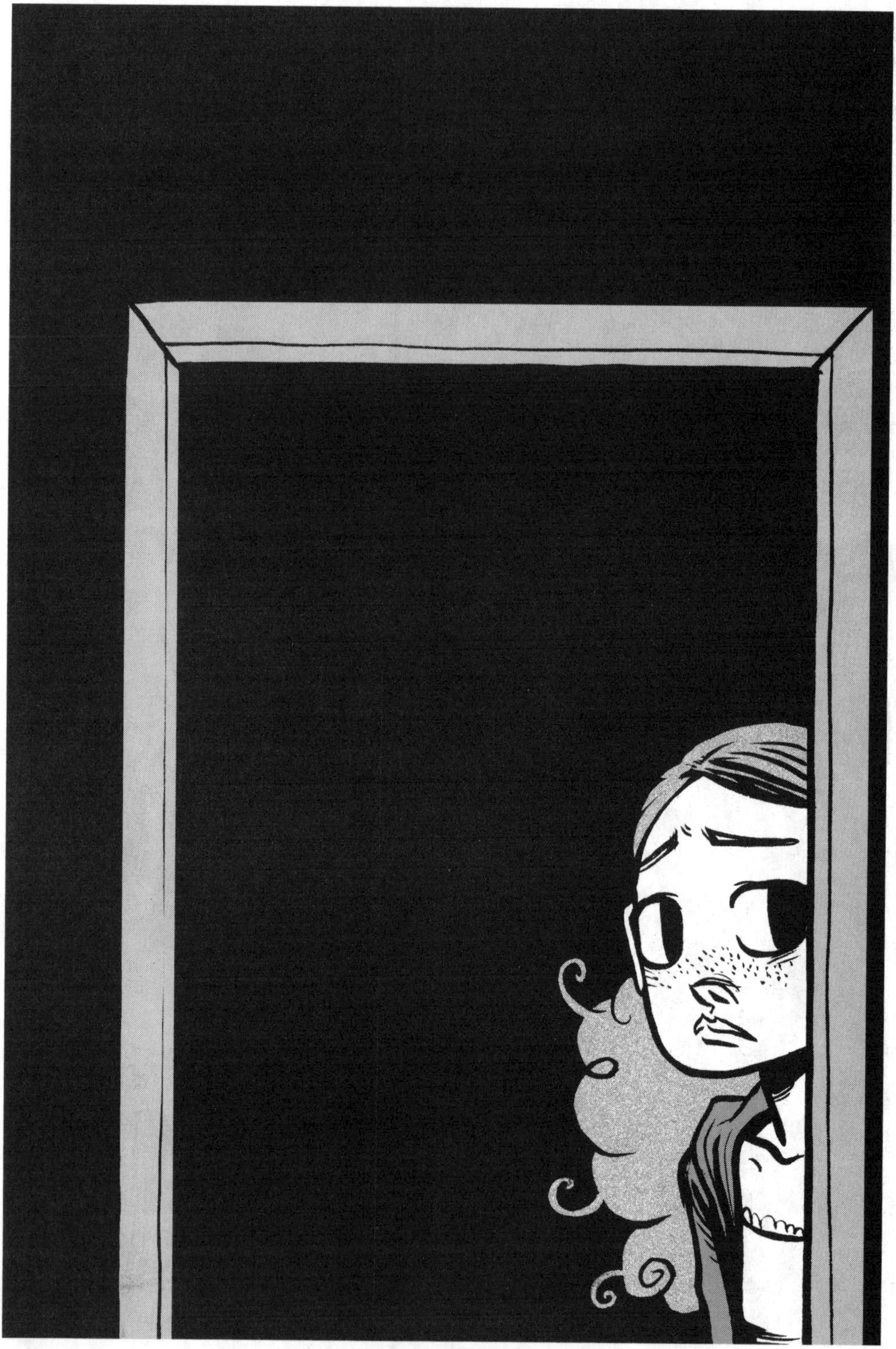

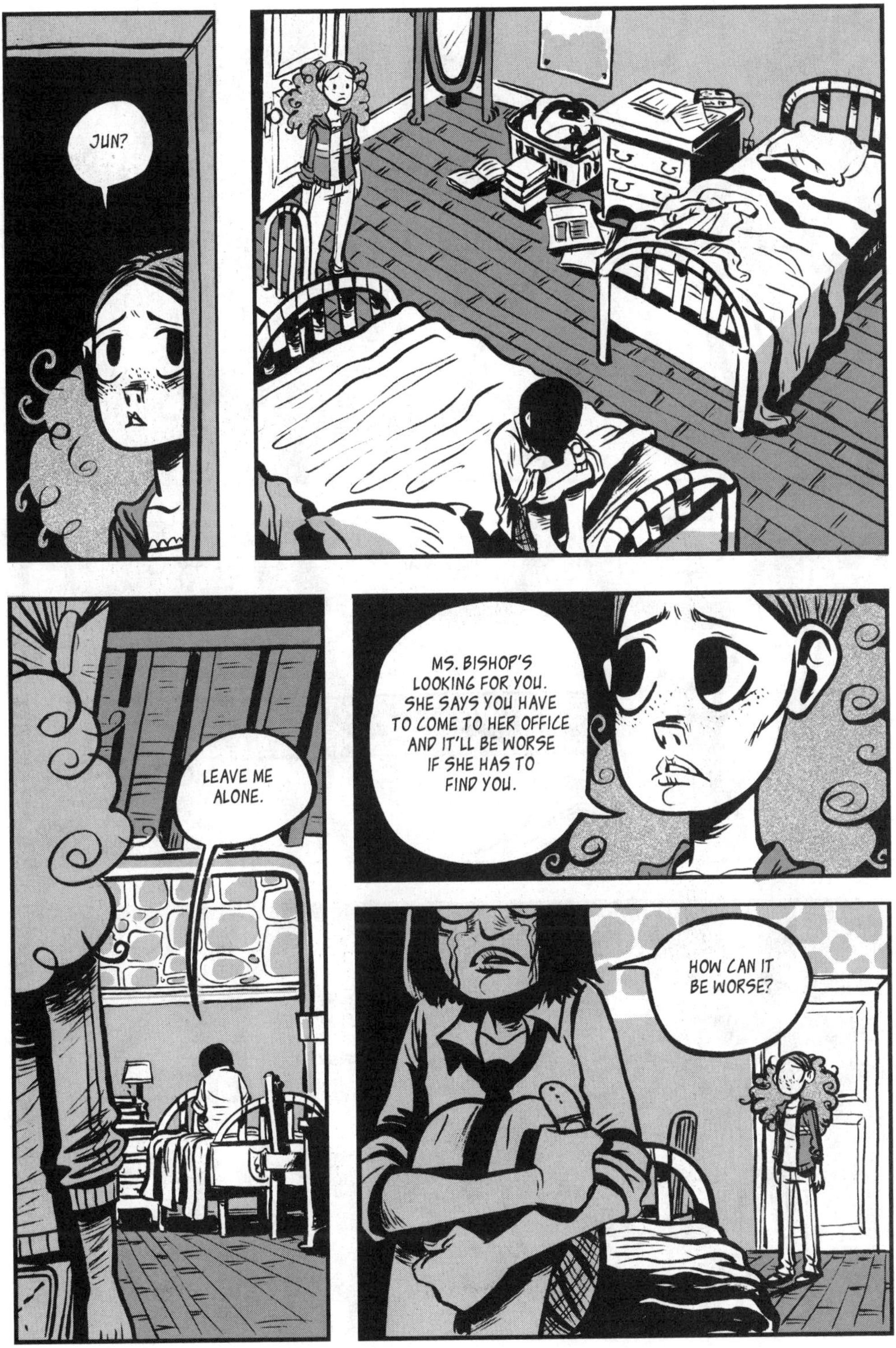
JUN?
LEAVE ME ALONE.
MS. BISHOP'S LOOKING FOR YOU. SHE SAYS YOU HAVE TO COME TO HER OFFICE AND IT'LL BE WORSE IF SHE HAS TO FIND YOU.
HOW CAN IT BE WORSE?

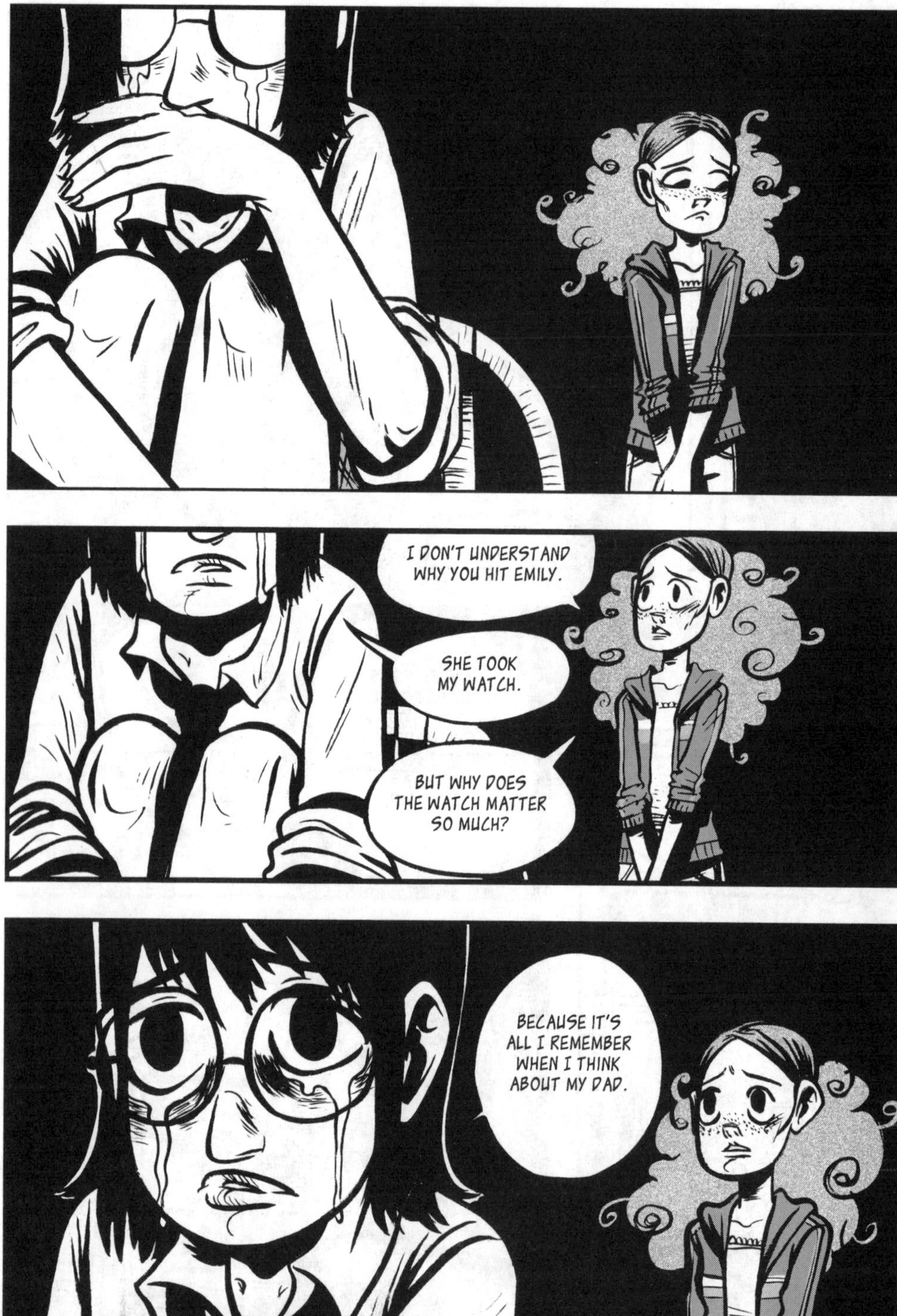
I DON'T UNDERSTAND WHY YOU HIT EMILY.
SHE TOOK MY WATCH.
BUT WHY DOES THE WATCH MATTER SO MUCH?
BECAUSE IT'S ALL I REMEMBER WHEN I THINK ABOUT MY DAD.

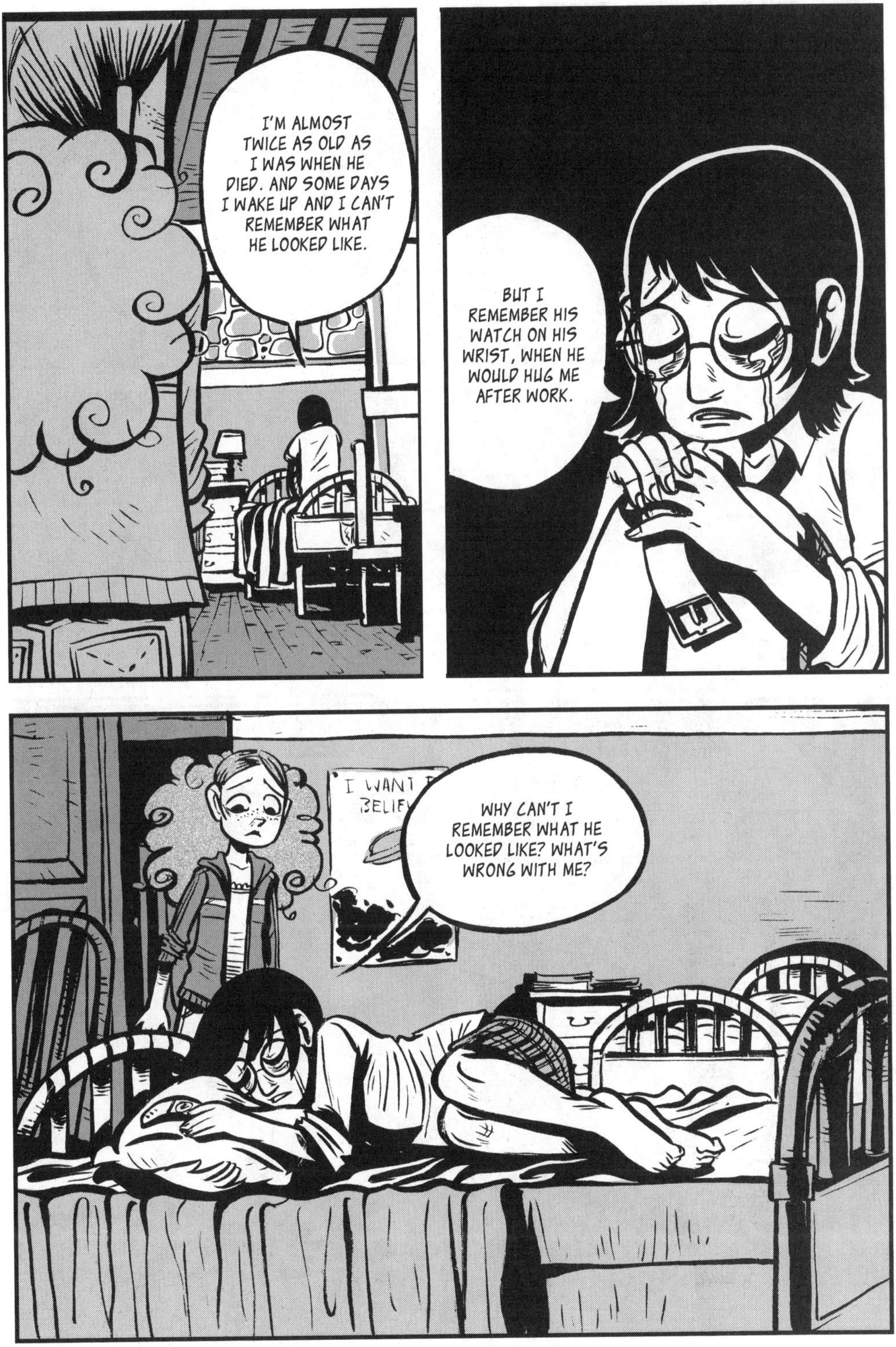
I'M ALMOST TWICE AS OLD AS I WAS WHEN HE DIED. AND SOME DAYS I WAKE UP AND I CAN'T REMEMBER WHAT HE LOOKED LIKE.
BUT I REMEMBER HIS WATCH ON HIS WRIST, WHEN HE WOULD HUG ME AFTER WORK.
WHY CAN'T I REMEMBER WHAT HE LOOKED LIKE? WHAT'S WRONG WITH ME?

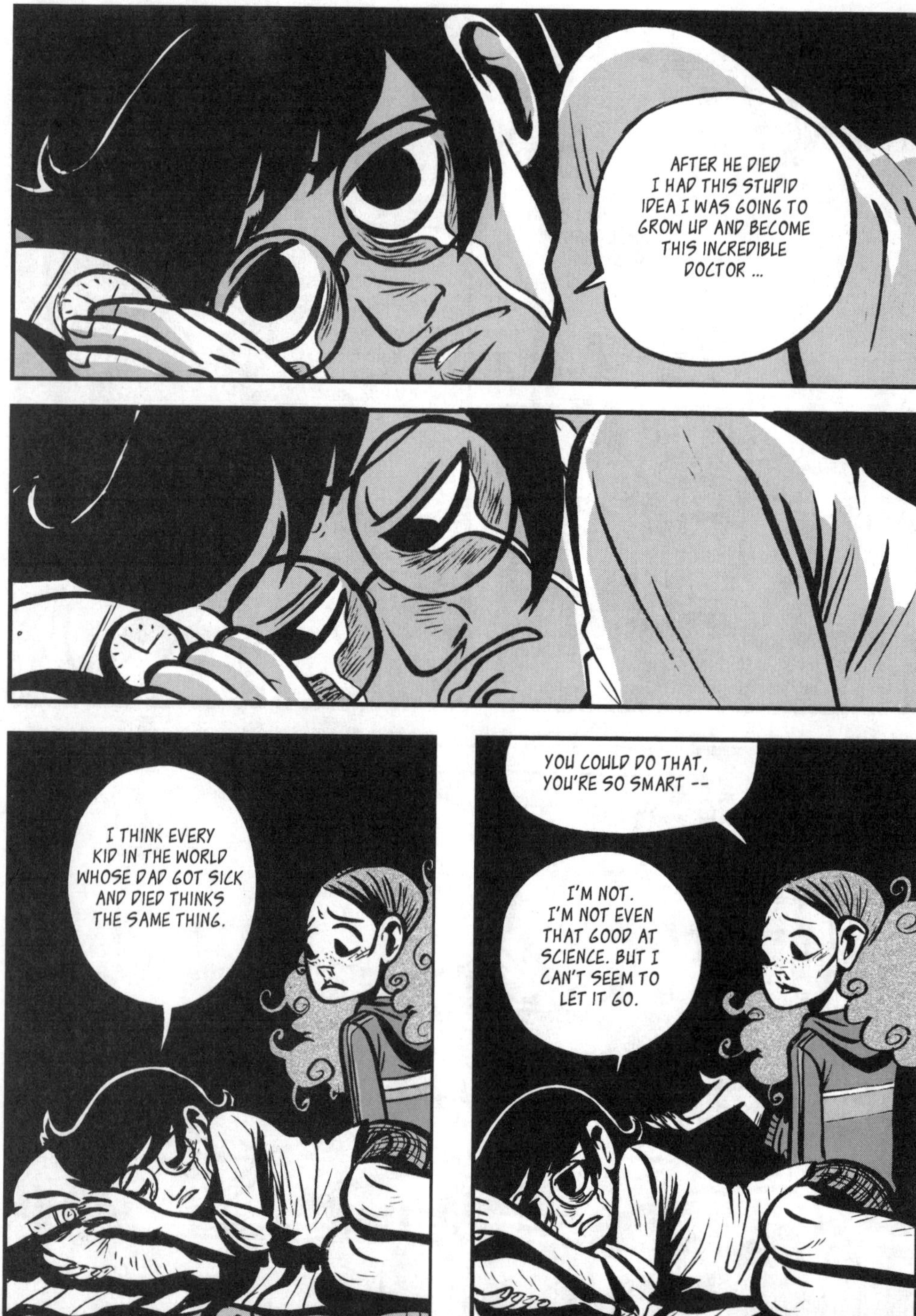
AFTER HE DIED I HAD THIS STUPID IDEA I WAS GOING TO GROW UP AND BECOME THIS INCREDIBLE DOCTOR ...
I THINK EVERY KID IN THE WORLD WHOSE DAD GOT SICK AND DIED THINKS THE SAME THING.
YOU COULD DO THAT, YOU'RE SO SMART --
I'M NOT. I'M NOT EVEN THAT GOOD AT SCIENCE. BUT I CAN'T SEEM TO LET IT GO.

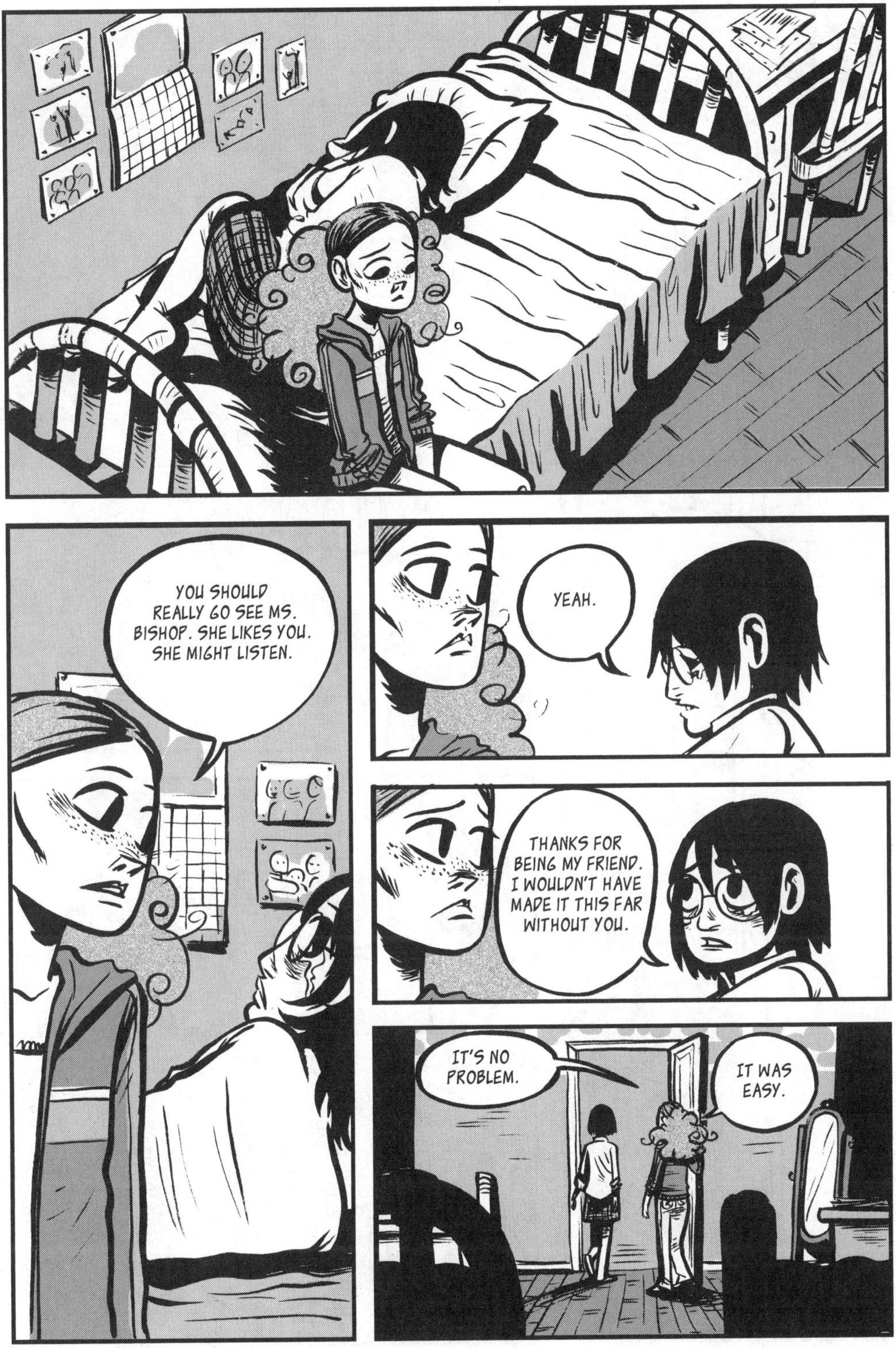
YOU SHOULD REALLY GO SEE MS. BISHOP. SHE LIKES YOU. SHE MIGHT LISTEN.
YEAH.
THANKS FOR BEING MY FRIEND. I WOULDN'T HAVE MADE IT THIS FAR WITHOUT YOU.
IT'S NO PROBLEM.
IT WAS EASY.

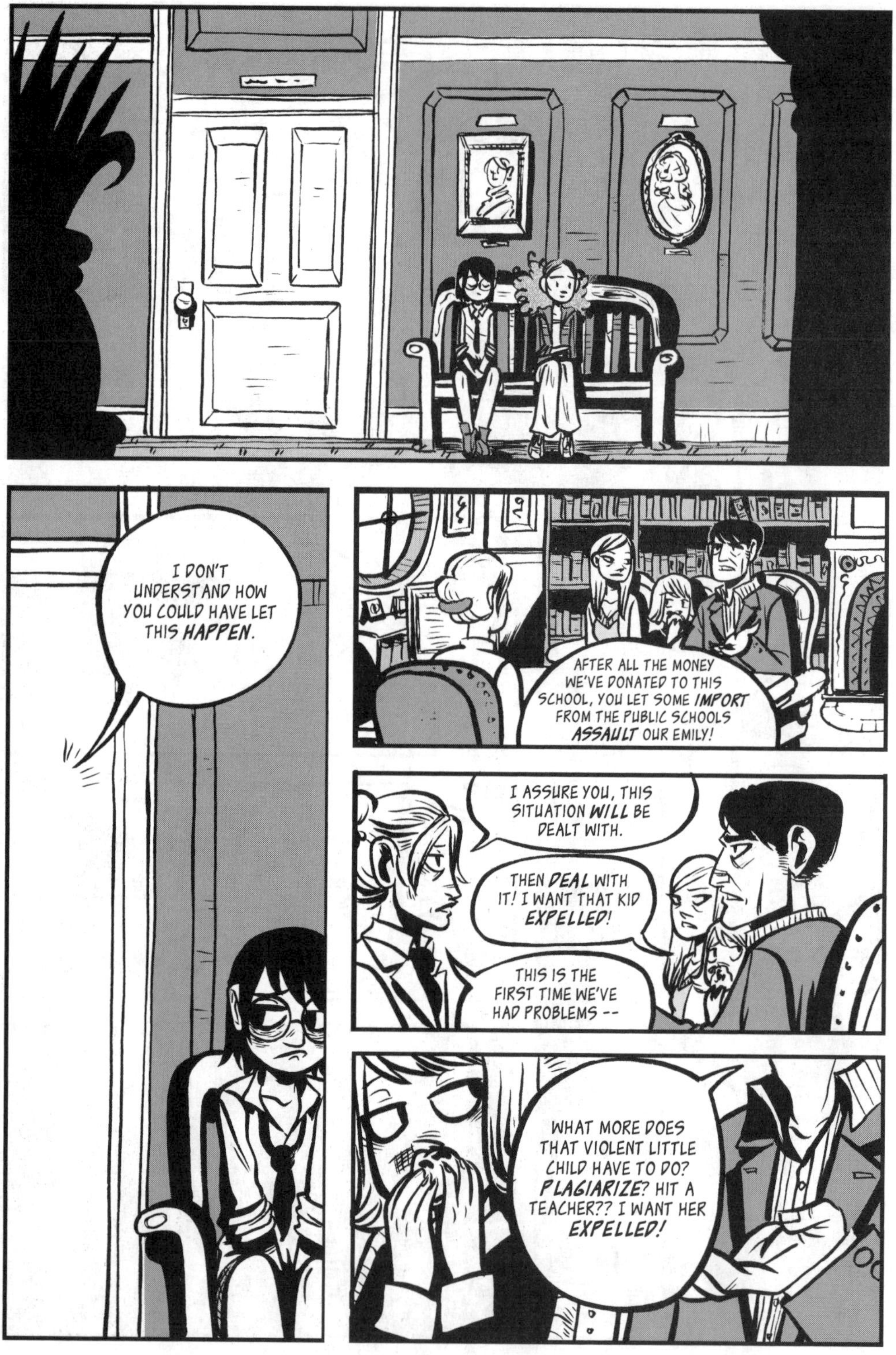
I DON'T UNDERSTAND HOW YOU COULD HAVE LET THIS HAPPEN.
AFTER ALL THE MONEY WE'VE DONATED TO THIS SCHOOL, YOU LET SOME IMPORT FROM THE PUBLIC SCHOOLS ASSAULT OUR EMILY!
I ASSURE YOU, THIS SITUATION WILL BE DEALT WITH.
THEN DEAL WITH IT! I WANT THAT KID EXPELLED!
THIS IS THE FIRST TIME WE'VE HAD PROBLEMS --
WHAT MORE DOES THAT VIOLENT LITTLE CHILD HAVE TO DO? PLAGIARIZE? HIT A TEACHER?? I WANT HER EXPELLED!

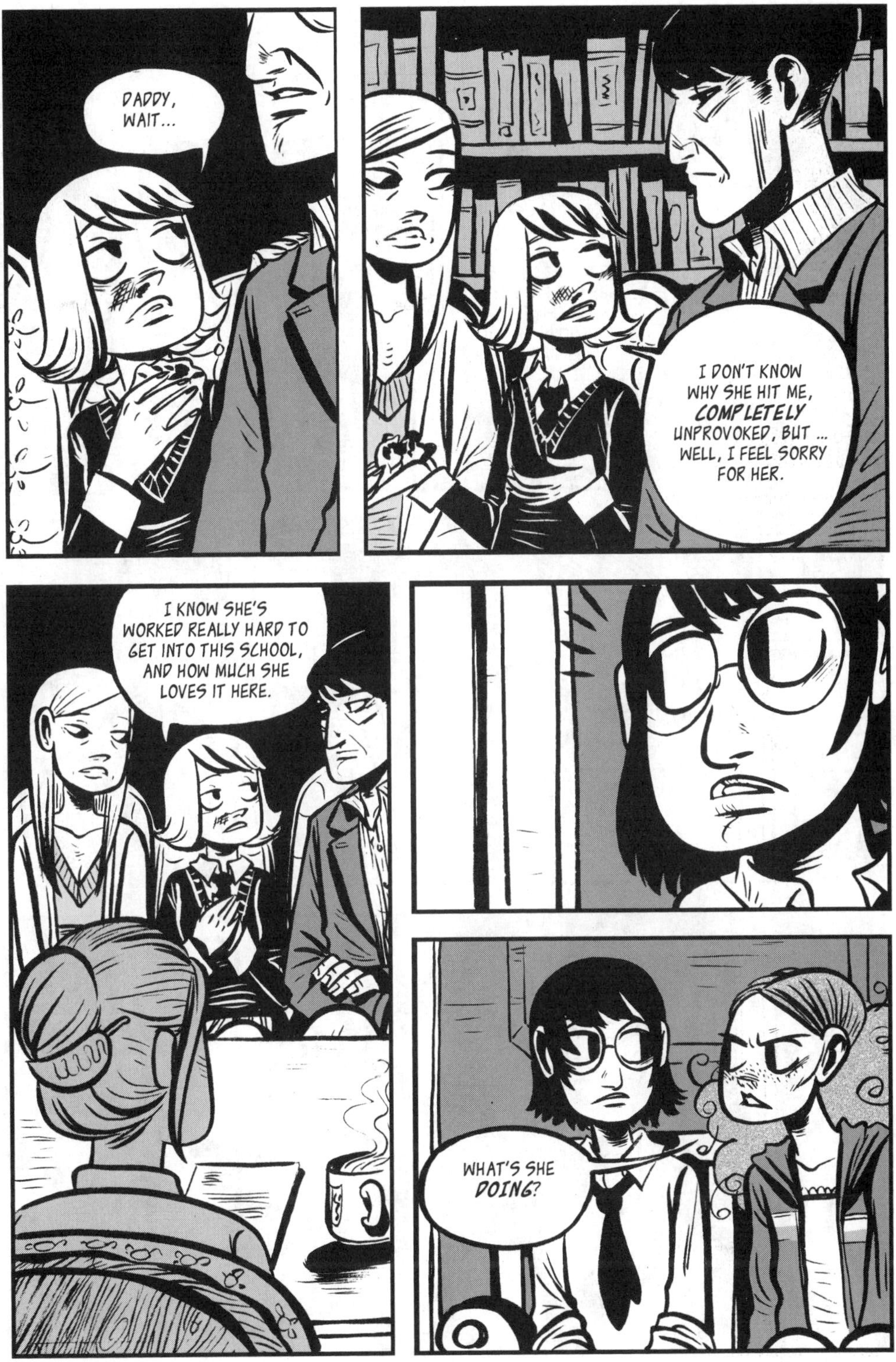
DADDY, WAIT...
I DON'T KNOW WHY SHE HIT ME, COMPLETELY UNPROVOKED, BUT ... WELL, I FEEL SORRY FOR HER.
I KNOW SHE'S WORKED REALLY HARD TO GET INTO THIS SCHOOL, AND HOW MUCH SHE LOVES IT HERE.
WHAT'S SHE DOING?

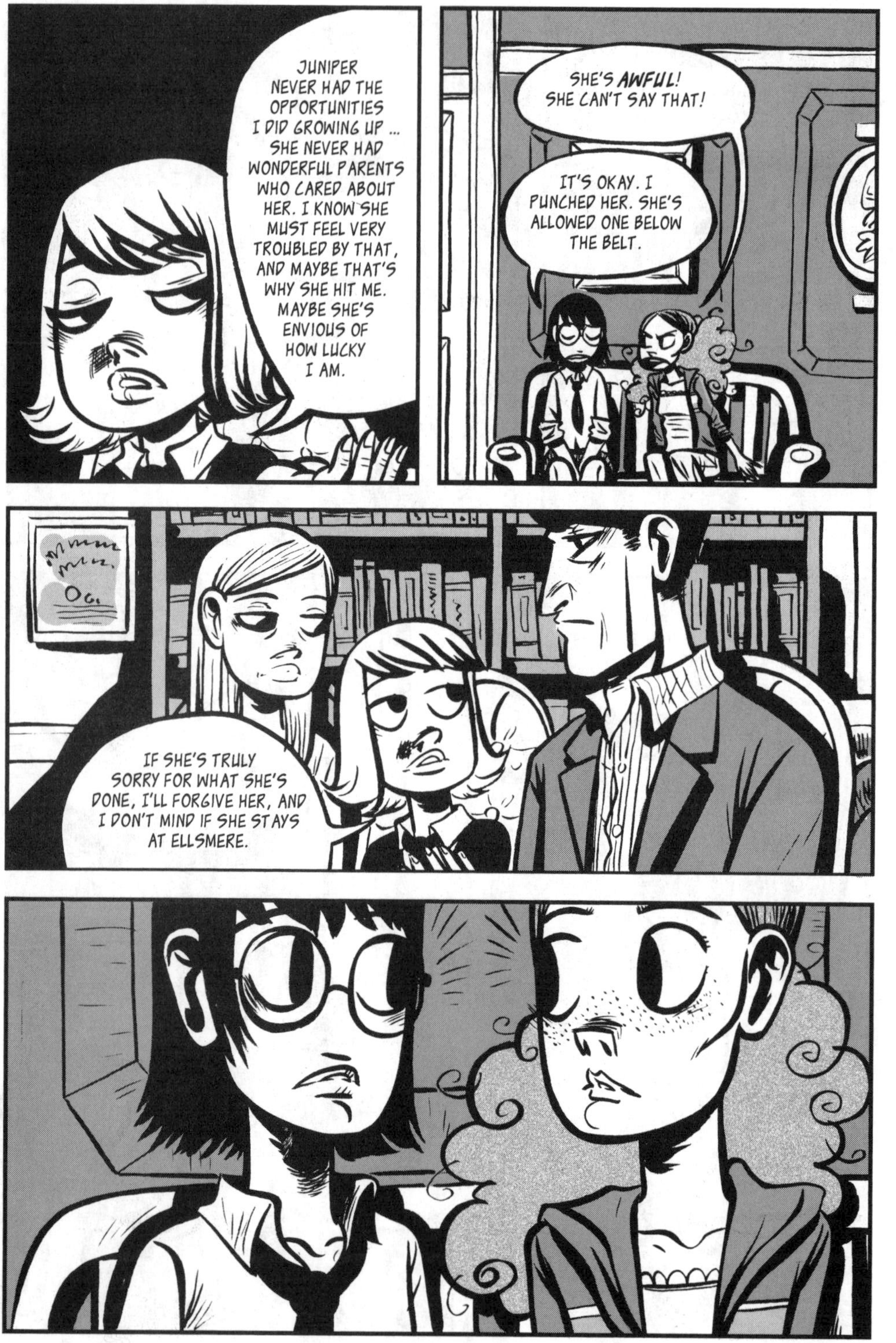
JUNIPER NEVER HAD THE OPPORTUNITIES I DID GROWING UP ... SHE NEVER HAD WONDERFUL PARENTS WHO CARED ABOUT HER. I KNOW SHE MUST FEEL VERY TROUBLED BY THAT, AND MAYBE THAT'S WHY SHE HIT ME. MAYBE SHE'S ENVIOUS OF HOW LUCKY I AM.
SHE'S **AWFUL**! SHE CAN'T SAY THAT!
IT'S OKAY. I PUNCHED HER. SHE'S ALLOWED ONE BELOW THE BELT.
IF SHE'S TRULY SORRY FOR WHAT SHE'S DONE, I'LL FORGIVE HER, AND I DON'T MIND IF SHE STAYS AT ELLSMERE.

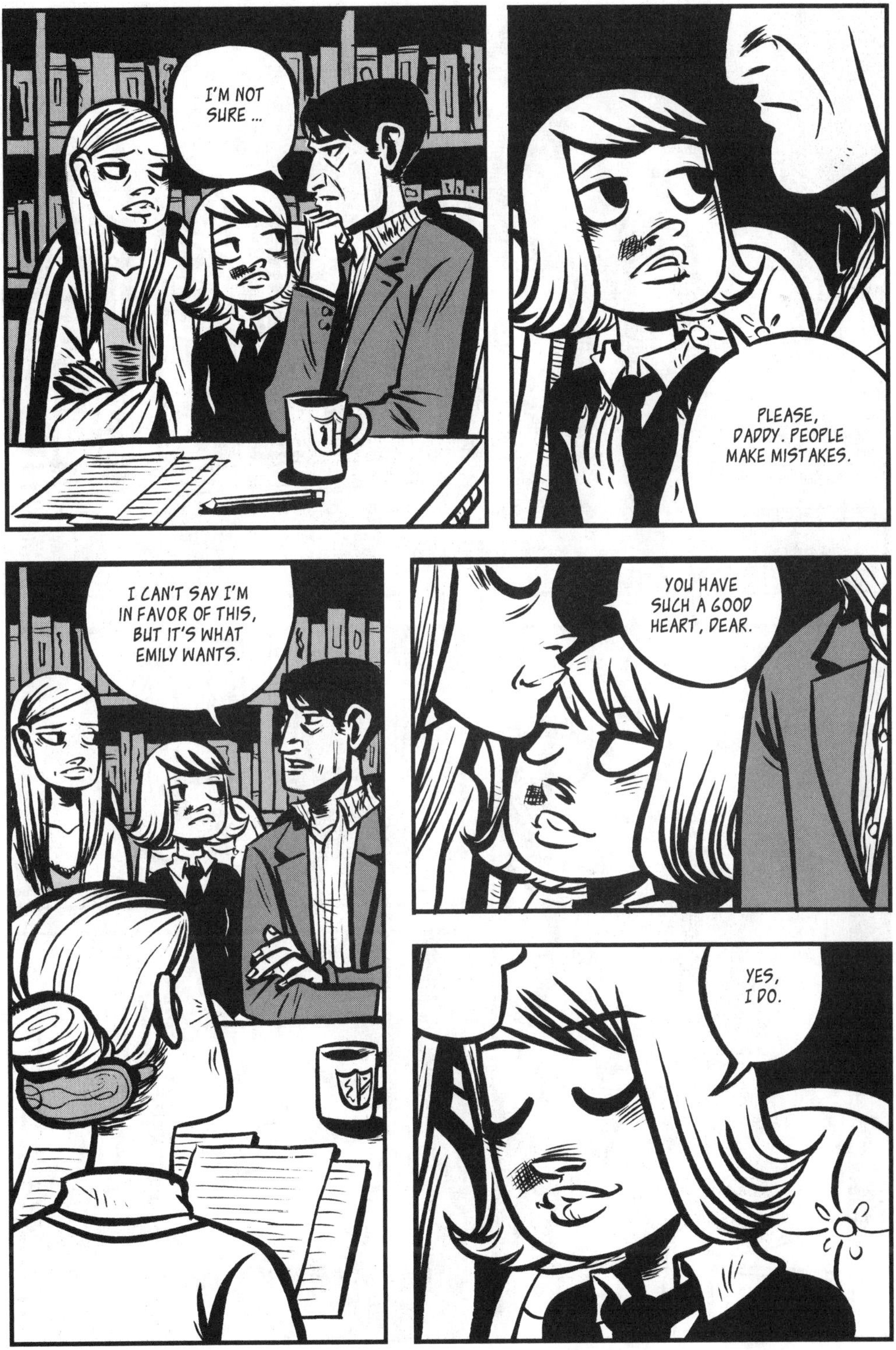
I'M NOT SURE ...
PLEASE, DADDY. PEOPLE MAKE MISTAKES.
I CAN'T SAY I'M IN FAVOR OF THIS, BUT IT'S WHAT EMILY WANTS.
YOU HAVE SUCH A GOOD HEART, DEAR.
YES, I DO.

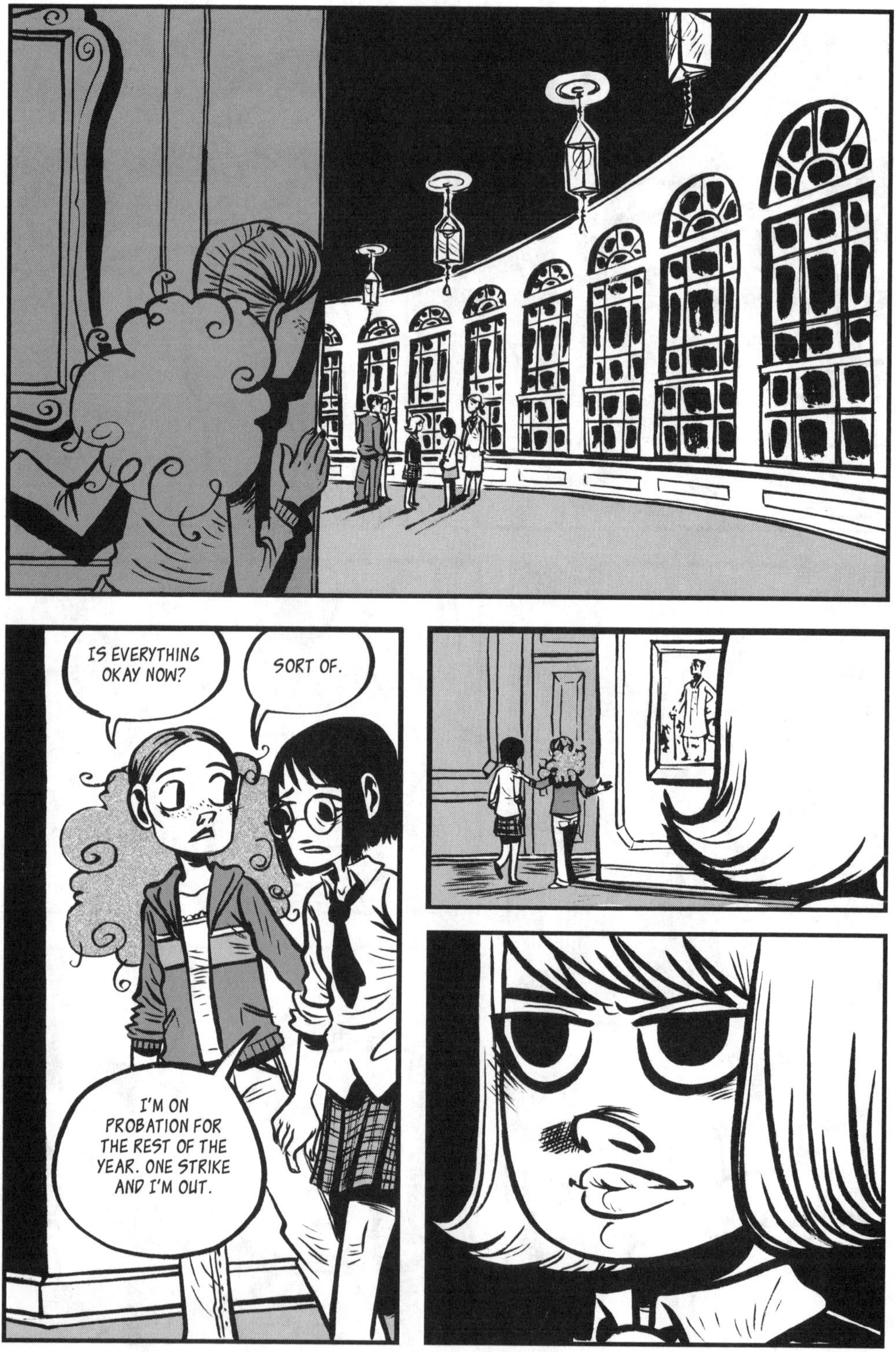
IS EVERYTHING OKAY NOW?
SORT OF.
I'M ON PROBATION FOR THE REST OF THE YEAR. ONE STRIKE AND I'M OUT.

chapter seven

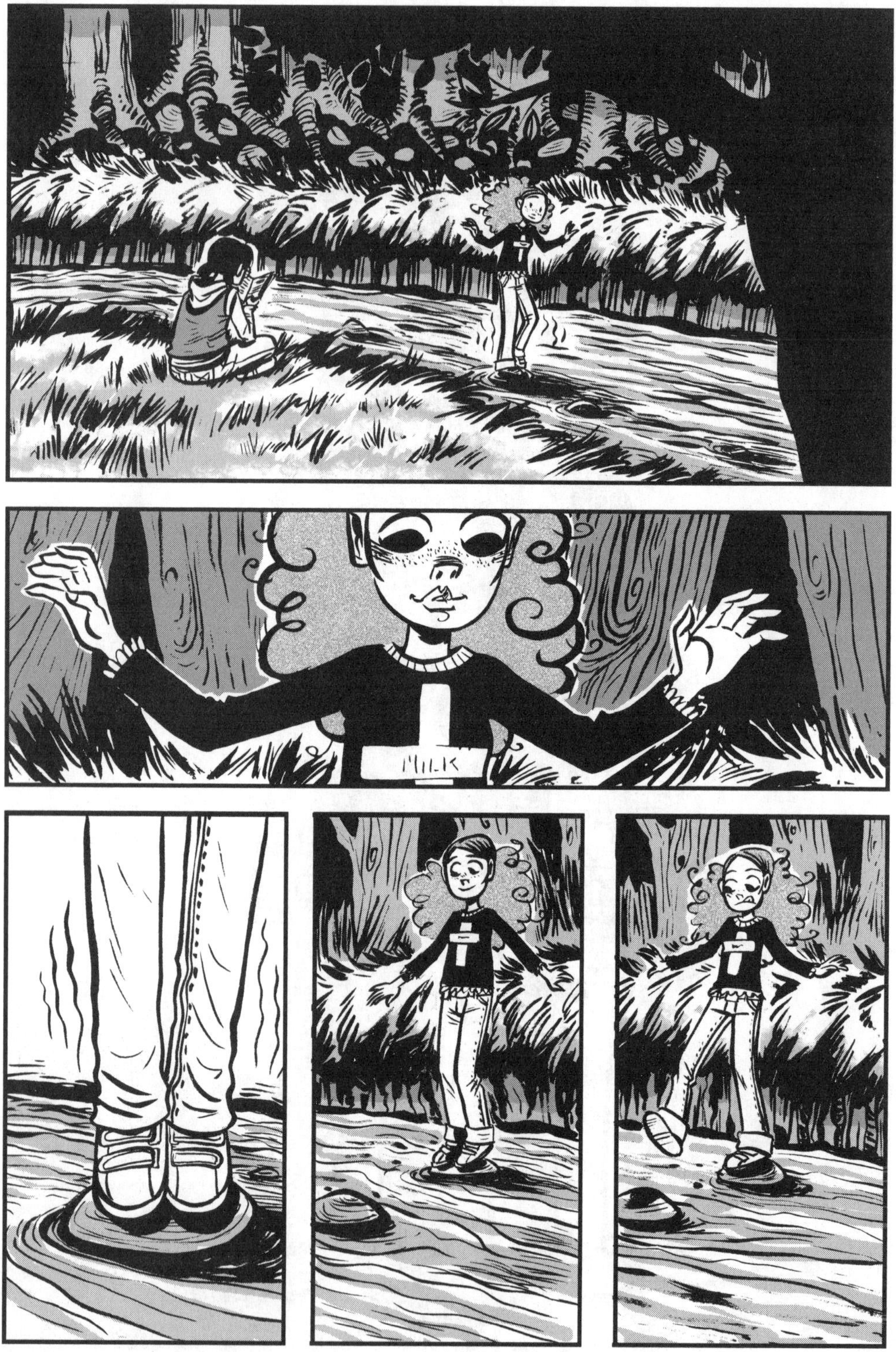
MILK

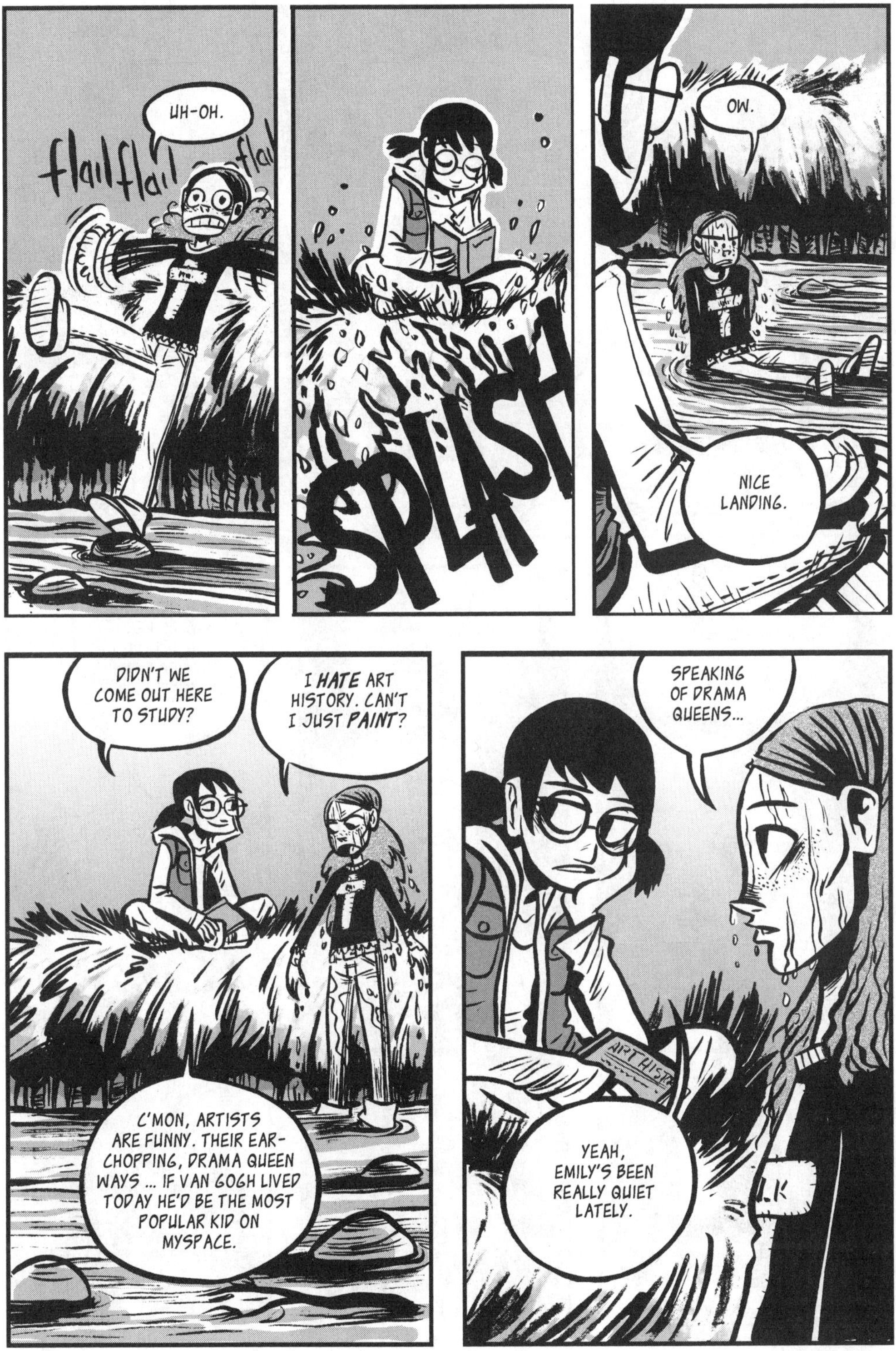
flailflail
flail
UH-OH.
SPLASH
OW.
NICE LANDING.
DIDN'T WE COME OUT HERE TO STUDY?
I **HATE** ART HISTORY. CAN'T I JUST **PAINT**?
C'MON, ARTISTS ARE FUNNY. THEIR EAR-CHOPPING, DRAMA QUEEN WAYS ... IF VAN GOGH LIVED TODAY HE'D BE THE MOST POPULAR KID ON MYSPACE.
SPEAKING OF DRAMA QUEENS...
YEAH, EMILY'S BEEN REALLY QUIET LATELY.

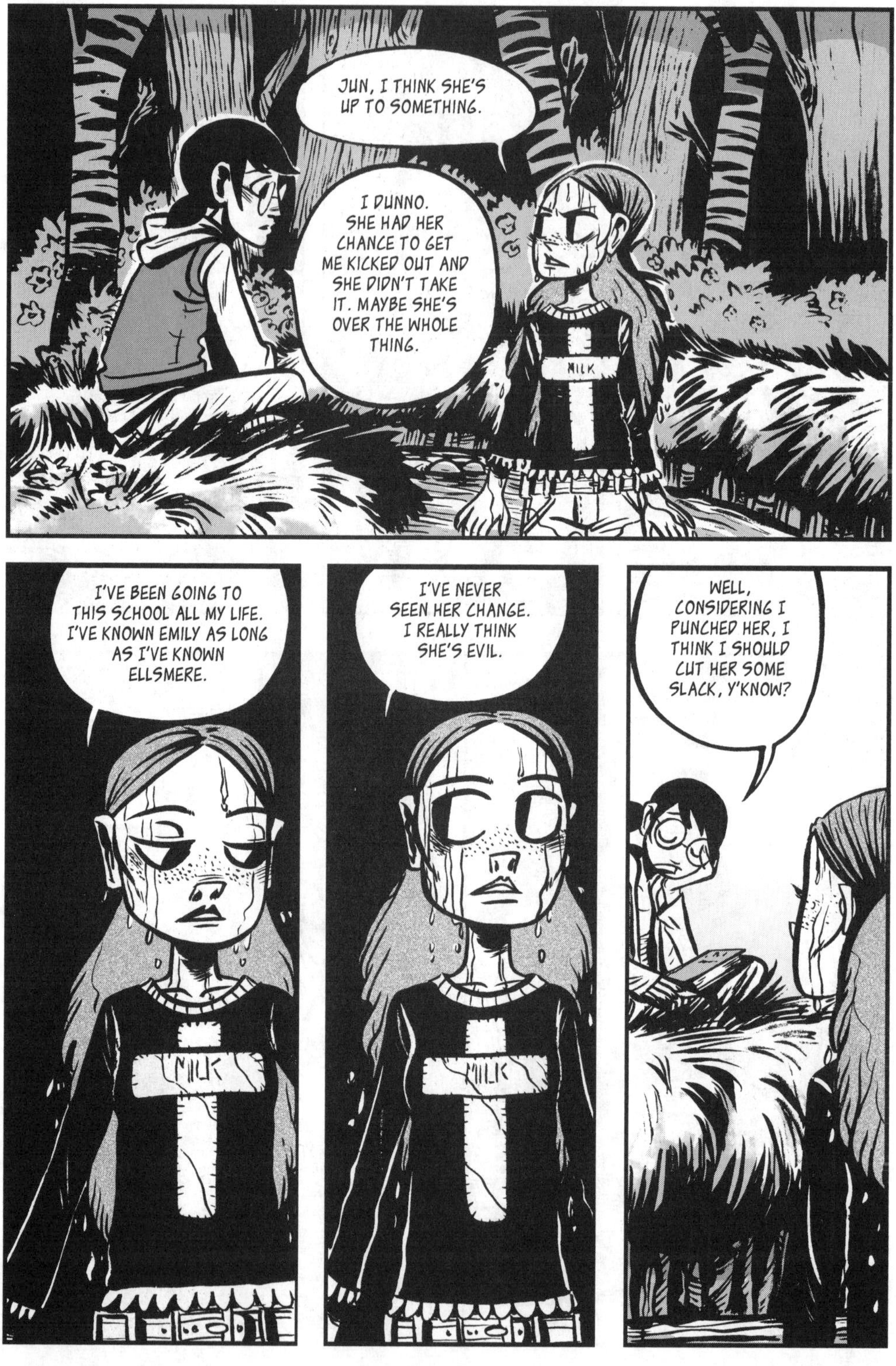
JUN, I THINK SHE'S UP TO SOMETHING.
I DUNNO. SHE HAD HER CHANCE TO GET ME KICKED OUT AND SHE DIDN'T TAKE IT. MAYBE SHE'S OVER THE WHOLE THING.
MILK
I'VE BEEN GOING TO THIS SCHOOL ALL MY LIFE. I'VE KNOWN EMILY AS LONG AS I'VE KNOWN ELLSMERE.
MILK
I'VE NEVER SEEN HER CHANGE. I REALLY THINK SHE'S EVIL.
MILK
WELL, CONSIDERING I PUNCHED HER, I THINK I SHOULD CUT HER SOME SLACK, Y'KNOW?

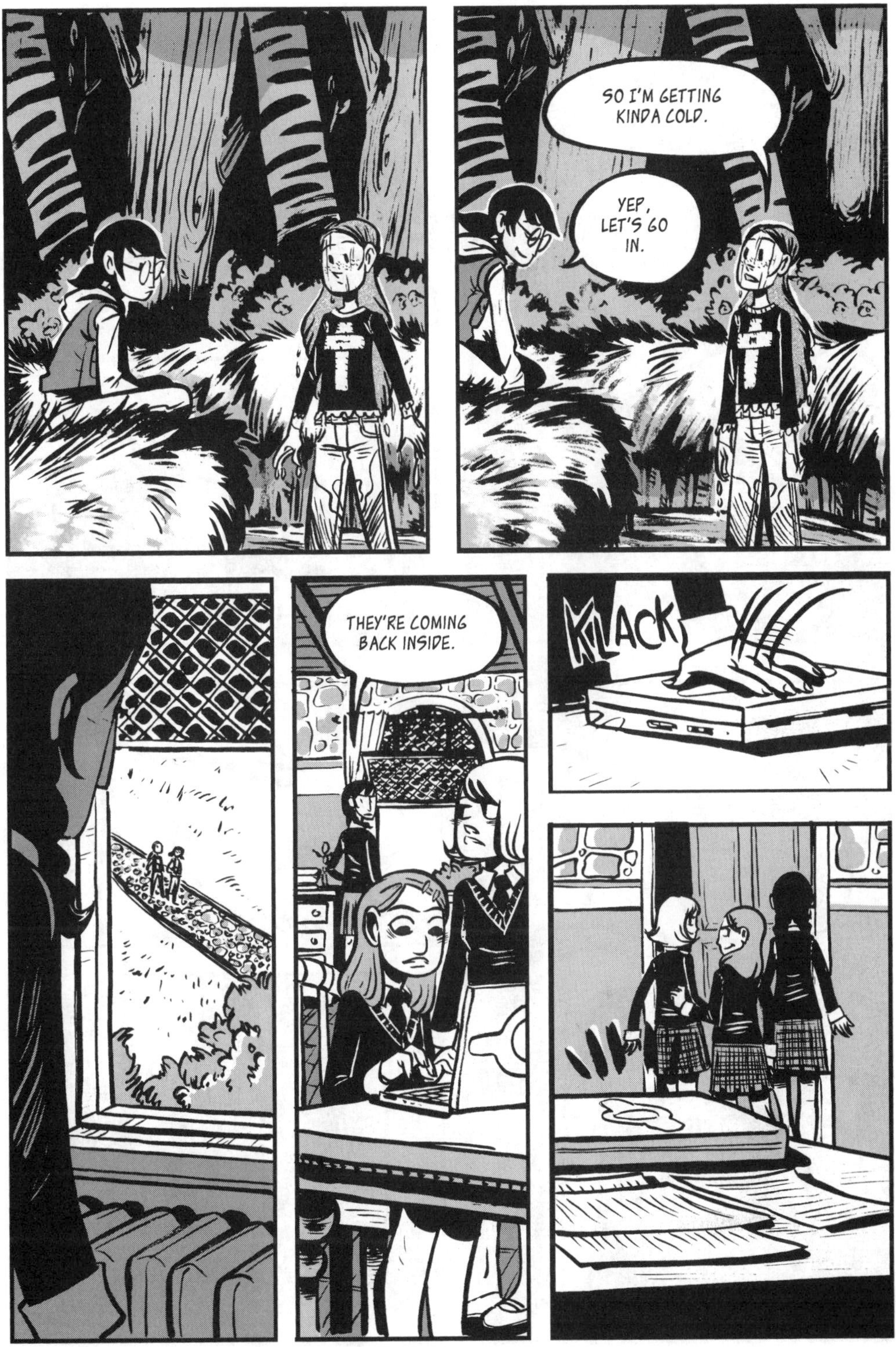
SO I'M GETTING KINDA COLD.
YEP, LET'S GO IN.
THEY'RE COMING BACK INSIDE.
KLACK

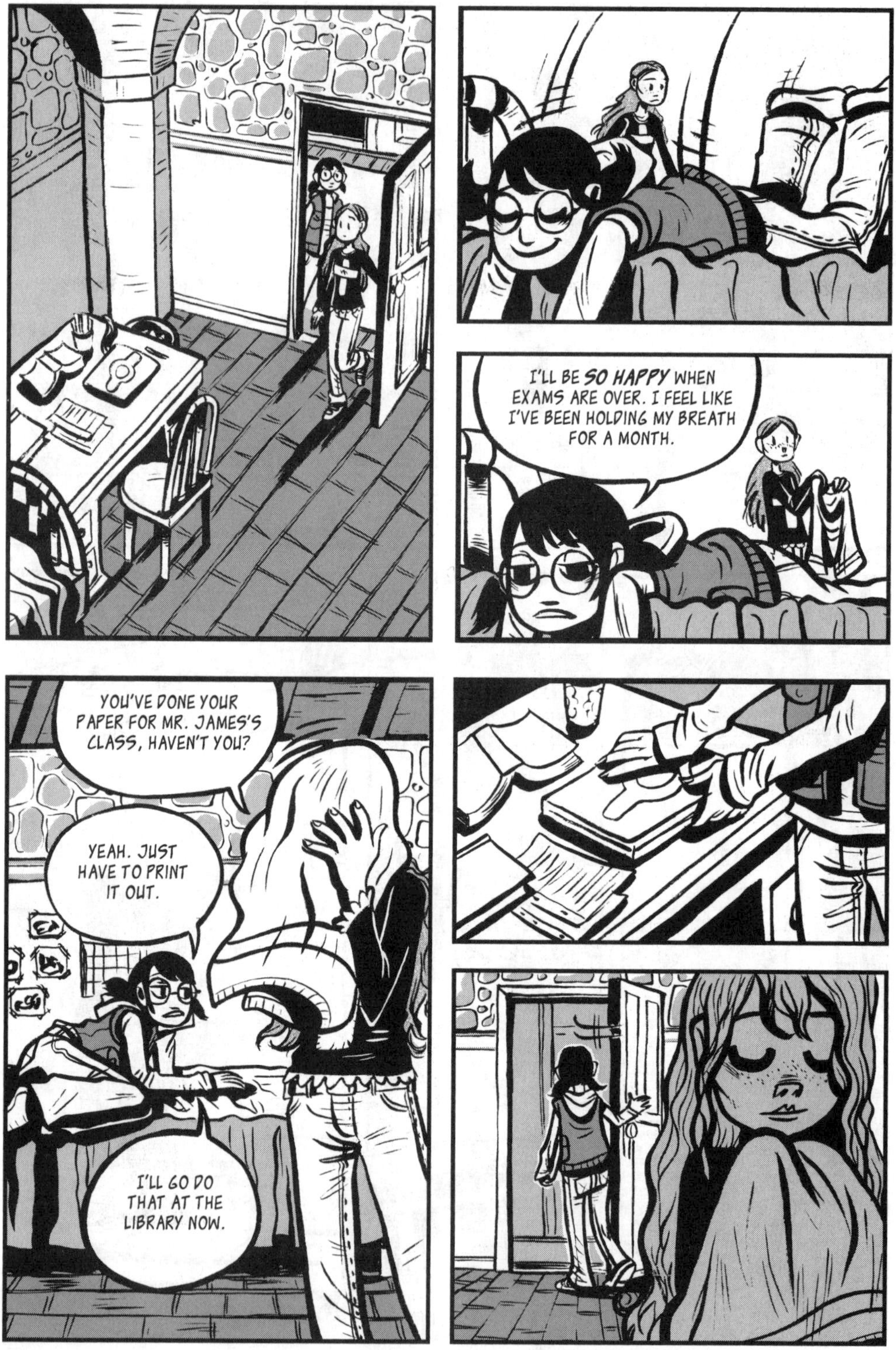
I'LL BE SO HAPPY WHEN EXAMS ARE OVER. I FEEL LIKE I'VE BEEN HOLDING MY BREATH FOR A MONTH.
YOU'VE DONE YOUR PAPER FOR MR. JAMES'S CLASS, HAVEN'T YOU?
YEAH. JUST HAVE TO PRINT IT OUT.
I'LL GO DO THAT AT THE LIBRARY NOW.

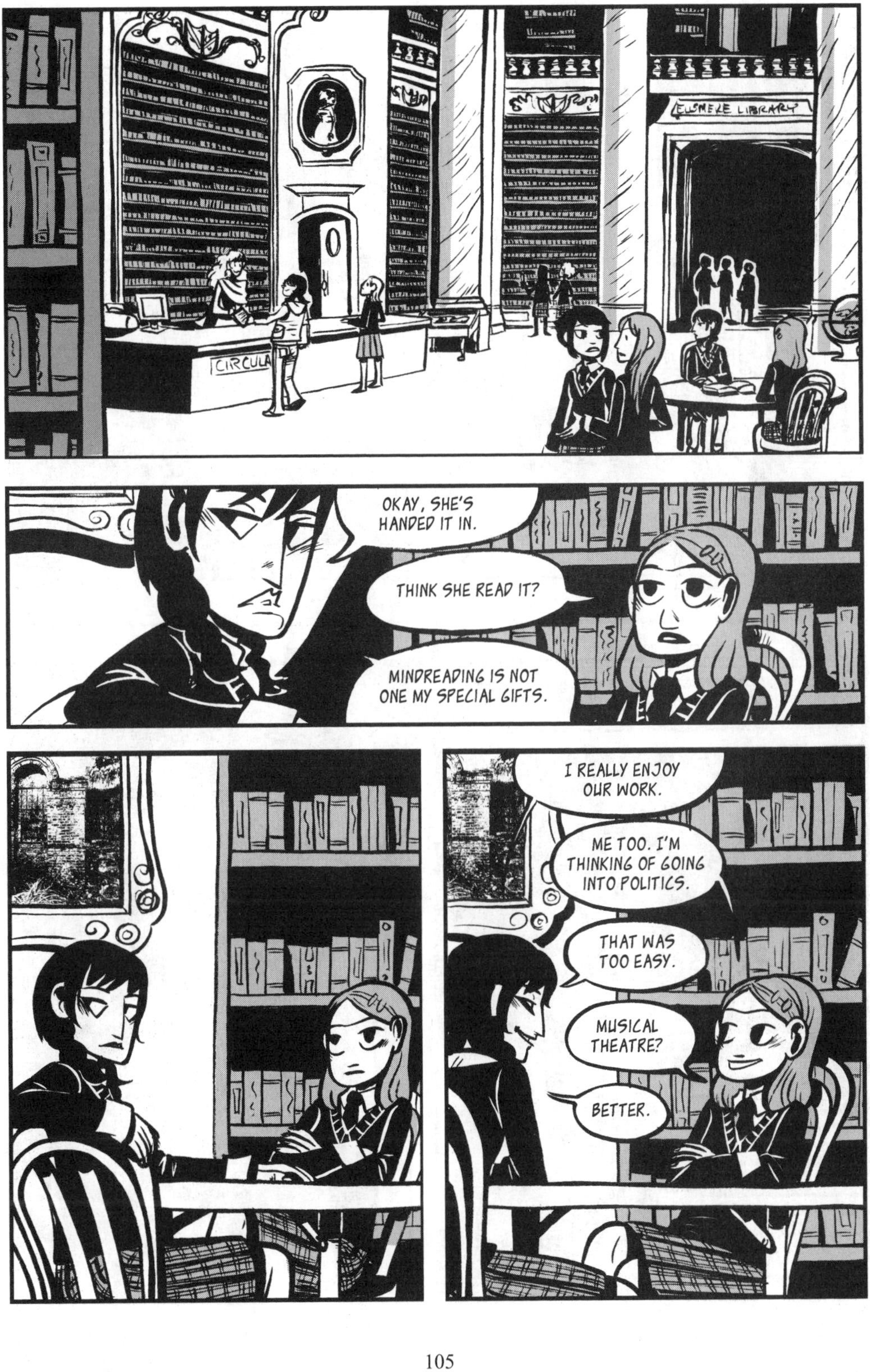

CIRCULA
ELLSMERE LIBRARY
OKAY, SHE'S HANDED IT IN.
THINK SHE READ IT?
MINDREADING IS NOT ONE MY SPECIAL GIFTS.
I REALLY ENJOY OUR WORK.
ME TOO. I'M THINKING OF GOING INTO POLITICS.
THAT WAS TOO EASY.
MUSICAL THEATRE?
BETTER.

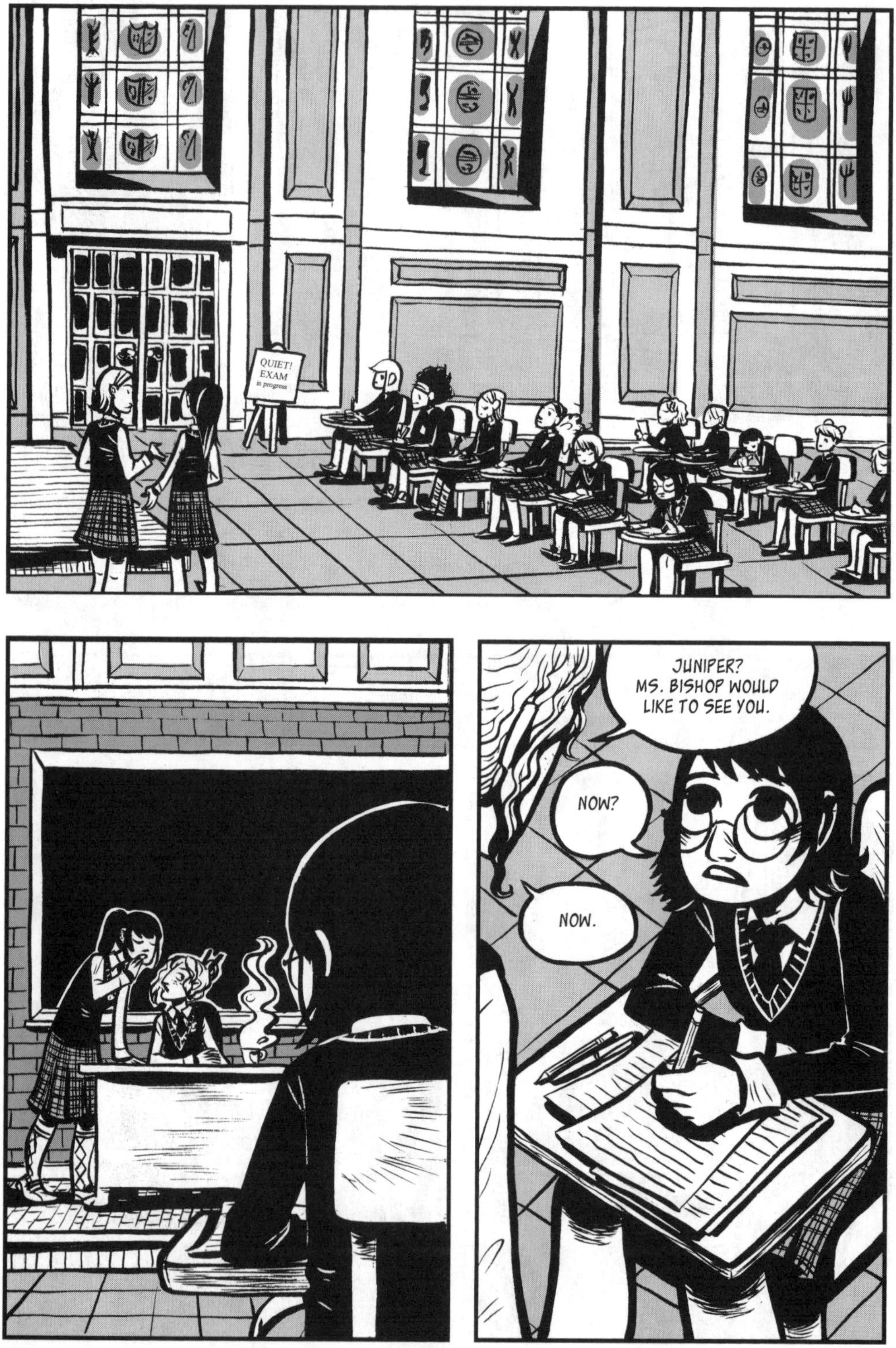
QUIET! EXAM in progress
JUNIPER? MS. BISHOP WOULD LIKE TO SEE YOU.
NOW?
NOW.

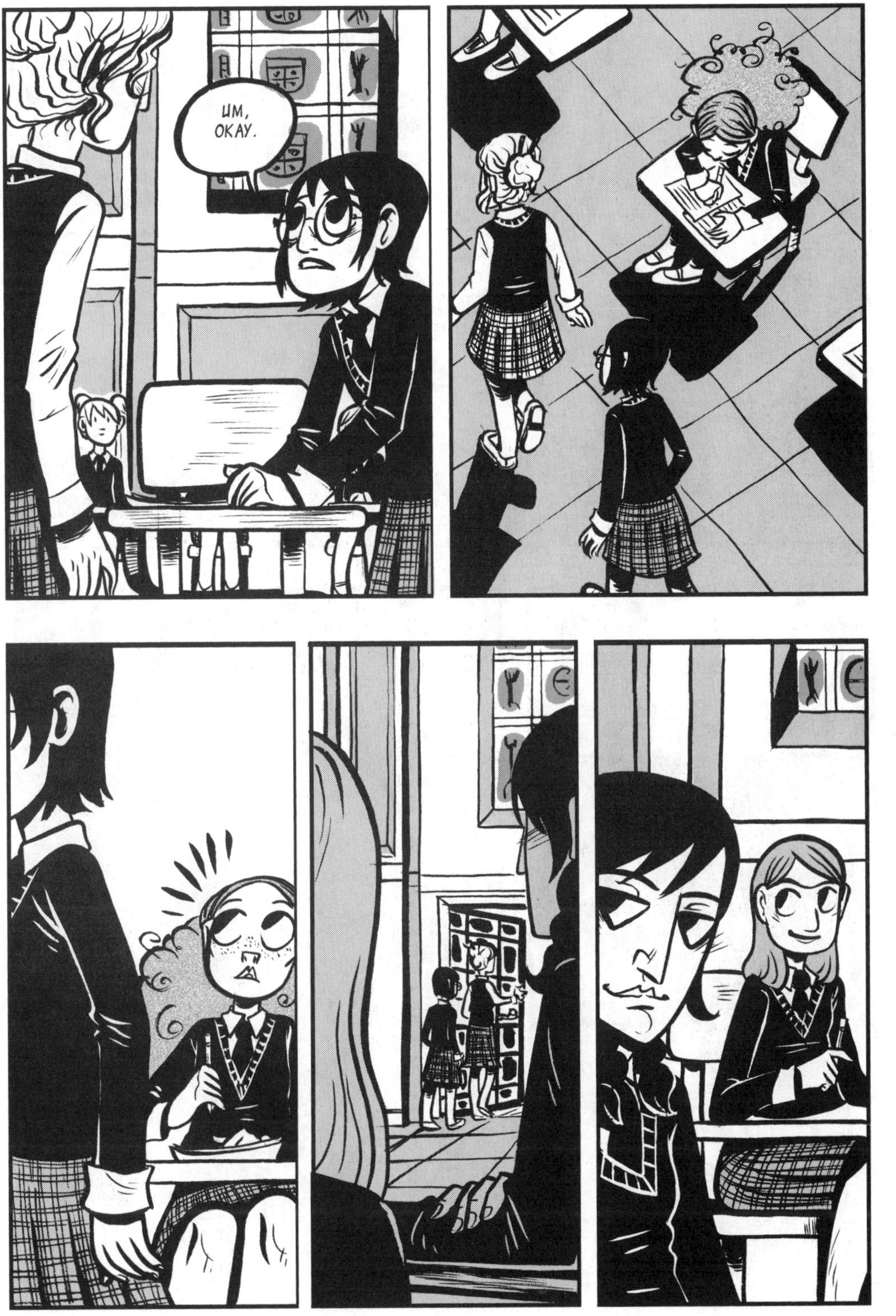
UM, OKAY.

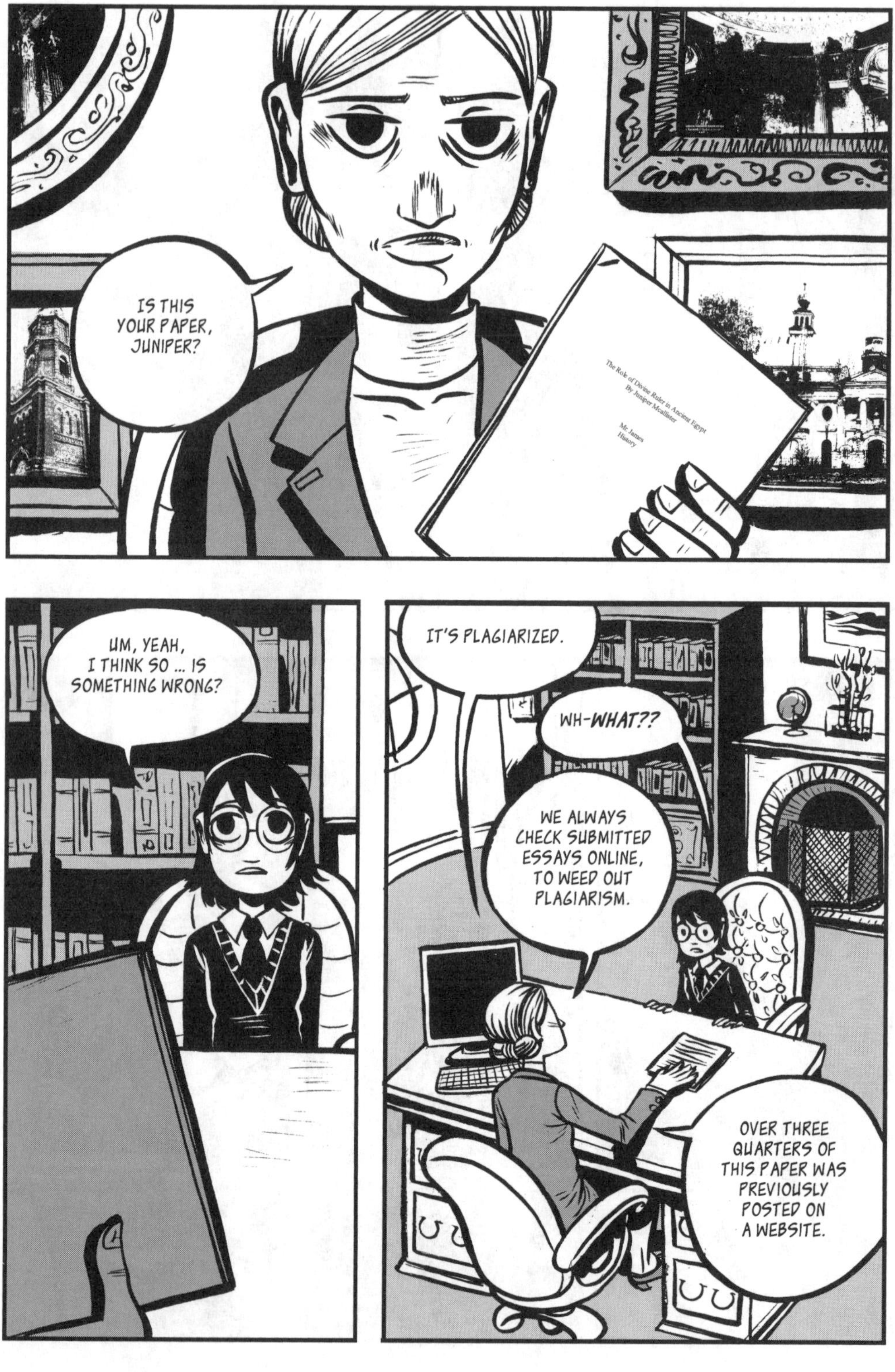
IS THIS YOUR PAPER, JUNIPER?
The Role of Divine Ruler in Ancient Egypt
By Juniper Mcallister
Mr. James
History
UM, YEAH, I THINK SO ... IS SOMETHING WRONG?
IT'S PLAGIARIZED.
WH-WHAT??
WE ALWAYS CHECK SUBMITTED ESSAYS ONLINE, TO WEED OUT PLAGIARISM.
OVER THREE QUARTERS OF THIS PAPER WAS PREVIOUSLY POSTED ON A WEBSITE.

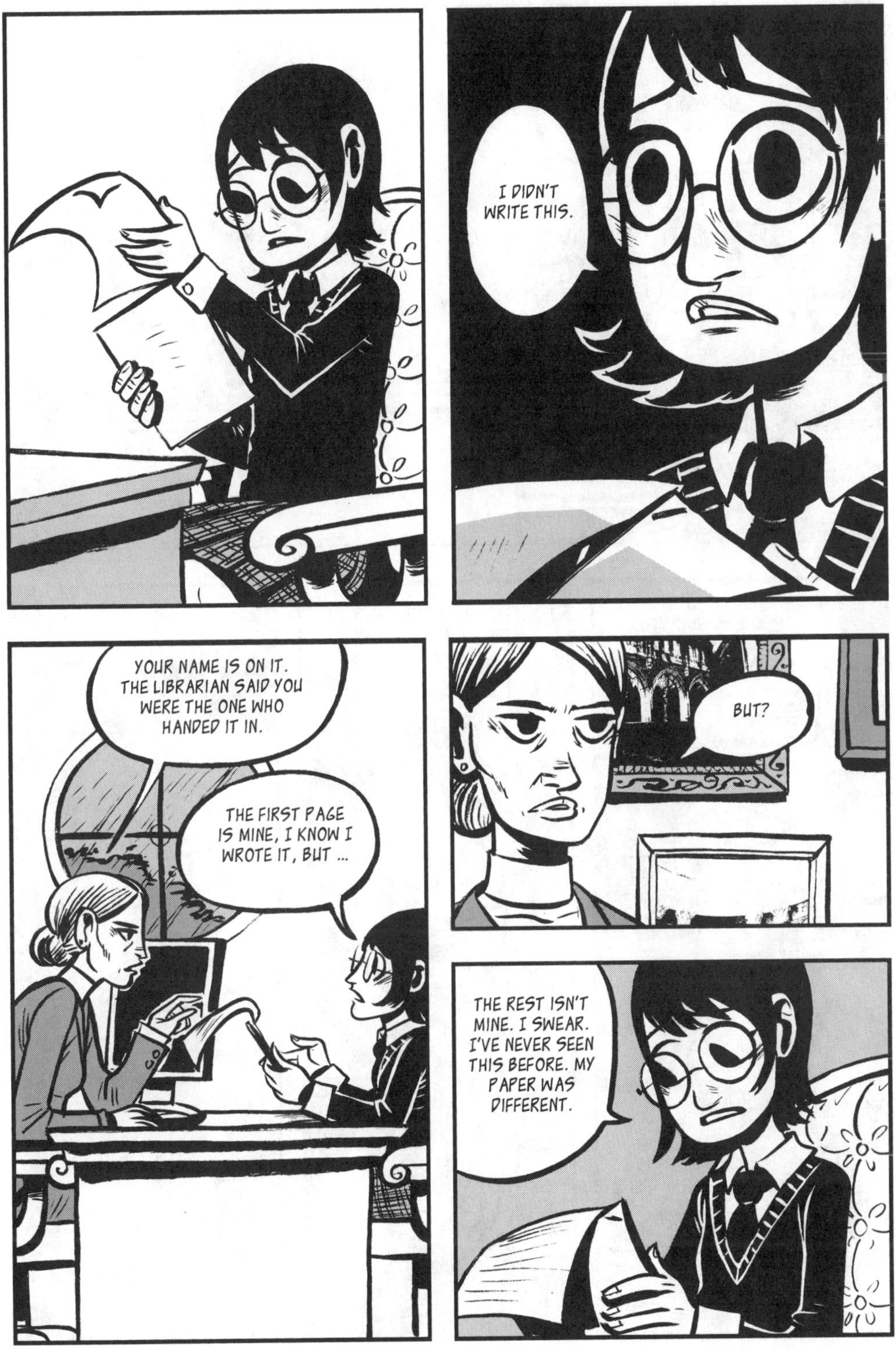
I DIDN'T WRITE THIS.
YOUR NAME IS ON IT. THE LIBRARIAN SAID YOU WERE THE ONE WHO HANDED IT IN.
THE FIRST PAGE IS MINE, I KNOW I WROTE IT, BUT ...
BUT?
THE REST ISN'T MINE. I SWEAR. I'VE NEVER SEEN THIS BEFORE. MY PAPER WAS DIFFERENT.

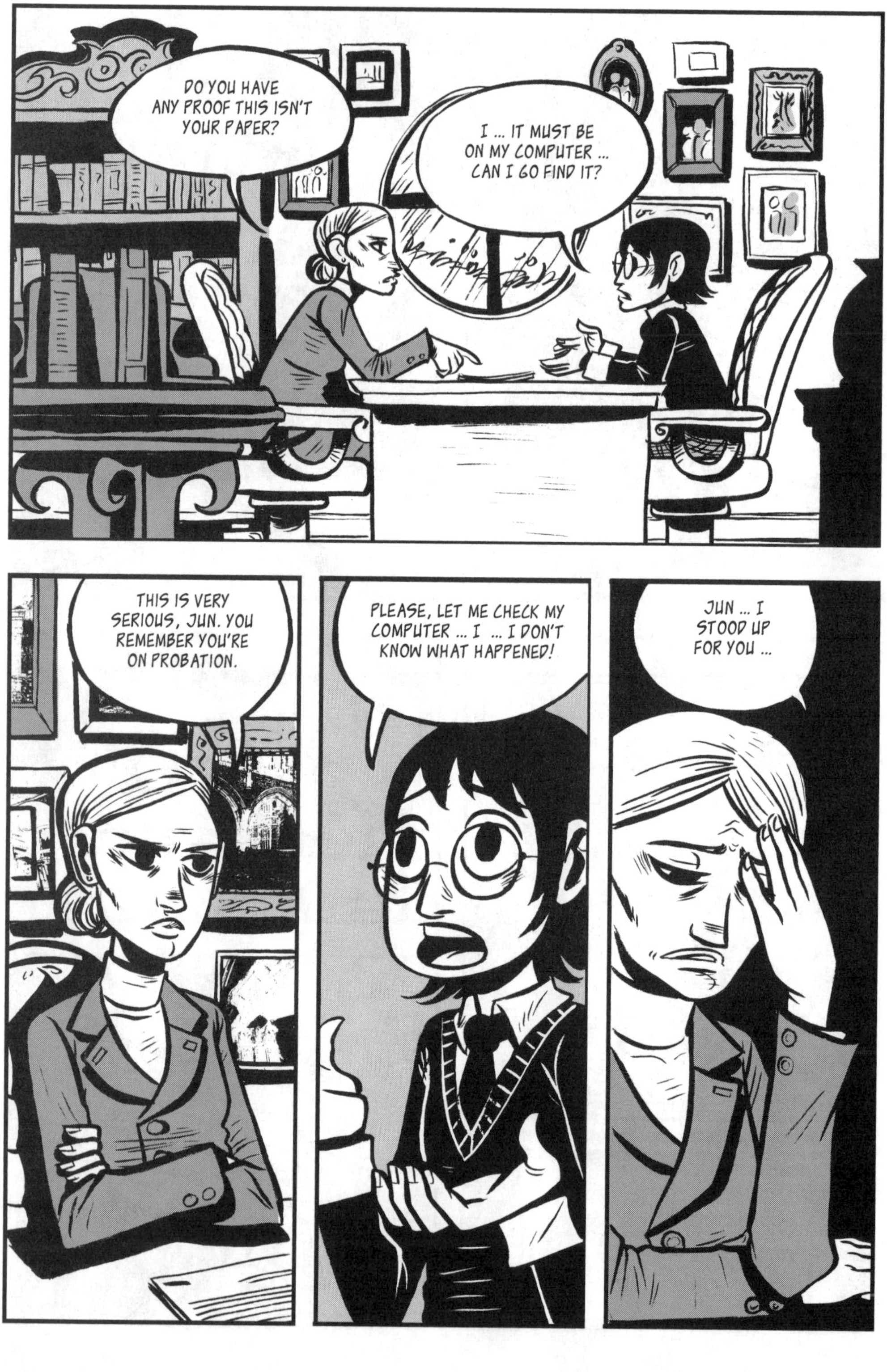
DO YOU HAVE ANY PROOF THIS ISN'T YOUR PAPER?
I ... IT MUST BE ON MY COMPUTER ... CAN I GO FIND IT?
THIS IS VERY SERIOUS, JUN. YOU REMEMBER YOU'RE ON PROBATION.
PLEASE, LET ME CHECK MY COMPUTER ... I ... I DON'T KNOW WHAT HAPPENED!
JUN ... I STOOD UP FOR YOU ...

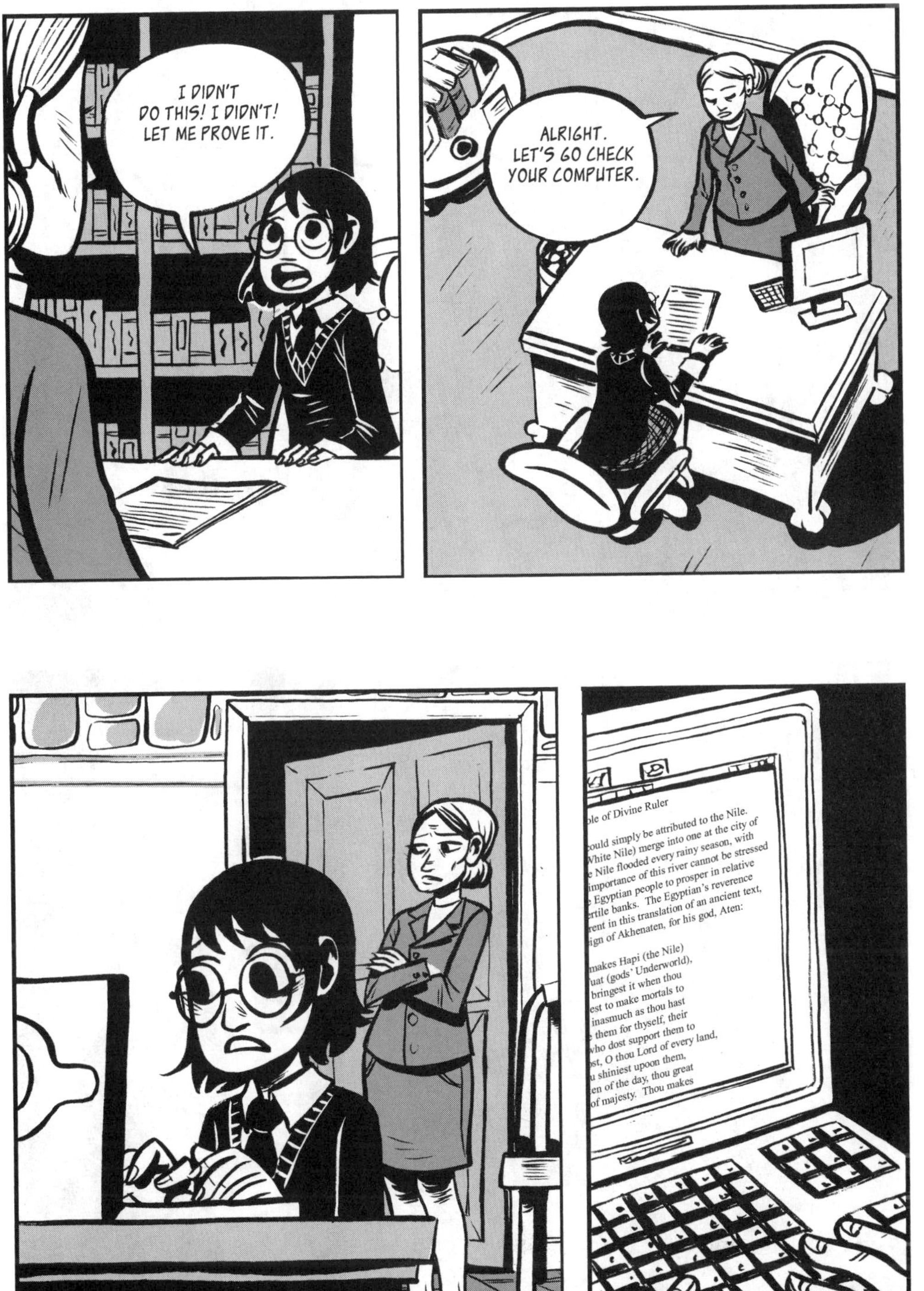
I DIDN'T DO THIS! I DIDN'T! LET ME PROVE IT.
ALRIGHT. LET'S GO CHECK YOUR COMPUTER.
ble of Divine Ruler
could simply be attributed to the Nile.
White Nile) merge into one at the city of
e Nile flooded every rainy season, with
importance of this river cannot be stressed
e Egyptian people to prosper in relative
ertile banks. The Egyptian's reverence
rent in this translation of an ancient text,
ign of Akhenaten, for his god, Aten:
makes Hapi (the Nile)
uat (gods' Underworld),
bringest it when thou
est to make mortals to
inasmuch as thou hast
them for thyself, their
who dost support them to
st, O thou Lord of every land,
u shiniest upoon them,
en of the day, thou great
of majesty. Thou makes

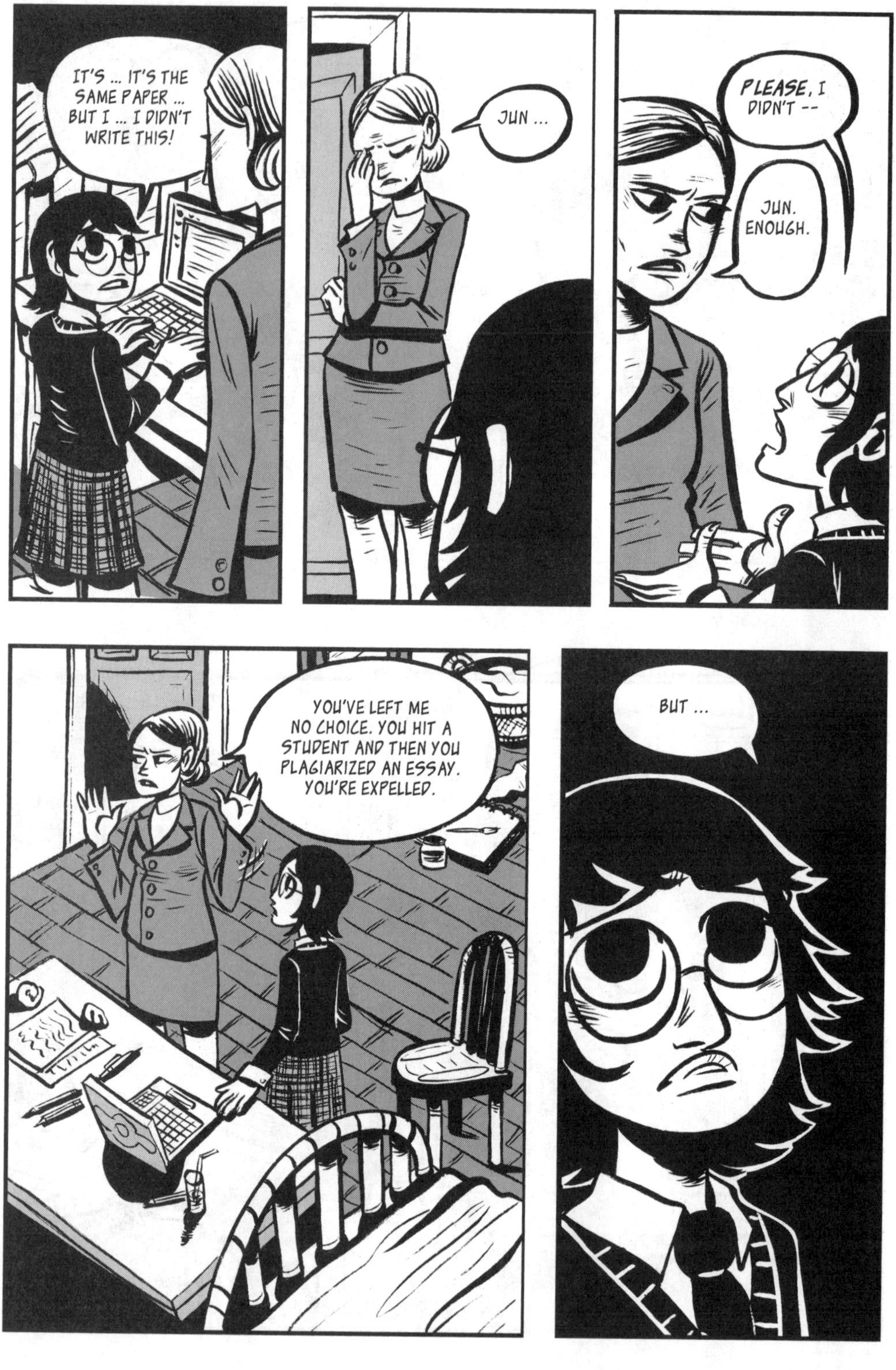
IT'S ... IT'S THE SAME PAPER ... BUT I ... I DIDN'T WRITE THIS!
JUN ...
PLEASE, I DIDN'T --
JUN. ENOUGH.
YOU'VE LEFT ME NO CHOICE. YOU HIT A STUDENT AND THEN YOU PLAGIARIZED AN ESSAY. YOU'RE EXPELLED.
BUT ...

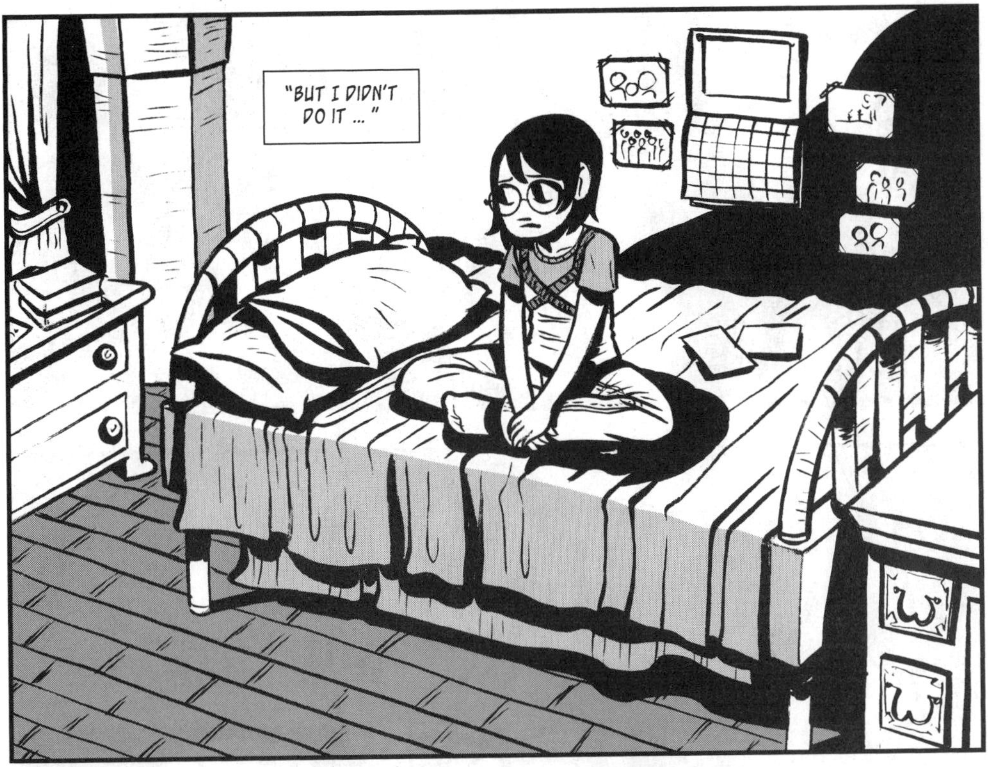
"BUT I DIDN'T DO IT ..."

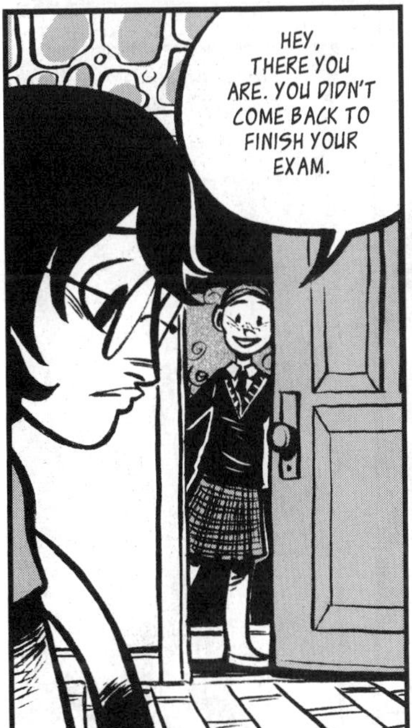
HEY, THERE YOU ARE. YOU DIDN'T COME BACK TO FINISH YOUR EXAM.

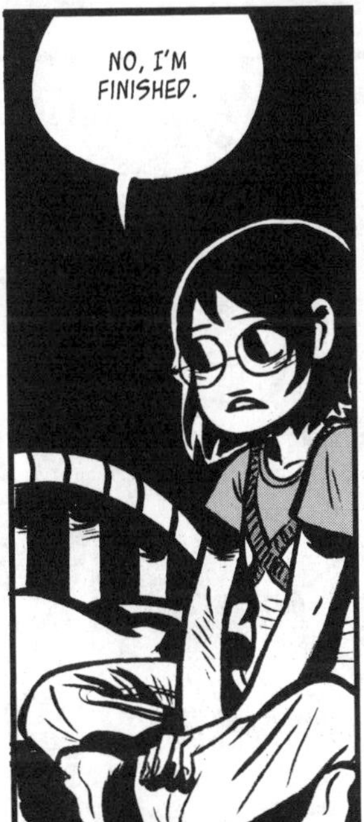
NO, I'M FINISHED.

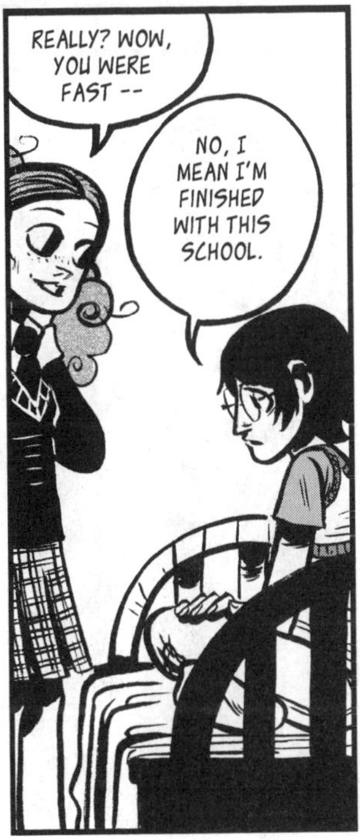
REALLY? WOW, YOU WERE FAST --
NO, I MEAN I'M FINISHED WITH THIS SCHOOL.

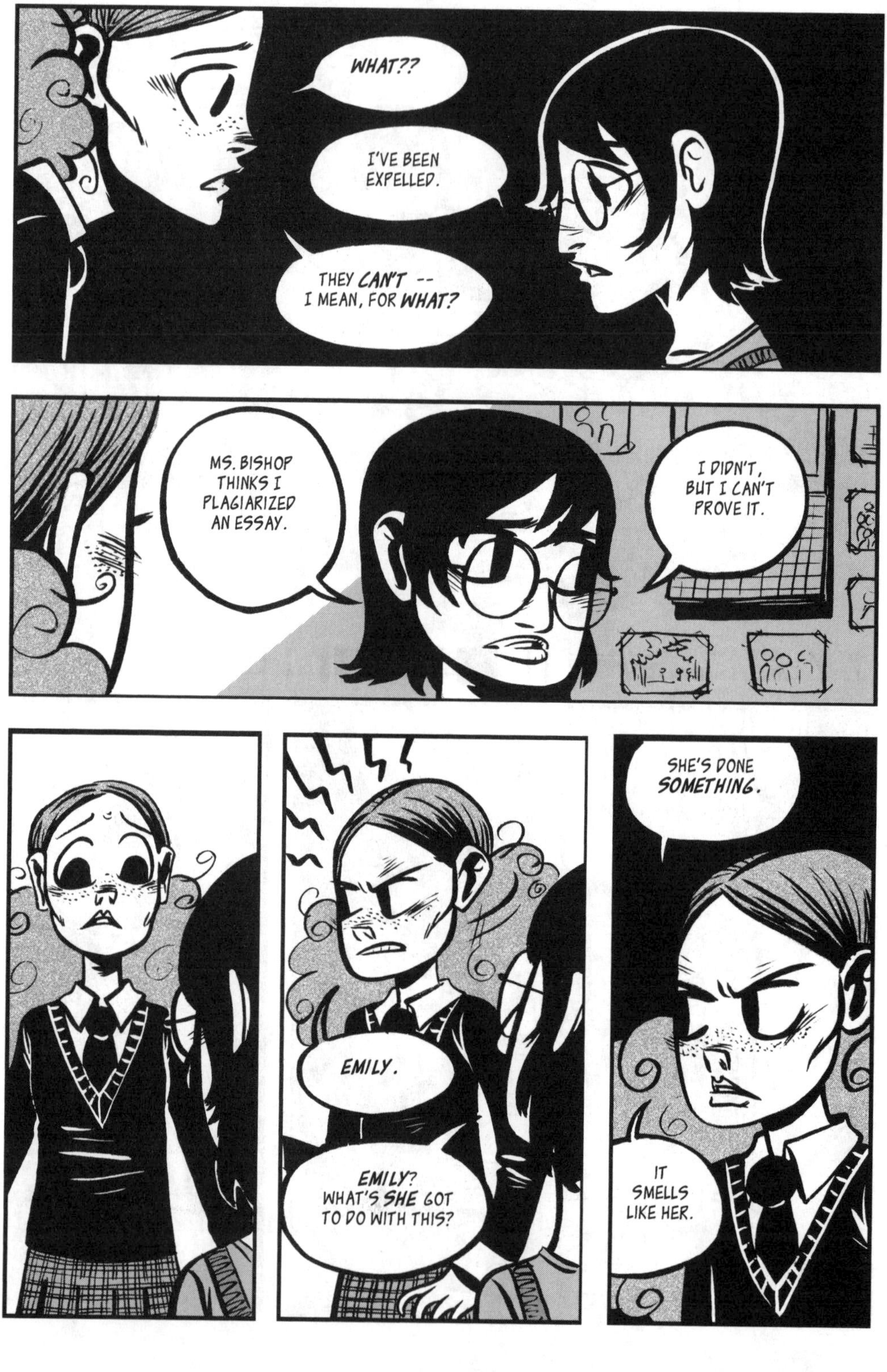
WHAT??
I'VE BEEN EXPELLED.
THEY CAN'T -- I MEAN, FOR WHAT?
MS. BISHOP THINKS I PLAGIARIZED AN ESSAY.
I DIDN'T, BUT I CAN'T PROVE IT.
EMILY.
EMILY? WHAT'S SHE GOT TO DO WITH THIS?
SHE'S DONE SOMETHING.
IT SMELLS LIKE HER.

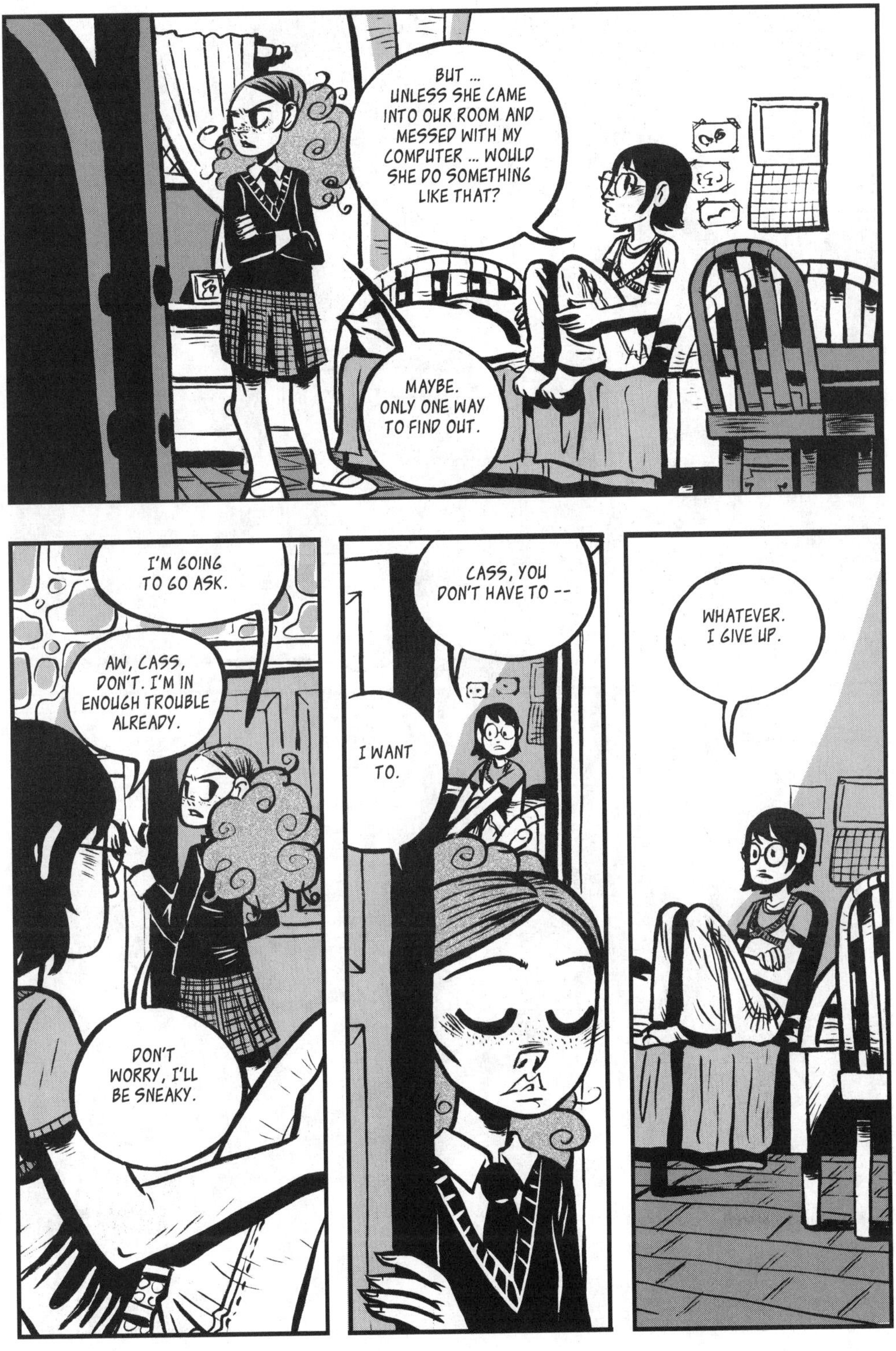
BUT ... UNLESS SHE CAME INTO OUR ROOM AND MESSED WITH MY COMPUTER ... WOULD SHE DO SOMETHING LIKE THAT?
MAYBE. ONLY ONE WAY TO FIND OUT.
I'M GOING TO GO ASK.
AW, CASS, DON'T. I'M IN ENOUGH TROUBLE ALREADY.
DON'T WORRY, I'LL BE SNEAKY.
CASS, YOU DON'T HAVE TO --
I WANT TO.
WHATEVER. I GIVE UP.

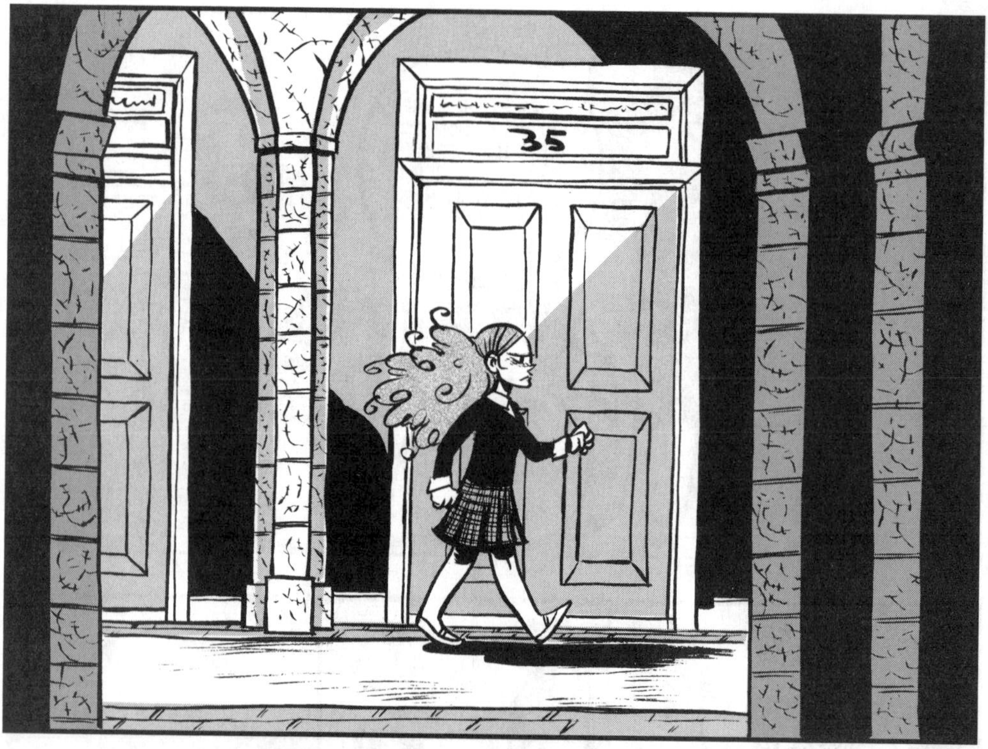

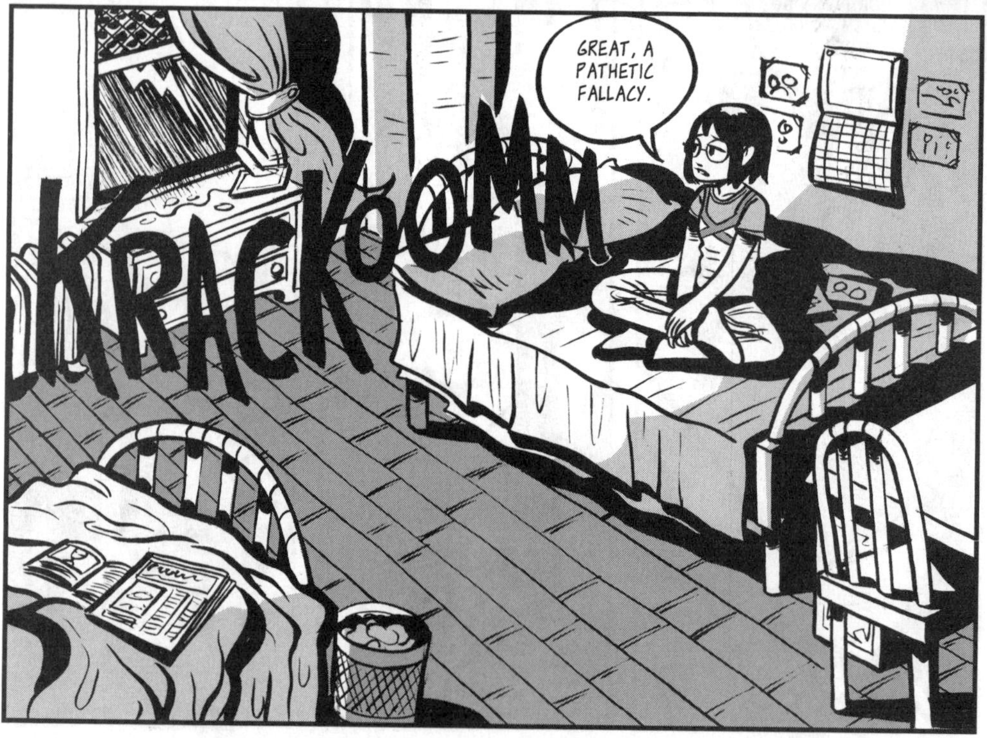
GREAT, A PATHETIC FALLACY.
KRACKOOMM

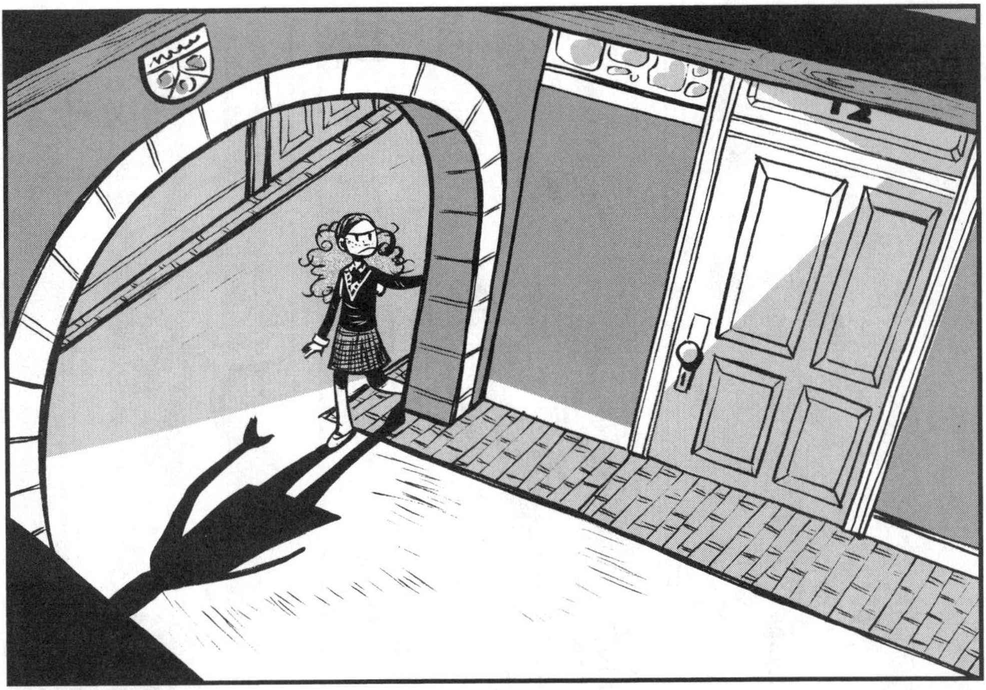

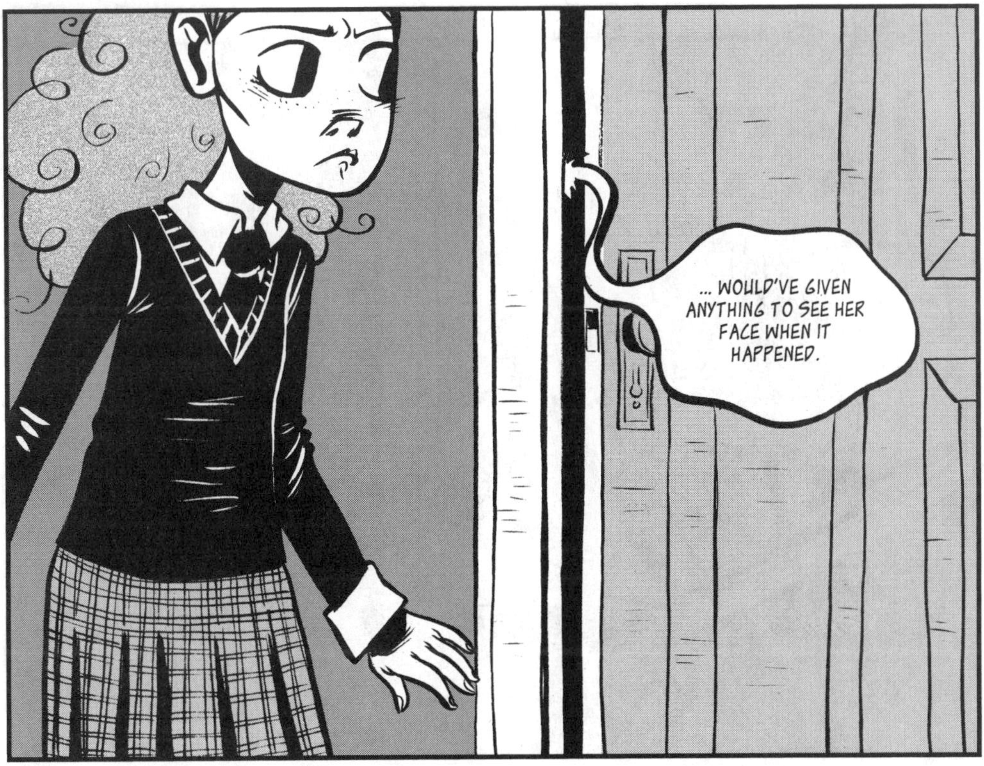
... WOULD'VE GIVEN ANYTHING TO SEE HER FACE WHEN IT HAPPENED.

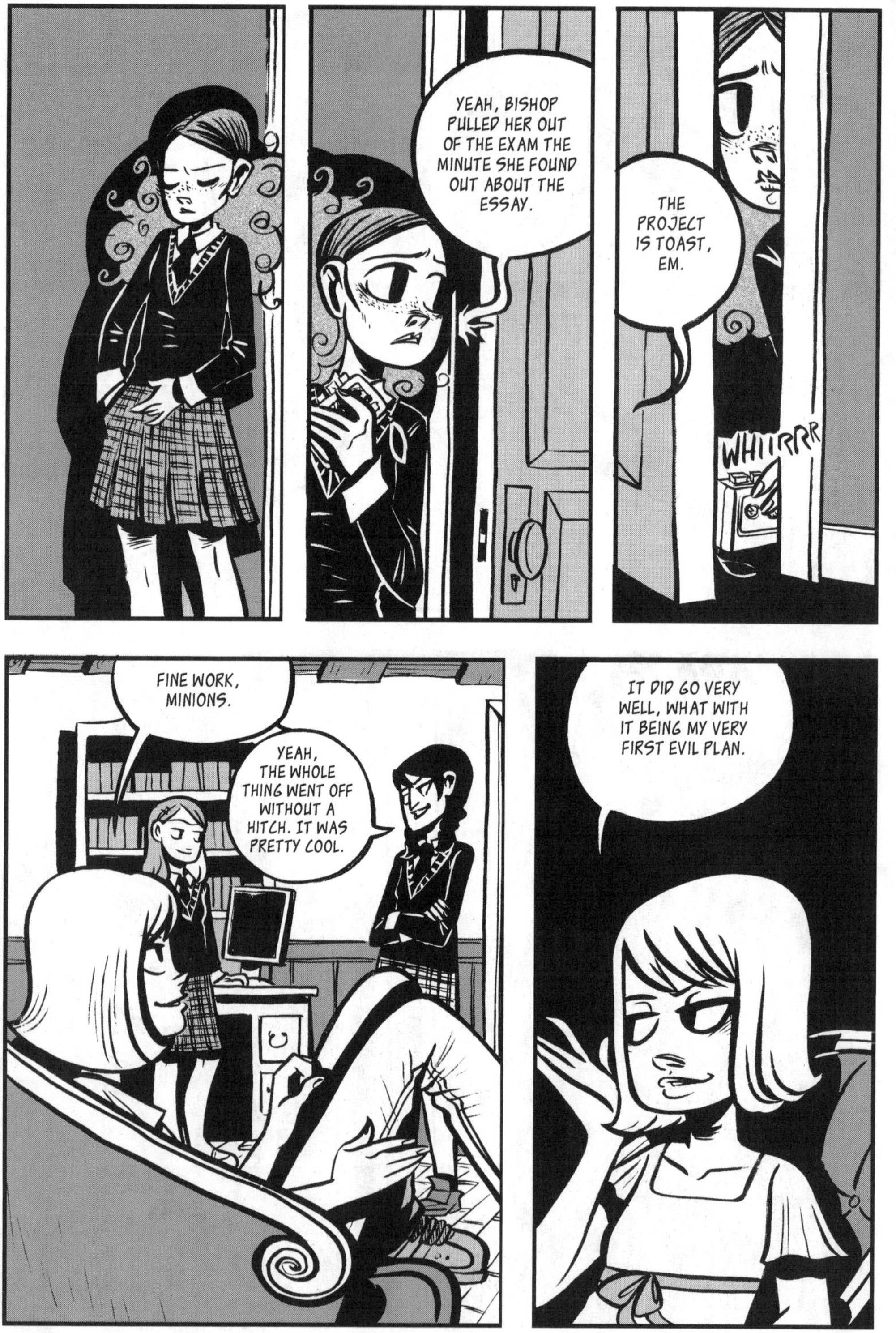
YEAH, BISHOP PULLED HER OUT OF THE EXAM THE MINUTE SHE FOUND OUT ABOUT THE ESSAY.
THE PROJECT IS TOAST, EM.
WHIIRRR
FINE WORK, MINIONS.
YEAH, THE WHOLE THING WENT OFF WITHOUT A HITCH. IT WAS PRETTY COOL.
IT DID GO VERY WELL, WHAT WITH IT BEING MY VERY FIRST EVIL PLAN.

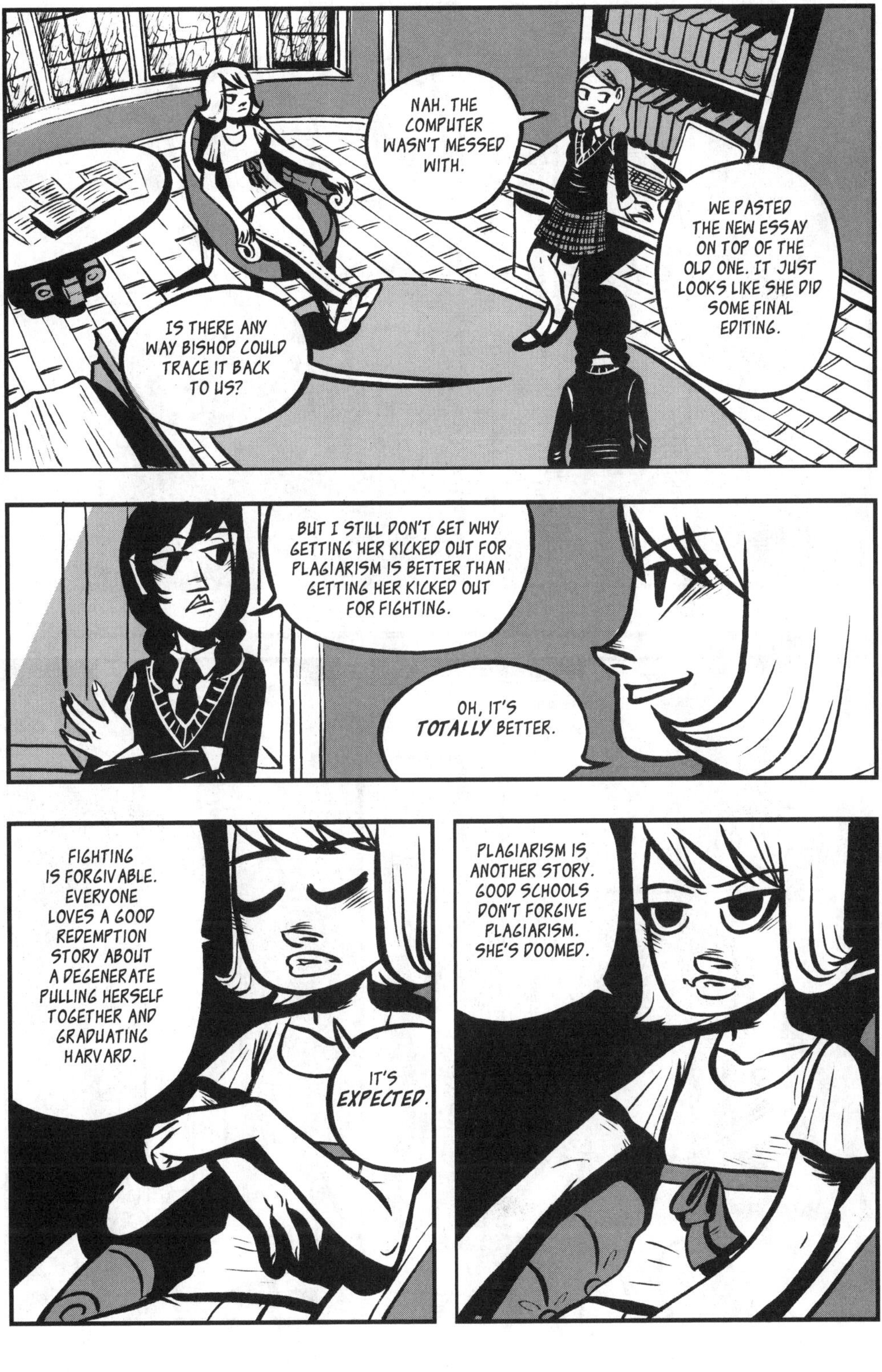
NAH. THE COMPUTER WASN'T MESSED WITH.
WE PASTED THE NEW ESSAY ON TOP OF THE OLD ONE. IT JUST LOOKS LIKE SHE DID SOME FINAL EDITING.
IS THERE ANY WAY BISHOP COULD TRACE IT BACK TO US?
BUT I STILL DON'T GET WHY GETTING HER KICKED OUT FOR PLAGIARISM IS BETTER THAN GETTING HER KICKED OUT FOR FIGHTING.
OH, IT'S *TOTALLY* BETTER.
FIGHTING IS FORGIVABLE. EVERYONE LOVES A GOOD REDEMPTION STORY ABOUT A DEGENERATE PULLING HERSELF TOGETHER AND GRADUATING HARVARD.
IT'S *EXPECTED*.
PLAGIARISM IS ANOTHER STORY. GOOD SCHOOLS DON'T FORGIVE PLAGIARISM. SHE'S DOOMED.

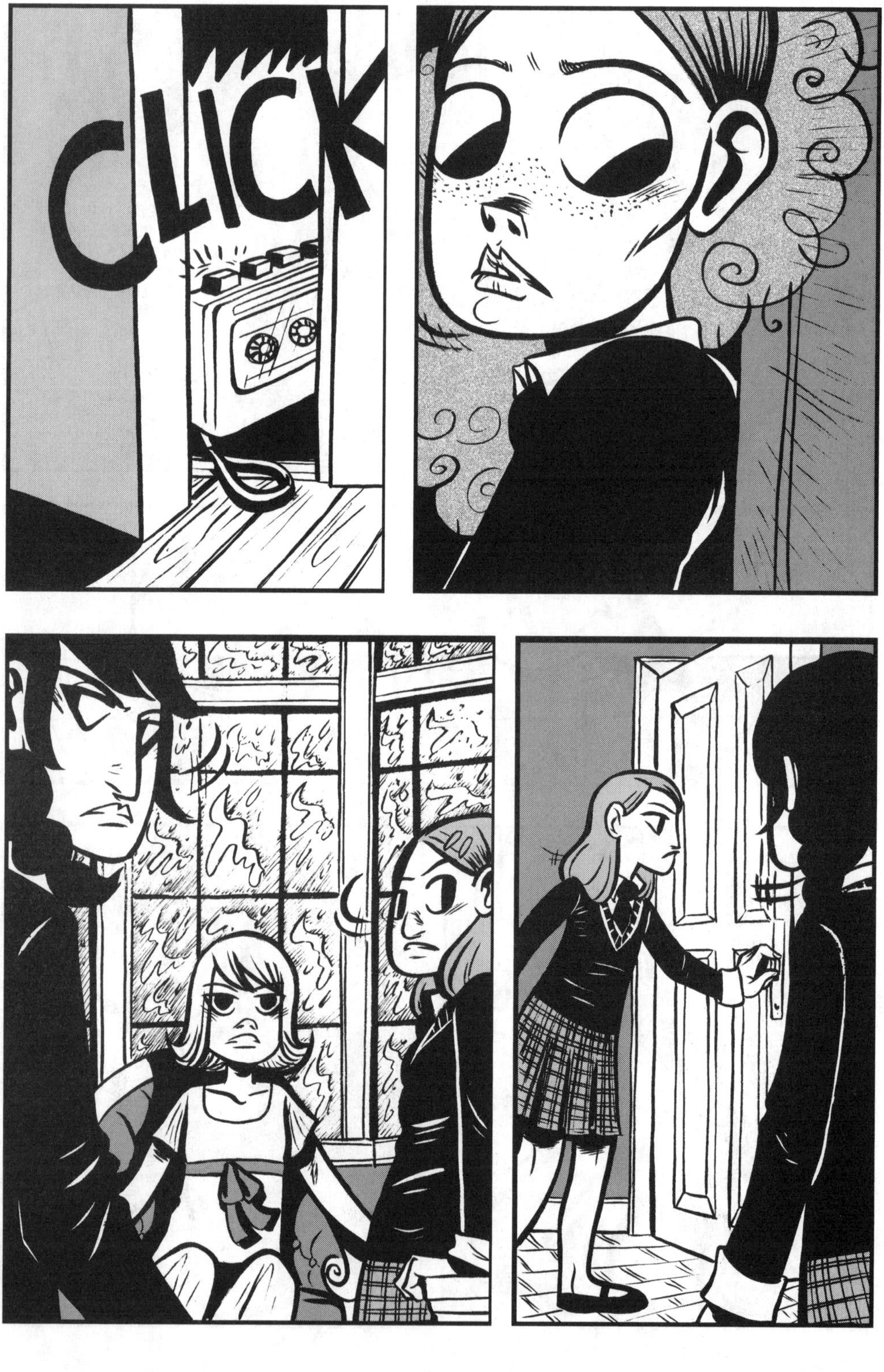
CLICK

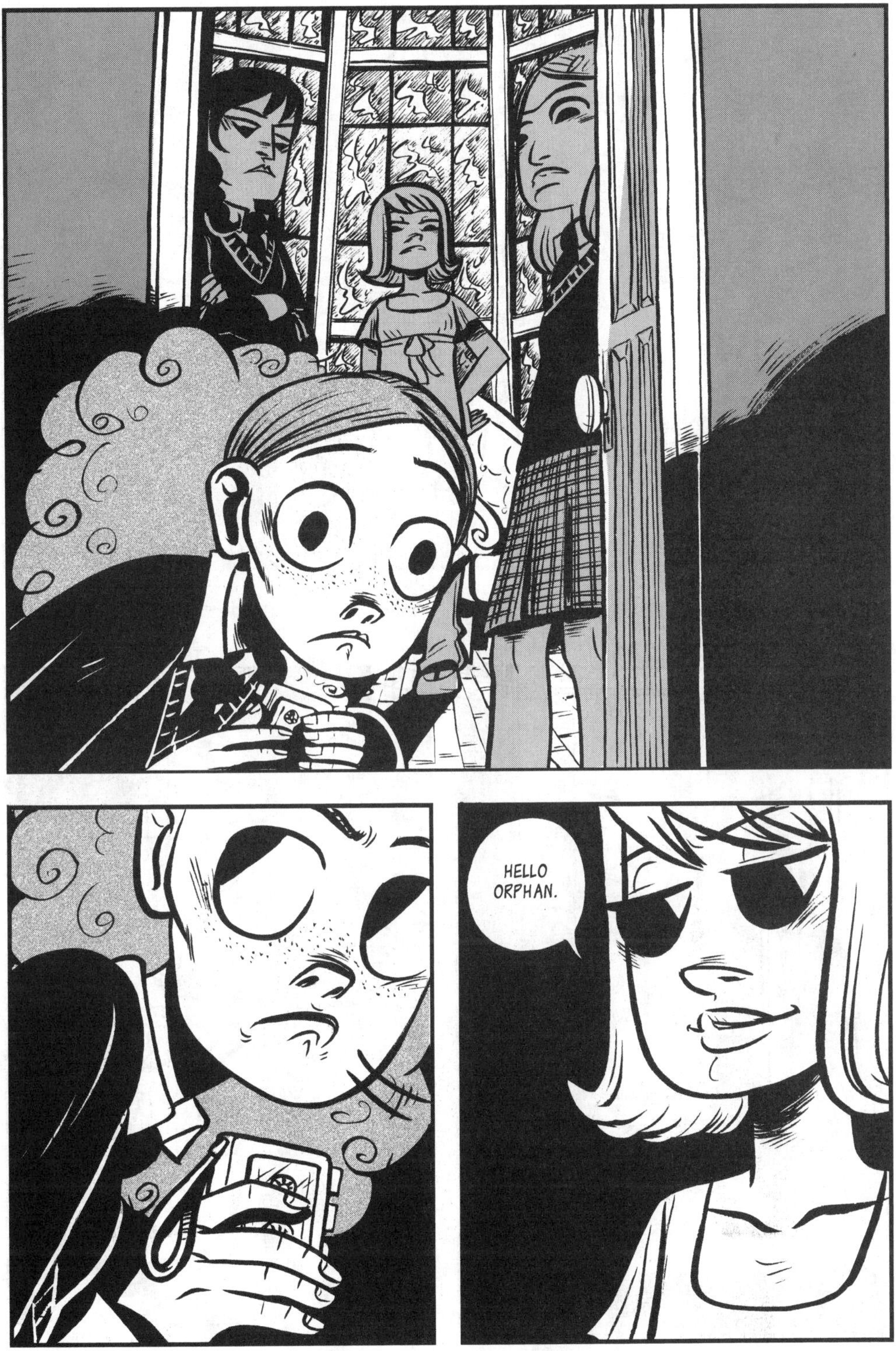
HELLO ORPHAN.

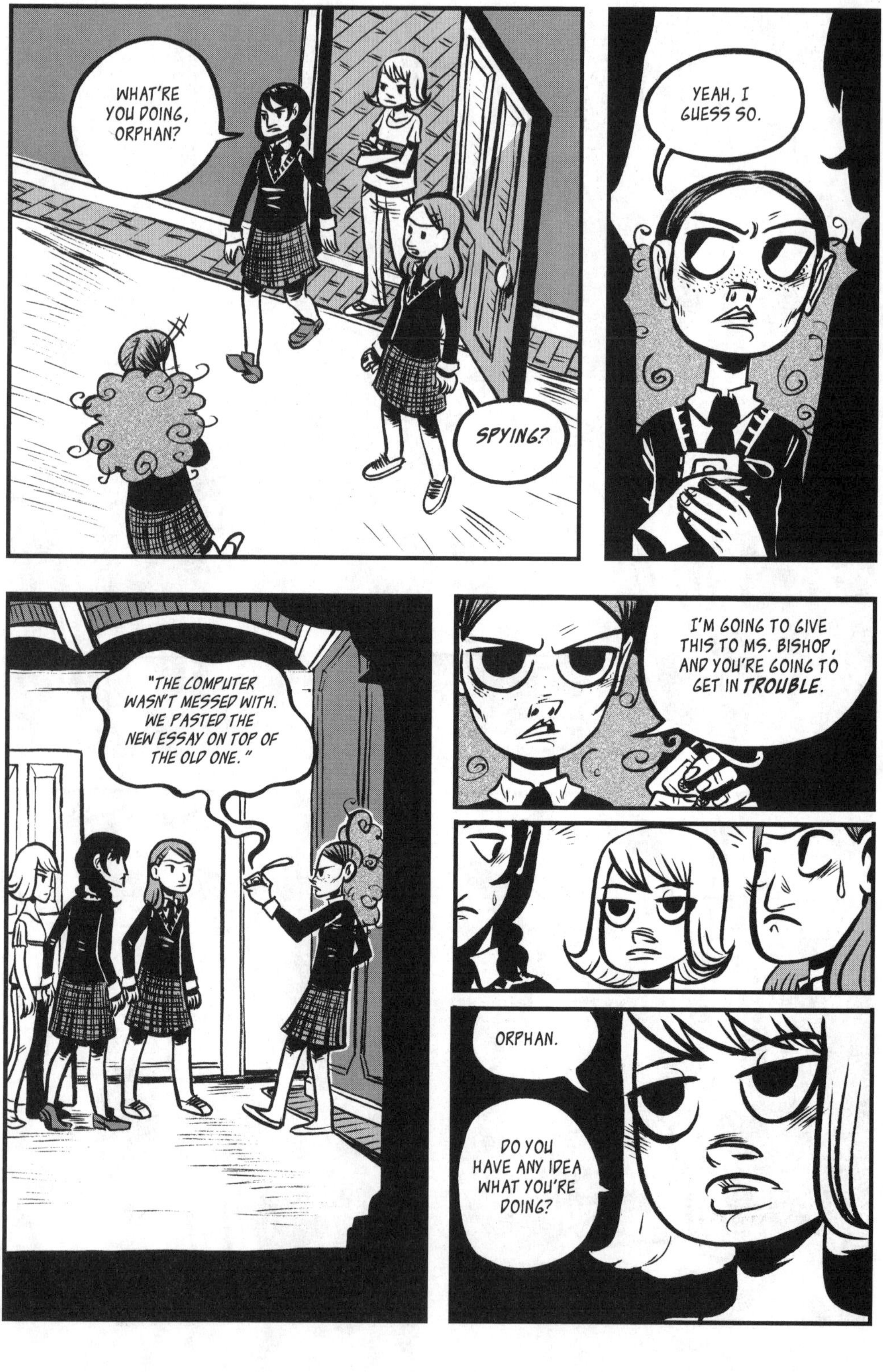
WHAT'RE YOU DOING, ORPHAN?
SPYING?
YEAH, I GUESS SO.
"THE COMPUTER WASN'T MESSED WITH. WE PASTED THE NEW ESSAY ON TOP OF THE OLD ONE."
I'M GOING TO GIVE THIS TO MS. BISHOP, AND YOU'RE GOING TO GET IN TROUBLE.
ORPHAN.
DO YOU HAVE ANY IDEA WHAT YOU'RE DOING?

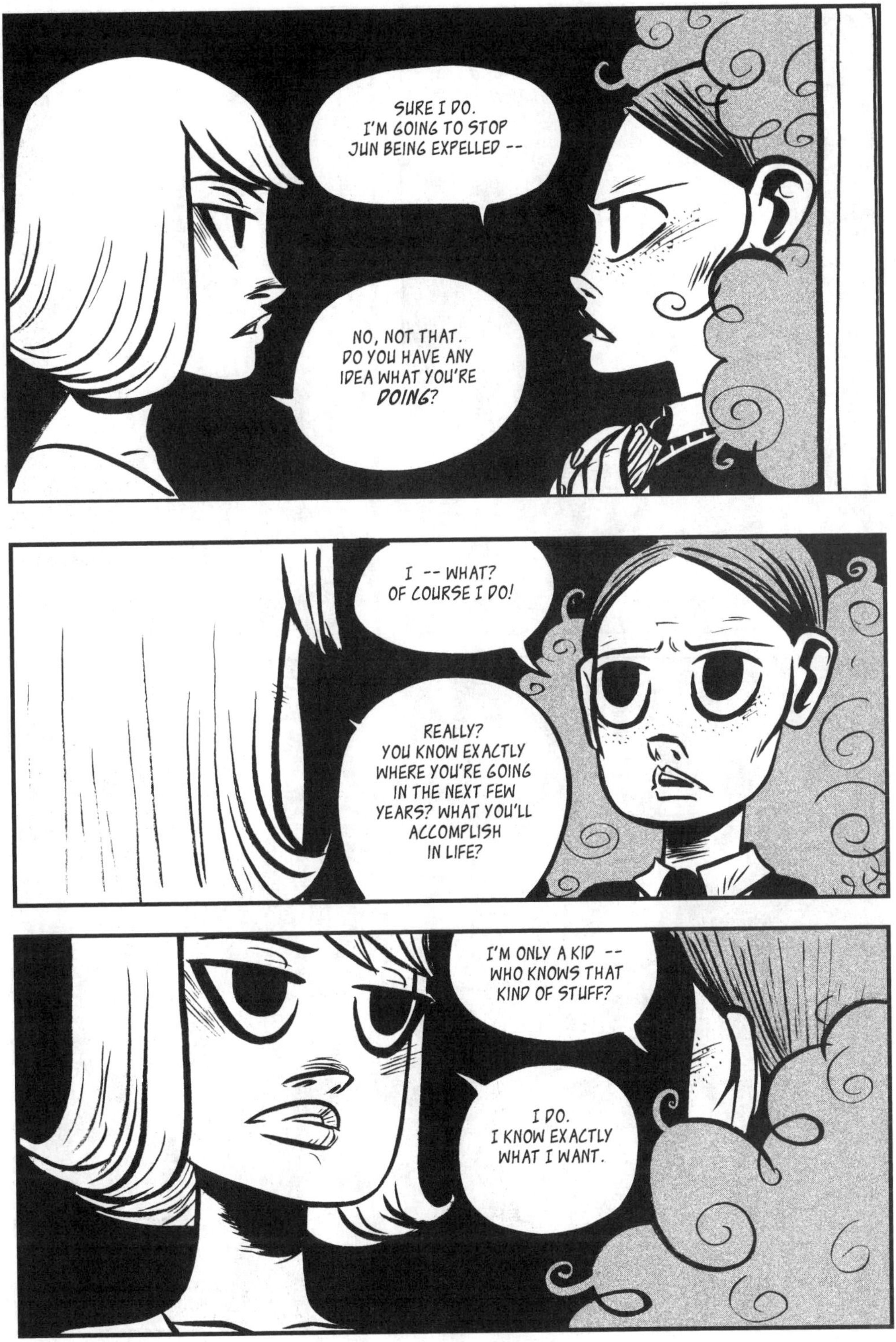
SURE I DO. I'M GOING TO STOP JUN BEING EXPELLED --
NO, NOT THAT. DO YOU HAVE ANY IDEA WHAT YOU'RE ***DOING***?
I -- WHAT? OF COURSE I DO!
REALLY? YOU KNOW EXACTLY WHERE YOU'RE GOING IN THE NEXT FEW YEARS? WHAT YOU'LL ACCOMPLISH IN LIFE?
I'M ONLY A KID -- WHO KNOWS THAT KIND OF STUFF?
I DO. I KNOW EXACTLY WHAT I WANT.

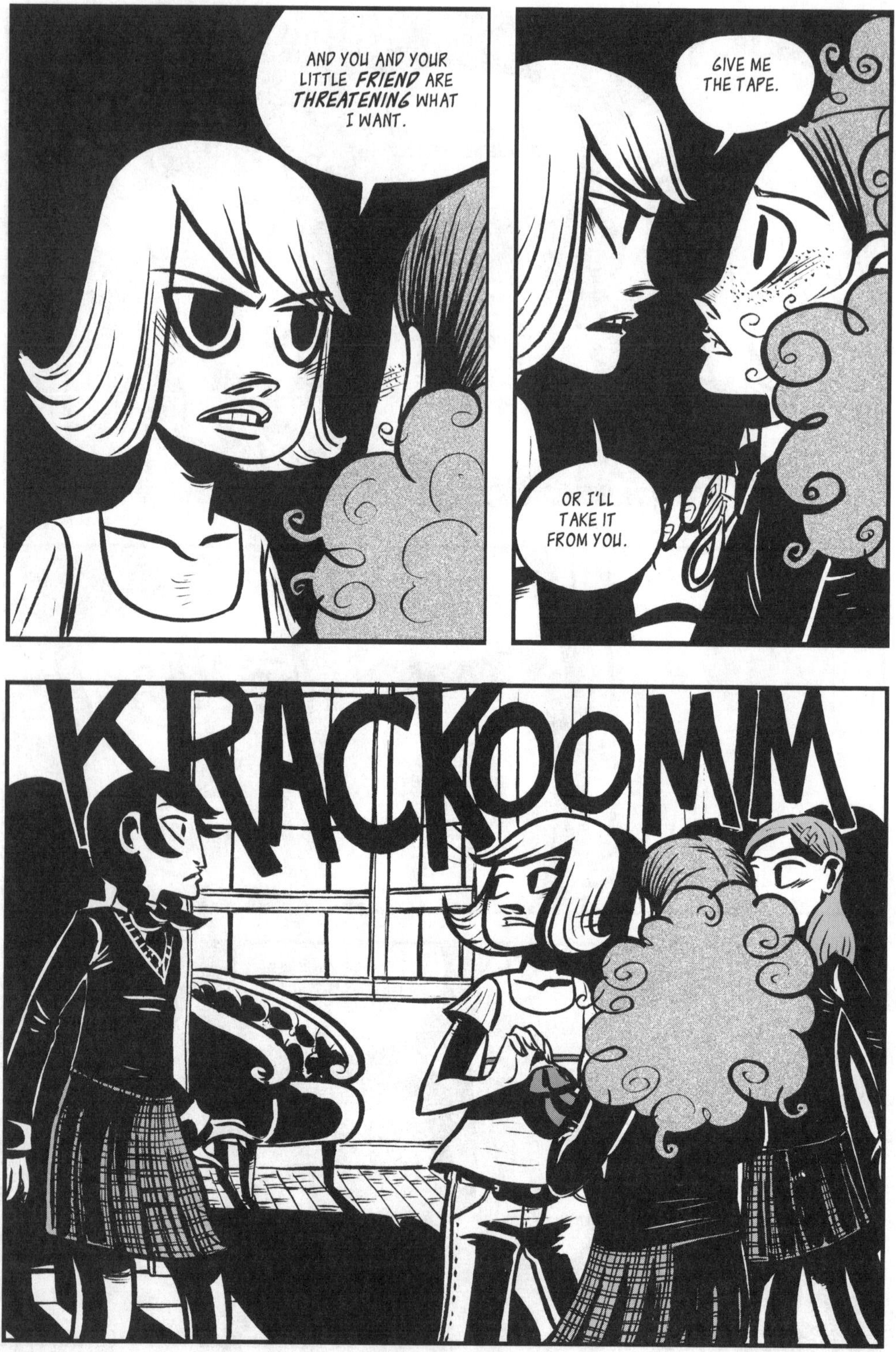
AND YOU AND YOUR LITTLE FRIEND ARE THREATENING WHAT I WANT.
GIVE ME THE TAPE.
OR I'LL TAKE IT FROM YOU.
KRACKOOMM

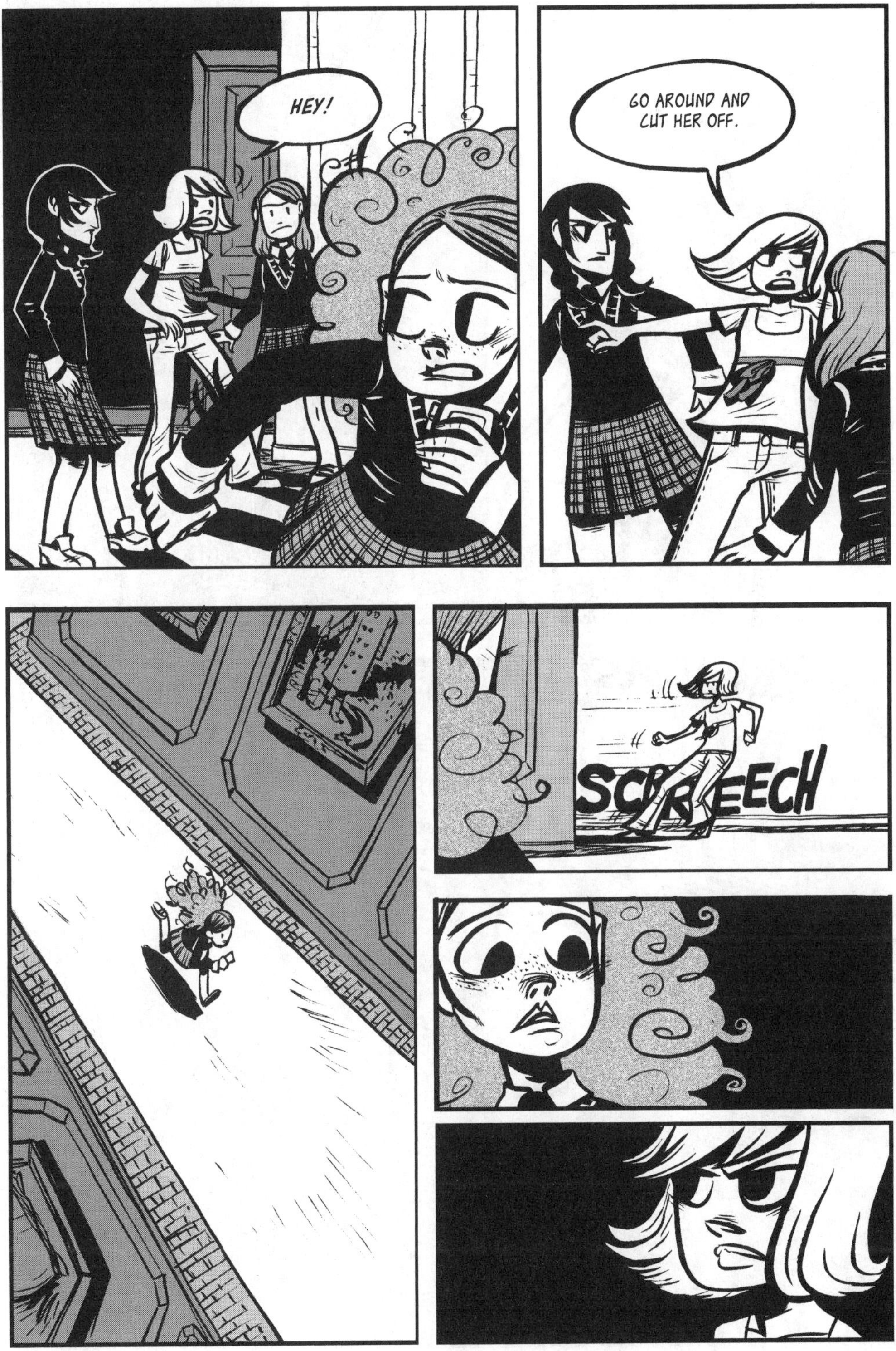
HEY!
GO AROUND AND CUT HER OFF.
SCREECH

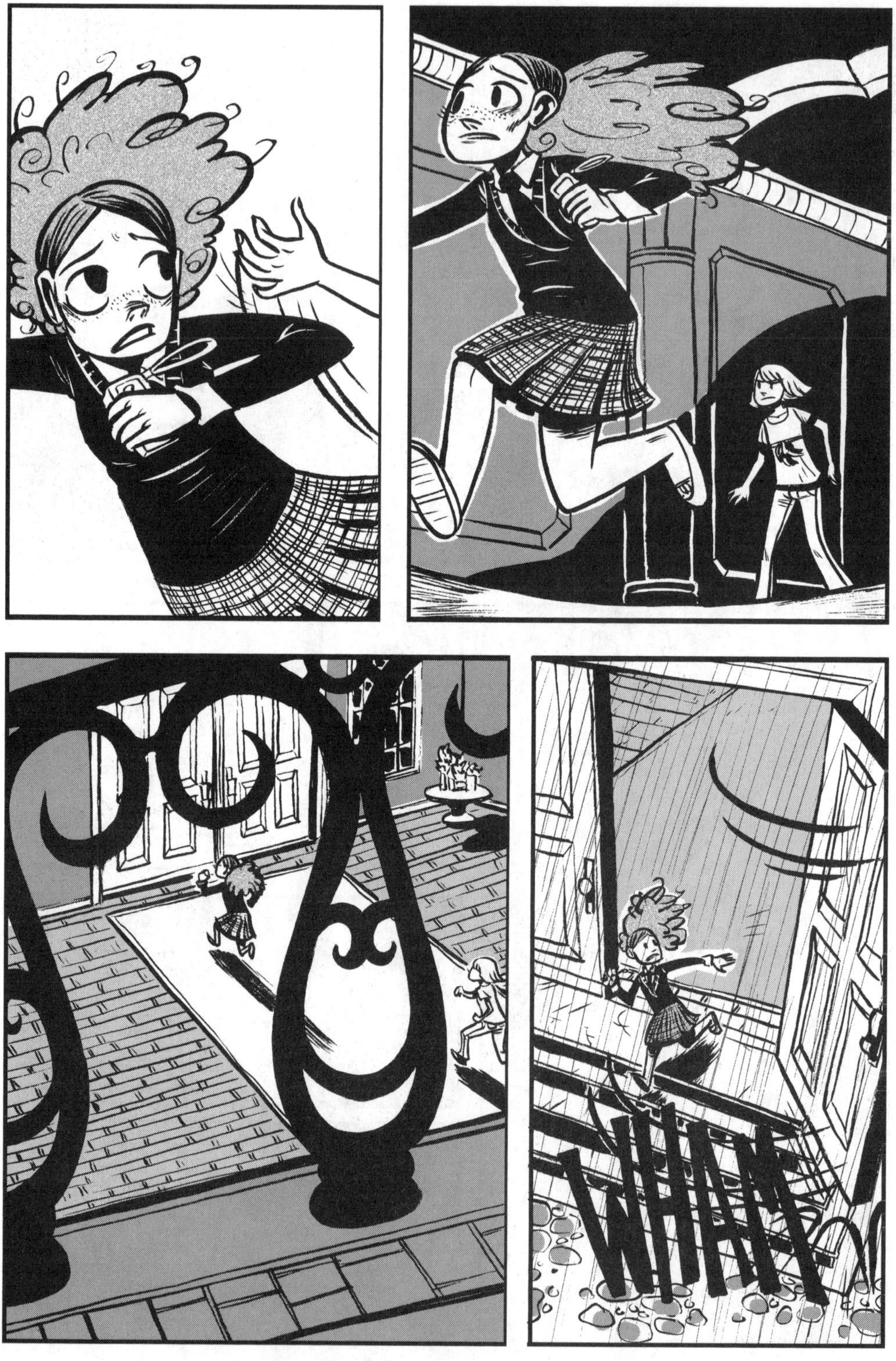
WHAM

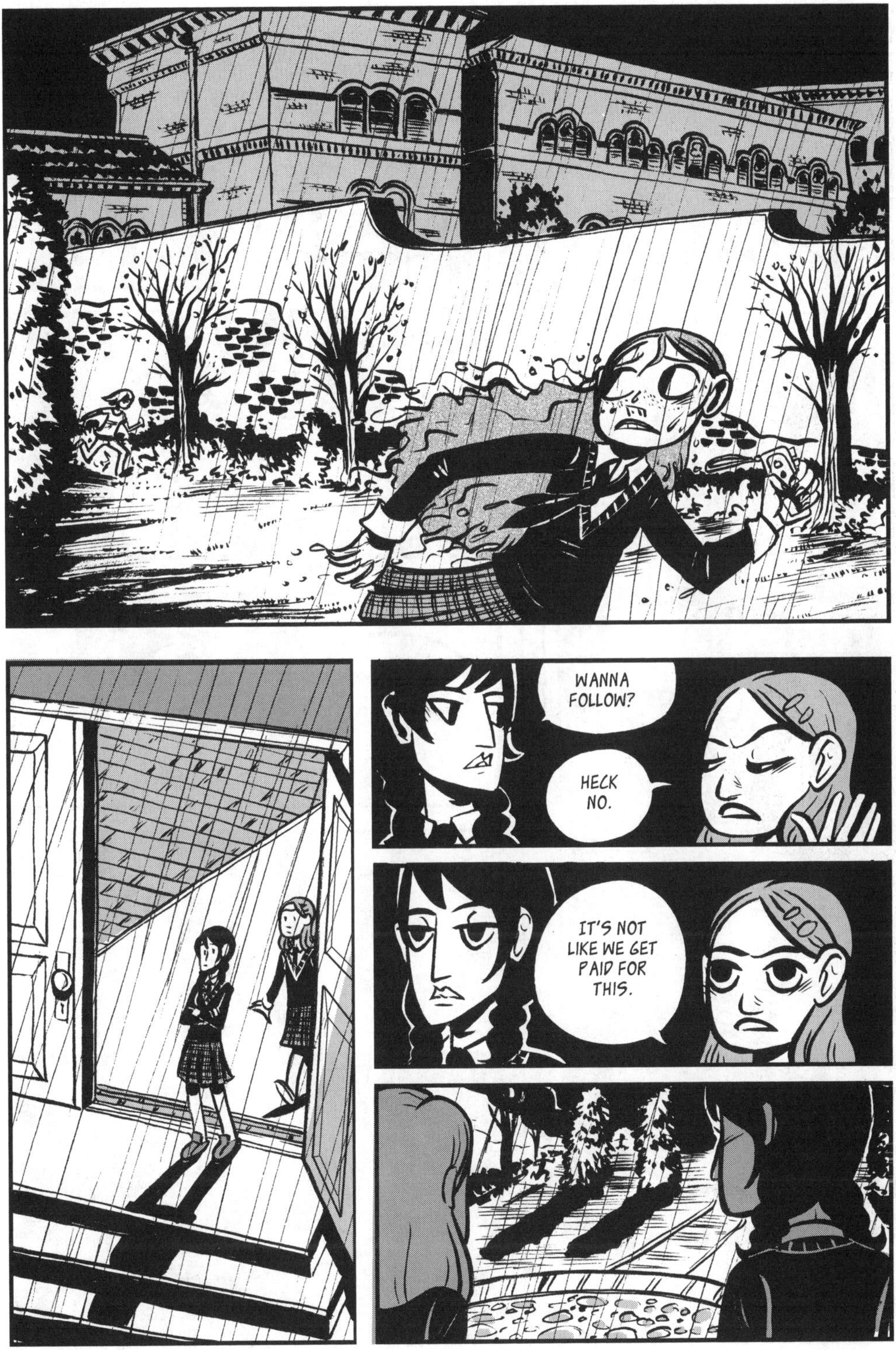
WANNA FOLLOW?
HECK NO.
IT'S NOT LIKE WE GET PAID FOR THIS.

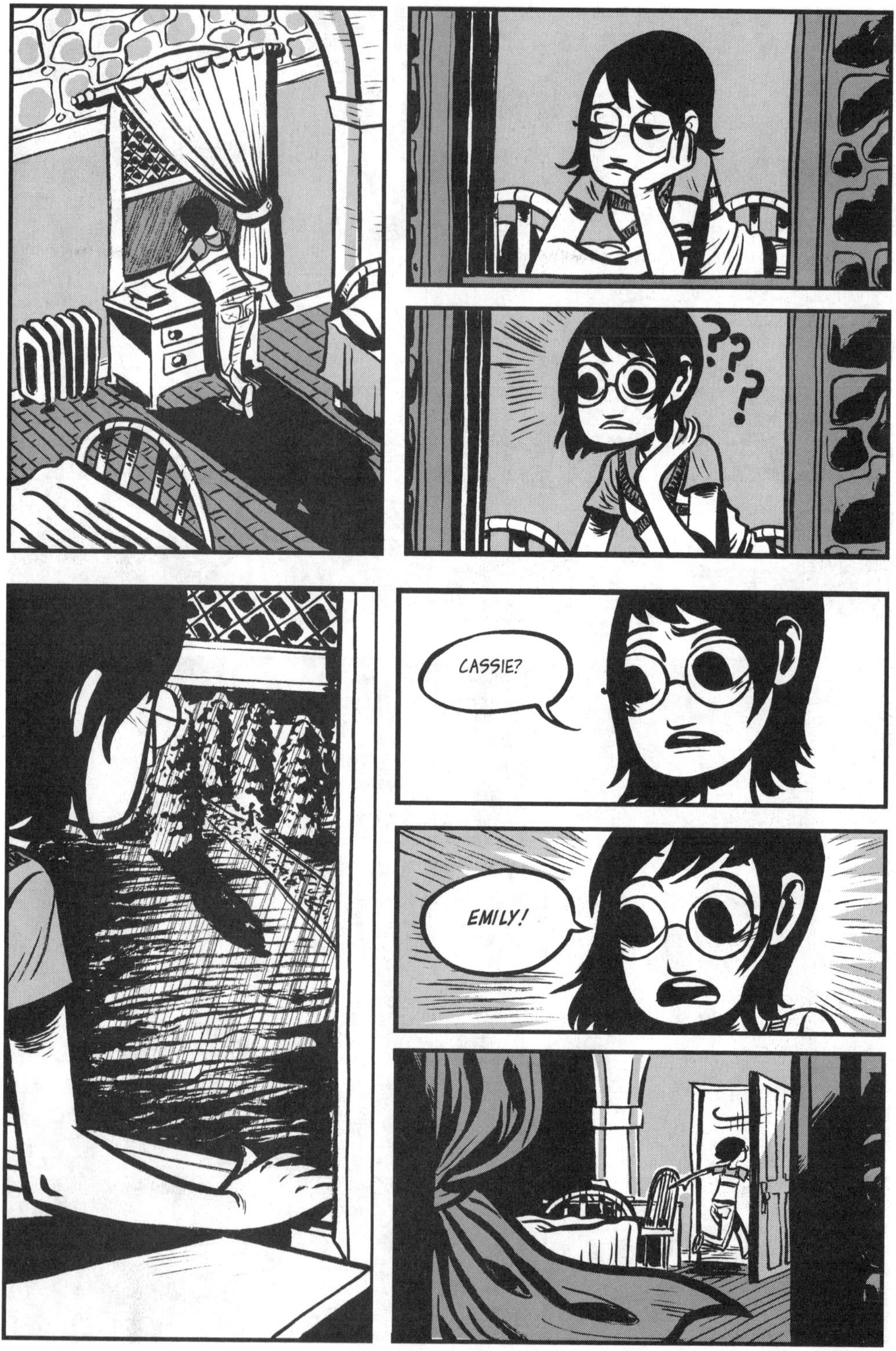
CASSIE?
EMILY!

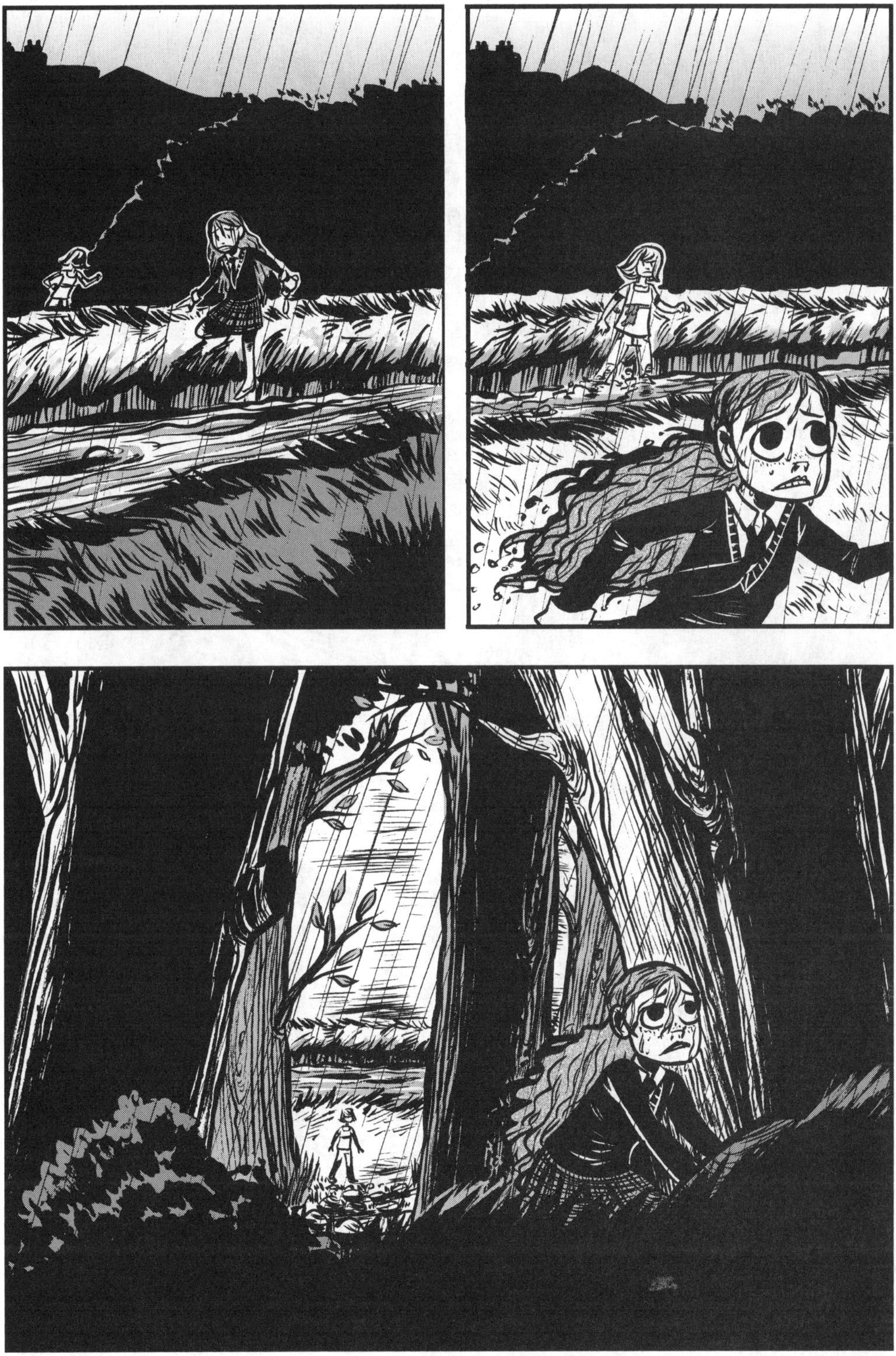

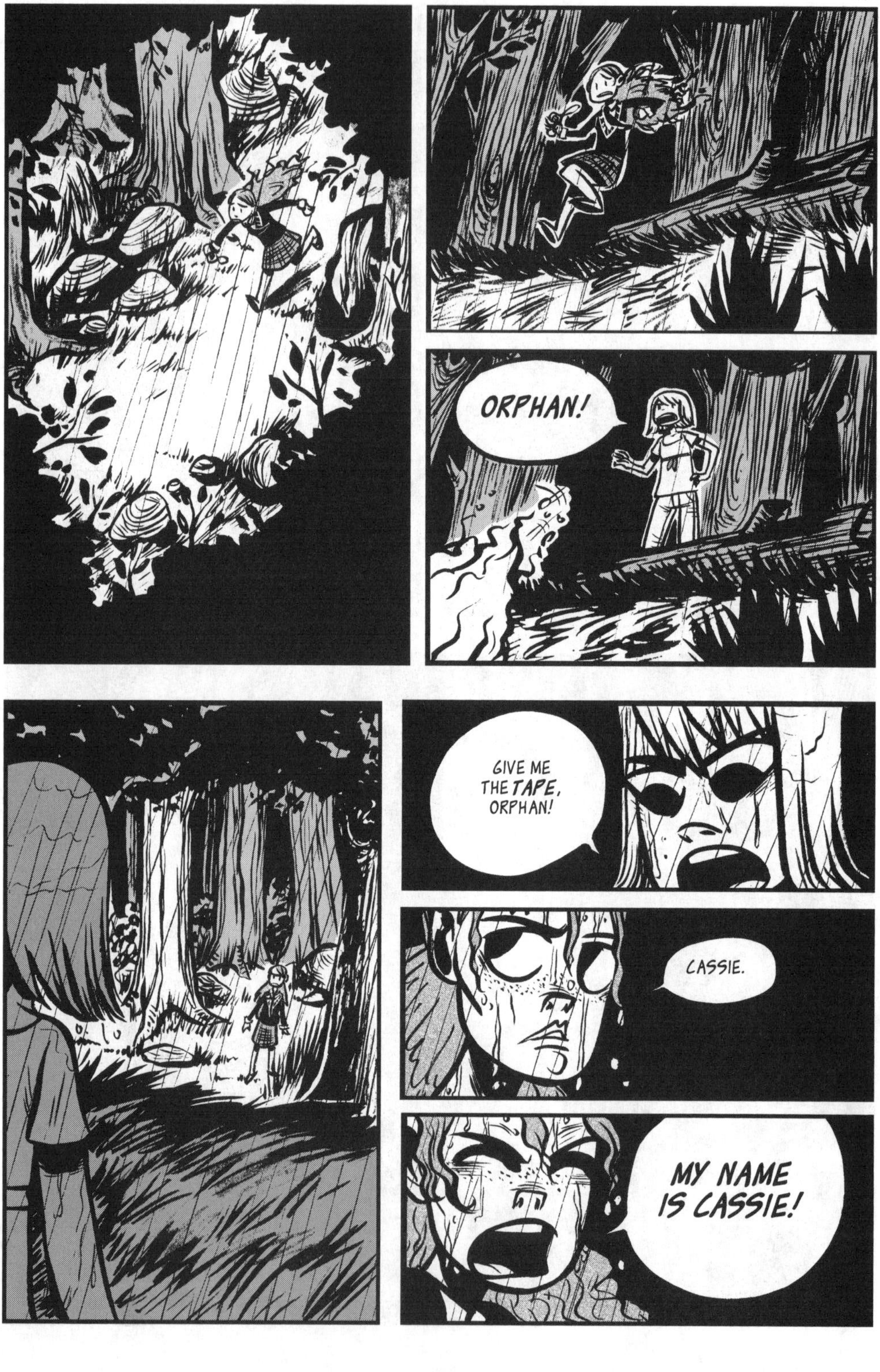
ORPHAN!
GIVE ME THE TAPE, ORPHAN!
CASSIE.
MY NAME IS CASSIE!

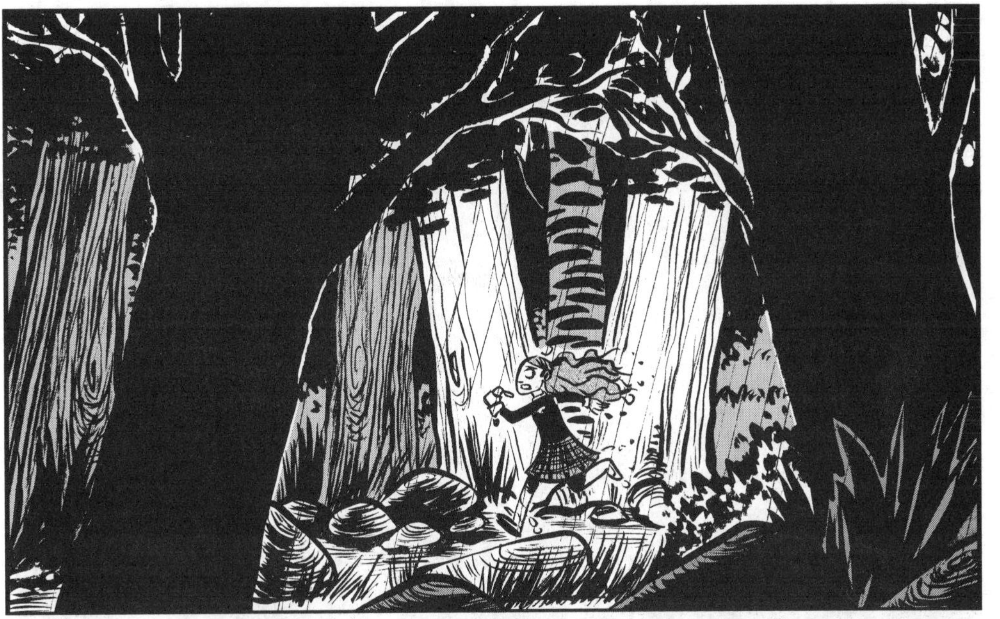

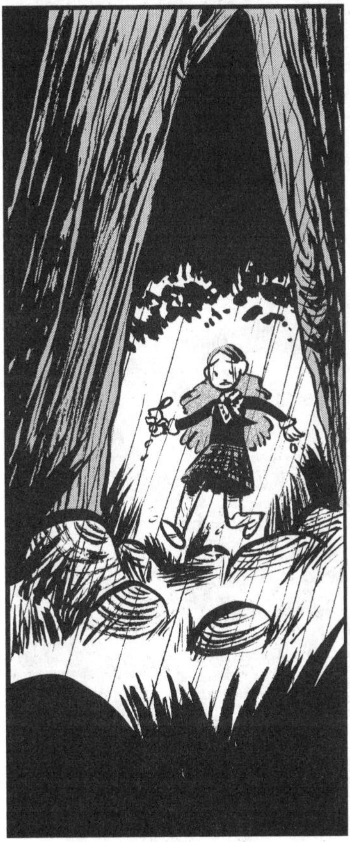

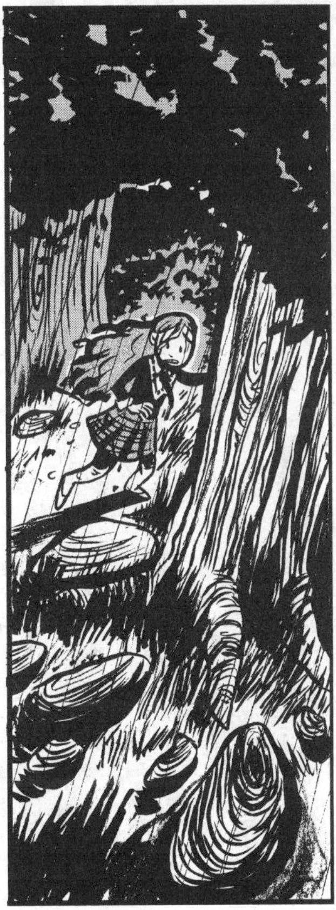

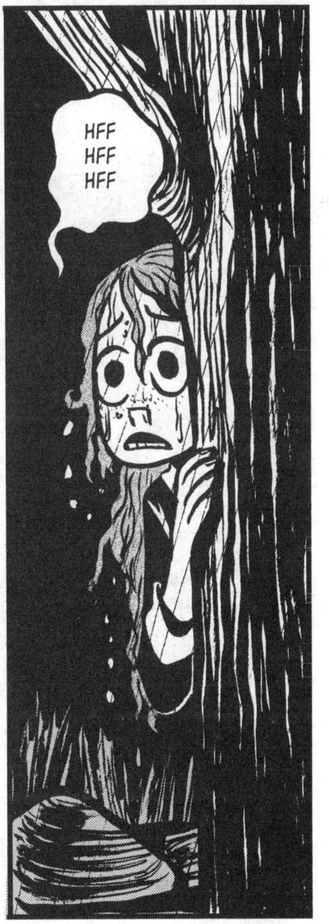
HFF
HFF
HFF

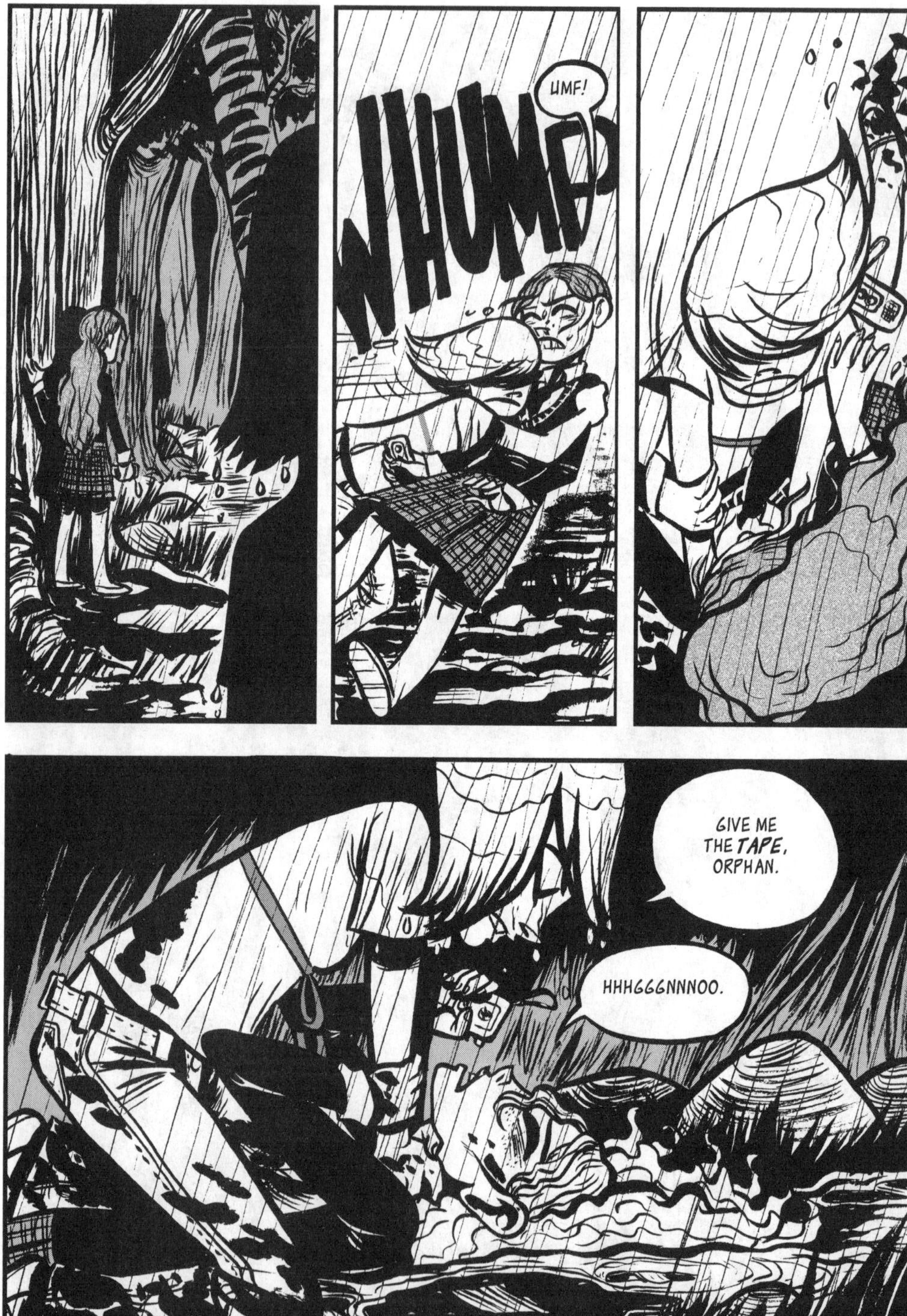
UMF!
WHUMP
GIVE ME THE *TAPE*, ORPHAN.
HHHGGGNNNOO.

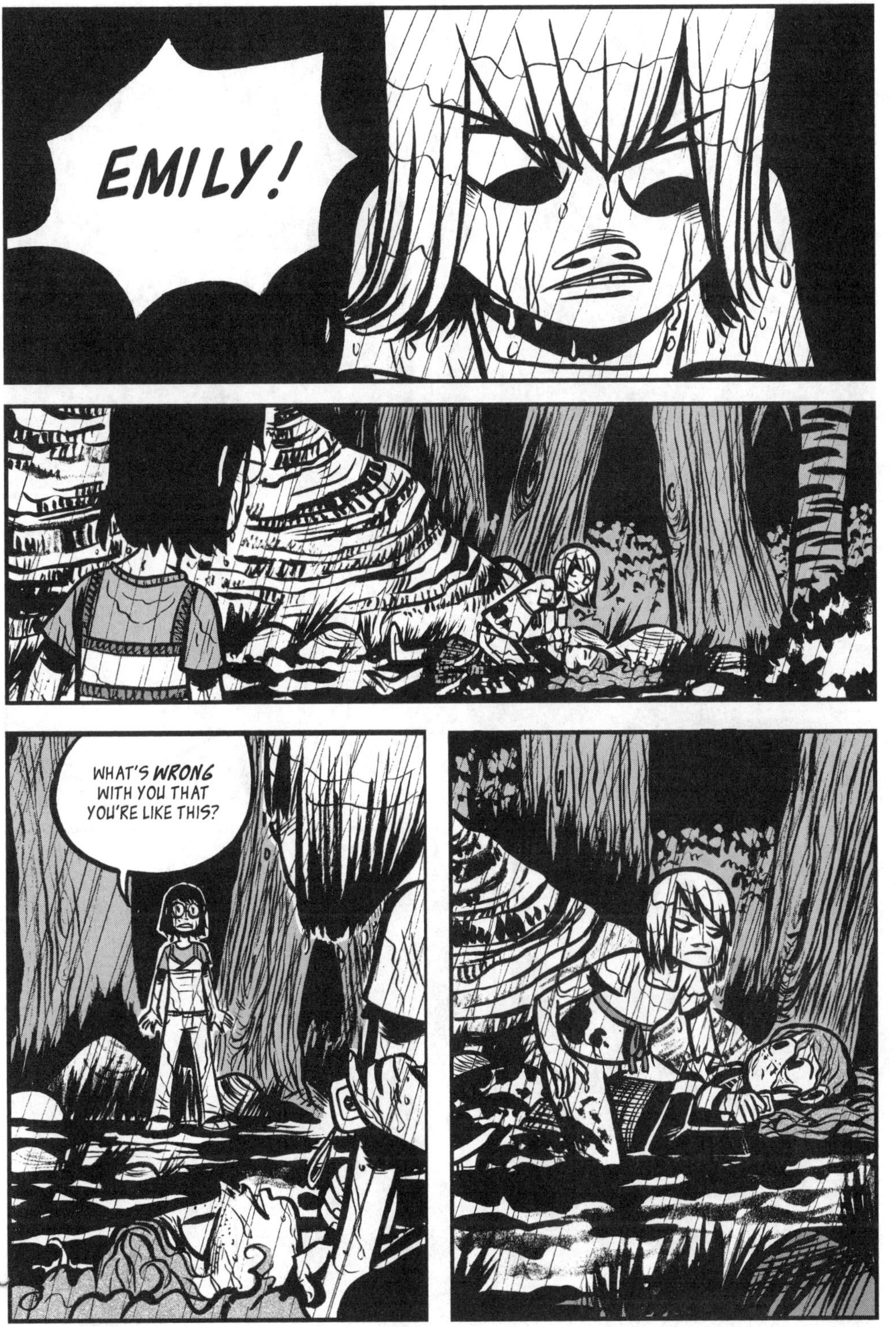
EMILY!
WHAT'S **WRONG** WITH YOU THAT YOU'RE LIKE THIS?

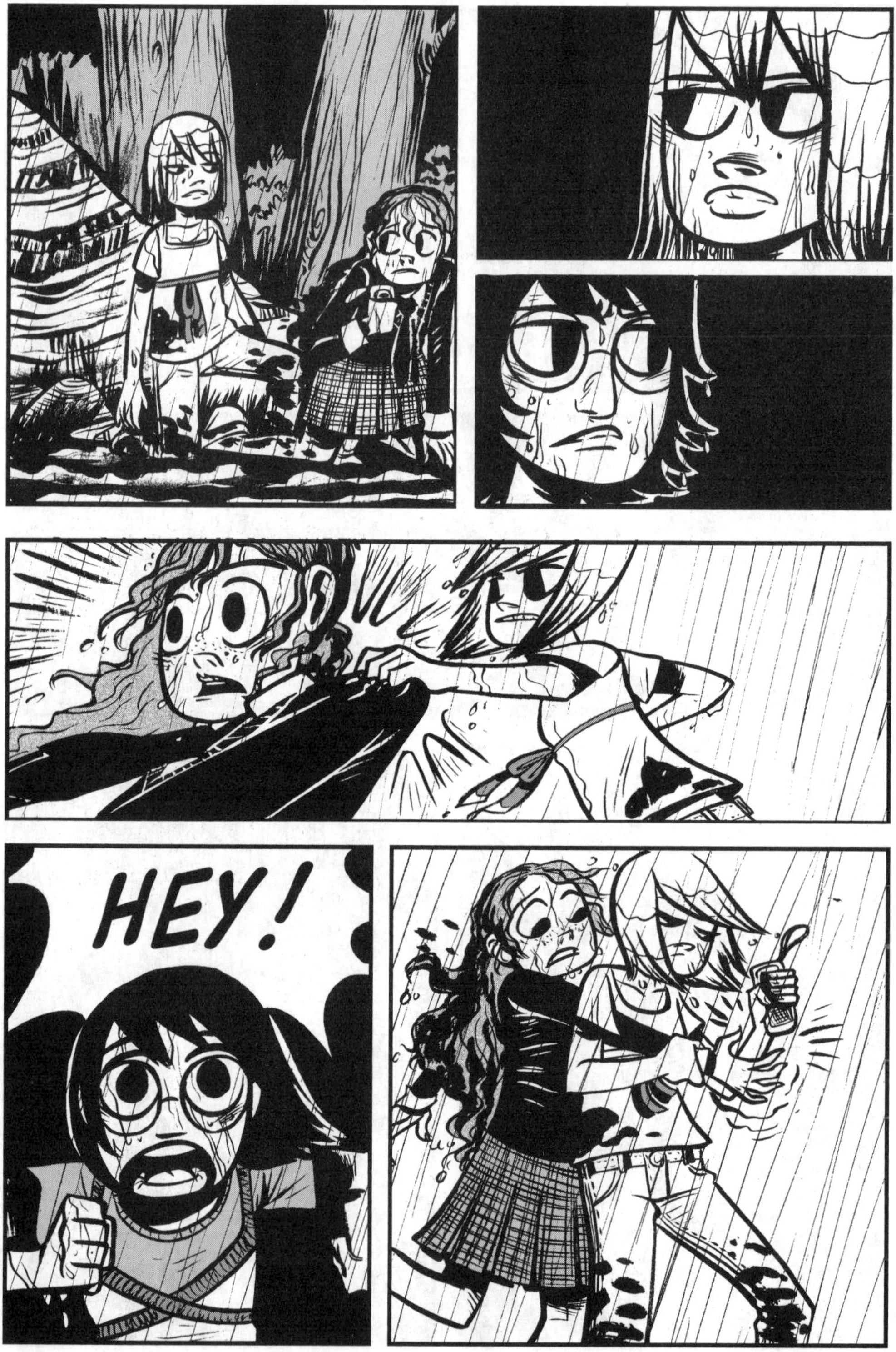
HEY!

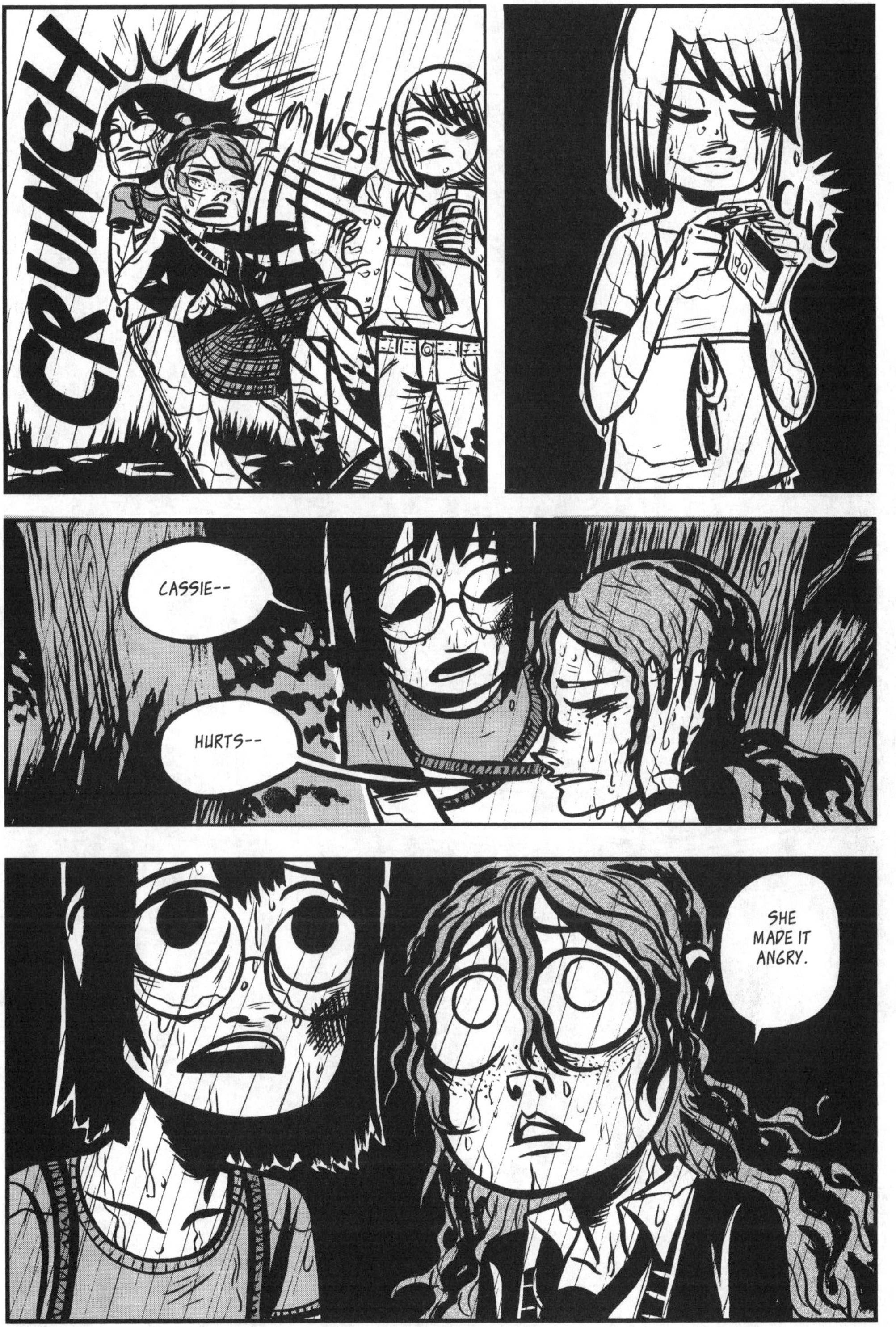
CRUNCH
WSST
CLIC
CASSIE--
HURTS--
SHE MADE IT ANGRY.

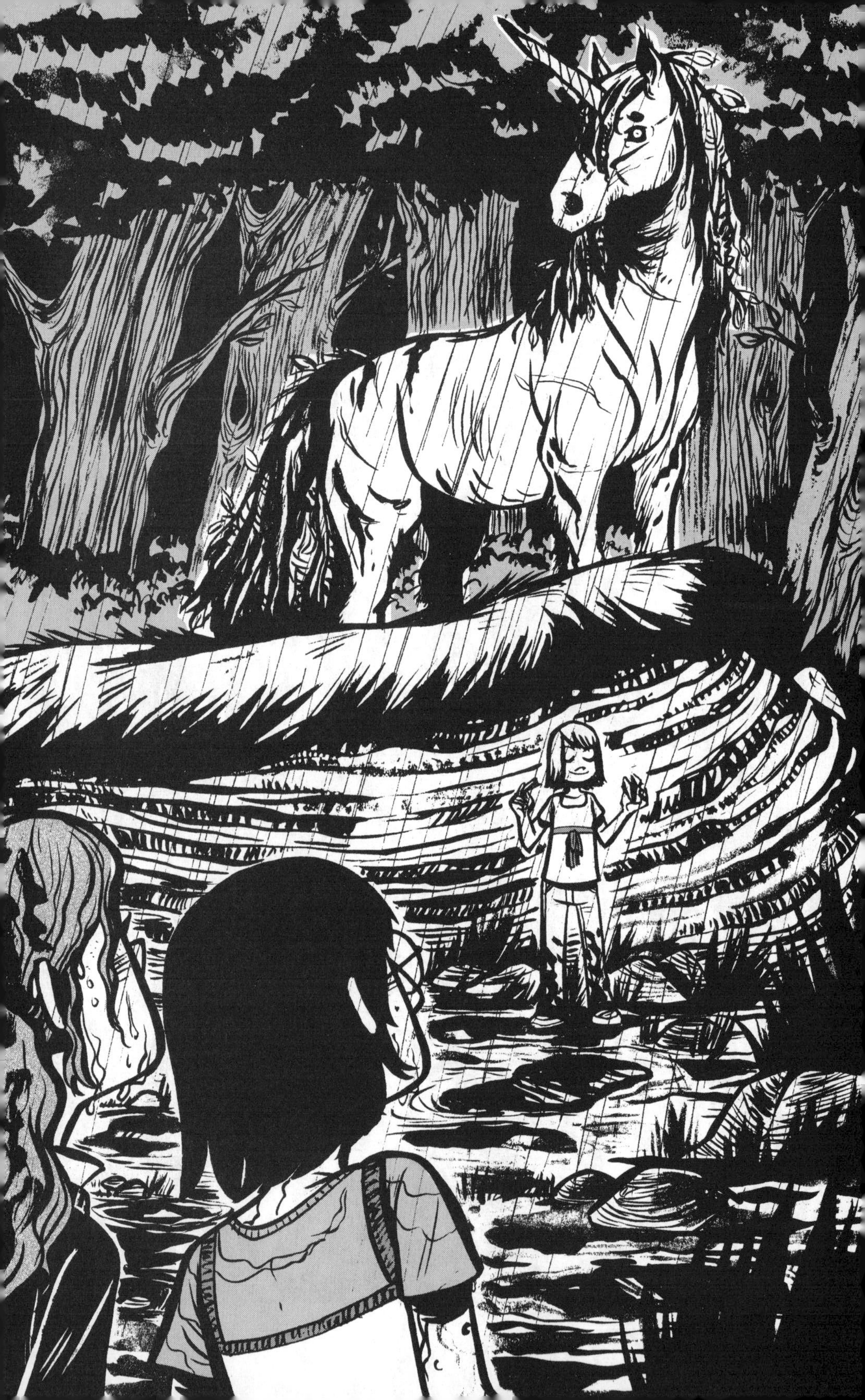

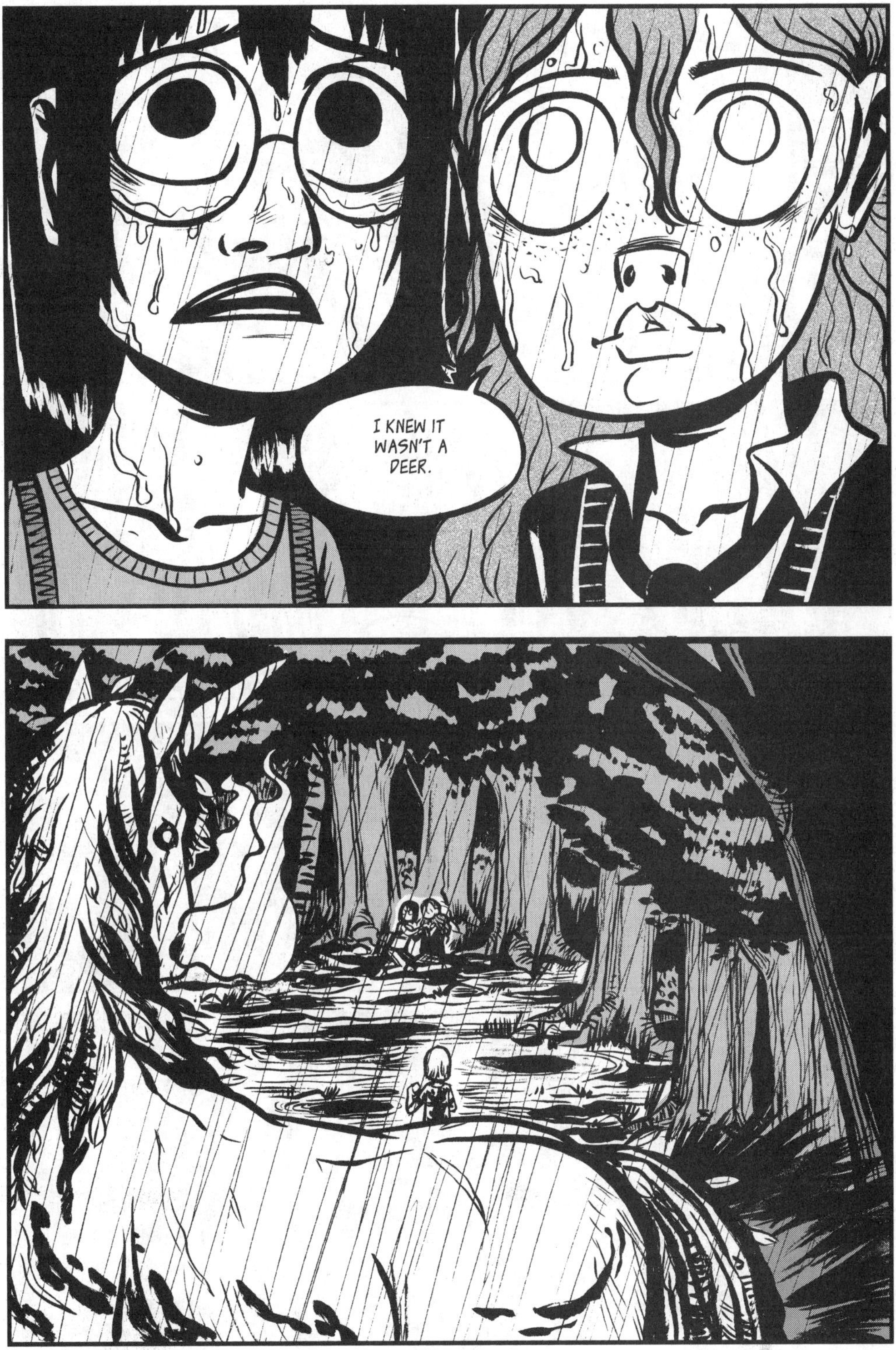
I KNEW IT WASN'T A DEER.

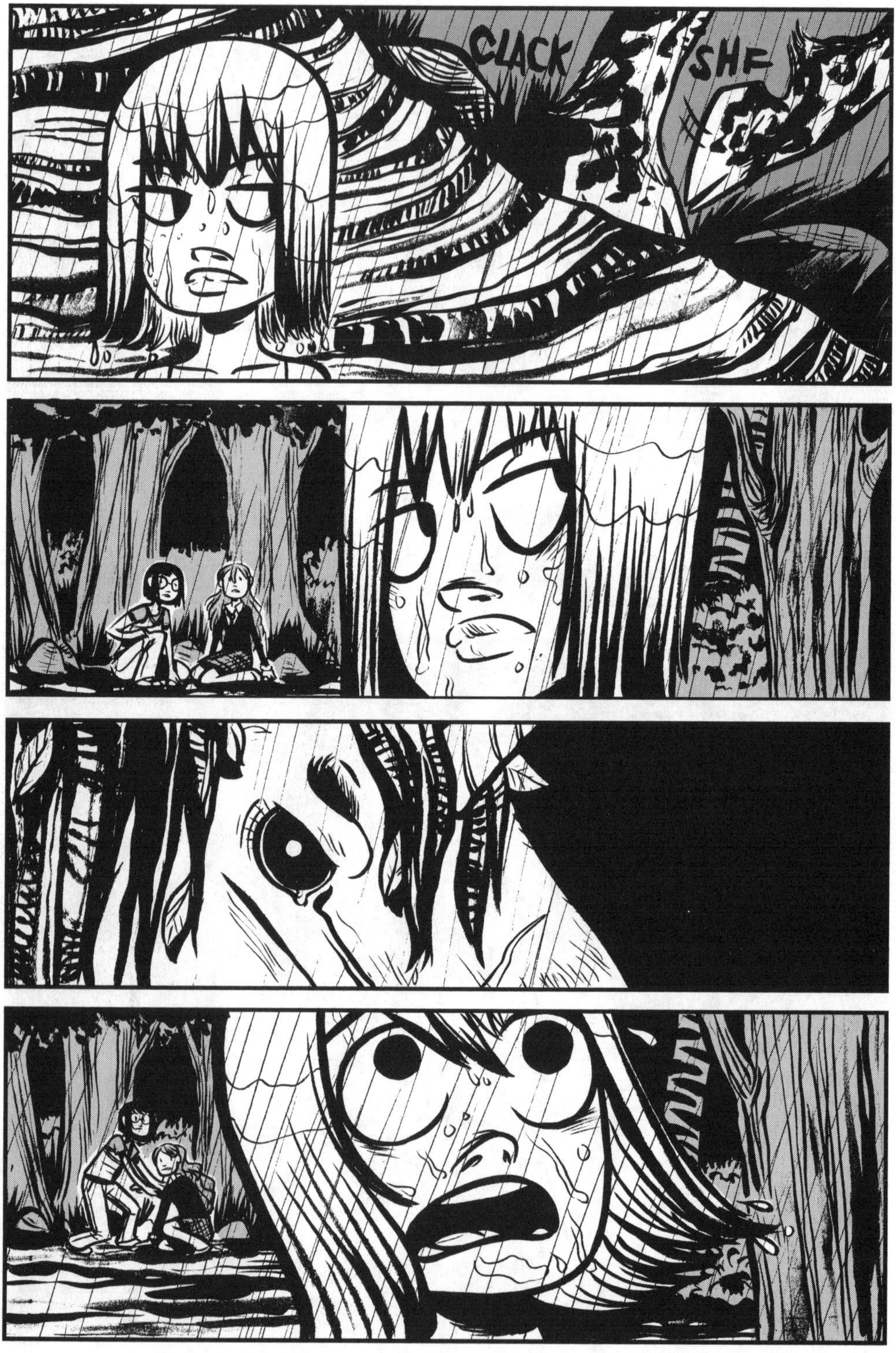
CLACK
SHF

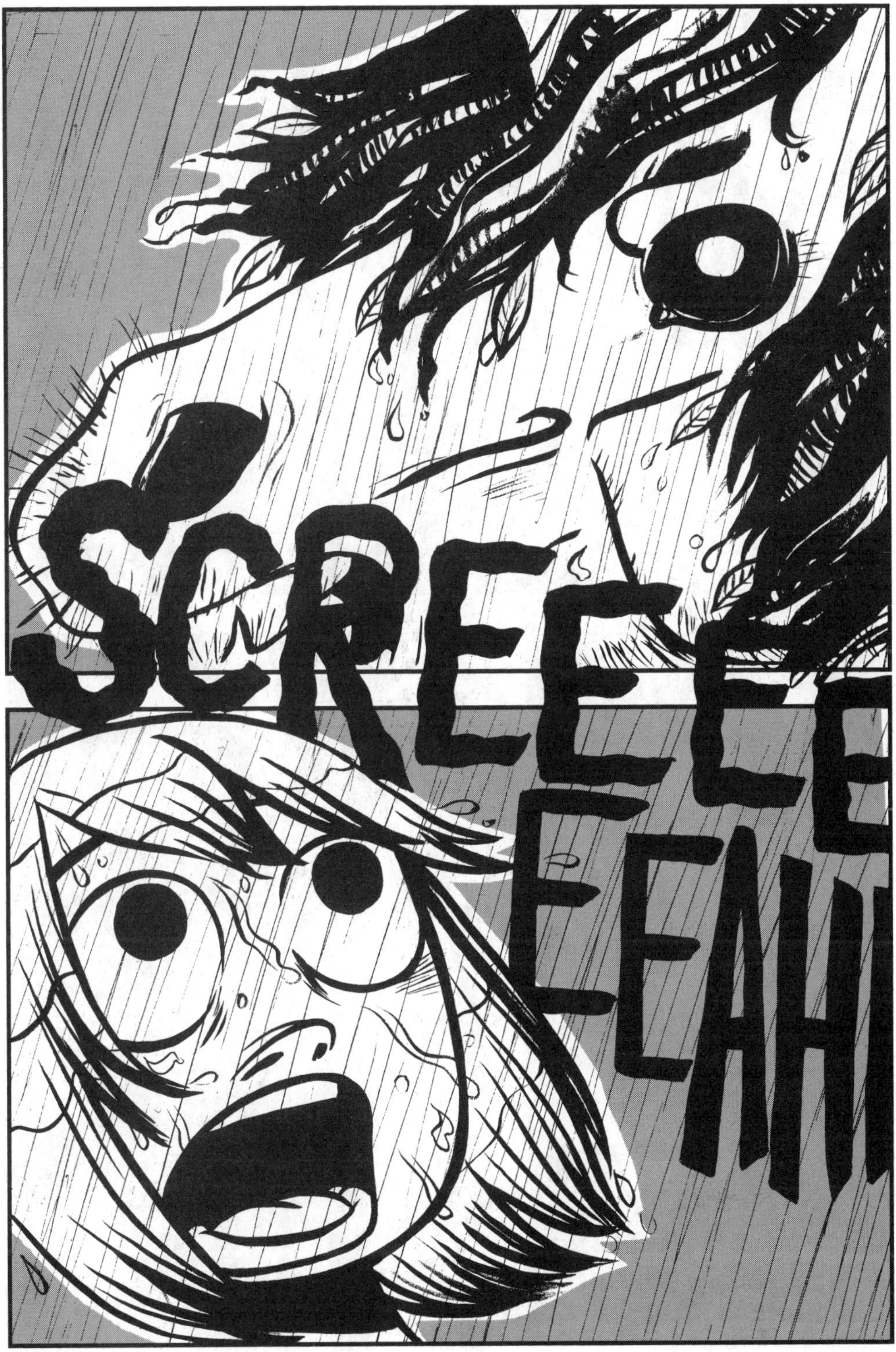
SCREEE
EEAH

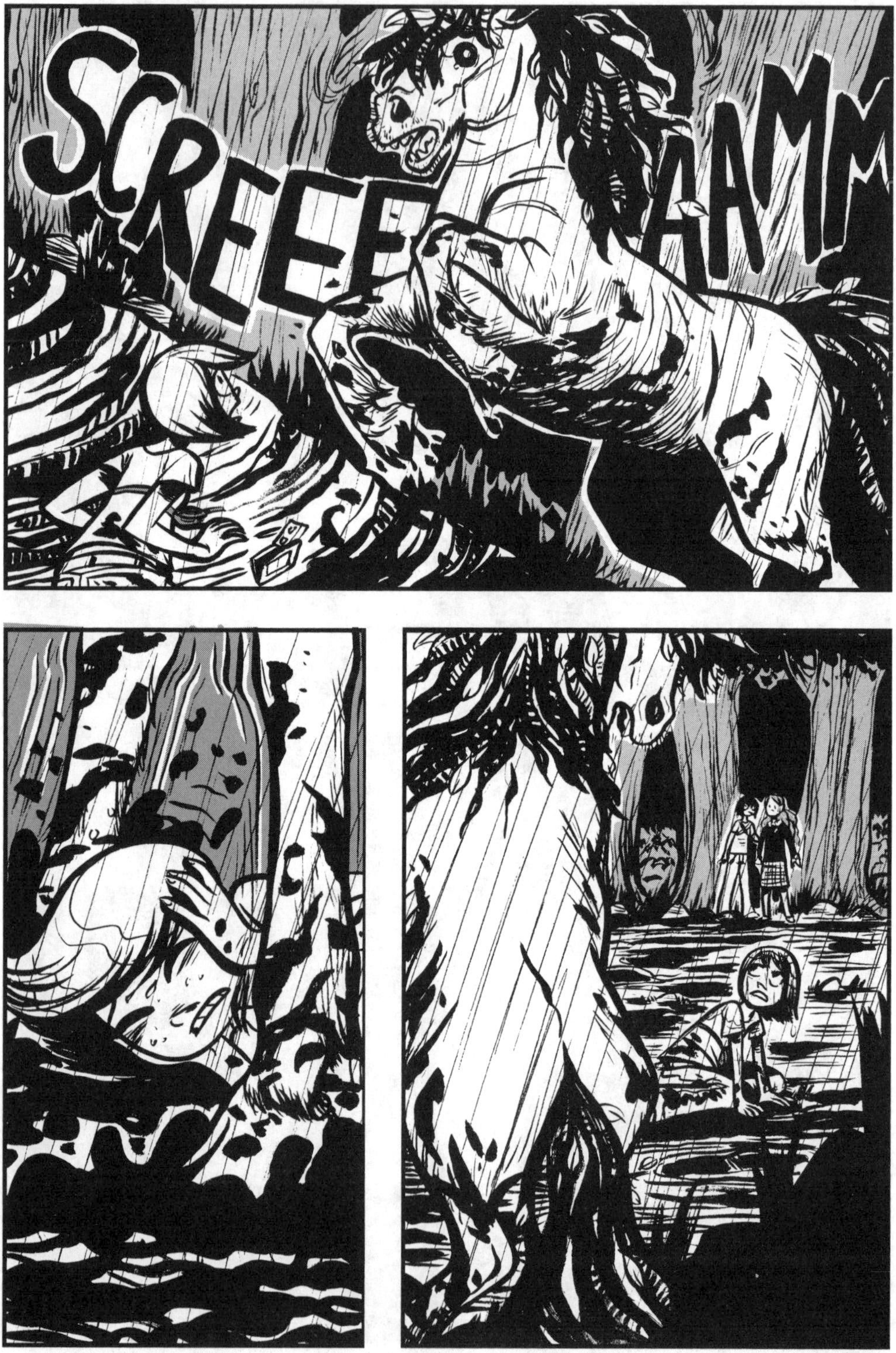
SCREEEAAMM

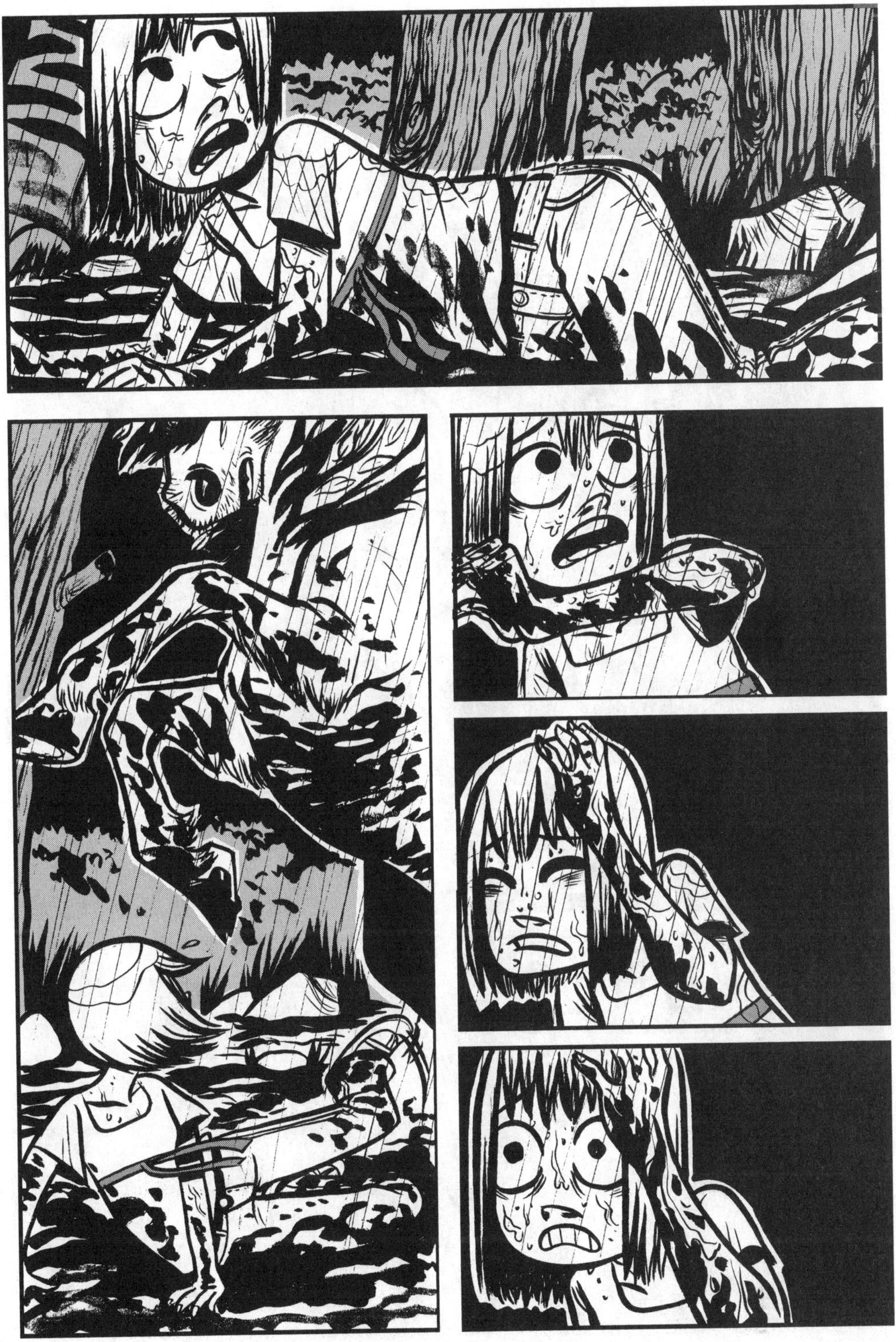

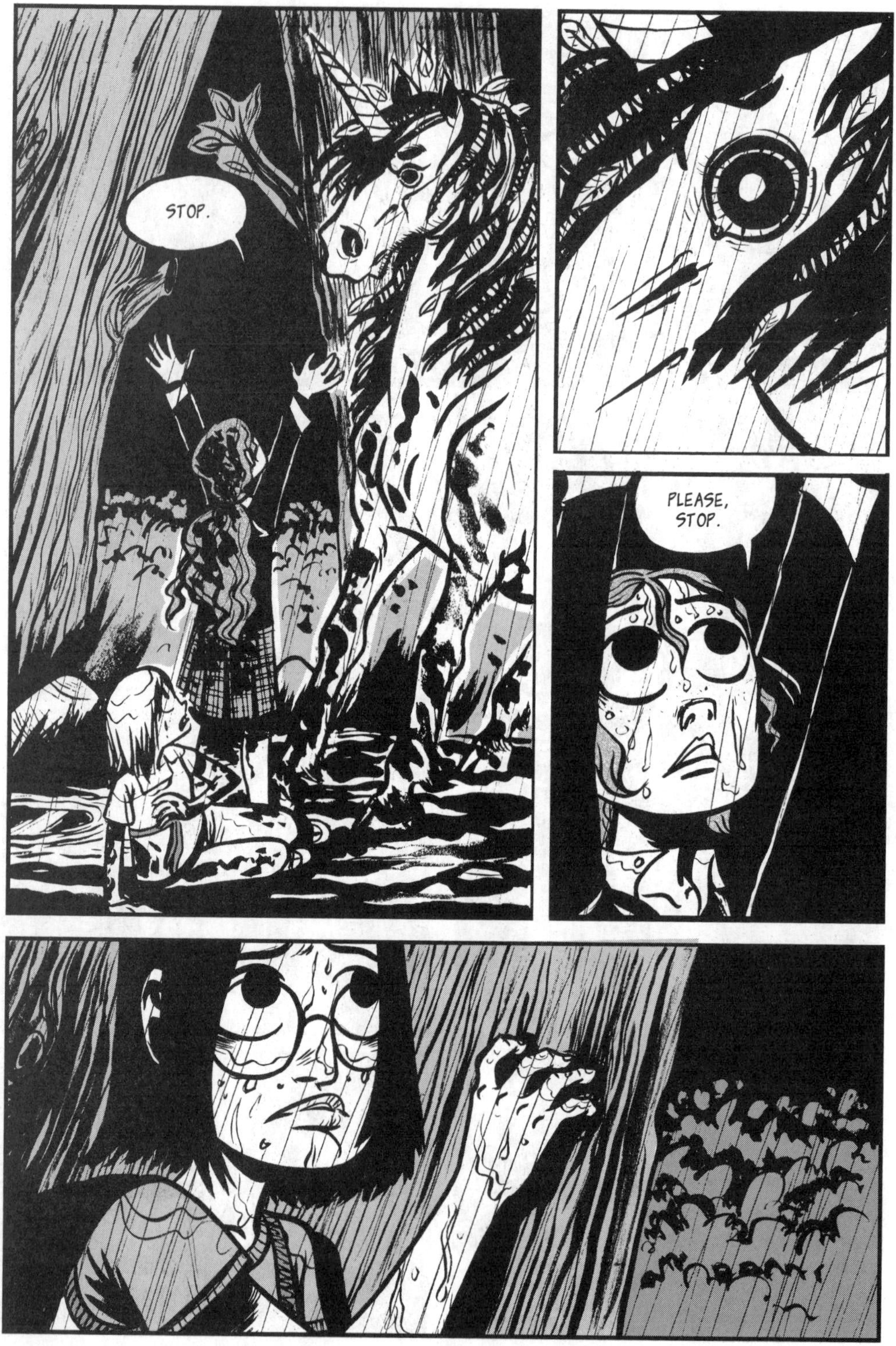
STOP.
PLEASE, STOP.

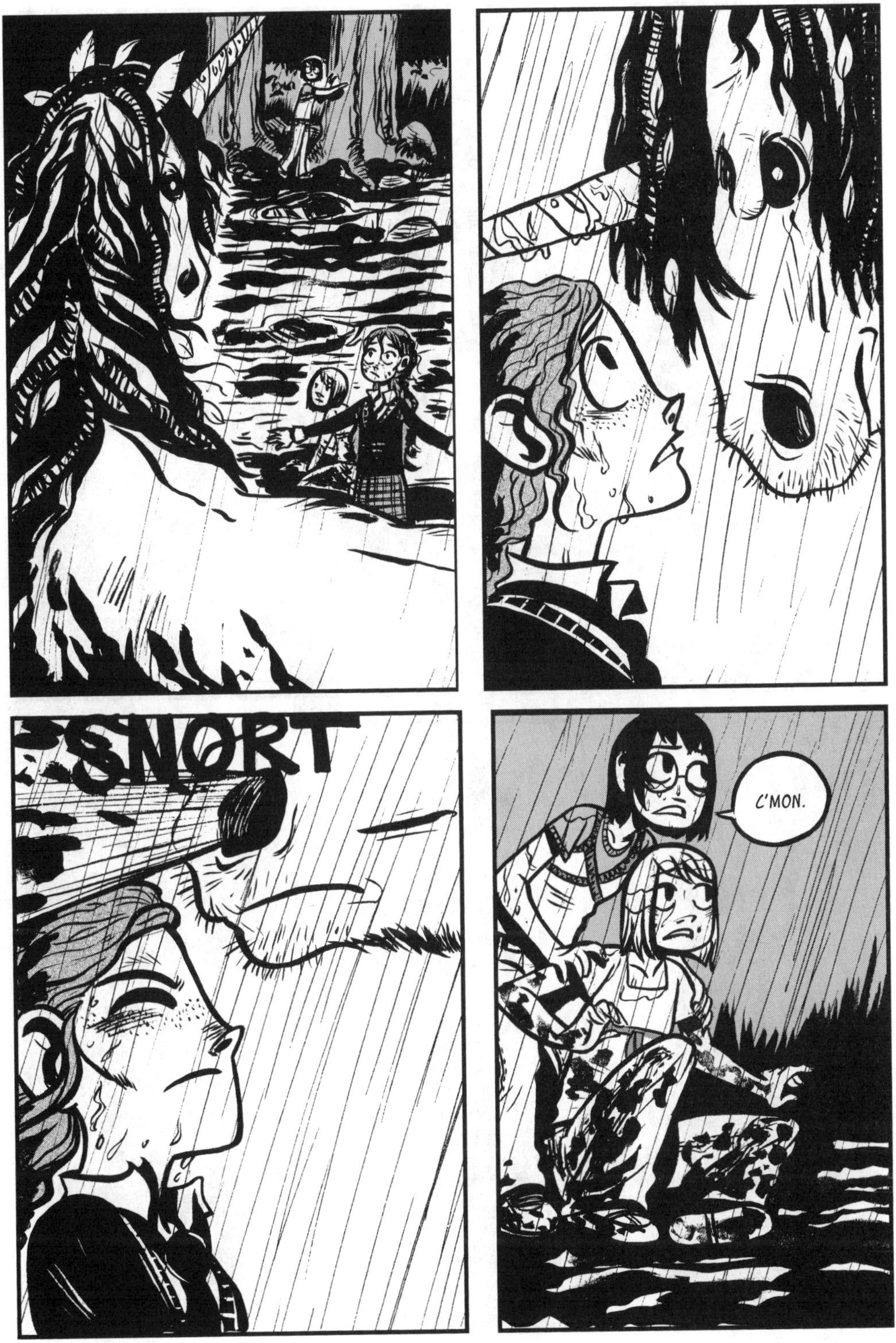
SNORT
C'MON.

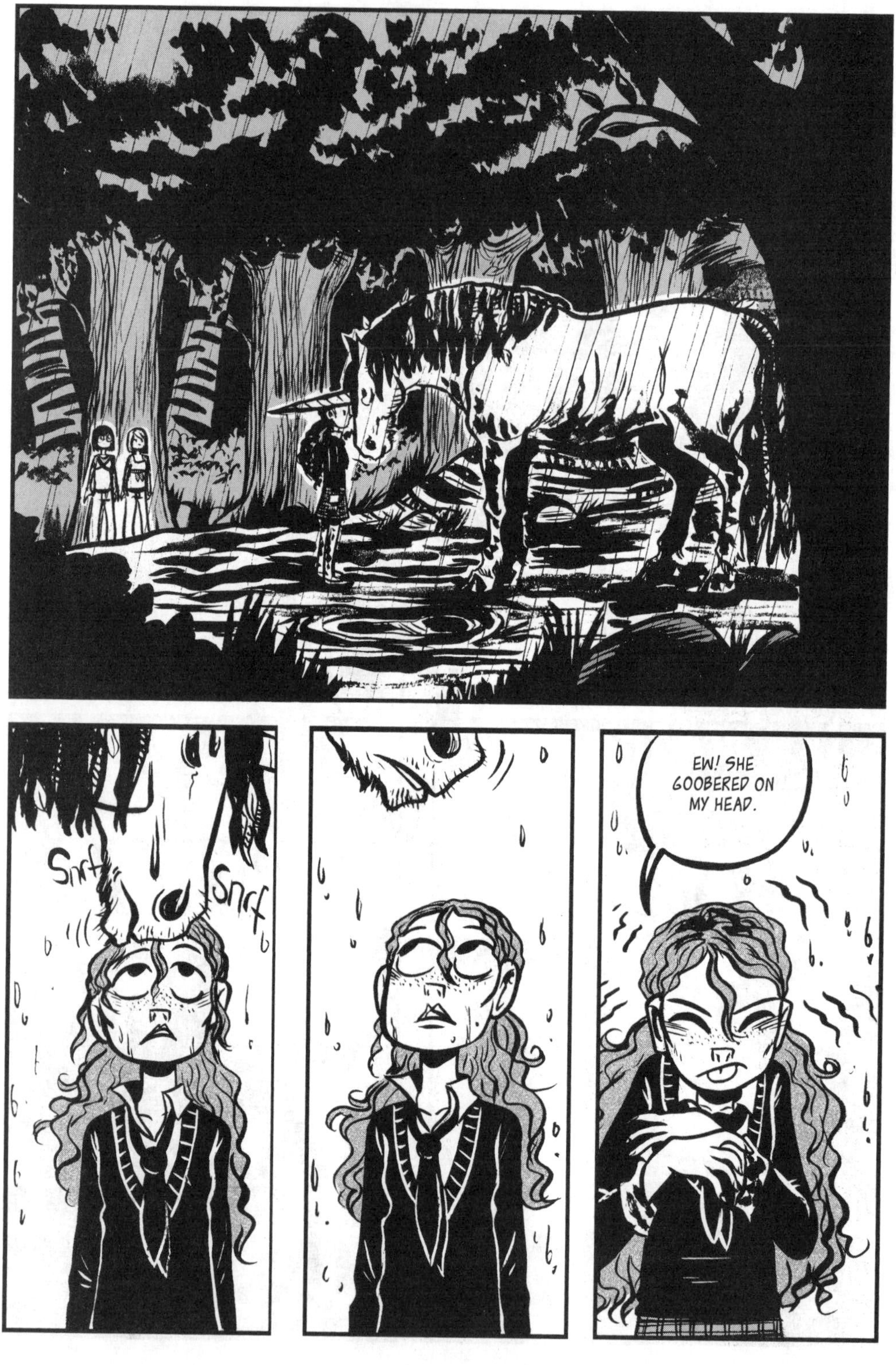
Snrf
Snrf
EW! SHE GOOBERED ON MY HEAD.

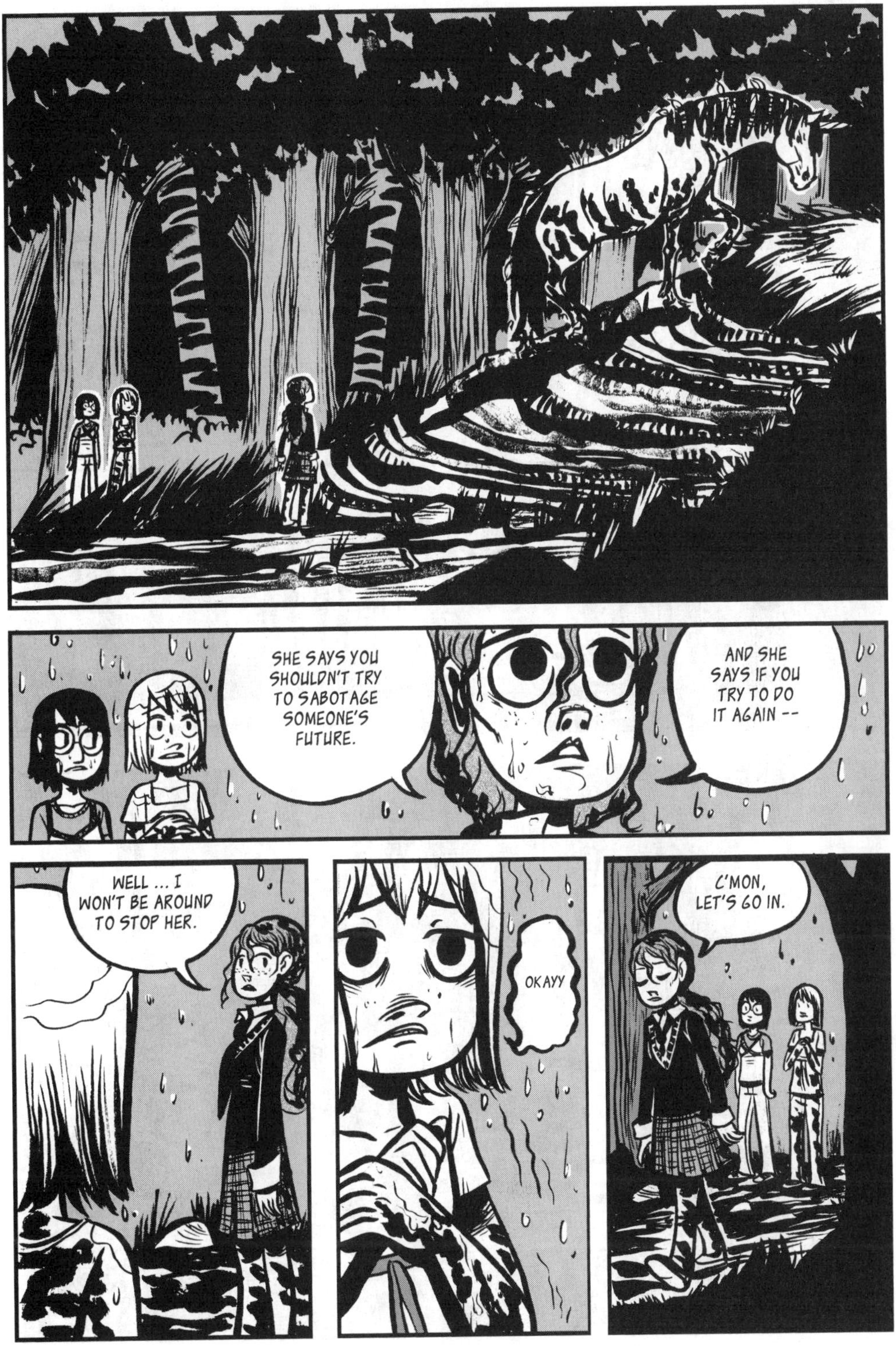
SHE SAYS YOU SHOULDN'T TRY TO SABOTAGE SOMEONE'S FUTURE.
AND SHE SAYS IF YOU TRY TO DO IT AGAIN --
WELL ... I WON'T BE AROUND TO STOP HER.
OKAYY
C'MON, LET'S GO IN.

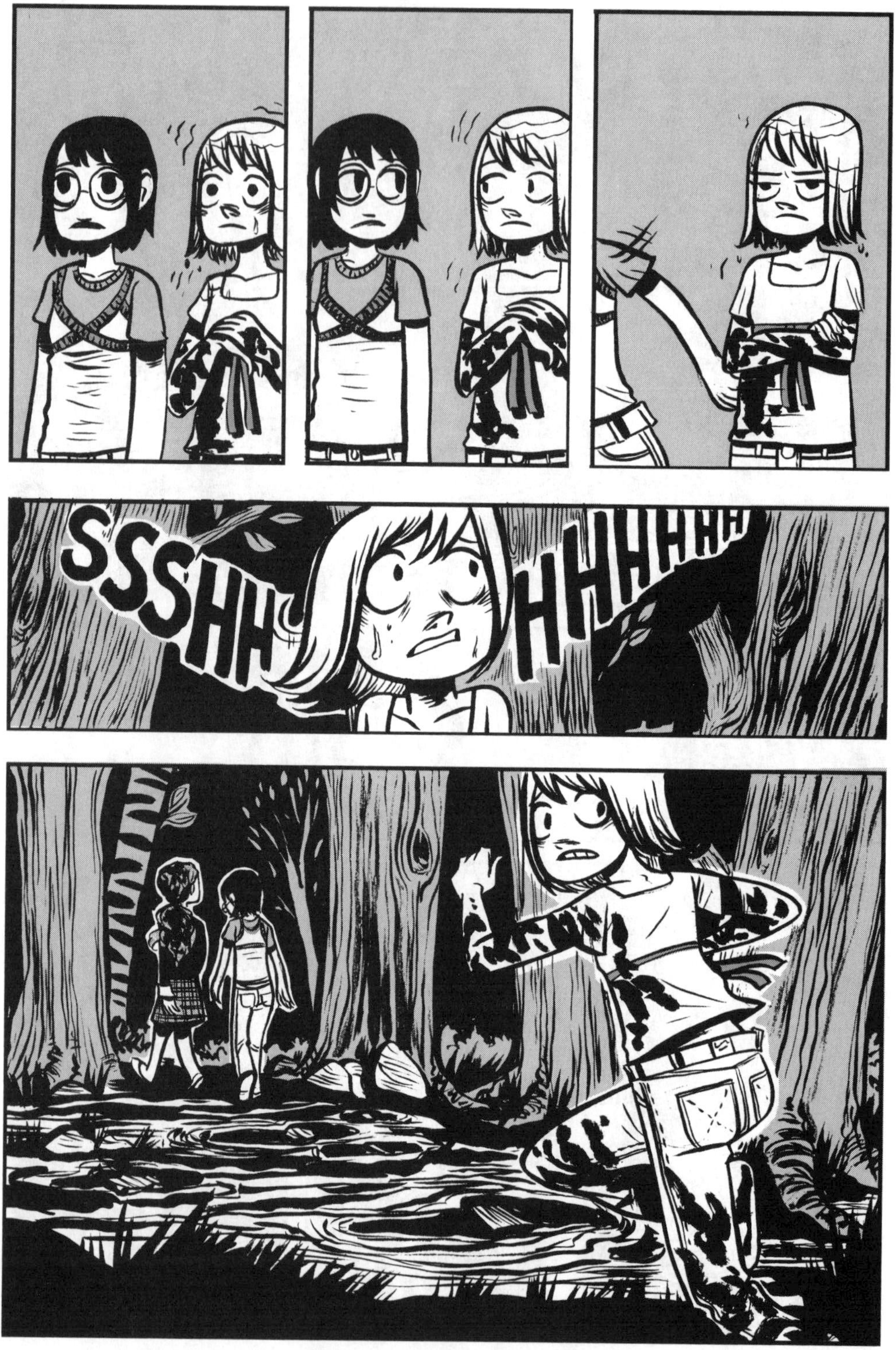
SSSHHHHHHHHHH

chapter eight

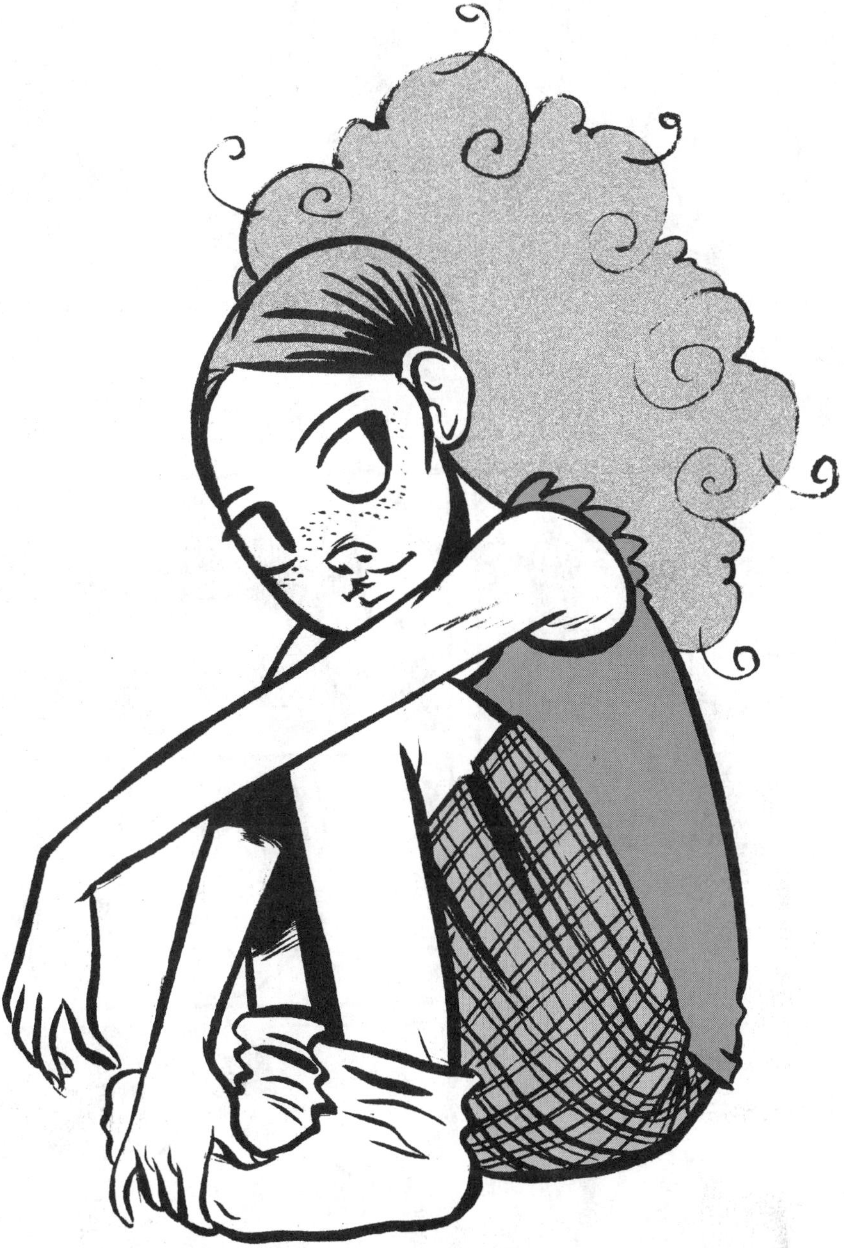

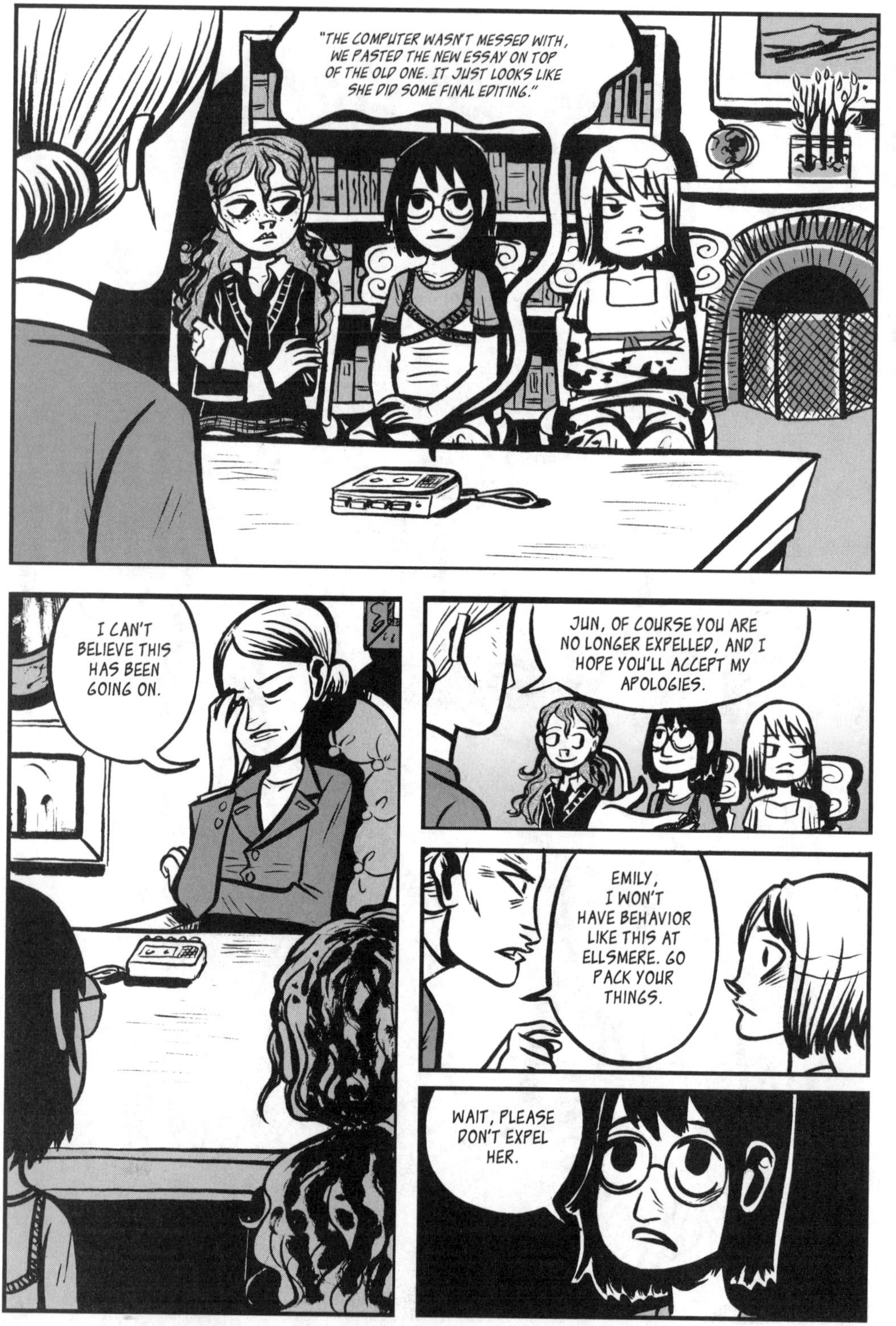
"THE COMPUTER WASN'T MESSED WITH, WE PASTED THE NEW ESSAY ON TOP OF THE OLD ONE. IT JUST LOOKS LIKE SHE DID SOME FINAL EDITING."
I CAN'T BELIEVE THIS HAS BEEN GOING ON.
JUN, OF COURSE YOU ARE NO LONGER EXPELLED, AND I HOPE YOU'LL ACCEPT MY APOLOGIES.
EMILY, I WON'T HAVE BEHAVIOR LIKE THIS AT ELLSMERE. GO PACK YOUR THINGS.
WAIT, PLEASE DON'T EXPEL HER.

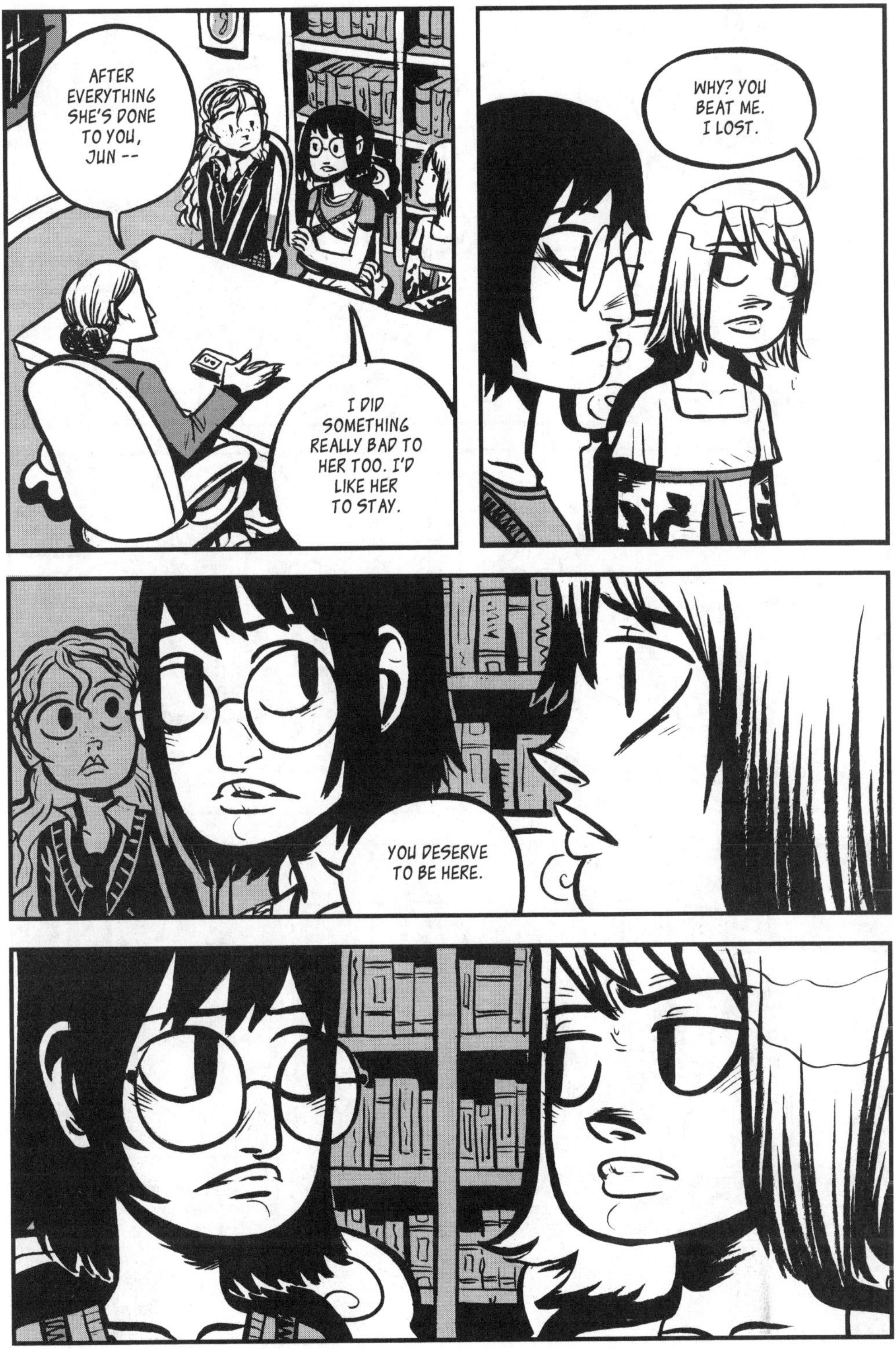
AFTER EVERYTHING SHE'S DONE TO YOU, JUN --
I DID SOMETHING REALLY BAD TO HER TOO. I'D LIKE HER TO STAY.
WHY? YOU BEAT ME. I LOST.
YOU DESERVE TO BE HERE.

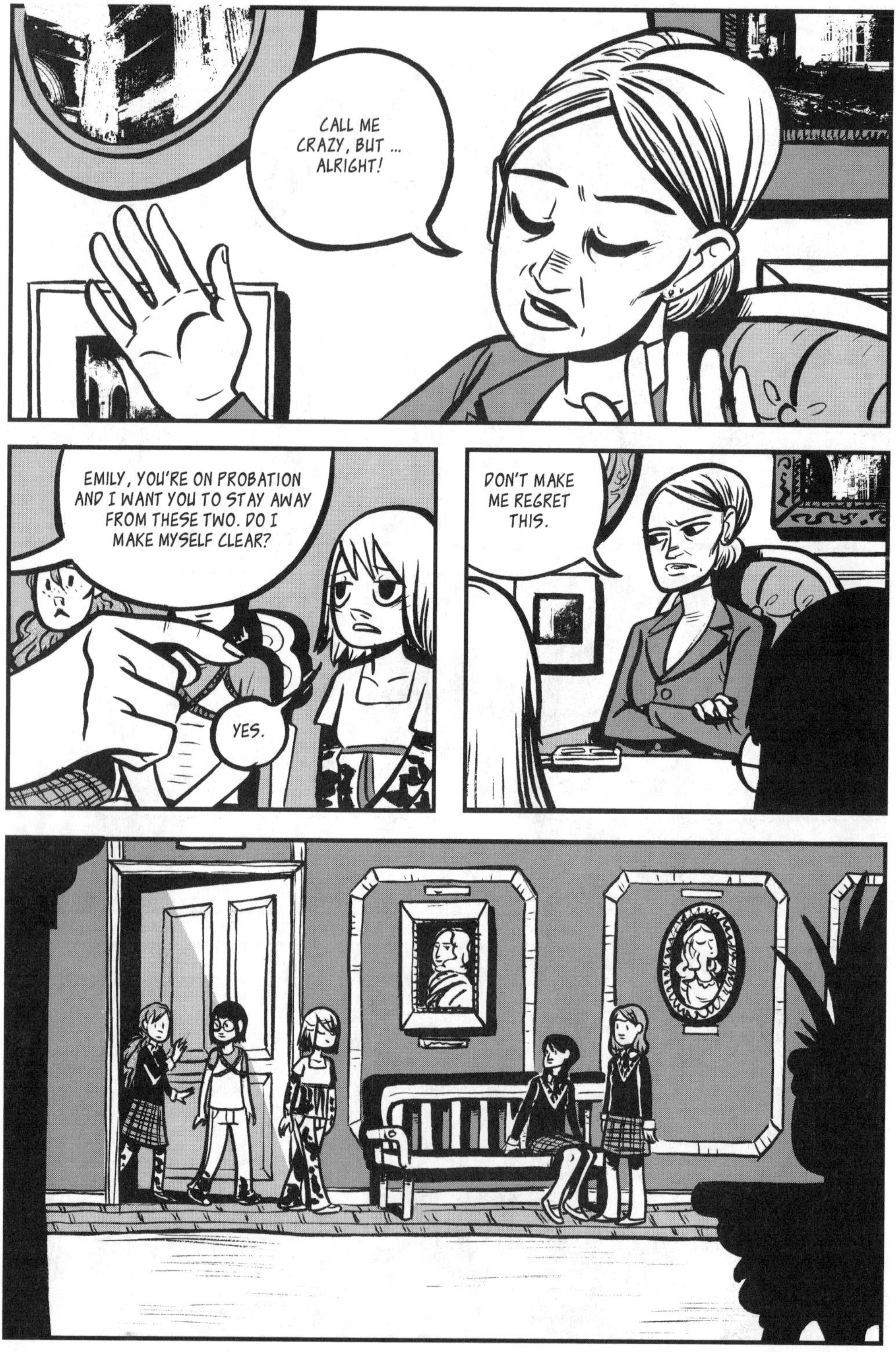
CALL ME CRAZY, BUT ... ALRIGHT!
EMILY, YOU'RE ON PROBATION AND I WANT YOU TO STAY AWAY FROM THESE TWO. DO I MAKE MYSELF CLEAR?
YES.
DON'T MAKE ME REGRET THIS.

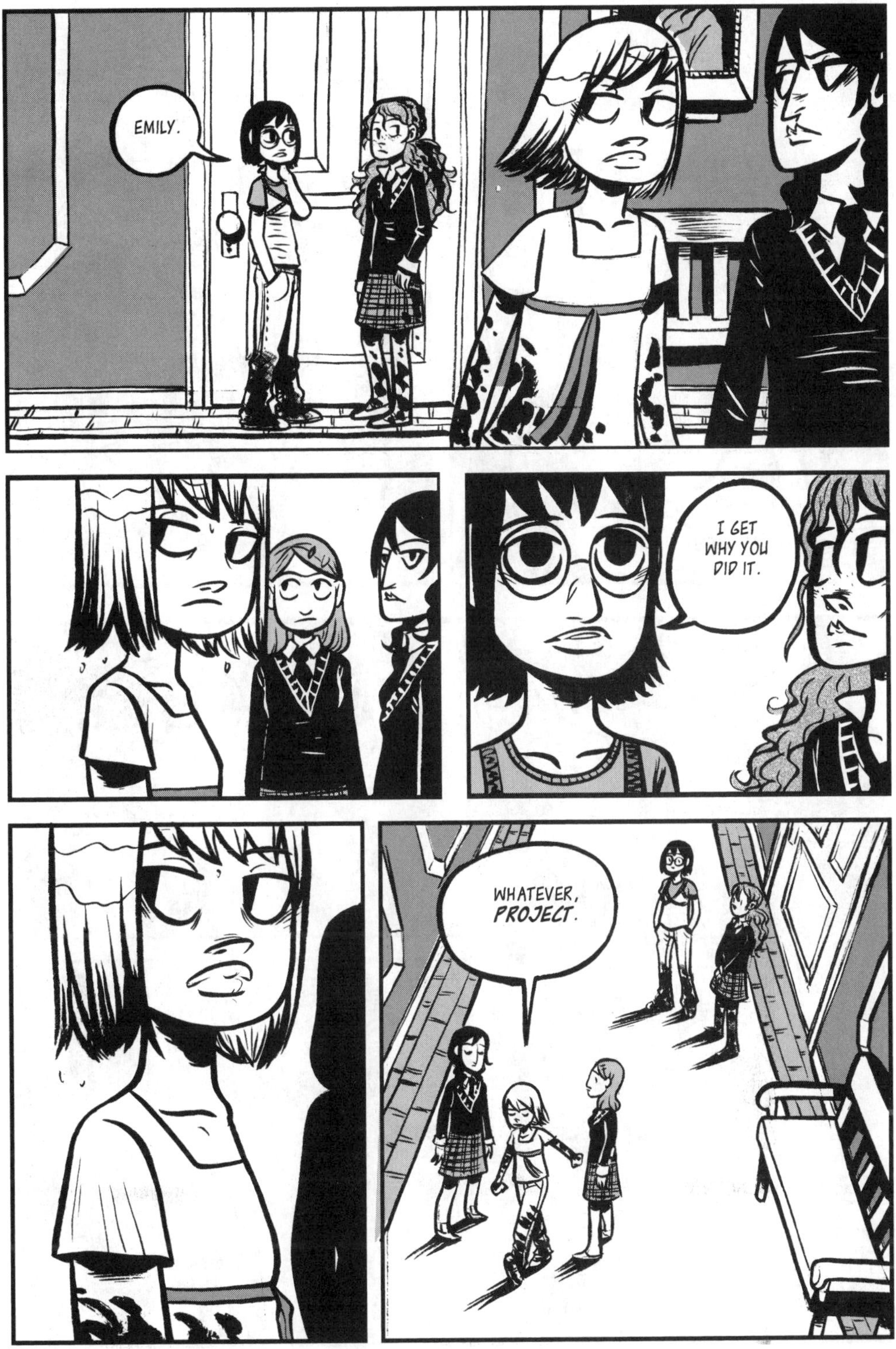
EMILY.
I GET WHY YOU DID IT.
WHATEVER, PROJECT.

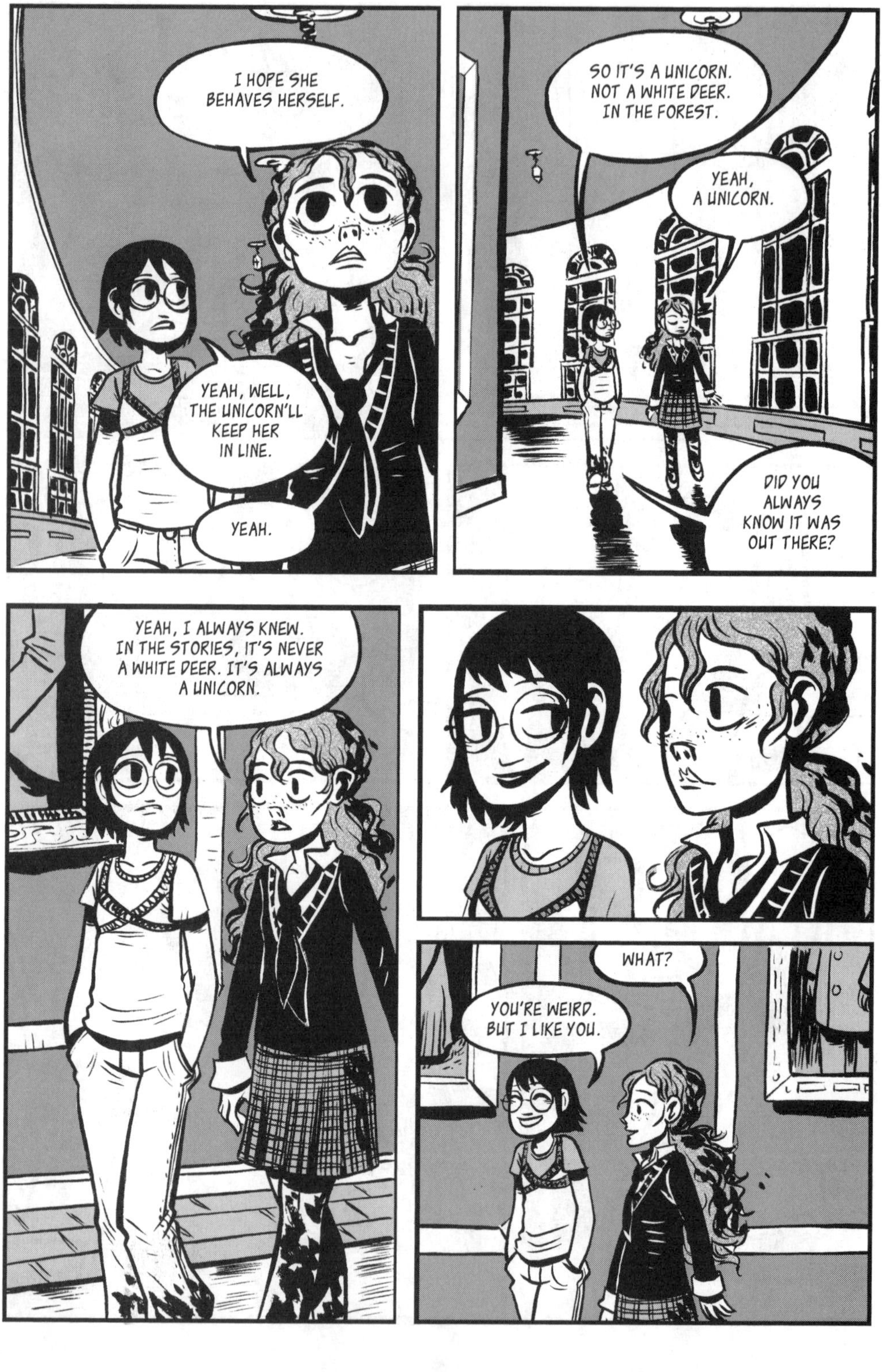
I HOPE SHE BEHAVES HERSELF.
YEAH, WELL, THE UNICORN'LL KEEP HER IN LINE.
YEAH.
SO IT'S A UNICORN. NOT A WHITE DEER. IN THE FOREST.
YEAH, A UNICORN.
DID YOU ALWAYS KNOW IT WAS OUT THERE?
YEAH, I ALWAYS KNEW. IN THE STORIES, IT'S NEVER A WHITE DEER. IT'S ALWAYS A UNICORN.
WHAT?
YOU'RE WEIRD. BUT I LIKE YOU.

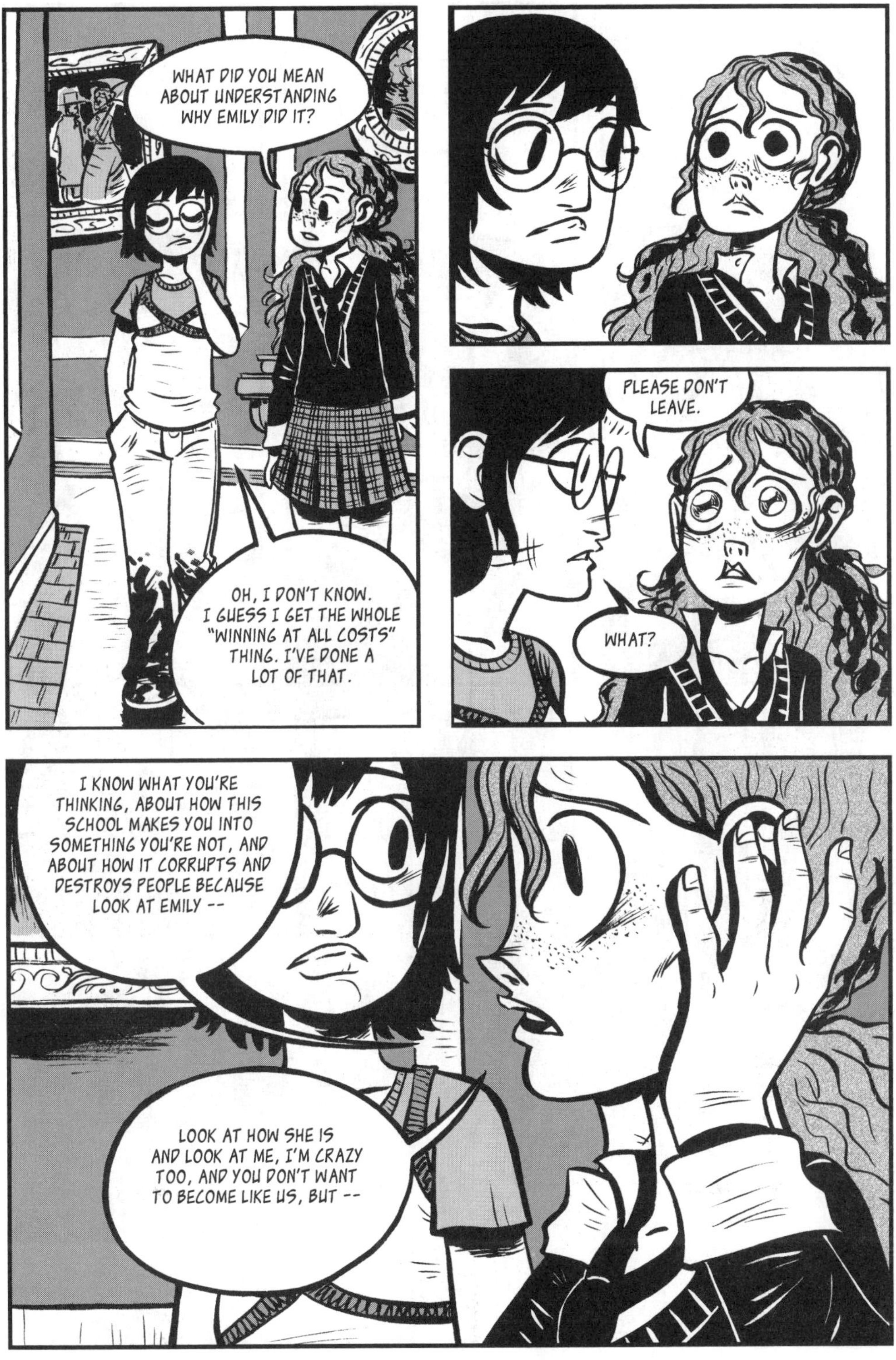
WHAT DID YOU MEAN ABOUT UNDERSTANDING WHY EMILY DID IT?
OH, I DON'T KNOW. I GUESS I GET THE WHOLE "WINNING AT ALL COSTS" THING. I'VE DONE A LOT OF THAT.
PLEASE DON'T LEAVE.
WHAT?
I KNOW WHAT YOU'RE THINKING, ABOUT HOW THIS SCHOOL MAKES YOU INTO SOMETHING YOU'RE NOT, AND ABOUT HOW IT CORRUPTS AND DESTROYS PEOPLE BECAUSE LOOK AT EMILY --
LOOK AT HOW SHE IS AND LOOK AT ME, I'M CRAZY TOO, AND YOU DON'T WANT TO BECOME LIKE US, BUT --

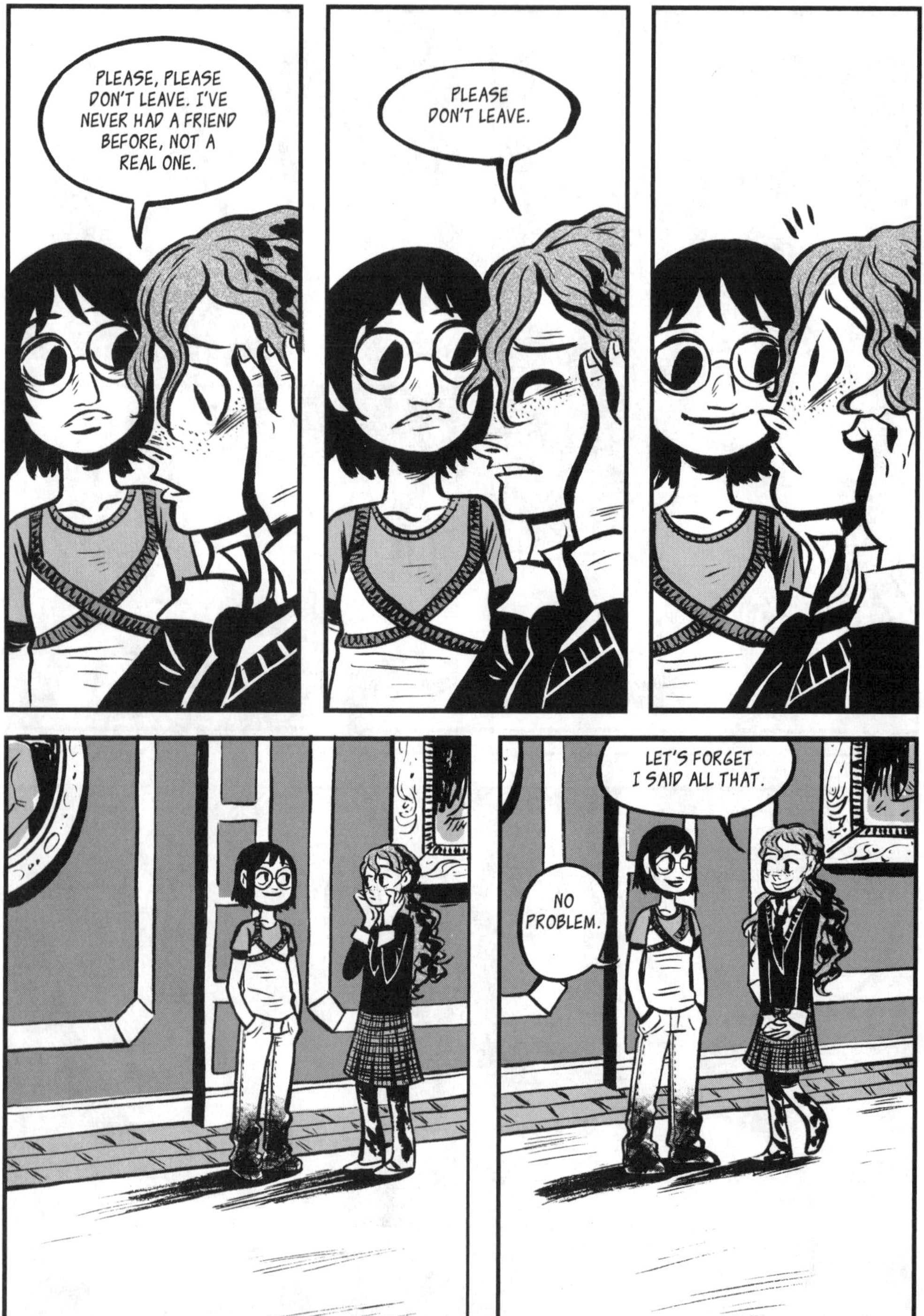
PLEASE, PLEASE DON'T LEAVE. I'VE NEVER HAD A FRIEND BEFORE, NOT A REAL ONE.
PLEASE DON'T LEAVE.
LET'S FORGET I SAID ALL THAT.
NO PROBLEM.

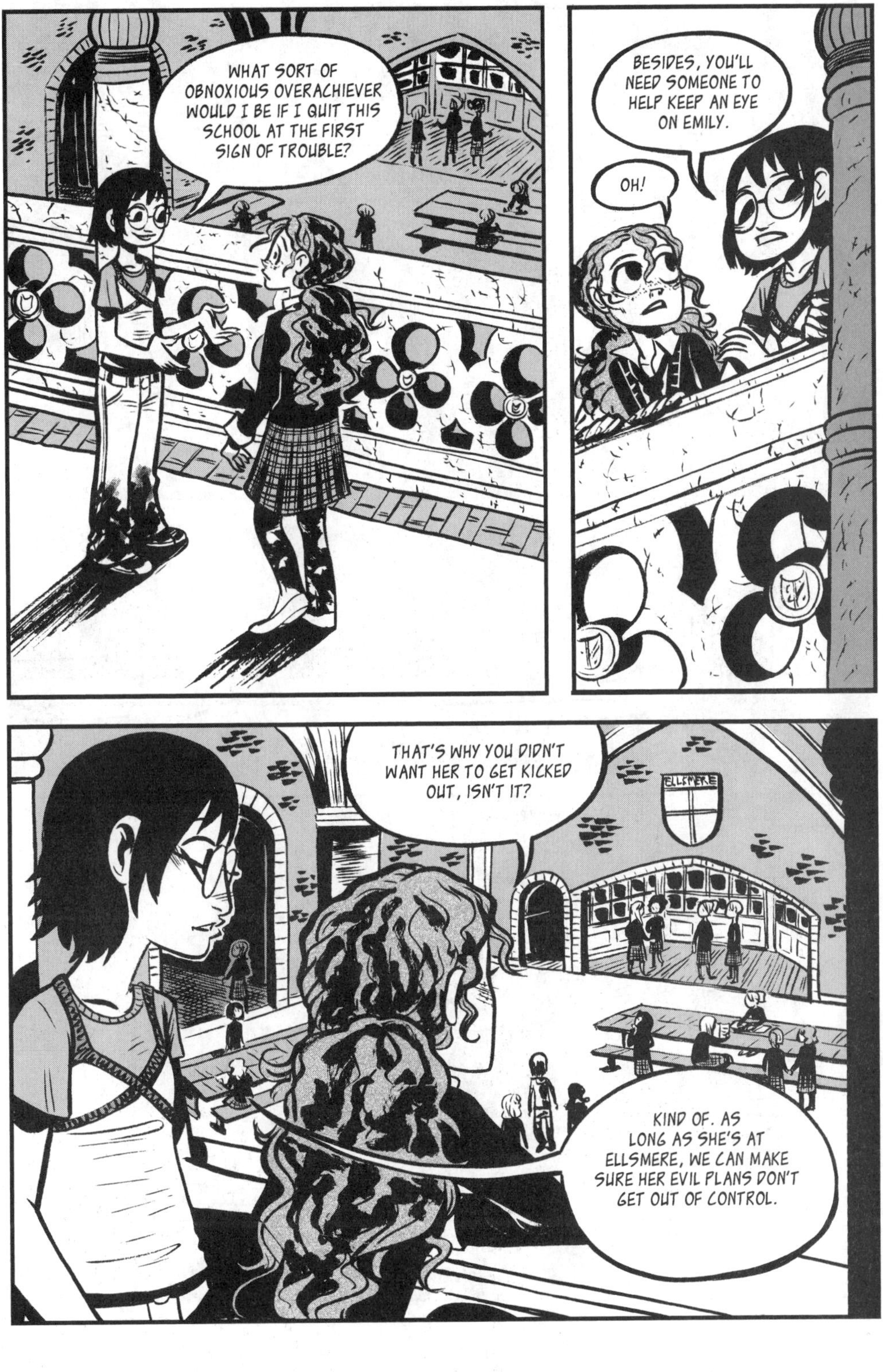
WHAT SORT OF OBNOXIOUS OVERACHIEVER WOULD I BE IF I QUIT THIS SCHOOL AT THE FIRST SIGN OF TROUBLE?
BESIDES, YOU'LL NEED SOMEONE TO HELP KEEP AN EYE ON EMILY.
OH!
THAT'S WHY YOU DIDN'T WANT HER TO GET KICKED OUT, ISN'T IT?
ELLSMERE
KIND OF. AS LONG AS SHE'S AT ELLSMERE, WE CAN MAKE SURE HER EVIL PLANS DON'T GET OUT OF CONTROL.

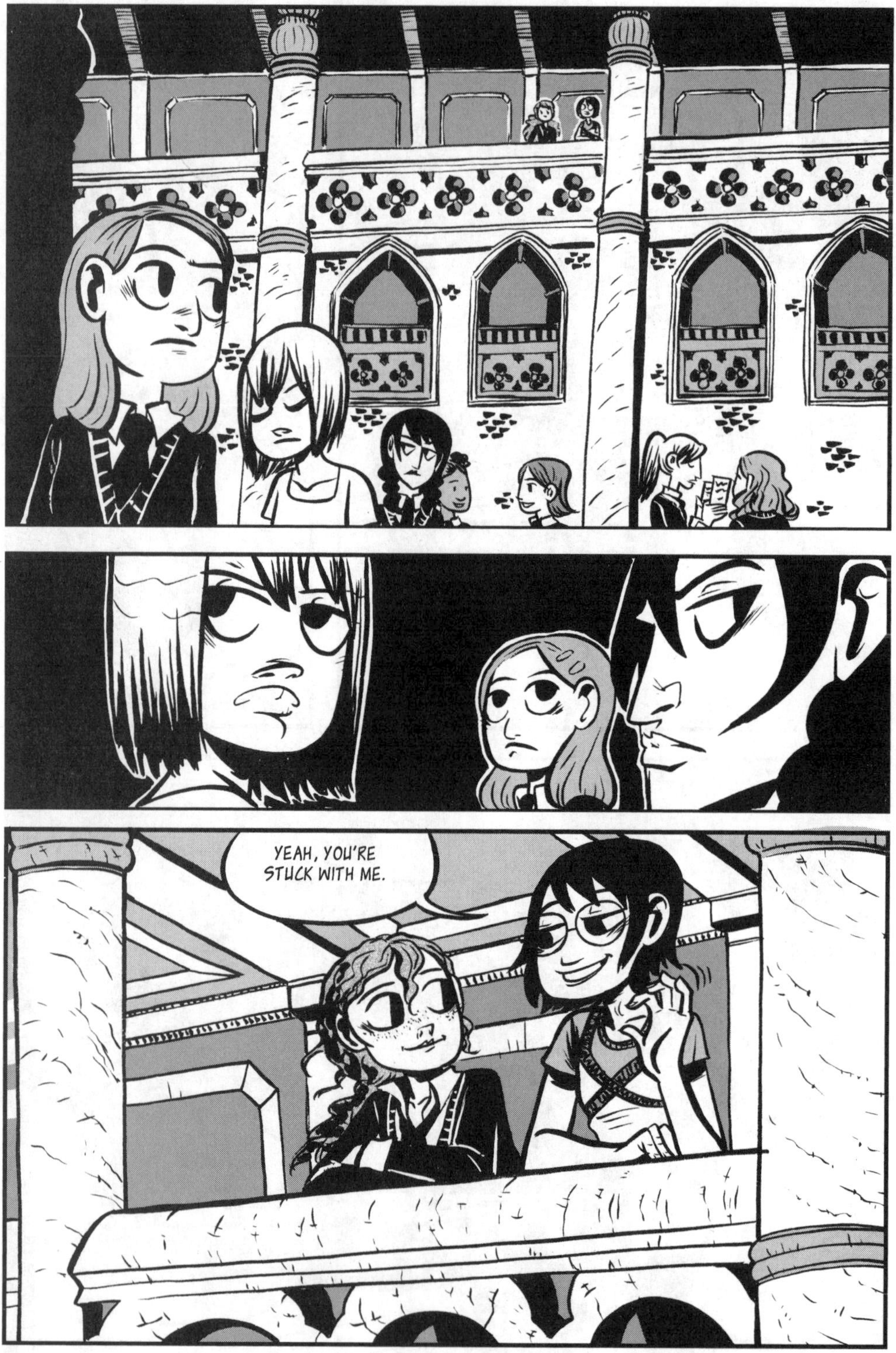
YEAH, YOU'RE STUCK WITH ME.

the End